Forbes **WATSON**

Forbes
WATSON

Independent Revolutionary

Lenore Clark

THE KENT STATE UNIVERSITY PRESS
KENT, OHIO, & LONDON

Frontis: Forbes Watson, sometime between 1943 and 1946.
Photograph courtesy of Maria Ealand.

© 2001 by The Kent State University Press, Kent, Ohio 44242
ALL RIGHTS RESERVED.
Library of Congress Catalog Card Number 2001029601
ISBN 0-87338-710-4
Manufactured in the United States of America

05 04 03 02 01   5 4 3 2 1

Library of Congress Cataloging-in-Publication Data

Clark, Lenore.
Forbes Watson: independent revolutionary / Lenore Clark.
p. cm.
Includes bibliographical references and index.
ISBN 0-87338-710-4 (alk. paper)
1. Watson, Forbes, 1880–1960.
2. Art critics—United States— Biography.
3. Periodical editors—United States—Biography.
4. Arts—History.
I. Title.

N7483.W3635 C58 2001
709'.2—dc21
[B]   2001029601

British Library Cataloging-in-Publication data are available.

For **MERV**

CONTENTS

PREFACE

For years after he retired, Forbes Watson made sporadic starts on a memoir he planned to publish. An assortment of notes and clippings, a few drafts of fragmentary reminiscences, and correspondence with friends offer glimpses into his general scheme for the book. It was to contain recollections of his early life and career. There would be the insider's vignettes of personalities in the arts, friends and adversaries, both of whom he had in abundance. Watson was ready to tell all about some people he could not have gossiped about during his career. He planned a scathing chapter on museums in America and a laudatory one on Edward "Ned" Bruce, the inspirational chief of the Treasury art programs. The centerpiece of the memoir would be a look back at what he as well as art historians regarded as his finest achievement, *The Arts* magazine, which for eleven years had been at the forefront of art periodicals in America.

Watson apparently made little progress with the project, which is unfortunate. A coherent autobiography by a figure who was both a penetrating commentator and a key participant in the rise of modernism and the democratization of art in America would have been an invaluable addition to the literature.

This biography of Forbes Watson is an effort to sort out and elucidate some of the experiences and observations he would have shared. In doing so, it chronicles the development of his ideas and the impact they had on American art and its reception during the period from the Armory Show to World War II.

I have corrected misspelled words, punctuation, and minor errors in Forbes Watson's writings, which do not affect the meaning of the text, in order to promote readability and clarity. I have also added Watson's name to citations where he is the known author, even though his name does not appear.

The subject of money comes up from time to time in the narrative. To estimate its relative value at the beginning of the twenty-first century, the reader is advised to multiply the amount specified in the text by ten: that is, one dollar during Forbes Watson's time would be worth at least ten dollars today.

I am indebted to a number of persons for assistance in writing this book, but to no one more than H. Wayne Morgan. His formidable knowledge and generous interest in my work made me more conscious of historical perspective and kept me focused. For bibliographic access to the all-important resources at the Archives of American Art, I am especially grateful to Judy Throm and her competent staff, all of whom were unfailingly responsive and helpful in providing assistance. The prodding and encouragement of my husband and children were awesome by any standard.

INTRODUCTION

The name Forbes Watson crops up throughout the literature of early-twentieth-century American art, in references to his trenchant commentary, and in his pithy one-liners, quoted by historians to key up their narratives. The magazine he edited, *The Arts*, illuminated more vividly than any other periodical of the day the art issues of the twenties. Watson began his career in 1912 as art critic for the *New York Evening Post* newspaper on the eve of the historic Armory Show, in which European modernism was first introduced to the American public on a large scale. It was the era of progressivism, when reformers enacted a wide array of measures to redress social and economic abuses and restore democracy to politics. Challenges to the orthodoxies of nineteenth-century culture were taking shape all around. In the sphere of art, the conservative National Academy of Design, which had dominated American taste for more than eighty years, faced disruptions from two groups: Robert Henri's urban realists, who sought to democratize American art, and the Alfred Stieglitz circle, emissaries of European avant-garde art. Watson quickly gained a reputation as an outspoken progressive, a critical ally of independent American artists, and a witty annihilator of those who got in the way.

It is difficult to imagine today—when modernism is taken for granted, and museums and galleries are eager to introduce novel, radical, even shocking art to a public both receptive and outraged—that institutions in Watson's day resisted modern art, particularly if it was American. The likelihood that an established museum or dealer would show contemporary American art, or that a timid public would take it seriously, was remote. That situation changed during the course of Watson's career. With Watson's appearance on the art scene, modernists' ad hoc assaults on the conservative monopoly escalated into a full-scale war; in Watson, young American artists found a high-profile, articulate champion.

Brought up in a well-to-do New England family, Watson imbibed early on the independent spirit of the American Revolutionary War and the mugwump's sense of guardianship and democratic reform. A close relationship with an

1

older brother-in-law, the respected artist Alfred Quinton Collins, nurtured a love of art and fostered a sense of identity with American artists. His marriage to the artist Nan Paterson deepened that empathy. As the child of a privileged broker's family, Watson received not only early schooling abroad but opportunities to appreciate the great art of Europe, an appreciation he retained throughout his life.

Watson's impact on the history of art and art criticism in America was greatest during the period between the two world wars. As editor of *The Arts*, the liveliest and most vital art magazine of the twenties, and discriminating art critic for the *New York World* newspaper, he widened Americans' exposure to the modern movement and engaged readers as allies in his war against the stodgy National Academy on one side and the faddist School of Paris on the other. He was the crusading cheerleader for independent contemporary American art, an exhorter to an unconfident public that had for decades looked beyond America for guidance in art taste and certified masters.

What distinguished Watson's commentary from that of his contemporaries was not only his ideas, which coalesced a reverence for the great traditions with a confidence in the modern spirit, but his style. Sardonic, independent, combative—some called him the H. L. Mencken of art criticism. His friends—artists, collectors, dealers—were legion, but so were his adversaries. The most knowledgeable and urbane member of the Gertrude Whitney–Juliana Force circle, he helped guide the women's artistic decisions and added editorial clout to their liberal collecting and exhibiting tendencies. He was a key figure in the decision to establish the Whitney Museum of American Art, although he did not get to participate in its development.

In the thirties, Watson became technical director and then consultant for the New Deal's Treasury art programs, where his advocacy of the American artist took a more material and social direction. Whereas art historians of the 1920s considered him a modernist critic, a decade later he was viewed as a conservative.[1] Forbes Watson fit neither formula. He was independent, liberal, and democratic; pro-modernist in some respects and conservative in others. It was he who referred to himself as an independent revolutionary. This is the story of his development from Progressive art critic to New Deal art critic. Throughout, he left an important legacy of foresighted, influential, and highly readable commentary.

1 BACKGROUND AND EARLY
YEARS, 1879–1912

In a letter to Van Wyck Brooks written in May 1953 at the age of seventy-three, Forbes Watson praised Brooks's recent book *The Writer in America,* in which he urged a return to humanitarian liberalism. What had become of "the humanitarian, the liberal, the progressive," Brooks asked, "*without* which we could never have attained the planetary mind?" Watson affirmed his own commitment to this ideal in painting and art criticism and reminisced about its roots. "I was born in Cambridge, Mass, went to school with the Danas and the Jameses, played baseball in the Longfellow backyard and in a field behind the James and Royce houses, was brought up to speak the words Concord and Emerson under my breath."[1]

Watson's childhood and youth reflected the genteel upbringing of an established, affluent New England family during the Gilded Age. Born in Cambridge on November 27, 1879, he was one of seven children of John Calquhour Watson, a broker, and Mary Robinson Shute Watson. His paternal grandparents, John Watson and Jane Peacock Watson, were Scottish, and his mother's parents, James and Mary Shute, were English. His father was born in Cranston, Rhode Island, and had fought in the Civil War, soon after which he moved to Somerville, Massachusetts, a bustling commercial town three miles northwest of Boston. There he met Mary Shute, a native Bostonian. They were married in Somerville on New Year's Day 1863 and moved to Cambridge several months later; John Calquhour was twenty-four years old and Mary was twenty. Cambridge was an hour's ride by horsecar from Boston and had been founded in the same year, 1630, as the larger city. Cambridge too was steeped in the history of the War for Independence, Gen. George Washington having taken command of the American army there. With Harvard College its focal point, the city attracted a large proportion of lawyers, clergy, doctors, and successful businessmen. The Watsons lived in West Cambridge, west of Harvard Square, where residents smugly adopted the language of the stock market to signify their superior status. West Cambridge was "Cambridge Preferred," as distinguished from Old Cambridge, or "Cambridge Common." Mary and John's first child, Mary, was born in September, and over the next fifteen years they had six more children, all sons: Ashley, Morrill, Arthur, Lucian Carr, Carroll, and Forbes. The youngest, Forbes never knew his brother Lucian, who died at two of tubercular meningitis six years before Forbes was born. The family enjoyed the typical advantages of a prosperous broker's household. Two Portuguese servants were in residence to see to their comforts. The children were well groomed and outfitted in quality, impeccably tailored clothing. Their parents always had the children's shoes custom made, a practice Watson would recall with particular poignancy during the depression.[2]

John Watson frequently took the family abroad. As a result the children received much of their early education in Germany and France, achieving fluency in French and other languages. Forbes began school in Paris at age eleven, an experience he remembered as much for the daily trek "from the Opera House to the Louvre and from the Louvre to the Montparnasse" as for the education itself.[3] Travel abroad also afforded abundant opportunities to visit the great European art centers. Forbes never forgot the exhilaration of accompanying his mother to the museums of Florence, where they spent an entire winter, and to Paris, London, Munich, and Berlin.

As business flourished John Watson moved the family to progressively finer, more spacious homes on Harvard Street, then Martin Street, and during Forbes's senior year of high school, to 175 Brattle Street, a site with splendid spreading elms and prestigious architecture; Henry Wadsworth Longfellow's famous yellow clapboard house was just down the street at 105 Brattle. The Brattle Street home, a three-story Georgian style mansion overlooking the Charles River, was built in 1764 and had served as a hospital following the battle of Bunker Hill. Some eighty years after the Watsons moved from Cambridge to Boston in 1904, the house, known as the Ruggles-Fayerweather House, was entered on the National Register of Historic Places.

Three of Forbes's brothers, Carroll, Ashley, and Morrill, pursued financial careers. Carroll started out in insurance and Morrill and Ashley went into the stock brokerage business, joining their father's firm for a time. Arthur chose a mariner's vocation. Of all the Watson males, only Forbes lacked an inclination toward business or the practical professions. Temperamentally, he had little in common with his brothers. He described Carroll, four years his senior and closest to him in age, as "built like an ox, fearless and generous with a great big heart undiluted by intellect." Carroll had become a "phenomenal cook," Watson recalled in later years, "which he learned as a miner in his youth after he had been fired from St. Paul's school for beating up one of the teachers."[4]

He was most attached to the women in the family, sharing their antimaterialist impulses and artistic sensibilities. Excursions with his mother and sister to the historic landmarks surrounding Cambridge ignited in young Forbes a lifelong reverence for the Emersonian lessons of individualism and social obligation and for the ideals of the Revolutionary War. In later years he would trace his passion for independence back to the experience of Bunker Hill and Concord.

Forbes's sister, Mary, sixteen years his senior, had married the well-known painter Alfred Quinton Collins when Forbes was only three years old, and despite a twenty-four-year gap in their ages, Forbes felt a greater kinship with Collins than with his brothers. Forbes liked to relate how, as a rising young painter with a studio in Cambridge, Collins passed the Watson home almost daily, never seeing Mary, a fledgling art student at the time. The couple did not meet until Collins sailed for Paris, and Mary and Watson's brother happened to be aboard the same ship. "Mary brought me up," he wrote a friend, "and I have been close to her since I was six years old." Extended vacations in the Collins home nourished Forbes's interest in art, affording him the stimulation of living among artists and learning firsthand from his brother-in-law "the processes of painting," which probably referred not only to technique but also to Collins's construction of models to simulate changing light on figures. The American expatriate painter Mary Cassatt was one of Collins's admirers, and in time also Forbes's friend. She had become acquainted with Collins when he was a student in Paris, and they remained lifelong friends, exchanging letters and portrait sketches. Forbes later inherited Cassatt's sketch. Collins died in 1903 at age forty-eight, and Mary never remarried.[5]

When the family was home in Cambridge, Forbes attended a private school, which Miss Sarah Page operated in her house on Everett Street. At age twelve he entered the fifth grade at Browne and Nichols Preparatory School located on Appian Way and Garden Street near the Cambridge Common, the present site of Harvard Medical School. Browne and Nichols was an appropriate place for a young man of Forbes's background. Its announced mission was to provide boys between the ages of twelve and seventeen "thorough training in all the studies required for admission to Harvard" and at the same time "meet the wants of boys who do not intend to enter college, by giving special prominence to the English and Scientific branches."[6] Except for seasons in Europe

Young gentleman Forbes Watson, sometime between 1894 and 1897. Forbes Watson Papers, Archives of American Art, Smithsonian Institution.

and one term at Phillips Academy in Andover in 1896, Forbes attended Browne and Nichols until graduation in 1898. Both there and at Phillips Academy he followed the classics program of study in preference to the science curriculum, the classics core consisting of Latin, Greek, French, German, English, history, mathematics, and natural science. Among his schoolmates were Henry and Richard Dana, William James Jr., Francis Peabody, and Homer Saint-Gaudens.

Boys' school curricula did not include art when Forbes was growing up, but his mother engaged private instructors for him despite his apparently undistinguished gift. "Drawing teachers seemed to enjoy nothing better than telling my family I had no talent," he remembered. Among his teachers was the esteemed Boston painter and Harvard lecturer Denman Waldo Ross, in whose Cambridge studio in Washburn Square Forbes studied color scales. Years later

Watson would recall more vividly than the lessons in "Washtub Square" Ross's conservatism and his "execrable" taste in "matters occidental."[7]

After graduating from Browne and Nichols, Forbes attended Harvard, the only Watson offspring to do so. He was a poor student, however, and was placed on academic probation in 1902, the year he should have graduated. It took two more years and several repeated classes before he received his bachelor's degree. One of his short stories, "Denis and I," published in *The Bellman* a few years after he graduated, contained suggestive insights into Watson's advantaged youth, carefree work ethic, and his relationship with a practical-minded father who was less indulgent than his doting mother. The story opened with the first-person narrator, a college student, and his cousin Denis "lolling about" the tennis courts in their white flannels, smoking and dreaming up "bully" ways to enliven their leisure. Their fathers strode over, furious at their sons' failing performances in college and sternly informed them that they would not be allowed to return next term. Instead, they would be put to work in the family brokerage and banking firm to change them "from gentlemen into men." The breezy plot centered on the boys' blithe inattention to business and their merry schemes to gain permission to return to college. Despite their free-and-easy conduct—indeed, as a result of one of their numerous blunders—the youths made a large sum of money for their parents. "In any case," the story concluded, "Denis and I got an A.B. three years later, and nowadays we and the enemy get on harmoniously."[8]

Forbes intended to be an artist, "but," he reflected in later years, "writing seemed to go a little more naturally for me than painting, which is to this day my first love." Recalling that his enthusiasm for writing and art had remained steady and undiminished from the age of ten, Watson wrote in the *Harvard Fiftieth Anniversary Report*: "if 'I had it to do all over again,' I'd rather be a painter than a writer. Actually I'd rather be both." His most vivid memories of Harvard were his written themes; the English professors Charles Townsend Copeland, Barrett Wendell, William Allan Neilson, and George Lyman Kittredge; and his work on the *Harvard Advocate*, in which two of his stories, "At the House of the Countess" and "A Spool of Thread," were published in 1900. Both were lavishly tapestried narratives, the first set in France and the second in Italy. Both related the exploits of radiantly handsome young heroes, doubtlessly surrogates for the romantic twenty-year-old author, struggling earnestly to save poor but virtuous women from the clutches of mercenary predators. The sophomore left no doubt about his contempt for Gilded Age greed, as in the end honor and respect triumphed over coarse materialism. In "At the House of the Countess," the narrator, a handsome young student, rescued an impoverished but noble old countess from the tyranny of insolent "provision-men" and "dunners." In "A Spool of Thread," a poor fruit dealer, also young and handsome, in love with a comely lace maker thwarted a rich rival who had gotten his money in "crooked ways no one knew about."[9]

Forbes's parents wanted him to become a lawyer, and acceding to their wishes, he enrolled in Columbia University Law School in the fall of 1902 before receiving his degree from Harvard. He failed all his first-year courses, however, except equity. The next academic year he enrolled in New York Law School but soon dropped out. New York City offered too many allurements. Artists came there from all over America to escape the fetters of small-town conventions, study with the celebrated teachers, gather with other artists, pore over the latest art, and hopefully exhibit and sell their own works. Watson's apartment at 64 West Fifty-sixth Street was just a short walk from one of the most popular art schools, the Art Students League on West Fifty-seventh Street. Robert Henri had joined Everett Shinn, William Glackens, and George Luks there in 1900, forming the informal nucleus of an independent school of urban realists in America.

After graduating from Harvard in spring 1904, Watson abandoned law and went abroad, where he spent most of his time writing and studying painting, "but with no intention of becoming a professional artist, merely to get a more intimate knowledge of art."[10] Meanwhile, the family had moved from the Brattle Street mansion in Cambridge to another on Bay State Road in Boston (that house today serves as a dormitory for Boston University). When Watson returned to the United States in 1906, he decided to settle in Manhattan.

Twenty-seven years old, sometime law student, and a cosmopolite, he was confident about himself and his country and was wholly in accord with the forward thinking of the day. He was quite dashing, with brown hair, straight nose, and full mustache. His dark, prominently arched eyebrows angled steeply above clear blue eyes, suggesting a roguish masculinity. In profile, the back of his head was rather flat, creating, despite sloping shoulders, a silhouette of erect carriage. With a high forehead, a long smooth-complexioned face, and a rather square jaw, the young man projected, for all his five feet, seven-and-a-half inches, an image of self-assurance and authority. His voice was soft, inflected with the cultivated accents of the well-bred. In spite of his distaste for the common rituals of moneymaking, he never outgrew his fondness for the things it bought—finely cut tweeds, aged scotch whiskey, and parties. The debonair flirt had no difficulty attracting women. In one final gesture toward a law degree, Watson reenrolled in New York Law School but soon withdrew again. He would thereafter try his hand at writing for a living.

Watson had grown up during a time of unprecedented industrialization and urbanization in the United States. Electricity and telephones were introduced into the home when he was a boy. Railroad lines crisscrossed the nation. Technological advances in manufacturing and mining helped promote the creation of large corporations. The mechanical typesetter, the electric streetcar, and the automobile, each invented during Watson's youth, facilitated rapid communication and broadened opportunities for association. Between early childhood and young adulthood, Watson witnessed the sudden proliferation of consolidations in railroads, utilities, and a broad variety of industries, as well as the mounting opposition to them. Merchants in big eastern cities and in the West amassed fortunes almost overnight. Not impressed, Watson's New England elders valued character, high ethical standards, and a sober humanitarian spirit above mercenary achievement. They saw newly rich tycoons as socially inferior, and although their own leadership was no longer prominent, they never relinquished a sense of moral responsibility to reform society.

The grim side of America's new expansiveness was also magnified during those years. Poverty and slums; gross health and safety abuses in industry; factory exploitation of women, children, and foreigners; labor strikes and riots; and flagrant corruption in politics and business all accompanied the aggregation of national wealth. By the turn of the century, moral outrage over these indecencies and high confidence in the goodness and ingenuity of the American public and in the powers of modern science were translated into prodigious reform activity. From local action by professional and social organizations to legislation at the national level, progressives moved to restore democracy and individualism to politics and economics, revising electoral procedures, regulating monopolies, and outlawing unfair business practices. They sought honesty, order, and efficiency in business and government, better living conditions, and a richer cultural environment for all segments of society. Progressive reform activity was in full swing when Watson returned to the United States in 1906.

Watson's story "Denis and I" appeared in *The Bellman* in 1907 and was well reviewed in the press. The following year "The Bet" was published in Frank Munsey's *Scrap Book,* where Watson had been hired as a manuscript reader.[11] "The Bet," subtitled "How a Daring Chauffeur Tore a Line of Terror through a Great City and Met a Greater Terror," told the story of two chauffeurs, an American and a Frenchman, in an automobile race from South Ferry to Harlem. To win the bet and prove his toughness, the American sped recklessly through crowded New York City streets, nearly killing several pedestrians. Finally, imagining that he actually had killed a man and that the police were pursuing him, he tore through the city at an increasingly frantic speed and died of a heart attack. Watson could well have been commenting on American culture, its hectic pace, and its excesses and irresponsibility compared to Europe.

In 1909 Watson took and passed the New York State bar examination without having completed law school and was admitted to the bar in March. Although law was not his career preference, he probably considered practicing at that time, since at age thirty he had not yet supported himself with a steady job or with freelance writing. That same year, however, he advanced from reader to assistant editor of *The Scrap Book,* and if he had been contemplating law practice, he abandoned the idea. Employed in a real job for the first time, he moved to 84 Grove Street in Greenwich Village to live among artists. One of the poorer quarters of New York City, though by no means a slum, the Village offered cheap rents and restaurants, and artists and writers liked the easy egalitarian camaraderie. It was a picturesque and pleasant place to live.

Up until that time, American art had been relatively static and, like American music of the period, neither unique nor highly esteemed. Museums and galleries generally preferred traditional and academic art from Europe, and the new millionaires, eager to acquire culture and demonstrate their respectability, bought up the Old World paintings and sculpture. European art was the accepted model for Americans, and, from colonial days, study in Europe was considered the appropriate path to artistic validation. It was not uncommon for American artists to rent galleries in France in which to exhibit their work, purchase space in the newspaper to publicize it, and then return to the United States with proper "credentials" in hand.

Few stylistic changes had occurred in painting since Watson's childhood. Except for the work of a small number of original native geniuses, including Winslow Homer, Thomas Eakins, and Albert Pinkham Ryder along with important expatriates such as James Abbott McNeill Whistler and Mary Cassatt, American art was generally traditional. "It was a period," in Watson's words, when "a mild and temperate refinement was much in evidence in American art, and, to a great extent, in literature—the period of William Dean Howell's gently discreet novels and of Henry James's elaborate and allusive style, of Abbott Thayer's lofty idealizations of womanhood and St. Gaudens's elegance. In fact the American woman was in danger of being etherealized out of existence. . . . It was a period when not only the lusty breezes were not allowed to enter the refined studios but even the daylight was discreetly veiled."[12] The National Academy of Design (NAD), the most powerful artists organization in the country, dictated art etiquette. There was no single formula, but academic painting usually emphasized discreet, pleasant, moral subject matter and technical tidiness. Independent artists who did not conform were effectively excluded not only from NAD exhibits but also from major galleries, since few dealers showed works that deviated from the accepted standards.

From the early nineteenth century, nature painting was America's premier genre, embodying the pastoral ideal of the United States as an unspoiled, guileless oasis. Leading nature painters, while generally faithful to the facts, swelled and accented the mystical vastness and virginal grandeur of America's wilderness. Portrait painting, derived from Continental examples, featured handsome, aristocratically posed subjects and technically dexterous canvases. The undisputed master of portraiture was John Singer Sargent, whose stunning virtuosity was widely imitated both in the United States and abroad. Historical art, anecdotal work, and still life had changed little from pre–Civil War days, and America's venerated muralists Kenyon Cox, Edwin Blashfield, John Alexander, and Elihu Vedder safeguarded the conventions of traditional mural art.

The most illustrious style was the classical, or traditional, based on the Old Masters and transmitted to America via the École des Beaux-Arts, the chief official art school of Paris. High-minded subject matter, proficient drawing, and well-ordered composition were mandatory. A kind of inert solemnity pervaded the most revered classical-style paintings. Photographically accurate realism was admired, but so too was the impressionist style of landscape and figure painting, respectable since the late 1890s when "The Ten American Painters" held their first exhibition. Adapting the French impressionists' fragmentary, atmospheric approach, American impressionists Childe Hassam, J. Alden Weir, and others recorded glimpses of nature, cityscapes, and genteel domesticity, relying on reflected light and color more than outline. Another style had also gained prominence by then, derived not from France but from Germany: the Munich style. Frank Duveneck and William Merritt Chase popularized its broad, flashy brush strokes and high color. Robert Henri and other urban realists adopted the rapid brushwork of the Munich school as much to capture a feeling of immediacy as for the bravura surface effects.

By 1908 two major agents of modern art in America—The Eight and Alfred Stieglitz—were stirring things up in New York art circles. Robert Henri led The Eight—including John Sloan, Everett Shinn, William Glackens, George Luks, Arthur B. Davies, Maurice Prendergast, and Ernest Lawson. They were drawn together through friendship, a common preference for nonacademic subject matter, and a mutual frustration with the NAD's exhibition policies, which they believed penalized their viewpoint. Henri had enunciated their confidence in a living democratic art and galvanized their efforts to gain recognition independent of the academy. The first exhibition of The Eight at Macbeth Gallery in 1908 marked the beginning of their successful revolt. It "proved conclusively, and for the first time in America, that a group of artists who were strongly anti-academic could attract wide public notice and financial returns—not as curiosities but as significant artists who honestly spoke the language of their own time and place." Although formally their compositions diverged little from prevailing representational styles, their mundane subject matter—lower-class life in the city, saloons, shop girls, and dirty-faced waifs—violated the accepted notion that beauty and politeness were the proper content for art. Works of their ilk were "too brash for the tea table." But the notoriety their "unhealthy," "coarse," and "vulgar" works generated, rather than defeating them, advanced their case. The Eight and other urban realists believed in the primacy of daily life as the source of art and in art as the expression of life. Even where fantasy was the object, as in the works of Davies, their subjects were readily recognizable. As resolutely as they embraced an art of life, they rejected art devoid of the vigor of daily living.[13]

In contrast, Alfred Stieglitz and his circle exalted an art disengaged from life, art for its own sake. In his Little Galleries of the Photo-Secession at 291 Fifth Avenue, which promulgated photography as an art form, Stieglitz created a center for the avant-garde. In 1908 he began exhibiting advanced and experimental art, introducing works by Auguste Rodin, Henri Matisse, and other European moderns as well as several Americans who were working in a modern idiom. The Stieglitz gallery, known as the 291, brought cubism, fauvism, and other vanguard movements to the United States. Only a small elite public viewed them, however, and not everyone appreciated these works. Many urban realists shared Robert Henri's contention that their art was "faddist." For their part, Stieglitz and his coterie scorned the work of the realists, if they noticed it at all.

A handful of other New York galleries also showed modern art. The Macbeth, Montross, Haas, Madison, Berlin, Folsom, and Cosmopolitan Galleries exhibited the work of America's progressive realists and several avant-garde artists such as Max Weber and Abraham Walkowitz. That took courage, Watson later recalled, because those were days "when even the mildest Sloan, the mildest Henri, the mildest Glackens, Luks and Bellows were considered belligerently radical by a public made up of people just like you and me."[14]

When he was not at work, Watson's social life centered on art. He gravitated to those spots where the young artists congregated, in the Village, at the congenial galleries, and at the Art Students League. The league's rosters of students and instructors contained some of the most distinguished names in American art, among them William Merritt Chase, Frank Duveneck, Kenyon Cox, J. Alden Weir, John H. Twachtman, Daniel Chester French, Thomas Eakins, and

Childe Hassam. Its educational policies were liberal, in some respects radical, which made it a popular alternative to the NAD for many young art students.

Through his widening circle of artist friends, Watson became acquainted with Agnes Christian Paterson, a painter from Buffalo who studied with William Merritt Chase. She and Forbes "could not have been more unlike one another," but the two got on beautifully.[15] She came from a large family also. Born in Edinburgh, Scotland, the daughter of William Paterson and Gemina Hardie Paterson, "Nannie," later "Nan," had come to the United States in 1878 with her parents; two older sisters, Lizzie and Maggie; an older brother, William; and baby sister, Alice. She was two years old when the family settled in New Haven, Connecticut, where her father was a dry-goods merchant. Another brother, John Hardie, was born four years later. Even though she moved to America at an early age, Nan remained quite Scottish, speaking with a slight burr all her life and returning to Scotland faithfully to visit her outspread, pious clan. In 1894 at age eighteen, she went to Paris to study art at the highly regarded Académie Colarossi in the Montparnasse, which, along with the Académie Julian, was a favorite studio of American art students; Paul Gauguin had studied at Colarossi's. A number of emerging American modernists had attended, among them Charles Demuth, Thomas Hart Benton, Walt Kuhn, and Max Weber. There was always a model at Colarossi's, and, unlike the Académie Julian, seats were not assigned so that by coming early the artist could get close enough to see.[16] Upon returning to the United States, Nan settled in Buffalo, where her family had recently moved, to paint and give lessons in their home on Jersey Street near the Niagara River. But she craved greater artistic stimulation, and two years later, in 1901, she joined the numerous young artists who had migrated to New York City. There, she concentrated increasingly on portraits and still lifes.

Forbes never lacked for female company, but he felt especially drawn to Nan. There was a natural personal compatibility between them, as well as common interests and outlook. She was astute, though quietly so, and her modesty appealed to him. "You couldn't ever get a boast out of Nan," he would comment in later years.[17] He appreciated her art too. She was taken with his brilliance and panache. The closeness between them quickly deepened.

Forbes and Nan were married in Buffalo on September 14, 1910, with her family in attendance, after which they honeymooned briefly in Wilmington, Vermont. Despite the contrast in their personalities and Watson's lifelong promiscuity, their nearly fifty-year marriage was harmonious. Three years older than Forbes, Nan always looked older. Her hair turned gray years before his did, which added to her somewhat matronly appearance. Unlike many of her contemporaries, whose attire proclaimed their artistic calling, she did not go in for bohemian dress or flamboyant accouterments, nor did she have a flair for the high chic some favored. Small in stature, round faced, with little or no makeup over her ruddy Scots complexion, hair pulled back softly into a pug, and simply, though tastefully, dressed, Nan presented a rather conventional image. Her canny gaze seemed to confirm what her close friends said about her alert intelligence and wry sense of humor. She was "a person of very few words, very brief," but "very sound," friends observed. "She was a good listener for chatty Forbes," who was the lively one. A scintillating and at times contentious conversationalist, he was the life of any social gathering. One associate described him as the most entertaining man he ever knew. Forbes was always very close and affectionate toward Nan and respectful of her opinions, and she in turn "was very admiring of him." He was devoted to her family as well, more so than to his own, except Mary. Forbes's friends had a high regard for Nan and made a point of mentioning her in correspondence, referring to her as "a very kindly person," "a most charming person," and "a grand girl."[18]

In Manhattan they settled into the carefree artist's life, she to paint and he to edit and write freelance. Financial security did not concern them especially, as they enjoyed the camaraderie of other artists and pursued their liberal interests in art and politics. They lived in a studio in the Clinton Building at 253 West Forty-third Street between Seventh and Eighth Avenues, an apartment Nan had rented shortly after their marriage. "It was a wonderful building as far as tradition went but not as far as modern conveniences went. The first two floors of the building were occupied by 'ladies of dubious morals' and the top floor by artists entirely. It was all studios. Eugene Speicher had the only studio with a bath." Their neighbors, established and rising artists, included Speicher, Thomas Moran, Carl Rungius, William Ritschel, Gardner Symons, Leon Kroll, and Ben Foster. Speicher, a fellow Buffalonian, had been a classmate of Nan's, and when the two bumped into each other in the elevator, they were delighted to discover that since they last met both had married and now lived in the same building.[19] In later years Watson would recount with gossipy relish a number of personal anecdotes about the artists in the Clinton Building and their wives.

One Saturday morning after completing his work and handing in his copy, Forbes was taking Nan out to celebrate when, opening the door of the studio, they "ran smack into" Pres. Theodore Roosevelt. The president had been visiting Carl Rungius, "rather a dumb creature," according to Watson, "but very decent and without any sense of art whatsoever." He had a remarkable knowledge of wild animals, however, which he normally depicted in western scenes, and was probably Roosevelt's favorite artist. Watson recalled the elevator ride with the president. "I didn't know what to do about it but I bowed very formally and said, 'Good Morning, Mr. President.' Roosevelt acknowledged the greeting in an extremely polite manner, and we three went down in the little elevator together, passing the time of day as the old fashioned elevator banged itself downward. When we got to the first floor the President backed out of the elevator and bowed from the waist to Nan and me and said, 'I wish you a very good morning,' and then he departed."[20]

During those years the Watsons became part of a close-knit coterie of young artists associated with the Art Students League and the "ash can" school. There were gatherings at the studios of Robert Henri and George Bellows with William and Edith Glackens, Robert and Marjorie Henri, Eugene and Elsie Speicher, Guy and Floy Pène du Bois, and other progressive artists. Years later, describing parties at Bellows's East Nineteenth Street studio, Watson recalled, "the women formed one group to discuss domestic witticisms and problems and the men another group to discuss painting." In Bellows's eyes, the world of painting definitely belonged to the men. "We talked of Emma Goldman, Alexander Berkman or Isadora Duncan or the Ferrer School. The distraction from painting was comparatively short-lived. Emma Goldman was a great friend of Henri's and Bellows' and talk of her made us feel pleasantly liberal if not radically advanced." Watson was among the eighty-four men who marched with the women in the first joint suffrage parade in 1911. The object of boos, hisses, and shouted taunts about their wives' masculinity, he and Nan and the others got a good laugh from the "hooting on the sidewalks of Fifth Avenue."[21]

Two of the articles Watson sold during the first year and a half of their marriage dealt with the subject of athletics, and each demonstrated an easy familiarity with the more "civilized" sports of his youth. In "The Making of Tennis Champions," he examined the form of great tennis stars and recounted memorable moments from their careers. "Athletic Stars of the Year" was a review of the season's highlights in international polo, tennis, golf, and intercollegiate Ivy League track and boating. During this period, Watson also wrote a small book on sports, which explained how all sports developed from the original ball games played during medieval times.[22]

The Watsons had been married less than two years when Forbes was fired from his job at *The Scrap Book* because of rudeness to Mr. Munsey, "since I kept my feet on the desk and continued to read a manuscript and paid no attention to him when he came into my office. He was with a friend to whom he was showing his riches of several floors in the Flat Iron Building with attendant slaves editing his magazines. He slammed my office door so hard that it broke the glass and rushed into the next room where Bob Davis was acting as head of all seven magazines, and yelling so loud that I could easily hear him, said to Davis, 'Who is that next door?' Davis told him and Munsey said, 'Fire him.'" Faced with the prospect of impecuniousness, Watson nonetheless registered no remorse or second thoughts. Indeed, his account of the incident, recorded thirty-four years later, seemed mirthful, tinged with an arrogance that would permeate his attitude toward authority throughout his career. He referred to Munsey as "that incredible caricature of a stage Englishman."[23]

In retrospect, his dismissal was fortuitous. "This was a most fortunate circumstance," he observed, "because I had already written articles for the *International Studio* and that very night when I got home I was talking with Ben Foster who for years had been a critic on the *Post,* but he was becoming so successful as a painter that he wanted to give up the job. When he mentioned this fact, I pulled out my articles, showed them to him and he said he would get the job for me, which he immediately did." Watson's initial piece in *International Studio* had been devoted to Eugene Speicher, a rising young painter apprenticed in the tradition of the Old Masters but independent in point of view. It was Watson's first nationally published art criticism, and it signaled the direction his future commentary would take. That Speicher was "almost rampantly American" was good, Watson noted, for "a strong note of nationality indicates strength in an artist."[24]

Watson joined the *New York Evening Post* in October 1912. Like most other art critics of the day, his credentials were less a matter of systematic education than informally accrued knowledge. Family wealth and position had enabled him to develop a spacious but discerning love of art, and over the years he had cultivated a formidable connoisseurship. Growing up with artists, he understood almost instinctively their artistic aims and personal aspirations. His mugwump sense of guardianship fitted him for the role of illuminator to a public capable of progress in appreciating art.

During his first months on the *Evening Post,* Watson conducted an informal survey of American artists, among them Robert Henri, Childe Hassam, Arthur B. Davies, Gutzon Borglum, and J. Alden Weir. How, he queried, could criticism serve art, the artist, and the public? The artists' responses, as Watson excerpted them, seemed advance confirmation of his own critical approach: Interpret art to the public and promote public interest in art. Be serious and sincere, study carefully all points of view. Understand the vitality of today's art and train one's observation, intelligence, and knowledge. Know something about the medium being criticized and know something about the work being analyzed. Attack sham, including the good-natured commercialist.[25] Most reputable art critics of the decade subscribed to these caveats to some extent. But of the respondents' admonitions, those which Watson practiced most avidly, and which differentiated his criticism from that of his contemporaries, were to "understand the vitality of today's art," "promote public interest in art," and "attack sham." In Watson, the unique coalescence of a privileged background with a progressive confidence in Americans' potential to apprehend quality, a love of art matched only by a love of America, and a skeptical temperament that shrank neither from giants nor from battle suggested the way in which his criticism would serve art. By interpreting for Americans the aesthetic elements in a work of art extricated from the gimmickry of fashion and the strictures of tradition and removed from extraneous issues of morality and status, Watson sought to elevate their appreciation. Emancipated from material considerations, viewers would share the artist's spiritual vision and experience the unadulterated pleasures of art.

Four major issues dominated art criticism in the United States when Watson joined the *Evening Post:* The issue of academic versus modern art; representational art versus abstraction; socially useful art versus art for art's sake; and a national art in America versus internationalism.[26] The former delineated the conservative, the latter the modernist. The critic's stance on these issues more or less established his or her alignment in the conservative-versus-modernist controversy. Watson held modernist views on some issues and conservative ones on others. Where aesthetics and art principles were concerned, his predilections were generally moderate. However, a liberal perspective and an independent disposition brought him much closer to the modernists than the conservatives.

A kind of mugwump progressive in art matters as well as those political, for the next twenty years Watson the critic would vigorously champion individualism in art, battling both slavish adherence to tradition and uncritical embracement of the new. He would attack the monopoly of the conservative NAD and promote young and independent American artists. While urging originality and creative freedom, he would disdain radical experimentation for its own sake. His art criticism would advance not only an aesthetic viewpoint but also a confidence in America, its art, and the improvability of American taste. He would admonish his readers that the American artist was, after all, a member of society with the same material needs as others, but he would attack, with a scorn intensified perhaps by his mugwump heritage, the mercenary spirit of artists who painted primarily for the market. Applying to art the themes he would later identify in Van Wyck Brooks's "humanitarian liberalism," Watson would emphasize personal expression and democracy. Those views, most of which would change little over the years, were enunciated for the first time during his tenure on the *Evening Post.*

2 NEW YORK EVENING POST
YEARS, 1912–1917

Watson was nearly thirty-three years old when he became art critic for the *New York Evening Post*. He had not chosen this career in advance, but once he took on the assignment, it suited him immensely well. After all, art and writing were his primary interests, and his creative gifts were not sufficiently powerful to achieve success in literature or art alone. He joined the influential New York newspaper at a time when the country had experienced the exhilarating effects of half a century of rapid industrialization with, however, its attendant abuses. Americans were ready to redress injustices, to enact laws to bring about social reform, and to organize for civic, cultural, and personal improvement. America's moral ideals, little removed from the Victorian canons of respectability and optimism, supported the prevalent notion of progress and applied to all aspects of culture.

The *Evening Post*'s tradition of liberal reform was already well established when Watson signed on. Through a series of crusading owners and editors—Alexander Hamilton, William Cullen Bryant, Carl Schurz, William Legget, Edwin Lawrence Godkin, and John Bigelow—the newspaper had earned a reputation for vigilance, independence, and combativeness. In 1912, under the ownership and presidency of Oswald Garrison Villard, the son of journalist and financier Henry Villard and the grandson of abolitionist William Lloyd Garrison, the paper championed the progressive agenda and circulated its message to a discriminating readership. At once a strong practitioner of capitalist expansion in his railroad empire and a humanitarian crusader in his journalistic ventures, Villard was an unrelenting editorial writer who led the *Evening Post* and its weekly supplement, the *Nation,* in righteous support of women's suffrage, African American rights, and other progressive causes. Watson was in tune with the paper's campaigns. Before long he would be launching several of his own to liberalize artistic conventions in America.

Despite strong personal opinions, Villard characteristically promoted the kind of independence among his staff that he himself embodied. Here too the fit was right for Watson. The diversity among his illustrious new colleagues on the *Evening Post* offered the best proof of Villard's liberalism, as they jealously guarded their "absolute freedom of expression," even though, in Villard's opinion, there was no occasion to do so. The *Evening Post*'s venerable drama critic at this time, J. Ranken Towse, was a proper, conservative Englishman who made it a rule never to make the acquaintance of actors and actresses, a practice Villard urged Watson to emulate toward artists and dealers. "I did not confide in Mr. Villard when he interviewed me that nine-tenths of my friends were painters," Watson wrote thirty years later. Towse's uncompromising integrity contrasted starkly with Henry T. Finck, the music critic, who was "all emotion," in Villard's words. "Far from shunning musicians, Finck loved their company and especially adored the beautiful women among them. He saw no impropriety whatsoever in falling in love with them and raving about them in his writings." Simeon Strunsky, whose *Saturday Magazine* column, "Post Impressions," and other articles ranged from satirical stories of city politics and the state of education to international affairs, contributed eyewitness reports on many of the most important events of the day, including the war in France and the Versailles Peace Conference. Washington correspondent David Lawrence "scooped" William Jennings Bryan's resignation as secretary of state in 1915. He also refused to concede the presidential election to Charles Evans Hughes in 1916, making the *Evening Post* the only major newspaper in the country to call the outcome correctly. Other *Evening Post* colleagues who established major reputations were editorial writer and art critic Frank Jewett Mather Jr.; sportswriter Lawrence Perry; Harold Phelps Stokes, who succeeded Lawrence as Washington bureau chief; and V. J. Youmans, science editor.[1]

Between 1906, when Watson settled in New York, and 1912, when he became art critic for the *Evening Post,* the number of art societies, museums, and art schools in the United States had more than doubled, and museum attendance was on the rise. New York City was the hub of art and culture in the United States. Its museums, dealers, and critics dictated national acceptance. Despite conspicuous challenges from The Eight and Alfred Stieglitz, mainstream American art remained traditional and academic. As in the preceding century, the public wanted its visual creations to be veritable and idealistic.

Art criticism as a discipline had gradually achieved respect. Considered somewhat esoteric during the nineteenth century, published criticism and theory had been confined to magazines and usually consisted of undistinguished comments from writers of dubious authority and moralistic predisposition. As "culture" became a symbol of status in Gilded Age America, however, an eager, unsure public looked to the critics for guidance. Critics gained in authoritativeness and knowledge as they interpreted a bewildering variety of media, subjects, and styles in art. By the turn of the century, newspapers also published art criticism, and the major dailies added art critics to their staffs, though generally with divided assignments. Watson's colleague Frank Jewett Mather Jr., first served as an editorial writer on the *Evening Post,* then gradually concentrated on European politics and art criticism. News bureau correspondents in Paris and London usually covered Continental art events. By the time Watson joined the *Evening Post,* most New York dailies took art criticism seriously enough to pay their writers full-time wages.

Watson took over the column "Art Notes," which appeared once or twice a week, and wrote articles about current art topics. A little more than a year after he joined the staff, in November 1913, he began contributing full-page feature pieces to the *Illustrated Saturday Magazine* under a byline. The cover of the magazine section for February 1914 anticipated not only Valentine's Day but also Watson's ascending stature with a full-page color picture by his wife, Nan, entitled *'Tis Love that Makes the World Go Round.*[2]

Watson's immediate predecessors and contemporaries on the *Evening Post*—Ben Foster, who got him his job; Frank Jewett Mather Jr.; B. P. Stephenson; and Charles DeKay—tended to be conservative in their approach to art, and Watson's early reviews were not readily distinguishable from theirs. During the first several months, his notices were generally bland in tone and noncontroversial in content, barely hinting at the dauntless stances that would later mark him as an uncompromising champion of contemporary American art and a witty, pugnacious opponent of conservatism. Nor was his style distinctive. Words such as "agreeable" and "piquant" lent a note of Victorian primness to his remarks. He criticized only discreetly the leading artists and fashionable styles of the day and accepted "official" art, albeit without zest. In 1912 he wrote admiringly of The Ten, America's respectable impressionists, whom he would later describe as "boring," "prosaic," "commonplace," and "settled in ruts."[3] He indulged the popular portraitists, whose slick, flattering likenesses were especially offensive to him in subsequent years. Initially, he even treated the National Academy of Design, the prime target of his progressive attacks, with restraint.

A review of a Kenyon Cox exhibit written during Watson's second month on the *Evening Post* illustrated his initial forbearance. "However regular may be the features, or however perfect the figures, in his work," Watson wrote, "they are always infused by the life which inevitably goes into the work of the artist standing on the rock foundation of solid drawing." Within a few years, he would criticize Cox's portraits as incredibly hard, "positively stifling in the utter absence of the breath of life," marvels of "rigid exactness." Cox himself was "the determined leader of the reactionaries in their effort to stem the on-rush of the modernists."[4]

Similarly, his early comments concerning Edwin Blashfield's murals, which Watson would dismiss in 1920 as "merely covering the wall," were tactful. Allowing that "such an abundant use of the American flag in Blashfield's decorations for the Wisconsin state capitol sounded a little alarming," Watson nonetheless commended the artist for draping the figures in such a way as to make the flag a unifying color design. In 1914 he complained of a Blashfield exhibition, "It is all very methodical, very thoughtful, very 'educational,' the kind of schoolma'am art that has so long dominated mural decoration in America."[5]

That October when Watson started at the *Evening Post,* members of the Association of American Painters and Sculptors were completing final preparations for an upcoming exhibition at the Sixty-ninth Regiment Armory on Lexington Avenue in New York. Despite a certain reluctance on the part of Henri and many of his followers, European and American modernists were to be shown together under one roof along with a panorama of older artists. It was the intent of Arthur Bowen Davies, Walt Kuhn, and other sponsors of the exhibition to bring to America examples of the most significant new art in the Western Hemisphere. The Armory Show, which opened on February 17, 1913, and ran through March 15, was a landmark event in the history of American art, introducing European modernism to a public that for the most part had never before seen it. From New York City the exhibition traveled to Chicago and Boston, and by the time it closed, nearly three hundred thousand curious Americans had attended.[6] It elicited strong, often extreme reactions, from outrage to mania, although critical reviews were more adverse than favorable overall. As a front-page news story in a number of major American newspapers, the exhibition's effect was to expand public awareness of modern art far beyond the customary audience.

The momentous Armory Show was the subject of Watson's earliest columns. He attended it daily, from the preview through the final day. In four separate columns in the first week alone he hailed its groundbreaking importance in promulgating nonrepresentationalism. Yet he neither acclaimed nor analyzed the show's major attraction, European modernism. His initial notice took the form of a pseudo-suspense narrative in which he guided readers through the armory galleries, parodying the furor over the new art and twitting the abstractionists. If the gallery visitor survived the cubists "without flinching" and confronted the "shouting canvases" of Matisse, Watson mocked, he could proceed to Wassily Kandinsky's *Improvisation*. Once the viewer looked it "straight in the eye—if it contains an eye," the operation would be over. "Weird examples are decidedly in evidence," Watson concluded, but these held a minor position in the exhibition.[7]

In his second review, he praised the exciting postimpressionist art on display, especially that of Paul Cézanne and Vincent van Gogh, which broke through the ruts of impressionism and rigid representationalism. But regarding cubism, fauvism, and other avant-garde art he was skeptical. Remarkably, Watson even managed to forget the name of Marcel Duchamp, whose *Nude Descending a Staircase* was the *succès de scandale* of the show. Challenging the claim that the work of Francis Picabia or the "artist whose name has escaped for the moment" (Duchamp) could be considered art, let alone significant art, Watson scoffed, "without the aid of manifestoes, without the prop of titles, what do these pictures say?" Indeed, he asserted, there were rugs and wallpaper with nonrepresentational designs superior to those of the so-called abstract art. Thus dismissing Duchamp, Matisse, and Kandinsky, he moved on "to more significant work."[8]

Watson found the American section most satisfying. Enunciating his dominant credo of the special genius of American art, he singled out the paintings of the American Impressionists, The Eight and other urban realists, and a few abstract artists, praising in particular J. Alden Weir, Allen Tucker, John Twachtman, and Childe Hassam. Hardly pioneers in modernism compared to the European vanguard, these were nonetheless artists who asserted the modern note in American art by 1913. In their work Watson perceived a change from the old derivativeness that had characterized American output for decades and an all-important independence of spirit. Hold on to distinctiveness, he urged American artists, though adding a cautionary note: Assimilate some of the more splendid ideas of postimpressionism, yes, "but solemnly to imitate the little twisted offshoots, even if the offshoots are but six months old, will not develop originality."[9]

Conservative critics such as Frank Jewett Mather Jr. and Royal Cortissoz also praised the American art at the Armory Show and dismissed cubism, fauvism, and other forms of European abstract art. Where Watson differed from them, however, was in his enthusiasm for postimpressionism, which the conservatives regarded with suspicion, even repugnance.

A number of American artists had ventured into modernism well before the Armory Show. John Covert, Joseph Stella, Abraham Walkowitz, Max Weber, Marsden Hartley, Stanton MacDonald-Wright, and John Marin among others had been exploring figurative ambiguity and formal deviation for several years.

However, except for Arthur G. Dove, who had developed a nonobjective idiom by 1911, and Joseph Stella and Henry Patrick Bruce, who had exhibited with the futurists and orphists, respectively, few American artists had turned to total abstraction before the Armory Show. The majority had seen only isolated examples of European modernism. Now the show set off a ferment of experimentation with cubism, futurism, fauvism, dada, and other nonobjective styles. Stuart Davis, a gifted pupil of Robert Henri, recalled, "I was enormously excited by the show, . . . I resolved that I would quite definitely have to become a 'modern' artist." Assimilating one element, then another, American artists evolved through successive levels of abstractness from mild distortion to total nonobjectivity.[10]

A new group of collectors emerged as a direct result of the Armory Show. John Quinn, Walter Arensberg, Katherine Dreier, and others not only purchased works from the show but also went on to build significant modern collections of their own. Several such as Arthur Jerome Eddy and Albert E. Gallatin also became spokesmen for modern art, exhibiting their collections and promoting modernism in books and articles.

Galleries specializing in modern art also started up following the Armory Show, beginning with the Daniel Gallery in December 1913. Watson was enthusiastic about the Daniel, noting that it provided opportunities "to some of the least conventional, and at the same time most alive, of our artists." The Carroll, Bourgeois, and Washington Square Galleries opened the following year. Having held informal exhibitions in her studio in MacDougal Alley since 1907, Gertrude Vanderbilt Whitney established the Whitney Studio in 1914, one of only a few galleries dedicated to contemporary American artists. Marius de Zayas, who had been associated with Stieglitz's 291, started his own place for avant-garde art, the Modern Gallery, in 1915. There were also several others that emphasized modern art or featured it in an occasional show. Watson urged these owners "not to follow new chatter, but to exhibit a diversity of modern pictures, and let the poor layman take his choice and see what is going on in the world while he is choosing." Independence in creating art and in judging it, a cardinal theme in his Armory Show reviews, remained the dominant message.[11]

With a respectable salary from the *Evening Post* and a brimming social life, Forbes and Nan moved in 1913 from their studio apartment in the Clinton Building to more felicitous accommodations at the Hotel Chelsea at 222 West Twenty-third Street, a short walk from the Village. One of the first cooperative apartments in New York City, the legendary twelve-story red brick building, with its ornately decorated wrought-iron staircase and balconies, towered over the colorful Chelsea neighborhood of shops and lively happenings. Artists, writers, musicians, actors, and other creative clientele were attracted to the hotel's bohemian ambiance. "The Chelsea was not part of America," one illustrious resident commented, "had no vacuum cleaners, no rules, no taste, no shame. It was a ceaseless party."[12] Hard-up tenants sometimes traded their art for rent, and the hotel's lobby was filled with paintings and sculptures. Nan and Forbes resided in those convivial surroundings for four years.

In the summer they escaped the city heat in the small resort town of Harbor Springs in northern Michigan, where they savored the fresh breezes blowing in off Lake Michigan. The vacation marked the beginning of a thirty-two-year ritual. In 1916 they bought a small cottage there at the edge of a golf course and added a working studio for Nan, cutting down sixty-five trees to provide clear, uninterrupted light for her painting. They expanded the cottage again in 1938. Harbor Springs was "an awful distance," but despite the laborious train trip, Nan and Forbes loved to go there. Often, the weather "just showed off," and after several days of sleepiness and acclimatization, they felt its full benefit. Forbes "spent most of the time fooling around with the trees on the place and fooling around on the golf course." Something of a celebrity among his Harbor Springs neighbors, Watson regularly golfed with them, and, when he graciously presented talks on art, the local paper publicized the occasion and the community turned out. Nan always seemed to do her best work in Harbor Springs, and it was not unusual for her to stay for a month or so after Forbes returned east. Sometimes her sister, Alice Paterson, came out for visits, perfectly in her element, Watson remarked, among all the politically conservative residents.[13]

When Watson went abroad that year, he visited Mary Cassatt in her chateau, Beaufresne, at Mesnil-Théribus. It was his first face-to-face meeting with the sixty-nine-year-old expatriate artist. "She began to talk the instant that I alighted from the motor which she had sent to the station," he wrote, "and the talk went on all that day. . . . The real point of meeting her, even then, was that one couldn't listen to her, pouring out her ardor and her understanding, without feeling his conviction in the importance of art to civilization intensified. . . . She made you share her intense hatred of aesthetic prevarication and compromise."[14] Although that was his first encounter with the internationally acclaimed artist, by the time Cassatt died thirteen years later, Watson was generally recognized as the leading interpreter of her art and the critic who understood her best.

The National Academy of Design was the most powerful force in American art at the time Watson began his career on the *Evening Post*, as it had been since shortly after its establishment in 1827. It was "the one artist organization that had real standing, stability, and prestige, and the rest of it was an amorphous kind of movement that consisted of individuals," Lloyd Goodrich recalled.[15] Although the NAD had originally been founded to break the reactionary hold of the American Academy of Fine Arts, it too had become an exclusive bulwark of conservative art. Over the years various artist groups had mounted efforts to liberalize the organization and weaken its control over art in the United States, but they made few inroads. Even the most successful, the Society of American Artists founded in 1877, gradually lost its impetus, merging finally with the NAD in 1906. In the years following the highly publicized emergence of The Eight, Henri and his fellow progressives led the drive to open opportunities for independents, forming the American Painters and Sculptors in 1911, incorporating in 1912 as the Association of American Painters and Sculptors. The group had little impact, however, and came to be remembered almost exclusively for the Armory Show.

It was only a matter of months before Watson joined the fray, denouncing the NAD's monopoly over exhibition standards and taste in America and dismissing academic art as anemic and unoriginal. That a number of artists he respected were members or associate members of the academy did not deter him. Nan exhibited in three separate NAD shows during the years he was at the *Evening Post,* and his good friend William Glackens exhibited in many more. But Watson excepted Glackens, J. Alden Weir, Ernest Lawson, George Bellows, Childe Hassam, and others who were "academicians merely by title. . . . Theirs is not the kind of work that really touches the heart of the dyed-in-the-wool academicians," he explained. Years later Watson recalled that his first major article after joining the *Evening Post* was a review of the NAD's winter show, and that after it appeared, the sole artist in the building who would speak to him was Eugene Speicher, he being the only one who was not a member of the academy. "The others were dumbfounded by my criticism. . . . Foster treated me as a young man who was too bad to be associated with." Gardner Symons's wife "could never see me without angry tears and Mr. Symons chided her about this, not because he minded what she did but he thought it was too big a compliment to me to let me know that it mattered so much what I wrote."[16] Actually, Watson's first NAD notice was relatively tame. A few jabs at conservative artists such as Carroll Beckwith and dissenting comments about Symons's award-winning painting ("undistinguished" and lacking in warmth) were his harshest criticisms in December 1912. There was more sting in his review of the academy's spring exhibit, however, which began the day the Armory Show closed, as, for example, his observation that John Carlson's popular snow scenes were "degenerating into lifeless repetition of a mechanical color recipe."[17]

By the following December, when the NAD held its winter show, Watson had not only greeted more spiritedly the arrival of modernism in America but had also attacked less hesitantly its conservative adversaries. By then his liberalism and discriminating taste had melded into a cohesive aesthetic. An antielitist streak beaconed his perspective, and a zest for battle animated his phrasing. "He had a very very strong vein of sarcasm in his makeup," a colleague observed, and the NAD became his prime victim. "All is well at the Fine Arts building," he intoned, despite whispered fears that "those horrid influences emanating from last winter's international exhibition of the Society of American Painters and Sculptors would defile the purity" of the National Academy. "Lest one be convicted of predisposed ideas, and unjust generalizations," he jibed, proof was "generously supplied by the prize-winning pictures." That review marked roughly the beginning of nearly two decades of unrelenting assaults by Watson on the NAD and its adherents. In his campaign to gain recognition for American modernists, he not only led the chorus of encouragement but also took on all impediments to independent production: Conservative critics, dealers who ignored progressive art, old-line museum officials, architects who resisted contemporary decoration, and foreign competitors.[18]

Besides the NAD shows themselves, Watson criticized the invitational system, the jury system, and the prize system, each of which perpetuated the academic monopoly. Its practice of issuing red tickets, usually to entrenched members rather than to young artists, guaranteed acceptance of works that Watson was certain a conscientious jury would otherwise reject. A jurist had disclosed to him that more than one thousand pictures had been submitted to a show in which only fifty places remained after red tickets had been distributed. "In other words, about five thousand dollars, by moderate calculation, went out of the pockets of the very artists who can least afford waste, because they were deceived by pretenses which, if not technically false, were at least slightly misleading." As for the jury system, it discouraged individual expression, Watson asserted, because juries, especially large ones, represented the majority, which opposed experiment. "It is hard enough to find two men who will agree on a strongly individual and original picture, but everyone will agree on the moderately good picture, the mild and competent work." The prize system was insidious because it deluded the casual visitor, who, not having seen the ineligible pictures, would be overly regardful of the winners.[19]

Watson the progressive understood the value of organizing for strength, and he urged independent artists, denied exhibition opportunities, to band together. In 1916, seeking such an organizational breakthrough, a group of independent artists ranging from moderately progressive to avant-garde formed the Society of Independent Artists. Walter Pach, who had been instrumental in bringing modern European art to the Armory Show, took the lead and, with help from collector Walter Arensberg and artist Marcel Duchamp, organized the independent artist-run association. Modeled after the French Société des Artistes Indépendants, minimal dues and fees permitted any artist to show in the annual exhibitions. William Glackens was its first president; John Sloan, who succeeded him in 1918, held the position for life. From its inception until its demise in the mid-1940s, the Independents' staunchest advocates were Gertrude Vanderbilt Whitney, who covered its deficit for more than fifteen years, and Forbes Watson and Henry McBride, who supported it as much for its example of independence as for the art it exhibited. "It is the only way whereby we can throw off the shackles of officialdom, and let in fresh air on the art situation in general," Watson argued. The truth was that Watson had difficulty at times suppressing his distaste for the inevitably ordinary works that made their way into Independents shows. Yet he shared John Sloan's view that even if it "only introduced to the small appreciative audience of art lovers, one artist of significance a year, . . . the annual show was worthwhile."[20]

Wholeheartedly, he believed in the promise of a vital American art. More than merely sympathizing with artists' ambitions, Watson identified person-ally with them, sharing with the younger, lesser-known artists of his and Nan's generation an impatience with stodginess, a delight in the exercise of creative and social independence, and a deep aversion to regimentation. His aloofness from business and trade, evident from early youth, accorded closely with the artist's detachment from mundane commerce. In his mind, to be practical and efficient was somehow to be inartistic.[21] Family wealth, a genteel heritage, and assured social standing had nurtured a mugwump liberalism in Watson, and he felt little obligation to conform to upper-class conventions. His writings reflected simultaneously an ease with moderate forms of bohemianism and a responsibility to guide those with less civilized taste.

Brought up among artists, knowing them in a way few critics could lay claim to, he naturally became their critic rather than that of the dealers.[22] He "automatically gravitated toward Washington Square rather than the Plaza," a fellow art commentator wrote of him in later years. Watson pinpointed the illuminating influence of those friendships in a monograph about his best friend, painter Allen Tucker. "When one's entire life has been lived with artists there gradually emerges an abstract being—the *Artist*. He emerges out of, or is created by, countless contacts with countless different types of artists, under as many different social and economic conditions. . . . Out of these concrete be-ings, and many others, is evolved that disembodied being who stalks through the critic's subconsciousness, balancing and measuring." Indeed, it was not unusual for Watson to use the pronoun "we" when discussing artists' circum-stances and views.[23]

His artist-centered aesthetic was a familiar position among modernist critics, and among some important conservatives as well.[24] For Watson, the artist's unique sensibility enabled him to apprehend and transmute the world around him with a special intensity that distinguished him from ordinary persons. Works created by an endowed artist and perceived by a sensitive viewer elicited in the viewer feelings of exhilaration. Implicit in Watson's philosophy was the mission of the critic to emancipate and heighten that sensitivity. In contrast to the theorists and formalists of the day, who elucidated art through intellectualization and explication of formal elements, Watson's criticism tended to be expressionistic and affective. Recurring use of terms such as "exhilarating," "exciting," and "refreshing" pointed up the subjective link between artist and viewer. That Watson was aware of Clive Bell's formalist theories was evident in his occasional reference to "significant form" and other formal vocabulary of the avant-garde after 1914.[25] However, form per se did not interest him as much as character, artistic intent, and pictorial effect. Color, the one exception, was engaging for its emotional impact rather than its formal function.

With Robert Henri, Watson shared an abiding confidence in a democratic art. When Henri instituted the MacDowell Club gallery plan of jury-free rotating exhibits in 1912, Watson enthused: "This is the only gallery where the artist meets the public without the intervening judgment of jury or dealer. Each artist stands apart, his work not being joined to that of any other artist by the stamp of supervising authority."[26] Even then, however, the essential conflict within his mugwump progressivism was apparent: that is, the struggle between the democrat's receptiveness to all artistic endeavor and the critic's stern insistence on competence. Subsequent notices were not consistently sanguine. Between congratulatory reviews, Watson regretted the "somewhat amateurish" pictures and "the inundation of beginners' works."[27]

He was unequivocally democratic on the issue of women in art. "I always think that women can do everything that men can and then some," he declared, and as early as 1912 he rejected the phrase "woman artist" because it laid a false stress on sex, "for one is an artist or one isn't and stands accordingly." Women's rights, particularly the right to vote, was high on the progressive agenda during those years, and Villard's *Evening Post* was at the forefront of the movement. Avidly sympathetic, Watson reported a suffrage benefit exhibition at the Knoedler Galleries that featured Mary Cassatt, a suffragist herself and one "who appreciates all the obstacles which the reactionary attitude of mind places in the path of the woman of liberal and independent mentality." Undoubtedly, his strong attachment to his mother and sister, who kindled his love of art, and his marriage to Nan deepened Watson's empathy with women artists, but throughout his career he expressed certain feminist insights that could well have been stated in the 1980s.[28]

His democratic philosophy was two-sided. Not only did all artists deserve a chance to show their work but the public—every sector—also deserved an opportunity to appreciate it. Democratic art did not mean the uplifting public art pompous do-gooders prescribed. Didacticism and inspirationalism only diluted aesthetic power. Watson sneered at Kenyon Cox's lofty *The Marriage of the Atlantic and the Pacific,* which was destined for the wall of the Wisconsin State Senate Chamber. The question, he insisted, was whether the senate chamber would become more or less beautiful through the presence of the work, not whether the large illustration would fill the "little brains" of the earnest schoolteacher's pupils with its "educational" ideas. But then "the question would probably not be discussed, for no respectful school-teacher would question the beauty of a picture that is so large, particularly when her own government bought it, and an authority on art made it."[29]

The short-lived People's Art Guild, the first artists' cooperative in the United States, embodied the true democratic spirit, in Watson's view, bringing "artists and the people into closer and more genuine contact for the mutual enrichment of each." Organized in January 1915 by John Weichsel, the guild sponsored art classes and study groups and mounted art exhibitions in settlement houses, artists' studios, and other community centers in poor sections of New York.[30] Pictures by John Sloan, Thomas Hart Benton, William Glackens, Abraham Walkowitz, Marsden Hartley, John Marin, Stuart Davis, and other first-rate American artists were shown to young men and women at a receptive age in surroundings where they lived, making art more real, Watson believed, and enabling them to enjoy the same works as privileged members of the community.

Still, for all Watson's democratic convictions and belligerent assaults on elitism, a lingering snobbishness surfaced now and then, touching a personal relationship or inflecting a remark. He could relate to his late, celebrated brother-in-law, Alfred Collins, of whom he wrote revealingly that as a handsome young man, Collins "took naturally to superior people."[31] After all, Watson's two closest friends over the years, Allen Tucker and Olin Dows, were of indisputably patrician lineage. Nor, deep down, could he consistently reconcile his own cultivated tastes with those of the average citizen. Like a good many progressives, especially in the East, he was democratic in conviction but, in breeding, above the crowd.[32] Even as he encouraged Americans to shake off their timidity and rely on their native instincts in judging art, his barely concealed disdain implied they had a long way to go. "An elusive quality steals into pictures that are conceived partly with the expectation of pleasing the kindly unknown owner of a nice, agreeable house, who has arrived at the psychological point of prosperity when he is prompted to replace his photographs of old masters with paintings by young masters," he wrote. "Nearly always it is found in paintings that are just what a great many people expect a painting to be, not too searching and not too original."[33]

Secure in his opinions and unhesitating in expressing them, Watson quickly established himself as a presence in the post–Armory Show art scene. His style had become quite distinctive by then, urbane yet accessible, cultivated but anti-intellectual.[34] There were lecture invitations from museums and art organizations throughout the East and commissions from a variety of publications. In addition to the *Evening Post,* Watson contributed to *Arts & Decoration, Ladies Home Journal,* and *International Studio Supplement.* He also wrote the introduction to the 1914 *Yearbook of American Etching* and articles on art for the 1915 and 1916 editions of the *National Encyclopedia.* Testimony of his prominence appeared in a photo feature in the *Vanity Fair* issue of June 1915: "Eight Critics of Art without Whom No Artistic 'Movement' Can Be Launched in New York." The eight were Charles Caffin, art critic of the *New York American;* the *New York Tribune*'s Royal Cortissoz, "'dean' of the art critics"; Frank J. Mather Jr., professor of the fine arts at Princeton University and writer for the *Nation;* Christian Brinton, "author of many critical works on art subjects"; Henry McBride, art critic of the *New York Sun;* Frederick James Gregg, who had "been more or less engaged in the controversies incidental to the 'New Movement'"; Kenyon Cox, "a destructive critic of Post Impressionism"; and Forbes Watson. Watson's photograph was captioned: "Sits in the seat of judgment of the *New York Evening Post.* Is trusted by the conservatives, as well as by the 'new men.' Believes in the organization of artists."[35]

That both conservatives and modernists trusted Watson underscored the independent mix of his positions on the conservative-versus-modernist issues and his outspoken candor in stating them. Actually, distinctions between conservative and modernist were neither clear-cut nor consistent, and demarcations were further blurred as a result of imprecise terminology. Words such as "modernism," "cubism," "futurism," "expressionism," and even "postimpressionism" were used almost interchangeably. So indiscriminately was the term "modern" applied to the spectrum of contemporary art and theories antipathetic to academicism that it came to have only general meaning as a descriptor. Some critics and historians reduced ambiguity by narrowing their discussion to avant-garde art, a category of modernism signifying advanced currents emanating from Europe—cubist, futurist, expressionist, and other recent movements.[36] For most critics, however, modernism encompassed the art of Cézanne, van Gogh, Gauguin, and other postimpressionists as well as avant-garde artists. Watson took a still broader view, including several members of The Ten. Allusive at best, those of his statements that addressed the meaning of modernism only emphasized his aversion to labels and elaborately rationalized "isms." "Whatever the fashion suggested by a painter's style," he observed in one of his less-ambiguous comments, "his true modernity depends on how acutely he responds to the life of his day."[37]

Although unanimity was rare among modernists, several common "symptoms" distinguished them from conservatives. A belief in the predominance of inner feeling was fundamental to modernist thought. Modernists ignored the conventions of traditional art, subordinating theme, composition, and technique to personal creativity and rejecting conservatives' notion of the social function of art to instill culture or transmit a motivational message. While certain conservatives also believed in the primacy of artistic genius, they nonetheless considered the rules of moral, timeless subject matter and sound workmanship inviolable. Modernists, they believed, had carried inner expression to unacceptable extremes of unintelligibility and even fraud, degeneracy, and insanity.[38]

Indebted to, if not immersed in, recent European developments, modernists, in particular the avant-garde, were internationalists in matters of art. Conservatives, however, held widely varied attitudes toward Europe, from Kenyon Cox who emulated the European Beaux-Arts school to those who rejected European traditions altogether, convinced that art should express a nation's spirit. Cosmopolitans such as John Singer Sargent and James Abbott McNeill Whistler viewed all art as international and above time and place. But all conservatives concurred in repudiating the European avant-garde.

The most reliable common denominator among modernists was the rejection of the representational function of art. Antimimetic tendencies ranged from slight distortions of visible nature to the elimination of natural images altogether. For the formalists, line, color, mass, and their relationships were the source of aesthetic meaning.[39] Some looked to "new expression by color, not by the color of things, or color in historic art" for aesthetic effect. For conservatives, the purpose of form was to pictorialize images from life. A certain degree of interpretative license was allowed—for example, minor color intensification to heighten nature's glory—but not arbitrary distortion. Such revolutionary tendencies were attributed "to lack of skill and to a mistaken historical appreciation of non-Western cultures."[40]

On most of these issues in the modernist-versus-traditionalist quarrel, critics such as Henry McBride, Christian Brinton, Sadakichi Hartmann, Marius de Zayas, and Walter Pach were unmistakably on the pro-modern, pro-avant-garde side, while Kenyon Cox, Royal Cortissoz, Frank Jewett Mather Jr., and Leila Mechlin were firmly conservative. Watson, along with several older newspaper critics such as James Huneker, James Fitzgerald, and Frederick James Gregg, spoke for the moderate modernists. Watson managed to state his moderate positions immoderately, however.

Spontaneity and personal creativity were critical in Watson's artist-centered aesthetic. Yet his consonance with the avant-garde on this issue was limited, for he also stood with the conservatives in demanding sanity and respect for the fundamentals.[41] Sanity signified for Watson moderation, stability, and the absence of gimmickry in art. It bespoke character. Its antonym, "insanity," was an epithet conservatives used in attacking modernism. Indeed, Watson himself disparaged certain modernist works as "weird," "freakish," and lacking "mental equilibrium." His skepticism toward cubism, dada, futurism, and machine art arose in part out of such perceptions. In Watson's view, J. Alden Weir embodied sanity. To go from an exhibition of moderns to one of Weir was to submit the "perturbed and fevered spirit to the benign influence of one of the sanest artistic personalities which American art has produced." Whereas continual experiment in the hands of weak, clever artists led only to bewilderment, Watson observed, it became "a source of life and renewal of youth when practiced by a mind so broad, so well-poised and sane as that of Weir."[42]

Also qualifying the expressionist cast of Watson's criticism was his insistence on disciplined craftsmanship. Emotionalism was not a substitute for competent workmanship; slapdash technique diminished art. A great many artists who had neither time nor talent to master their craft chose the simpler method of being emotional, he observed. The cubists sought to conceal their ineptitudes by "offering the public the fascination of a Chinese puzzle." Even as he complained about the conservatism of the Pennsylvania Academy exhibition of 1914, he winced at the "untidy" entries it would attract: "In contrast to the ever-present prosaic and literal portrait, and the over-gentle interior, we are sure to have some insurgent burst of protest that verges on the grotesque in its insistence on the virtue of spontaneity." He derided a group of youthful artists at the studio of Gertrude Vanderbilt Whitney for their "introspective art," which he characterized as the art of looking at "your own dear soul when you should be looking at the model." Forget about the world, he counseled the young painters, and try to find out something about painting and drawing.[43]

But brilliant execution alone did not make a work artistic, and Watson berated artists who dazzled the beholder with fluency but failed to transmit a personal vision. The era's most celebrated American painter, the star of the National Academy, John Singer Sargent, epitomized for Watson the consummate technician, slick, superficial, weak in creative spirit. That Sargent enjoyed greater adulation than any other American painter both in Europe and the United States only intensified the corrosiveness of Watson's remarks, as he relished nothing better than deflating the famous. Readers were introduced to a whole new thesaurus of derogation for him and his disciples: "Sargentism," "Sargent-imitators," "Sargent worship," "Sargentesque performance." Cecilia Beaux, William Merritt Chase, Louis Betts, Irving Wiles, and other adherents came under attack for their "machine-made portraits," "hand-made photography," "brittle dexterity," "intentional facility," "fictitious brushwork," and "meaningless cleverness." Watson thus tersely dismissed a portrait by Louis Betts: "One cannot call such portraits ... art, because art has personality, and this has none. It has likeness and cleverness, but not vision. This kind of thing is a business proposition."[44]

American viewers were partly to blame, of course. Their admiration for "pyro-technical" feats in painting was simply one more indication of their unsophisticated taste. "So many people measure art by some queer standard of painting gymnastics, believing that the more difficult a thing is to do the better it must be," Watson complained. A lack of confidence in their own taste only made matters worse. Unwilling as buyers to trust their personal responses and leaning on someone else's judgment from the beginning, they never strengthened their own initiative.[45]

On the issue of nonrepresentationalism, Watson was a modernist, regarding distortion in line and color as essential to emotional power. Faithfully drab stretches of canvas were "about as inspiring in color as a plate of pea-soup that has been left overnight in the refrigerator," he wrote in defense of William Glackens's "juicy" hues and "daring," sometimes arbitrary, harmonies. In Arthur B. Davies's drawings, linear and figurative distortion conveyed "not the facts of anatomy, but a divine moment of movement." It was "significant drawing as opposed to correct drawing." To criticize figures and objects in such pictures according to realistic standards would be as absurd "as to criticize the fragrance of a wild flower because it lacked solidity," he contended.[46]

Nor was there such a thing as intrinsically inappropriate subject matter, since expressiveness and quality of interpretation were what counted. Whereas conservatives frowned on urban realists' uncouth subject matter, Watson admired the vitality of their images. He placed a higher premium on Jerome Myers's "sympathetic observations of street groups" and "poetic intuition" than on his subject matter per se. Furthermore, art did not need to convey an insistent message in order to be moving. Polemics and "strong-armed psychology" detracted from the artistry of a work, he believed, and Watson derided the notion among certain groups that "strength in art increases in direct proportion as you leave upper Fifth Avenue as a field of subjects and approach the lower East Side."[47]

The distortion Watson espoused was only a modest step away from representationalism, however, and quite distant from the abstractionism promulgated by the avant-garde. A long-standing belief in the primacy of nature, by which he meant all of life, undergirded an unwavering commitment to figuration. Even as he scoffed at conservatives' faith in the moralizing power of nature, he himself evinced at times an almost Emersonian reverence for nature, seeing there a source of inspiration from which the artist fortified his own creative impulses.[48] As late as 1952, a time when abstract expressionism was gaining international recognition as America's unique contribution to the modern canon, he reminisced: "If these interests [writing and English classes at Harvard] had not absorbed me and led me towards my profession, I should now be a painter and probably an unpopular one because my vision is objective, and nature interests me more than my own powers of invention." All through his *Evening Post* years, Watson deprecated the nonobjectivists—Picasso, Kandinsky, and the others—and even though he later acknowledged their importance, he never truly warmed to their art. Henri Matisse was one of the few French vanguard artists whom Watson would come to admire as a brilliant liberating force, but in 1915 he belittled him as a "wavering talent," "not valuable" to other artists. American painter Andrew Dasburg's art fell and rose in Watson's estimation as Dasburg took up cubism and later returned to figuration. "Mr. Dasburg has apparently recovered from the violent attack of pure abstractionism under which he seemed to be laboring on the last occasion of his exhibiting," he wrote. "The recovery is a decided sign of health."[49]

For Watson, all the tendencies of a premier art were present in the most vital examples of progressive American painting. Feature by feature he identified and elaborated on them over the next thirty years. They were: originality, spontaneity, energy, sincerity, and refinement. Aggregated and examined as prototypically "American," they also delineated Watson's mugwump temper and the point at which his liberal and conservative propensities converged. They reflected too the personal, intuitive nature of his critical disposition.

Like the era in which he flourished, Watson's outlook both in life and in art was characteristically optimistic. He relished the buoyant, downright traits of recent American artists such as George Luks and George Bellows. In Watson's paradigm, those earthy qualities were not at odds with the characteristic he valued most in the American style, refinement. He recognized refinement in paintings by Childe Hassam, J. Alden Weir, John Twachtman, and other members of The Ten. "Wherever seen," he commented of a Hassam exhibit at the Montross, "these pictures would be recognized as American. . . . Their note is in harmony with some of the most distinctive work that this country has produced. It is the note of delicacy, of refinement, of charm, not the rude, strong note of youth which foreigners are continually expecting to find here, and which leads them to repeat the oft-repeated superficiality that Walt Whitman and Winslow Homer are our only purely native artists. . . . It is a peculiarly American note." Not only did he dispute the assertion of James McNeill Whistler, America's renowned nineteenth-century expatriate painter, that art had no nationality, but he also discerned in Whistler's own work that same peculiarly American strain of refinement.[50]

American art was sincere. Sincerity was a watchword Watson shared with conservative critics. It, too, referred to the artist's character. But Watson's usage was anticonservative, connoting not high-mindedness, but "essential independence of soul." To be sincere was to be original, unaffected, "completely one's self." It also meant "the lack of showing off." Thomas Eakins's "spotless sincerity" and "unflinching honesty" kept him aloof from the dictates of the NAD, Watson observed, and he was largely neglected during his lifetime, though not by Watson. Eakins's whole approach to life—his blindness to the crowd, his indifference to Europe, his rejection of prudery—epitomized for Watson the integrity and independence he so revered. In the work of serious modernists such as Edward Hopper and Henry Lee McFee, there was also an "unmistakable note of sincerity"[51]

As often as he commended sincerity, Watson condemned its lack. Commercialism, ballyhoo, faddist "isms," intentional emotionalism, and all emblems of insincerity aroused his mugwump scorn. "Forbes had a very healthy cynicism," Lloyd Goodrich, a colleague during the 1920s, remembered, "a very good corrective to being taken in by things." With an almost exuberant sardonic wit, he pricked the bubbles of fashionmongers and self-conscious movements. Man Ray, the well-known American modernist, was a "movement-painter as distinguished from an individualist." Lacking a personal idiom, he had "tried a little Post-Impressionism, a little abstractionism, a little of almost everything," until he had become "an artistic cocoon wound round with the threads of literary ideas, a personality enclosed in the shell of a movement." But the cubists were the most egregiously insincere in Watson's estimation, masters of "humbug." Frenchmen, he wrote, never tired of boasting that only foreigners, "meaning, of course, barbarians, Americans, and others like them," bought up the "mathematical thought-records which hang themselves on the wall as if they were works of art."[52]

It exasperated him that so many American modernists groveled blindly at the feet of Matisse and Picasso in "servile imitation of Paris." Unabashedly chauvinistic, he challenged the commonly held notion that America lagged behind France and "that American art might perish if *le dernier cri* in the art quarters of Paris, Berlin, etc. was not instantly adopted by our young artists." "If the quest of the fourth dimension in art, or Cubism, had emanated from Oshkosh, would anyone have risen to accuse Paris of not being 'up-to-date' because she was ignorant of the latest advance thoughts that had stirred Oshkosh Bohemia to its innermost soul?" he bristled. The fact was, Watson insisted, American art possessed greater originality. After all, Arthur B. Davies was the most important man to experiment in the field of cubism, and he was American, a draughtsman as powerful as any living Frenchman. "No one suggested . . . when Davies held a one-man exhibition . . . that Paris needed to see the Davies exhibition." And despite Watson's generally low regard for American portraitists, they were "innocent lambs" compared to the legion of foreigners who came to America "with a bundle of portraits of princesses and duchesses to flatter and to fleece."[53]

Those were bitter words, but given the nearly total official and commercial neglect of progressive American art during the second decade of the twentieth century, Watson's extravagant scorn was understandable. Even following the Armory Show, after postimpressionism and other modern European art had ignited the interest of American collectors and dealers, modern American art attracted few buyers. In 1916 Cézanne's *Four Apples* sold for $20,000. That amounted to "$5,000 an apple," artist Jerome Myers reckoned, "while whole orchards painted by American artists went begging." They "*needed* a champion who might occasionally be a little intemperate," Lloyd Goodrich insisted. With bite and fervor, Watson urged Americans to emancipate themselves from French domination and trust their own aesthetic instincts. Art, he asserted, was the truest manifestation of a nation's spirit.[54]

Modern American artists, many of whom had felt overshadowed by the Europeans at the Armory Show, were the main attraction at the Forum Exhibition of Modern American Painters in March 1916. The organizing committee, composed of well-known promoters of contemporary art, selected some two hundred works by sixteen artists for the show, generally regarded as America's foremost exponents of cubism, fauvism, synchromism, and other avant-garde styles.[55] It was arguably the most important exhibition of modern American art since 1913; its stated purpose, "to turn public attention for the moment from European art and concentrate it on the excellent work being done in America; and to bring serious, deserving painters in direct contact with the public without a commercial intermediary." That being its liberal mission, Watson's somewhat snappish response seemed perplexing. His review, a brusque half-page, rejected the premise itself. The show was supposed to be an "advanced" exhibition, he sniffed, but in actuality, there was nothing particularly new about it. "Miles of such canvases" had been shown, and critics had already written "miles of comment." As for the committee, its assumption of "the functions of critic and jury" amounted to "the Prussianization of art criticism." Certainly, the committee's preference for the more modern painters partially explained Watson's grudging response. (William Zorach's compositions were decorative "to a certain extent"; other of Marsden Hartley's paintings were superior to those shown; the touch of live color in Arthur Dove's designs was "hardly enough to make them important.") But something in his petulant tone also suggested that Watson was antagonistic to the venture from the beginning. He had, after all, been ignored at its conception.[56]

It was a different story regarding the Society of Independent Artists' first exhibition the following year. Watson was as cordial toward the Independents' show as he had been finicky toward the Forum Exhibition, and not simply because of the relative merits of the art presented. Democracy and the independent concept were at work here, not to mention the show's diluting effect on the NAD and the latest Paris imports. "Art has been said truly to be aristocratic, not democratic," he wrote. But the aristocracy was spiritual rather than material, and a truly democratic method was needed to overcome material differences. The answer was the independent exhibition, which he visualized as "a gigantic filter into which fine and rough material is thrown, but only the fine comes through. . . . An independent exhibition cannot make all artists equal any more than a democracy can make all people equal," he wrote, "but it can and does give every one an equal opportunity." The exhibition, the largest ever held in New York, included 2,500 works by 1,200 artists from thirty-eight states and several European countries. More than 20,000 people attended over a four-week period. Watson was generous in his praise of the participants, who ranged from moderately conservative to modern. "There was tonic in the air," he enthused in one of his five notices. "Men and women . . . saw pictures by the men who have more circus than art instincts, they saw works by such leaders as William Glackens. Best of all, more than one visitor found a discovery, something that interested him, by a man he had never heard of."[57]

And it was a splendid opportunity to compare the various currents influencing contemporary artists. "The abstract movement was never before put to such a test," Watson commented. "The alphabetical arrangement has brought the cubist pictures into contact with all sorts of other pictures, and they hang together like lambs." Henri Matisse, whose pictures were "not announced by fife or drum," hardly caused a ripple in the great melting pot. "Never did 'isms' seem so dead. If this were all the Independent had accomplished it would be much," Watson exulted.[58]

For his first few years on the *Evening Post,* Watson had attempted to heed, partially at least, Villard's admonition to distance himself from artists and dealers whose shows he reviewed. His half-hearted compliance ended abruptly in January 1917, however, when following a Whitney Studio show he returned for exhibit photographs he had forgotten to pick up earlier. "I snooped about the galleries until I came to a large table covered with photographs for press," Watson recalled. "While attempting to insert about four of these photographs into a large envelope, a lady, who had been observing my actions, caught me just before I got to the door and said very agreeably, 'Are you from the press?' I said 'Yes.' She then asked me my name. That lady's name was Juliana R. Force." The unexpected encounter with Gertrude Whitney's assistant ended for Watson "the cold tradition of the critic toward the creator, which Mr. Oswald Villard doubtless inherited from his distinguished father."[59] It signaled much more, however, initiating as it did a powerful, mutually productive alliance between Watson and two of the most influential women in early-twentieth-century American art, Gertrude Vanderbilt Whitney and her invaluable assistant, Juliana Force.

Whitney and Force were, in Lloyd Goodrich's words, "absolutely dissimilar." Gertrude Vanderbilt Whitney was an aristocrat, the great-granddaughter of millionaire "Commodore" Cornelius Vanderbilt; daughter of Cornelius Vanderbilt II, the richest man in America; and married to millionaire Harry Payne Whitney. Never simply a society matron, she had taken up sculpture early in their marriage, establishing herself not only as an artist but also as a generous patron. Juliana Force, who began as Gertrude Whitney's secretary, was one of ten children of a Hoboken, New Jersey, working-class family and "the only one with real brains," according to Goodrich.[60] Although she had no training or background in art, she was quick, ambitious, and keen to learn about it.

Whitney exhibitions in those days had not been very advanced. "There was an element of social relationship among the artists they picked," Goodrich remarked, having less to do with talent than with their connections to Gertrude Whitney. Easily forgotten society artists such as Count von Laszlo and Count Arnaldo Tambourini exhibited side by side with John Sloan and other promising American talents. Occasionally favorable but usually not, Watson's reviews made scant allowance for personal circumstances behind the women's choices. While he applauded Whitney's benevolence toward unknown artists, he deprecated her misguided generosity. Years later he was less sparing, commenting that before he came on the scene, the Whitney gallery exhibitions consisted of works by second-rate foreign artists, most of whom came with letters of introduction from Whitney's social friends. "Uptown swillage," he called them. He scoffed at the title of a Whitney Studio exhibit in 1916, "Modern Paintings by American and Foreign Artists." "The word 'modern' is used only by way of stating the fact that the pictures are the work of our own time," he observed. All those "cautious souls" who were disturbed by art that challenged "the cherished tradition that a picture 'should look like something'" were hereby reassured. "They may go to Mrs. Whitney's studio with the guarantee that nearly every picture looks like what it is supposed to represent." At that first encounter in January 1917, Force asked Watson how he liked the current show. It was terrible, he replied, and he proceeded to tell her why.[61]

Soon thereafter, Watson became the women's friend and advisor, introducing them to the work of promising talents and appearing as a guest at their social gatherings. Out of the women's respect for Watson's connoisseurship, and a common desire to foster interest in young American artists and a progressive American art grew a symbiotic relationship that lasted more than fourteen years. For Juliana Force, friendships with artists and involvement in their careers were inseparable from her job as assistant to Gertrude Whitney.[62] Force "was nothing if not personal in her choice of artists," Watson commented in later years. Sunday morning breakfasts with artist friends at her Thirty-sixth Street apartment were "small and gay and warmly hospitable, . . . began late enough and lasted long enough to lead gracefully into the luncheon cocktail period, to the countless openings and other parties, swarming with guests." When the women decided to establish a club, one with a similarly "friendly, festive" environment in which young artists could exhibit their work and meet fellow artists, they agreed that Forbes Watson was the ideal choice for artistic adviser.[63] But the war intervened.

From the time hostilities erupted in Europe in 1914, Watson had been troubled over the plight of America's friends in France and Belgium. France's battle was a struggle to protect civilization and freedom, he wrote, "which mean life to the artist, against the onrush of materialism, which is death to the artist." He accorded generous coverage to war relief exhibitions, noting that artists, with their gift of imagination, felt a special empathy for war victims. Sympathy did not dilute his critical objectivity, however. Despite the praiseworthy intent of a sculpture competition with war as its theme, which the philanthropic society Friends of the Young Artists sponsored, Watson's review was severe. Mainly, he observed, the show was weak because the designation of the subject, "war," had too constricting an effect on the artistic imagination.[64]

Watson's passport application photo, taken before he left for ambulance service, 1917. Forbes Watson Papers.

As the United States drew closer to entering the European war, Watson appealed to readers to support benefit exhibitions and contribute to war relief. The Allies had "a divine cause," he wrote. Among the letters to the editor in the *Evening Post* of May 23, 1916, one, signed "F.W.," most likely written by Watson, took to task those who caricatured Uncle Sam: "I should like to draw attention to the representation of 'Uncle Sam' in cartoons, and the effect it must have on the people," the letter stated. "It is wrong to believe that the American public is unable to appreciate artistic things. To keep before its eyes these odious, badly drawn images of an old crank dressed like a clown, the invention of some English cartoonist, who was anything but sympathetic toward Americans, is an insult to its taste. . . . 'Marianne,' 'Michel,' etc. are not served up every day in almost every daily paper; they remain the property of the comic weekly publications, and appear in such clever executions that they do not offend. It is hard for me to believe that an artist, or rather illustrator, with any patriotic ideals, could lend himself to such a work as we see here." Absent was his easy drollery, but where the country was concerned, Watson was earnest to the core.[65]

Early in 1917, no longer willing to stand back as a distant observer, Watson volunteered for ambulance service in France. In June, two months after the United States declared war on Germany, he was inducted as a private into the Norton-Harjes Ambulance Corps. His final column for the *Evening Post* appeared on May 5, 1917. For Watson, as for many others of his background including Richard Norton, cofounder of the ambulance unit, France represented a cultural ideal, the spiritual home of civilization, which must be preserved. Several months before he left, the *Evening Post* surpassed the earlier *Vanity Fair* tribute and enshrined its popular art critic among the historical greats. Juxtaposing a full-page portrait of Watson with the nineteenth-century British giants John Ruskin, Philip Gilbert Hamerton, and Theodore Watts-Dunton, the article praised Watson for his forthrightness and independence.[66]

While for the majority of young American artists the European war seemed less compelling than the beguilements of modernism, many of them volunteered for service, some out of a sense of idealism, others seeking adventure. Although well over age, Allen Tucker joined the American Ambulance Field Service in France in 1914, and after the United States entered the war, he worked in a Red Cross hospital. Samuel Chamberlain joined the French army; Edward Steichen served as an aviation photographer; Abraham Rattner was a camouflage artist in France; George Biddle became a commissioned officer with the occupation forces there. The sculptor Janet Scudder, who owned a home in Paris, joined the YMCA's entertainment department in Paris as a concert manager for the singer Camille Lane. When Lane's voice gave out, the women turned to decorating mess halls and restrooms for the troops, "splashing about through France" as "traveling house painters."[67] For some artists such as Arnold Blanch, army service offered an otherwise unavailable opportunity to travel to Europe. Sculptor John B. Flannagan, who had enlisted as a seaman in the merchant marines, stayed on for two years after the Armistice, making several trips to France, Germany, and South America.

Watson sailed aboard the *French Line* on August 3, 1917, carrying with him a letter of introduction from Guy Pène du Bois, in which he praised Watson as "one of the truest Americans" he knew. Watson arrived in Paris on the seventeenth, where the corps joined the Seventh Section of the American Expeditionary Force serving the Twenty-fifth Division of the French army. Watson spent the first few days chopping wood and carrying water for the cook and her assistant.[68] After several weeks, his unit was sent to the Somme, a quiet section of the front, where he was billeted in a chateau for the duration of his assignment in France.

The volunteer ambulance drivers were a close-knit group made up of men who mostly had been academics, leaders in college, or successful businessmen. More than 650 Americans from Ivy League schools had volunteered for the ambulance service. French civilians soon identified *les ambulanciers américains,* whose camaraderie was not unlike that of a fraternity, as young men of means and fashion, *"tous fils de familles riches."*[69] None of the horror or bitter nihilist sentiment prominent in the world-war literature of John Dos Passos, Ernest Hemingway, and others appeared in their writings. Rather, one found in them a striking devotion to cause and country. Excerpts from Watson's letters from France, published in the *Evening Post,* praised the valor of the French, particularly the common foot soldier, or *poilu,* who bore the brunt of the fighting. He marveled at the beautiful countryside and the excellent food. Watson also found time to travel to Paris and visit the site of the new Rodin Museum. Even though he experienced little of actual warfare, he felt he had become a different person since arriving in France. He noted too that his command of the French language made all the difference in the world.[70]

Following America's entry into the war, all volunteer ambulance units were absorbed into the United States Army Ambulance Service, and the Norton-Harjes corps was disbanded the fall after Watson arrived in France. Because of his newspaper experience, however, Watson was asked to join the Public Information Branch of the Military Affairs Division of the American Red Cross with the rank of lieutenant. In that capacity he traveled throughout France, except for the British front, reporting on Red Cross war-relief work. His articles and press releases appeared in magazines and newspapers throughout the United States, including his own *New York Evening Post.* The job offered the raconteur in Watson a golden outlet. In a typical piece for *Red Cross Magazine,* he wrote of dropping by an American Red Cross canteen one evening. Through vignettes and snippets of conversations, he animated the bustling atmosphere, the throngs of French servicemen, and the dedicated workers. One silent *poilu* who sat opposite him had the saddest face he had ever seen, Watson wrote. "Some personal loss hung over him, too poignant for me to approach." Later the soldier talked to one of the Red Cross women. "He talked to her as he never would have talked to a man, because she knew how to talk to him." Afterward, Watson learned that the *poilu* had suffered the loss of four brothers in the war, the youngest only recently: "Two weeks later he wrote her . . . telling her that her sympathy had torn apart the black veil that seemed to have settled down forever between him and life." It had "given him back the courage to go on. '*Vive l'Union Franco-Americaine!*' . . . Was it an exaggeration to say that 'American Red Cross women are the front ranks of our diplomacy?'"[71]

Nan Watson, sometime between 1920 and 1925. Forbes Watson Papers.

At home after Forbes left for France, his wife, Nan, had moved from the Hotel Chelsea back to Greenwich Village to an apartment just north of Washington Square. Her career had advanced during the years Watson was at the *Evening Post*. In 1915 the National Academy exhibited one of her paintings for the first time, *Miss Alice Paterson*, a portrait of her sister. It captured the prim, diffident demeanor of the high-school teacher in her bluntly striped jacket and sensible hat. The following winter she exhibited in another NAD show, and during the next several years she showed at the Arden Gallery, the Whitney Studio, Knoedler's, and other galleries. Her portrait *Miss Gladys Brown* was exhibited in the winter NAD show in time for Forbes's return in 1919. Nan's apartment at 12 West Eighth Street, together with its MacDougal Alley studio, was owned by the eminent sculptor Daniel Chester French. A number of artists had studios there as well, including Gertrude Vanderbilt Whitney, whose place at 19 MacDougal Alley fronted at 8 West Eighth Street, two doors from Nan's apartment. MacDougal Alley had been the center of rebellion against the academy ten years earlier, when The Eight first displayed their "ash can" art, and it continued to be a popular neighborhood for young and progressive artists. Beginning in 1907, Whitney held informal shows of works by fellow artists in her studio, and in

1914 she converted the adjoining house at 8 West Eighth Street into the Whitney Studio gallery.[72] Nan exhibited there several times and later at the Whitney Studio Club, which she had joined as a charter member.

The war did not discourage Nan from joining Forbes in Paris in 1918. They took a "romantic little house" on 20, rue Jacob surrounded by garden with a studio for Nan, and she stayed on for a good part of the year.[73] Wartime Paris was full of American artists, and the Watsons saw scores of friends. As fortune had it, Forbes's brother Arthur, whom he had seen only infrequently since youth, was also there, quartered just down the street. Twenty-seven years later, while on assignment in Paris for the Treasury Department, Watson recalled that time. "Do you remember the night in March 1918 when we sat at Arthur's window on the rue Jacob listening to the barrage at Compiegne eighteen miles away?" he wrote Nan. "I asked a Frenchman about the little hotels in the quartier Montparnasse which I used to know in the last war. He replied: '*Vous trouverez vos petits hotels, mais pas vos petites amies.*'"[74]

In January 1919, several months after the Armistice, Watson was transferred to Bologne and then Rome. From there he sent a final article to the *Evening Post,* the only art commentary he published during the war. It was transitional, in a sense, mixing sentimental war drama with critical straight talk. The subject was the French painter Jean-Julien Lemordant, whose heroic actions on the battlefield in France had resulted in blindness. Lemordant's work was currently on exhibit in New York, and Watson's article, which appeared in the art section, noted that while the paintings themselves might not interest contemporary American painters, Lemordant's talks on French art would.[75]

The following spring Watson left for the States. He never forgot his wartime duty and would refer to the experience all his life. Within weeks after he arrived in France, he had felt in himself a renewed idealism and a reinvigorated devotion to France and its civilization. On a more practical level, his public relations work for the Red Cross summoned a professional side that Watson had not previously explored, joining his considerable writing skills with a deep-felt patriotism and irrepressible crusader's instinct. It was a natural combination that would serve him well in future years.

3 LAUNCHING *THE ARTS*, 1921–1932

The world war and the subsequent peace treaty brought shifts in opinion in the United States, and by the time Watson returned home from Europe in June 1919, the national mood had changed. Split over America's entry into the war and other issues of internationalism and isolationism, progressives turned from common reform interests to more divisive issues, and the momentum of the Progressive Era quickly dissipated. While the 1918 summer and fall counteroffensives in France had had an exhilarating effect on some of the troops overseas and on some civilians at home, accounts of combat and trench warfare horrified others. Moral questions concerning United States involvement in the war and challenges to traditional ideals heightened the general sense of disillusionment.

America had continued to prosper during the war, promoting a general mood of expansiveness. Inflation produced an estimated forty-two thousand new millionaires, primarily those who had profited from land investments and shares in corporations and industry. The number of people earning between thirty thousand and forty thousand dollars tripled. Superior to any in the world, the American automobile, airplane, radio, and film served as conspicuous symbols of the nation's spectacular technological progress. Hailing the achievements of business and industry in elevating the United States to world status, the average citizen lionized the businessman as the model for success in life.

Not everyone participated in the new prosperity, however. Once affluent people who had depended on income from bonds, mortgages, and rents as well as others who lived on fixed incomes—government officials, teachers, intellectuals—were suddenly poorer. Social positions shifted as material success became the dominant standard against which virtue and personal merit were measured. A powerful sense of alienation gripped those who had fallen in status as well as those who did not share the businessman's credo. Many who despised the materialism and immorality of the metropolis conjured up idyllic memories of past innocence, yearning to return to the rural simplicity of earlier decades. Some turned to religious fundamentalism. Popular evangelists such as Billy Sunday and Aimee Semple McPherson attracted huge followings, while William Jennings Bryan and his adherents sought to save a sinful society from Darwin's evolutionary theories and other godless ideas. In the minds of many who clung to the Victorian values of nineteenth-century America, aberrance was at the root of the country's problems. The passage of the Eighteenth Amendment to the Constitution, along with the Volstead Act of 1919, which initiated the era of Prohibition, was only one of a host of measures aimed at restoring national righteousness.

The war in Europe had intensified the spirit of nationalism in America, evident not only in strident displays of patriotism but also in prejudice against immigrants, whose numbers increased by nearly seven hundred thousand between 1919 and 1921. Bolshevik uprisings in several European countries in the years following the Russian Revolution of 1917 aroused fears among many Americans that a communist revolution could erupt in their own country. Aggravating this "Red scare," a series of bombings and strikes at home raised popular demands for an end to radicalism in the United States. Laws establishing immigration quotas were enacted to keep American ways inviolate. Membership in the Ku Klux Klan soared following the Armistice, reaching a peak of five million by the early twenties. Klansmen attacked not only African Americans, Jews, Catholics, and immigrants but also deviancies such as birth control, Darwinism, pacifism, and internationalism.

For progressive intellectuals such as Malcolm Cowley, Randolph Bourne, and others, the war had confirmed the fallibility of traditional ideals and prewar reform propositions. The chortling materialism that dominated the country repulsed and alienated them. Seeing only sham in the accepted standards of conduct, intellectuals explored new philosophical systems and personal codes of living. A number of them abandoned the United States for the more hospitable culture of Europe, particularly Paris. Artists who had fled the continent during the war and returned were joined now by numbers of disillusioned Americans. Young people also rebelled. Declaring themselves emancipated from their elders' moral codes, they smoked cigarettes, swilled bootleg liquor, defied puritanical sexual taboos, and generally flaunted bohemian lifestyles.

With all the social and economic shifts that occurred during the war years, American art reflected few concomitant changes. That wholesale fascination with abstraction, ignited at the Armory Show, continued unabated, so much so that by 1920 modern American art had assumed a greater degree of nonobjectivity than at any previous time in history. As the twenties progressed, however, the allure gradually faded, and the majority of American modernists returned to figuration, though now it was distorted in line, color, and juxtapositions. With the exception of Arthur Dove, Stuart Davis, and a few others who continued to work in purely abstract styles, the typical mid-decade American abstract artist reduced life forms to exaggerated or generalized geometric areas of dense, arbitrary color and fractured masses while retaining identifiable references to reality.

One effect of the war had been to hamper the transport of art works from Europe. That, and the fragmentation of international support of the avant-garde, caused a drop in modern-art exhibitions and purchases and ultimately the demise of several modern art galleries, the most vital of which, Alfred Stieglitz's 291, closed in 1917; his avant-garde journal, *Camera Work,* ceased that same year. Once the world war ended, however, and despite a wave of isolationism in the country, Americans were eager to see more modern European art. The School of Paris was the rage.[1]

Watson's return to the United States in 1919 coincided with the culmination of abstractionism in American art and a revived impulse on behalf of European modernism. Greater affluence had brought greater art consciousness. Puffed with financial success, the American businessman shopped for art, seeking, "by means of his hard-earned fortune, some of the glamour which he understood sheds itself upon the collector." The market flourished at an unprecedented rate. Art galleries dotted Fifth Avenue. Between 1921 and 1930, as civic pride and a quest for culture fueled the public's interest, sixty new museums were established in cities throughout the United States, and thirteen new museum buildings were constructed at an estimated cost of $16,000,000.[2]

Despite high-powered resistance from conservative critics, modern art had gained broader acceptance. Having closed his Modern Gallery in 1918, Marius de Zayas opened the de Zayas Gallery in 1919, where he featured modern European art, African art, and postimpressionist works. The Weyhe Gallery, which opened in 1919 under the direction of Carl Zigrosser, introduced Americans to modern printmaking on a significant scale for the first time. In 1920 Katherine Dreier, with cofounders Marcel Duchamp and Man Ray, established the Société Anonyme, an organization that not only exhibited innovative international art but also programmatically sought to demonstrate the importance of modern art in the spiritual regeneration of society. Frank K. M. Rehn promoted progressive American art in a small private studio gallery in 1918, then in the early twenties he opened a public gallery on Fifth Avenue specializing in American painting. Over time, Rehn became the sole agent for Edward Hopper, Charles Burchfield, Henry Lee McFee, Andrew Dasburg, and other pioneer American modernists. Like Watson, who was a good friend, Rehn had grown up among artists (his father was a respected marine and landscape painter) and was close to many of them. Even the more staid dealers and museums such as Knoedler's, the Pennsylvania Academy of Fine Arts, and the Metropolitan Museum of Art exhibited modern art from time to time, although they were not apt to purchase such pieces for their permanent collections. The modernists "may fairly be said to have finally arrived at a state of classicism," Henry McBride wrote in his *New York Herald* column in March 1921.[3]

Yet with a few notable exceptions, museums and collectors continued to ignore American modernists. Chances were that if an older, established gallery exhibited the work of a nonacademic American painter, the artist had paid the gallery owner to do so. "The American artist was very much the stepchild of the art world," particularly the contemporary artist, Goodrich recalled.[4] Those wealthy collectors who did buy advanced art purchased Matisse, Picasso, Fernand Léger, and others from the School of Paris. Modernist Max Weber, and even John Marin, Charles Demuth, Marsden Hartley, and Georgia O'Keeffe of the Stieglitz group, had no real standing except with a small audience.

It had been agreed when Watson left for the war that his place at the *Evening Post* would be waiting for him, but it was not.[5] Joining Nan in the Eighth Street apartment in June 1919, he turned once again to freelance writing, publishing several articles about the New York art scene in the *Detroit News* and contributing regularly to *Arts & Decoration*. The editor of *Arts & Decoration* was Guy Pène du Bois, an old friend going back to the early years of Forbes and Nan's courtship, and they shared not only opinions but also companionable social habits.[6] Watson's artistic posture had not altered appreciably during the two years he had been away. In his first report for the *Detroit News,* he roasted the humdrum winter National Academy and its selection for the Altman Prize, "a shocking piece of bad taste." His three initial articles for *Arts & Decoration* were all explicitly antibusiness. Although not of a mind with the "lost generation," he nevertheless shared their repugnance for the materialism and hypocrisy that pervaded America. In "Playing the Game," the most biting of the three, he warned against applying the businessman's rule of merit to art: "that a good thing costs money and that a poorer thing costs less money."[7]

During Watson's absence, Juliana Force and Gertrude Vanderbilt Whitney had sought the advice of a number of artists who were sympathetic to contemporary American art, among them Pène du Bois, Robert Henri, John Sloan, Eugene Speicher, and Henry Schnakenberg. Now, upon his return, Watson once again assumed that role, guiding the women's decisions concerning shows and purchases and unofficially helping shape their policies. Even the Whitney Studio Club secretary, a Miss Warren, was hired on the recommendation of her friend Forbes Watson. "They saw eye to eye," Lloyd Goodrich commented concerning Watson and the two women, Force and Whitney. "And I think probably the initiative in many cases came from him. He would tell them about younger people, tell Mrs. Force that they should be exhibited."[8]

Each new show at the Whitney Studio Club opened with a tea, offering also fancy cakes and sandwiches. "The artists would line up and literally grab the food, particularly the ones who were hard up," one artist recalled. Critics from the New York area and neighboring cities attended quite regularly. After 1923 when the Whitney Studio Club moved from West Fourth Street to West Eighth Street, there were big parties with "lots of wine, an orchestra and dancing, and wonderful buffet suppers." Openings sometimes turned rather wild, Carl Zigrosser remembered. "The spectacle of seemingly unlimited supplies of liquor . . . sometimes was too upsetting for the self-control of the guests and there were lapses in decorum."[9]

Watson fit right in. "He had a great social instinct" and a knack for making "very acute personal observations." A touch of malice only increased his entertainment value.[10] Pène du Bois recalled that he, Juliana Force, Watson, and sculptor Jack Gregory were "most constantly in attendance" at Whitney's private affairs also, where a wide assortment of artists, musicians, writers, politicians, and other celebrities were present for jolly afternoons and evenings filled with animated talk, high jinks, and liberal quantities of food and Prohibition alcohol. One of forty-two or so friends, artists, and critics on Whitney's "List of Men for Opera," from which she invited escorts when her husband was out of town, Watson was chummy with the elite of art society. Fittingly, a golf tournament at the Winged Foot Country Club in Mamaroneck, in which Watson participated along with a virtual who's who of artists, dealers, critics, and patrons, was a social item in *Art News*. Each of the forty-six participants was named.[11]

When in early 1920 the directors of the Venice International Art Exhibition invited Gertrude Whitney to submit an exhibit, the women turned to Watson for help in assembling it. In March he accompanied Juliana Force to Venice as co-commissioner and director of the exhibition. The fact that he represented the Whitney galleries certainly did not have a neutralizing effect on his reviews, however, which appeared in two issues of *Arts & Decoration* that summer. The small, retrospective exhibition was "sane and agreeable," he declared, showing "refinement and good taste." Taking up the nationalist themes of his *Evening Post* years, he rebuked Americans who deferred to European art and

Juliana in her drawing room, circa 1931. Cecil Beaton, *Portrait of Juliana Force,* circa 1931. Whitney Museum of American Art, New York. Gift of Gertrude Vanderbilt Whitney.

Europeans who ignored American art. "No country has more . . . expatriated artists and saint-hunting spinsters . . . actively misrepresenting her than America," he complained, adding that the expatriates had produced "no one who matters much" since Whistler and Cassatt's generation. As for the European response to the exhibit, he noted sardonically that "Italy did not declare a national holiday" after seeing the Americans' works. Prince Udine, representing the king of Italy, "did the French pavilion in about five minutes, the American in something under seven and a half, and the Polish in a similar period, and finally the royal party was wafted away in gondolas of state toward Venice and a well-earned lunch." From Venice, Watson moved the show to London and Paris, taking the opportunity while in Paris to spend a day with his friend Mary Cassatt in her apartment on the rue Marignan. It turned out to be his last visit with the great painter, who died in 1926.[12]

By now Watson and Juliana Force had become lovers, beginning an affair that would continue for eleven years. Juliana and her husband, Dr. Willard Force, a dentist, lived only two blocks from the Watsons at the time. In late 1922 they moved closer still when, following a legal dispute with the landlord, Daniel Chester French, the Watsons moved from 12 West Eighth Street to a top-floor apartment next door at 14 West Eighth. Dr. Force moved to an apartment in number fourteen also, and for a year and a half (until June 1924) Juliana rented an apartment for herself at number twelve. Proximity made the liaison all the more convenient. The lovers did not go out of their way to conceal their affair from Juliana's husband, as by now the marriage had become little more than a friendly alliance "in which they politely ignored each other's comings and goings." Dr. Force was "undoubtedly the deadliest bore God ever created," in Forbes's view, besides which "his grammar was faulty." But it was different with Nan and Forbes. Their marriage was grounded on common interests and mutual regard—except for Forbes's well-known philandering. Friends tended to overlook his promiscuity as "just his personality," and when they teased him about his women, he protested with the coy good humor of one who had been flattered. Nan could not have been unaware of his repeated adulteries, yet she chose not to see. It was inimical to her nature to acknowledge this unsavory side of Forbes's character, let alone confront him or retaliate in kind. For his part, Forbes did not perceive his behavior as aberrant. Through one romping love affair after another, he remained close to Nan, his affection unwavering and unforced. It was as if all three—husband, wife, and current inamorata— were bosom friends. The Watsons' marriage endured, apparently harmonious and guilt-free.[13]

Juliana Force was a homely woman. No amount of style and elegance could mitigate that. Her nose was large and coarse looking; her eyes were narrow and undistinguished. "She was ugly, and she knew it," Lloyd Goodrich said. "But she had such a magnetism and such power that you forgot all about it. She could have been a very exciting person to be in love with." Friends' accounts of both Forbes and Juliana noted the remarkable similarity in their temperaments. Both were strong, extroverted personalities and great "fun" to be around. Each was a captivating talker, especially expansive over cocktails and cigarettes, in which both indulged heavily. When it came to sarcasm, Juliana could hold her own with the master annihilator, Forbes. They were activists who took issues very personally, "wonderful fighters" who "loved to do battle," and in those days, Goodrich observed, "fighting was needed, because the forces of conservatism were very heavily entrenched, and the younger artist didn't have an awful lot of chance."[14]

Watson was appointed to the faculty of the Art Students League of New York in the fall of 1921, where he lectured on art history each term for the next five years. A number of his friends had been added to the faculty since the war, including Robert Henri, John Sloan, Boardman Robinson, Maurice Sterne, Max Weber, Guy Pène du Bois, George Luks, and Andrew Dasburg. It was an honor to teach there, artist Raphael Soyer remembered. The league "had a very great tradition," and the teachers "were all very well known painters." Though Watson was one of the few who was not a practicing artist, in outlook there was hardly a difference. League policies encouraged liberalism, and the school itself was, as Allen Tucker described it, "an experiment in democracy" with open membership and member governance.[15] There were no attendance requirements, no examinations, and no degrees or certificates. Teachers, hired on a yearly contract, were free to pursue their own aims and methods. They and the administrators of the Art Students League were more enlightened concerning the importance of art history than the students, who preferred to concentrate on painting and sculpting. As an inducement, the school offered Watson's class tuition-free, the only free course except for manufacturers' lectures on the chemical and physical properties of artists' pigments.[16]

That year also Watson joined the staff of a new magazine that Hamilton Easter Field had recently founded, *The Arts*. Field, the descendent of an old Brooklyn family, was a collector, painter, teacher, one-time editor of *Arts & Decoration*, and art critic for the *Brooklyn Daily Eagle*, known for his ebullient affirmation of "the new creative ferment in America." Although by no means a millionaire, he was well off and spent generously on art and artists. His "palatial" home in Columbia Heights, Brooklyn, was "filled with the fruits of travel and the spoils of collectorship." Next door, in one of three fine old houses he owned, Field opened a gallery, Ardsley Studios, in which he displayed the work of early modernists, among them Charles Demuth, Marsden Hartley, Max Weber, Bernard Karfiol, and Maurice Sterne, and was one of the first to buy their works. At his school in Ogonquit, Maine, he offered easy financial terms to artists who studied and lived in the dormitory.[17]

Field financed *The Arts* magazine entirely on his own and served both as publisher and editor. The magazine's mission, stated in the first number, issued in December 1920, was "to be an art magazine and a trade paper." It would feature painting and sculpture while also providing news of what artists were doing, what art patrons and museums were buying, and what was going on in the trade. There would also be articles on drama and music. Watson's first article for *The Arts*, "Sisley's Struggle for Recognition," appeared in the February–March 1921 issue.[18]

The publication was "strictly a personal operation," Watson remembered. More than half the articles and features in any given issue were written by Field. He "fought his personal battles in it endlessly. But he fought the battles of other artists also. He gossiped charmingly in one column like an old lady on a rainy day and in the next wrote like a warrior." As an editor he was "very slap dash," Goodrich observed, and the magazine was "a little amateurish.... Sometimes what they published was not very good, but it was always fun, interesting and so on." They published "all kinds of things that nobody had ever published before in the modern field, and he laid great stress on American art too." From its first issue, *The Arts* emphasized contemporary work. One of Watson's early contributions described an exhibition he had assembled for the Dallas Art Association in which the single aim was to "bring us into direct contact with the men of to-day and stimulate the interest and the support for their work which is quite as necessary to our own spiritual enrichment as to theirs."[19]

By the end of the first volume year, October 1921, the monthly had incorporated *Touchstone Magazine* and *The American Art Student* and had grown to eighty pages in length with eight regular contributors. In February 1922 it was announced that the magazine would be increased to ninety-six pages, the additional space to be devoted to the older forms of art.[20] But the same editorial disclosed that Field was suffering from bronchitis and under doctors' orders to rest. The following month *The Arts* suspended publication, owing to his worsening condition. On April 10, Hamilton Easter Field died of pneumonia, eleven days before his forty-ninth birthday. Many felt he had spent all his energy on the magazine and lacked the strength to fight the disease.

For some time Juliana Force had been discussing the idea of starting a magazine, and late that year, probably at the suggestion of Watson, she approached Gertrude Whitney about purchasing *The Arts*. Acting quickly, Whitney negotiated the rights to the magazine from Field's nephew, sculptor Robert Laurent, and had her attorneys draw up stock, incorporation, and agreement documents. She established an advisory board consisting of Laurent, architect Chester Aldrich, Bryson Burroughs, and William M. Ivins Jr., curator of the Print Department at the Metropolitan Museum of Art. If the magazine broadened the scope of its editorial and business departments, the incorporation papers stated, it could be profitable within two or three years. Watson was named editor and president of the Arts Publishing Corporation.[21] Over time, Vincent Astor, Abby Rockefeller, Ralph Pulitzer, and other wealthy patrons purchased shares of stock in the corporation, but Whitney really financed the magazine.

Her subsidization of *The Arts*, according to Lloyd Goodrich, who joined *The Arts* staff the following year, was part of a whole pattern of expanding involvement in exhibiting, purchasing, and publishing that emphasized American works and younger artists. Once Watson took over the magazine, as one contemporary art commentator put it, he "added the authoritative editorial we to the Whitney-Force combination." Together, at times as if in tandem, the Whitney galleries and *The Arts* represented the most embracing liberal force in American art during the twenties. The magazine had "a very welcoming atmosphere, editorially speaking," Goodrich recalled, similar in spirit to the Whitney galleries, in which artists "were taken in right away if they had any talent and given a chance to show." For the first time, there was a significant forum for an entire younger generation of liberal artists.[22]

With a salary of $50 per week and $8,500 in seed money, Watson set to work in the Arts Publishing Corporation office at 211 East Nineteenth Street with one secretary and a business manager, William A. Robb. Having previously worked for the publishers of *Outing Magazine* and *Yachting Magazine,* Robb was "quite unaesthetic," according to Lloyd Goodrich, but in business matters Watson considered him a "man of great ability." He and Watson agreed to separate the advertising and editorial aspects of the magazine, which worked very satisfactorily. Robb sold advertising, paid the bills, and served generally as a "kind of a mainstay so far as the practical end of things went."[23]

The first number of the revived *Arts* magazine appeared in January 1923. A bright light-blue cover replaced the bland gray of the earlier publication, and bold black horizontal bands at the top and bottom set off a mounted reproduction of a work of art. The first was an Indian sculpture from the Boston Museum's collection. This inaugural issue was an impressive eighty-five pages, although subsequent issues averaged around sixty. The price, fifty cents per copy or five dollars for a yearly subscription, represented a ten-cent increase over its predecessor, but lower advertising revenue necessitated the rise. Under Field, a single issue sometimes contained fifty or more advertisements, whereas the new *Arts* rarely carried thirty; one they could count on every month was a full- or half-page ad for the Whitney galleries. At the outset Watson initiated two bibliographic improvements: a table of contents in each issue and a semi-annual cumulative index.

In his opening editorial, Watson pledged to continue and extend Field's work. "From the first the scope of the magazine has been liberal and it will continue to be liberal," he wrote. The emphasis would be American, with qualifications. "*The Arts* is not afraid to enjoy American work just because it is American," he stated. "It does not intend to wave the flag, but quite frankly it does intend to stand with the American artist against timidity and snobbery. . . . Most important of all, its function is to offer art simply for enjoyment, not for educational purposes nor for any other ulterior motive than just for fun." Watson promised to publish material representing many different points of view, "and if it arouses discussion and sparks fly from the conflict so much the better."[24] Thus, in his first statement as editor, Watson reiterated positions of his *Evening Post* years, now as commitments, and reasserted his battle-readiness.

The first issue signaled the catholic mix of topics and authoritative writing that would forge its reputation as the premier magazine of the liberal art spirit in America. Following tributes to the late editor by Henry McBride, Maurice Sterne, and Bryson Burroughs, Watson's lead article broke the news of the establishment of the Barnes Foundation in Merion, Pennsylvania. "What this means is that we are to have, at last, a public museum of modern art—that is, of some of the most vital art that has been produced since about 1870 to the present day."[25] Watson recounted the history of Dr. Albert C. Barnes's intrepid acquisitions and illustrated in page after page of striking black-and-white reproductions some of the first-rate Renoirs, Cézannes, and other remarkable modern works in his collection. American modernist Charles Sheeler photographed a number of them and did so for articles in several subsequent issues too. That Watson made the first public announcement concerning the Barnes Foundation was acknowledgment both of his stature as a critic of modern art and of his personal friendship with the millionaire collector. *The Arts*'s celebration of the Barnes Foundation also underscored the importance Watson placed on private collectors in promoting art appreciation in the United States. In addition to Watson's centerpiece tribute to the Barnes Foundation, there was an article by the architect Paul Philippe Cret about the design of the museum and another by Dr. Barnes himself, a review of a book about the appreciation of painting.

The initial issue contained contributions by both liberals and conservatives. William Ivins discussed the function of the museum in modern society, and Ananda K. Coomaraswamy of the Boston Museum of Fine Arts described recent additions to the museum's respected Indian collection. Traditionalist architect Egerton Swartwout, in "The Machine in Architecture," examined the ambivalent situation of modern architecture, in which advances in engineering solved construction problems but created the potential for stagnation in separating the engineer's problems from the architect's. Scenic designer Lee Simonson lamented the average theatergoer's conservative preference for "background" sets, insisting that modern sets, with their positive play of color, light, and form, must be a dynamic part of producing the play. Henry McBride wrote sympathetically about the modernist Italian painter Amedeo Modigliani, who had died in 1920 at the age of thirty-six, tragically scorned because of his bohemianism and his defiance of formulaic styles. Watson keynoted *The Arts*'s predilection for moderate modernism in his essay on the genius of Charles Demuth's post-cubism, which assimilated certain elements of abstraction, though not all. Demuth's art was not intellectual, he declared, and not earnest. It had nothing to do with those "heavy-minded young artists who tramped into 'modernism' to the accompaniment of a kind of fog-horn chorus of blah."[26]

Even before the inaugural issue, the *New York Times* hailed *The Arts* as "precisely the kind of magazine grievously needed in America." And it was true that *The Arts* filled a gap. At that time, "American art magazines, with a few honorable but ineffective exceptions, were devoted either to the art of the past, or in the present, to the safely orthodox," Lloyd Goodrich observed. *International Studio*, perhaps the best known, was English-based but published an American edition; *American Art News* emphasized news over the aesthetic; and the conservative *American Magazine of Art* represented the academic point of view. Although *Arts & Decoration* was more liberal, much of its content was devoted to home furnishings, crafts, and decorative arts, and its treatment of modern art was more reactive than proactive. Another thing that distinguished *The Arts* was its emphasis on American art.[27]

Artists' responses to *The Arts* echoed the *Times*'s advance applause. "*Congratulations, Congratulations, and then Congratulations, on the new number,*" artist Eugene Speicher wrote in a letter filled with underlined superlatives. "*You also have a vigorous taste and refinement and every page is meaty.*" He concluded, "*there never has been published a better number of an art magazine anywhere.*" Pène du Bois wrote his friend: "I started looking at the Arts about two hours ago, in the book shop, the restaurant, a cab, an elevator, Floy's show room— nothing stopped my looking. Its the finest art magazine I ever saw. It makes me want to paint. It makes it seems [*sic*] good to be alive. Its so alive itself that to fully express that aliveness I feel as though the word should be written in great big electric letters on the sky." It was "the great hope of American art," according to Allen Tucker, "the soundest and livest art magazine" the country had yet produced in the opinion of one of America's first proselytizers and patrons of modern art, Albert E. Gallatin.[28]

Except for art market news, Watson continued most of the features Hamilton Easter Field had introduced. Differences between the old and new *Arts* reflected differences in the editors' personalities for the most part. Watson was nothing if not discriminating in his choice of topics and writers, far more critical than Field and more cynical. Articles were more substantive on the whole. Unlike Field, Watson contributed a relatively small portion of the total text. He wrote the monthly editorial, an article or two, commentary as issues stirred him, and selected exhibition and book reviews. The remainder of the writing was assigned to staff and other contributors, who were paid at the rate of one and a half cents per word, two and a half cents a word by the mid-twenties. The "Exhibitions" and "Comments" sections of the new *Arts* offered ample exhibition coverage and commentary but were not nearly as lengthy as Field's, who could chat on for as many as sixteen pages.

Watson also introduced several new features. The "Young America" series showcased "new talent springing up"—caricaturist Peggy Bacon, painter Henry Schnakenberg, puppeteer Remo Bufano, and others—all of whom achieved substantial recognition over time. He also inaugurated "The Skylight," a "colyum," as he playfully termed it, to serve as a safety valve for the large amount of serious material in *The Arts*. "If you have a good laugh on art," he invited readers, "send it to The Skylight."[29]

The bulk of articles in *The Arts* was devoted to painting, sculpture, architecture, and the decorative arts, with an occasional piece on commercial design, crafts, and garden art. In addition, there were essays on music, drama, and literature as well as the subjects of stage design and film. Book reviews were important to Watson for current awareness and discussion. Some of the early issues also contained original poetry. Although the emphasis was on contemporary and American art, full-length essays on European masters of all periods appeared quite regularly, filling a need for basic, in-depth information, which was not readily available in English in the United States at that time. Illustrations were extremely important to Watson not only as a means of acquainting readers with an artist's output but also to heighten the "visual satisfaction of the magazine." He spent hours selecting reproductions and formatting them on the page. It was "such fun" for him, sitting on the floor of Nan's large studio at night with the illustrations spread around him, keying them up to their greatest impact.[30]

For the first seven months Watson was a one-man editorial staff. There was much to do, however, and publication was chronically behind. By August, the magazine was doing well enough to add an associate editor and another secretary. Virgil Barker, the new associate editor, had studied at Harvard, and he had been director of the Kansas City Art Institute. His primary interest was art history, and during his years on *The Arts* he authored two books and began work on a comprehensive history of painting in America, which took more than twenty years to complete.[31] In October 1923 *The Arts* moved to more spacious offices at 19 East Fifty-ninth Street, which accommodated the staff of five—Watson, Barker, Robb, and two secretaries—quite comfortably.

Watson was always on the lookout for able writers, "people who had a fresh point of view on American art," and when Alexander Brook took a full-time position as assistant director of the Whitney Studio Club and no longer had

Lloyd Goodrich, photograph taken in Little Compton, Rhode Island, sometime between 1930 and 1940. Photograph courtesy of David Goodrich.

time to contribute to *The Arts,* he recommended Lloyd Goodrich, a friend from Art Students League days. Goodrich, raised in Nutley, New Jersey, the same town as the artist Reginald Marsh, also started out as a creative artist; he "lost faith," however, and turned to business. Six years later he had had enough and moved on to publishing and writing. Watson, as ready to offer opportunities to new writers as to unknown artists, started Goodrich out with two book reviews in April 1924, soon after assigning him articles. Like Barker, Goodrich's work was carefully researched and significant. In fact, three of the seven or more major monographs Goodrich wrote in later years, those on Winslow Homer, Edward Hopper, and Thomas Eakins, originated with his *Arts* essays. In December 1925 he was appointed associate editor, and when Barker left for

Europe a short time later to become European editor, Goodrich became second in command, responsible for producing the magazine. Compared to the high profile, intemperate Watson, Goodrich was steady, solid, and never showy. But despite the differences in personality, possibly because of them, their relationship was "very good." "Forbes became one of my best friends," Goodrich recalled. "We were very fond of each other, Forbes and Nan and Edith [Goodrich's wife] and myself." In addition to writing, reading manuscripts, and assisting Watson in the selection of topics and authors, Goodrich took charge of the physical production of each issue. Earlier employment at Macmillan publishers and an evening course on printing at Columbia University had prepared him well, as he introduced changes in typography and graphics: increasing the size of the print, initiating a system of runarounds (type set in columns narrower than the body of the text, which allowed for variations in the size of illustrations), adding quarter-page illustrations, and eliminating the "totally unfunctional" black bands from the cover. With its excellent black-and-white photographic reproductions and improved layout and typography, *The Arts* became a handsome publication.[32]

Watson depended heavily on his associate editors, as by then he was committed to a number of enterprises. Also, he preferred being out and about, mixing it up with artists and others in the field. Goodrich recalled that Watson came to the office once or twice, maybe three times a week, but not steadily and never according to a schedule. In April 1928 C. Adolph "Cook" Glassgold joined *The Arts* as a contributing editor. Glassgold, like Goodrich, had originally studied to be a painter, but he had turned to teaching and writing for economic reasons. He covered the decorative arts principally. Later that year, in December, Watson appointed Dorothy Lefferts Moore assistant editor. She too had begun with book reviews and gradually assumed additional duties. Watson's editors did not always concur with his critical assessments, but they almost uniformly shared his liberal angle of vision.

Regarded as the "most satisfying and unadulterated . . . sounding board for . . . independently minded artists," *The Arts* represented their viewpoint in a way no previous magazine had. Its familiar blue cover, a staple in their studios, appeared "in more paintings by American artists—that magazine kicking around, standing on a table with brushes around it." Artists not only subscribed, they also talked about it and freely offered advice and criticism. It was "a much more intimate relationship" than Goodrich ever encountered before or after in the publishing field.[33] Watson commissioned articles and reviews from artists whenever possible, believing they could comment on art matters with greater sympathy and insight than those who had not lived the creative life.

The list of artist-contributors was imposing, particularly considering the innate reluctance of some to verbalize about their craft. The taciturn Edward Hopper turned down as many requests from Watson as he accepted, declining to do an article on A. B. Frost, for example, because he could not "get up much enthusiasm" for the artist. Reluctantly declining to review exhibitions for the February 1927 issue of The Arts, Hopper wrote: "I write, or rather think with so little facility that I am afraid it would take too much time and thought from my painting.... It may seem foolish to you that I can not give a little spare time to writing but I sweat blood when I write, and a thing that you could probably do in a day would take me I am sure a week or two." Yet those pieces Hopper wrote, particularly on John Sloan and Charles Burchfield, had "the substance and clarity of his own painting." Tellingly, in writing about Burchfield, Hopper called upon Emerson's essay "Self Reliance" to point up the grand "obstinacy" and "isolated and vigorous originality" with which Burchfield depicted the poetic ordinariness of the American scene. Picasso, whom Watson knew personally, published one of his first comprehensive statements on his own art, "Picasso Speaks," in the May 1923 issue. Thomas Hart Benton, William Zorach, and Allen Tucker were only a few of the regular contributors who brought the artist's unique perspective and credibility to the pages of The Arts.[34]

Similarly, those who wrote about music, the stage, architecture, and literature for The Arts were usually themselves practitioners, mostly progressive in orientation. Igor Stravinsky's "Some Ideas about My Octuor" was the first article the avant-garde composer ever wrote for publication. More than ten years before his "international style" attracted critical acclaim, architect Philip Johnson, something of an anomaly among conservative architects, contributed several essays on architecture. Over the years the magazine's pertinence and prestige attracted world-renowned writers on the arts, including Virginia Woolf.[35]

As opposed to pomposity in criticism as in art itself, Watson preferred contributors with a nonacademic perspective. Charles Downing Lay's consonance with the editors was apparent in his scathing article on the Metropolitan Museum of Art's Hearn fund. In it, the distinguished artist and landscape architect took the museum to task for failing to administer the Hearn fund according to its benefactor's intent, which was to purchase works by living American painters. Something of an activist in his own right, Lay complained that after George A. Hearn died in 1913, the Metropolitan bought only a few American pictures, and those did not represent the modern tendencies. Not only was this an injustice to the artist and the public, he asserted, but also "it is humiliating to the New Yorker to be unable to show visitors from abroad a representative collection of modern American work."[36]

William M. Ivins Jr., another regular, evidenced a similarly lively disputatiousness. A bookman as well as an expert on graphic art, the independent-minded Ivins expressed ideas that in the view of colleagues were almost revolutionary in their originality. Like Watson, he "rejoiced in reducing the pretentious to pulp." In "A Note on Aesthetic Theory," Ivins enunciated the ultimate independent democratic proposition that the aesthetic value of a work of art resided in the response of the individual viewer. There is no way to discuss beauty, he declared, except "in terms of the first person singular. . . . The thing that really counts the most is not the rules of the union, or the expression of the artist, but the impression upon the beholder."[37]

Contributors also reflected the diverse vantage points that fed into the magazine's bracing editorial temperament, from Mabel Dodge Luhan, the flamboyant salon hostess, to the erudite Meyer Schapiro, who was only twenty-one years old when he first wrote for *The Arts*. In an essay published in 1925, Schapiro, who would rank among the preeminent art scholars of the twentieth century, linked modern art with ancient art as he interpreted the evolution from archaism to realism in Greek sculpture as a diminution in artistry. Composer Louis Durey, a member of *Les Six*, represented the recent rebellion against impressionism and romanticism in music, while Richard Offner and C. R. Morey, internationally recognized art historians, explicated Renaissance and medieval art, respectively.[38]

Differences of opinion made *The Arts* more stimulating for readers. It certainly did for Watson. In an early issue, modernist painter Andrew Dasburg hailed the liberating influence of cubism, and in a later one Oliver S. Tonks, professor of art at Vassar College, reasoned that abstract art, characteristically inward in its concentration, was selfish, psychopathic, and dubious as a province of art. Despite Leo Stein's foresighted discovery of modern art and redoubtable connoisseurship, his articles for *The Arts*, "Tradition and Art" and "Renoir," expressed a distinctly conservative position and reflected his disenchantment with modernism. Royal Cortissoz, the most powerful of Watson's conservative foes, and Frank Jewett Mather Jr., another venerated conservative, contributed to *The Arts*, although their essays were historical in nature and thus safely removed from current controversies.[39] But true traditionalists such as Cortissoz and especially Kenyon Cox were worthy adversaries in Watson's view. Their conservatism was as deep-felt and uncompromising as his own liberalism, and Watson respected them for that.[40]

Watson's imprint was palpable from the start, not only in the spirited, eclectic choice of topics but also in the magazine's concern with issues and its missionary relationship with readers. Themes of artistic independence, young American genius, and anticommercialism rang out in his chock-full-of-anecdotes editorials and in contributed commentary. Watson characterized *The Arts* as scholarly, and, indeed, articles were penetrating and carefully researched. But there were no iconological or attribution studies, no highly technical analyses, and the material was not abstruse. The editorial intent was to break down the barrier between artists and the public by vitalizing and personalizing art. Read cover-to-cover by artists and art lovers, *The Arts* was a core periodical in major library collections and assigned reading in a number of colleges and universities. Alfred H. Barr Jr., then professor of art at Wellesley College, considered *The Arts* "indispensable" in his modern art courses.[41]

In the words of one colleague, Watson "had a very good nose for what was important." "Prophetic," was the term Virgil Barker used. Bringing film under the rubric of art was just one example of his editorial vision and instinct for the potentiality of an idea or a trend. So was the treatment of American Indian works as art rather than ethnography.[42] Watson recognized countless unknown artists well ahead of the establishment. For example, he proclaimed the genius of Edward Hopper more than twenty years before Hopper became a "collectors' favorite" and the Museum of Modern Art held a one-man show of his works. As early as 1914 in his *New York Evening Post* columns, Watson commended his "sincerity," "unaffected" style, and "heart." Frequent favorable coverage in *The Arts* by Lloyd Goodrich, Virgil Barker, and Watson, along with a special *Arts* portfolio edition of his works, virtually guaranteed Hopper's reputation. There were also Watson's enthusiastic endorsements in the *New York World* and in an important *Vanity Fair* article. Looking back on Hopper's rise some thirty years later, his wife, Jo, credited Watson and Guy Pène du Bois with launching his career. "They told the world what to like," she recalled.[43]

Watson came early to appreciate the modern energy of African art, even though he was initially repelled by its "rude," "gross brutality."[44] Over the years, he commissioned authorities such as Alaine Locke, a major voice for black intellectuals; Melville Jean Herskovits, the Columbia University anthropologist; avant-garde critic Marius de Zayas; and Brooklyn Museum of Art curator Stewart Culin to explicate the essential nature of African art and synthesize it with the development of modern art.

Even in the sector of formal analysis, considered the exclusive preserve of avant-garde sages, *The Arts* was in the forefront. Thomas Hart Benton's series of five essays, the "Mechanics of Form Organization in Painting," explored the structural relationships among elements of form in figurative art, setting up the first important bridge between representational and nonobjective art.[45] Systematic examination of form such as Benton's was "almost unique" in American art during the twenties, and although Benton was later labeled a regionalist and a belligerent foe of modern art, his analyses helped prepare the ground for the abstract expressionist movement.[46]

Watson understood the immense impact of nineteenth-century French art on the rise of twentieth-century modernism, and bypassing the charlatanism in the School of Paris, he spotlighted the seminal French masters in essays by the world's most distinguished authorities. Raymond Escholier, curator of the Victor Hugo Museum and France's leading Delacroix scholar, discussed the Delacroix exhibition of 1928 in Paris. Raymond Régamey, curator at the Louvre and an authority on nineteenth-century painting, reviewed the Corot exhibition that same year. Claude Roger-Marx was at the beginning of a long and notable career when he wrote his first essay for *The Arts*, a review of the most celebrated art event of 1929, the Gustave Courbet retrospective exhibition in Paris.[47]

For all the magazine's smartness, however, production was never caught up financially, and *The Arts* continually ran a deficit. Contributors frequently had to wait for payment, which may have been due not only to strained finances but also to Watson's careless management of details. Goodrich was convinced at times that the magazine would never get published if not for his efforts. "*Someone* had to get the magazine out," and "Watson wasn't there a lot. He was in and out." Watson himself rarely met a deadline. *The Arts* "had a very bad record of coming out always at the end of the month and sometimes even . . . the next month, but this was the nature of the operation," Goodrich remembered. It was a habit that irritated advertisers. "They would say, 'This exhibition which I advertised in your magazine had been on three weeks by the time the magazine came out.'" Watson was unperturbed.[48]

Orderly or not, morale was high at the office. Watson's unreserved confidence in *The Arts* and intense personal involvement in contemporary issues generated an atmosphere of commitment and enthusiasm. Everyone believed the magazine was at the cutting edge, crusading for causes that mattered. His example of scrappy independence encouraged an open market for ideas, and fortunately the staff writers never had to concern themselves about the effect of their editorial positions on circulation and advertising. "More than once, dealers withdrew advertising because of Watson's frank comments," Goodrich recalled, but neither Force nor Whitney intervened or applied pressure as a consequence.[49] It was an atmosphere that tolerated, indeed fostered, experiment, something the older art magazines did not do.

Editorially, Watson was generous, receptive, and supportive. Regular and contributing editors were assigned articles or general topics, and other times they submitted material that they thought would be of interest. "Very little editorial excision followed," Glassgold recalled. They "never felt any real shackles . . . in expression, or in idea." Watson "would never censor, never edit, never obstruct in any way," Goodrich noted. He was "a wonderful man to work for, very affirmative." Both Inslee Hopper, Watson's young assistant during the thirties, and Goodrich considered him "a very important influence" on their thinking and writing, although Goodrich would later look upon this as a mixed blessing. In particular, Goodrich recalled his own negative treatment of Picasso, which he came to regret, and which he attributed, partially at least, to Watson's influence, "because he was a man of very decided opinions, and an older man who had a reputation, which I had not yet gotten myself."[50]

Watson was "extremely moody," according to Goodrich, but he was so "brilliant" and obviously enjoyed people and had such a delightful sense of humor, "always with the good story," that the pleasure of working with him far outweighed the negatives. Artists and other friends liked to drop by *The Arts* offices for the conviviality. William Robb looked back on his years with *The Arts* as the happiest of his life. "Just getting loaded with George Luks, if nothing else, made it all worthwhile."[51]

The issue of *The Arts* dated June 1924 carried a list of exhibitions in London, Paris, Berlin, Munich, and Lucerne that travelers to Europe might visit that summer. The Watsons, sailing on May 31 aboard the *Orduna* for the British Isles and France, planned to take in as many as possible. As usual, a number of friends were also abroad, including Juliana Force, and they had a high time. Most of Watson's editorials and essays that summer centered on the European art scene and contained strong international themes reaffirming the power of art to promote understanding among nations. His resentment at Parisian venality did not abate, however, even during his stay in Paris. In the dozen times he visited the Art Patrons of America show there that July, he saw "exactly one French person looking with dubious interest at the pictures." Whereas the French accepted American motion pictures and jazz because they considered them superior, when it came to painting and sculpture, they looked upon the United States only as a rich potential market. "Our problem is to intensify our own production and spread the interest in art among our own people," he asserted. "And when France wants to see our pictures she will not hesitate to come and get them."[52]

Following Paris and before returning to the United States in August, he and Nan traveled to Scotland to visit her relatives. There, obliged as usual to forego their free lifestyle for uprightness, Forbes grew bored. "Since I left Paris," he wrote Gertrude Whitney from Bowden St. Boswells, "I have been to church three times, heard grace at every meal, climbed the Cheviot Hills day after day, slept ten hours a night, read Anthony Trollope's autobiography, made no mention of any sex problem, sworn not once, and heard nothing of the existence of wine, liquor or cigars, had afternoon teas served as regular meals with forty different kinds of scones and oat cakes and a dozen different kinds of jams, discussed Scotch ecclesiastical laws, as well as ballads and legends and in general been a perfect imitation of a country parson. I feel rested, healthy, full of pep, grateful and amply ready to depart toward regions where life is not quite so 1860."[53]

Watson's articles from abroad that summer anticipated the magazine's expanded coverage of European art, particularly French. Debuting in January 1925, it contained reports from Paris, variously titled "Paris Postscripts," "Paris Chronicle," and "Paris Letter," and in the spring, Jacques Mauny, a sophisticated young French artist, became a regular correspondent. Over the years, Mauny's astute, impudent observations kept *Arts* readers abreast of the latest from Paris as only a savvy native could. Virgil Barker moved to France that summer to become European editor, initiating a series of descriptive essays on the state of art in London, Paris, and the provinces. Then, following Barker's return in 1927, Goodrich went to Paris as European editor. In addition to sending back his own articles, he served as intermediary between *The Arts* and European writers, commissioning, and in some instances translating, articles and negotiating for European advertising and sales outlets.

Around this time also, Watson increased local art coverage in towns outside New York, the first important metropolitan critic to counter the typical "who cares" attitude about culture beyond Manhattan.[54] Decentralization, after all, was the key to a democratic, antimonopolistic art. The local booster would do more for art and for his own pleasure, Watson admonished, by buying a painting or a piece of sculpture from a local artist than by spending money on ennobling community monuments. Of all the museums in America, the Cleveland Museum of Art was the "most courageous and . . . legitimately helpful . . . toward the artists of the community," he editorialized. Its trustees "do not wait to be told by New York and Paris collectors, dealers or writers." In addition to field reports from larger cities, *The Arts* occasionally featured small-town galleries, those with a progressive art spirit. The Little Gallery in Cedar Rapids, Iowa, so impressed Watson with its independence and imagination that he devoted an editorial to it and later brought its director, Edward B. Rowan, east to be his assistant.[55]

As the magazine evolved, certain features were eliminated and others were introduced. Original poetry was dropped early on. "Young America" ceased after 1926, but only nominally, since *The Arts* could always be depended on to encourage new talent. "The Skylight" and "Comment" features were also discontinued after 1926, but "Fresh Paint," introduced a year later, served a similar function. Items in "Fresh Paint" did not warrant serious editorial treatment, but readers contributed lively material. In one column, Watson wrote about Pres. Calvin Coolidge's remarks at a meeting of the American Federation of Arts, observing: "Mr. Coolidge betrays that he knows nothing about art whatever. . . . Well, that is certainly no crime. But . . . we squirm at the sight of the President hoisting his ignorance on the public rostrum and incorporating this dull mumbo-jumbo into an official state paper."[56] As time passed, there were minor changes in personnel and some shifting of titles and assignments, but the nonacademic viewpoint predominated and the issues addressed were continually provocative to independent-minded readers.

Watson's efforts to promote *The Arts* and achieve solvency led to a variety of enterprises. The Arts Publishing Corporation, established as a semi-independent for-profit operation, launched the Arts Monographs series, "small books on various artists and subjects of art" for the general reader and students.[57] The "monographs" were slightly revised versions of articles from *The Arts*, attractively printed with cloth covers and folio ties. Walter Pach's monograph on Georges Seurat and Watson's monograph on William Glackens were the only two issued, however.[58] The corporation also published books by Virgil Barker, Lloyd Goodrich, and Allen Tucker.[59]

Watson embarked on an ambitious letter-writing campaign. From his friends around the country—museum curators, critics, and collectors—Watson solicited lists of potential subscribers, following which he wrote individual letters, mentioning the person who recommended them and why, with their "great interest in art," they would appreciate *The Arts*.[60] He sent sample issues of the magazine to wealthy art lovers to entice them to subscribe. Authors of articles published in *The Arts* were asked to furnish names of persons with an interest in their work so they could be solicited for subscriptions.

In 1926 the corporation announced the establishment of a special printing department, which provided services ranging from ordering stock and supervising type selection and layout to final delivery, including "competent" proofreading. The Arts Book Service was introduced in December 1928, offering mail order books in the fields of general nonfiction, fiction, poetry, drama, and art. The following year *The Arts* also began vending imported color reproductions and paperbound monographs on popular European artists. There was also the Arts Portfolio Series, introduced in February 1929, each number of which contained twelve black-and-white reproductions and brief biographical, critical, and bibliographical material about an American or European artist. Watson, Dorothy Lefferts Moore, and Mildred Palmer wrote the accompanying texts. By May, fifty-five portfolios were offered, but as with the Arts Monographs series, only a small number were actually produced.[61] Despite ambitious plans, most of the Arts Corporation's promotional ventures were scaled down or aborted.

The Arts never got out of the red, and Gertrude Whitney came to the rescue every month. Even so, she and Juliana Force were neither sermonizing nor parsimonious, nor did they pressure Watson to solicit additional backers or advertisers. William Robb recalled one meeting with Force at which she asked how much salary he and Watson were drawing. "When I told her she acted shocked, and told me to double the salaries in both cases. On that occasion I beat a hasty retreat lest she change her mind."[62] Whitney left the internal operation of the magazine entirely to Watson. Months after The Arts was launched, she sent her compliments in a gracious handwritten note, saying: "I think it's time the Arts got a little of my attention, don't you? It is certainly doing a great thing and I am proud to be a distant relative. I send it and you my best wishes. We must have a talk about it some day."[63] In contrast, Juliana Force was avidly engaged, and not merely as banker and intermediary with Whitney. She too left editorial direction to Watson, however, aware that the magazine was in the most capable hands possible. This was fortunate, because Watson, unofficially her mentor in art matters, would not gladly have accepted her intrusion in this sphere.

Deficit notwithstanding, The Arts flourished, gaining in influence, circulation, and advertising. Growth necessitated another move, and in July 1928 The Arts relocated to larger offices at 139 East Fifty-fourth Street. By the end of 1928, the staff was at its largest, consisting of an associate editor, an assistant editor, and two contributing editors. Additional pages had been promised in 1927, but the size of the magazine remained relatively unchanged over the years.

4 ILLUMINATING THE TWENTIES ART SCENE: WATSON, *THE ARTS,* AND THE *NEW YORK WORLD,* 1921–1931

In October 1923, only nine months after he had assumed the editorship of *The Arts,* Watson was appointed to still another prestigious position, that of art critic for the *New York World* newspaper, succeeding Henry Tyrrell, who was assigned to other features. Possibly, Gertrude Whitney had helped Watson secure the post since the publisher, Ralph Pulitzer, and his wife were friends of hers. Thus, almost from the beginning of *The Arts* and for more than three years, Watson simultaneously handled the daunting duties of editor of a front-ranking art magazine and art critic for a prominent New York newspaper.[1] He and Nan moved from Greenwich Village during those years to a midtown apartment at 315 East Fifty-first Street, which put him nearer his offices and the major galleries.[2]

As with the *New York Evening Post* earlier, Watson's outlook harmonized with that of the *World,* the most liberal, entertaining, and contentious daily newspaper in the city. Describing his colleagues at the *World,* a staff reporter wrote: "We tried to write lucidly and simply.... We also tried, as unobtrusively as we knew how, to give the reader our eyes, to make him see people and events as we saw them. Such editorializing in the news was a sin. But we were shriven if we could sin honestly and expertly enough.... The fighting music always sounded clear."[3] That reporter could easily have been writing about Watson as well.

The executive editor of the *New York World* was the legendary journalist Herbert Bayard Swope. Walter Lippmann, whom Swope had hired away from the *New Republic,* was the editorial page editor, and Arthur Krock, hired away from the Louisville *Courier-Journal,* was the assistant to Ralph Pulitzer. Among his numerous accomplishments, Swope turned the paper's relatively lackluster arts section into the finest in the country, assembling "probably the most gifted group of critics and columnists ever associated at the same time with an American newspaper." Many of them appeared in the lively "Op-Ed" section (opposite the editorial page), which turned out to be one of Swope's most successful and widely imitated ideas. The format served his intent of bringing the opinions of gifted writers to the forefront, ahead of facts, and with a minimum of advertising. For the first two years, Watson's popular "Reviews and Notes of Current Events in Art" and "Art News of the Week" appeared weekly during the art season, usually in the "Metropolitan Section." Then, in 1925, he added a second weekly column for the Op-Ed.[4]

Although only one of a host of stellar writers for the *World,* Watson made no concessions to team protocol where art-publishing standards were concerned. Within a span of two months, Watson's complaints of "colossally ignorant tampering by staff" occasioned at least ten written exchanges among Watson, Swope, and Louis Weitzenkorn, the Sunday feature editor. Furious over their "unenlightened interference" in the art page, Watson alternately chastised, lectured, and raged over incidents such as the rejection of a photograph of a fourth-century Greek statue because it was too nude; "a diligent staff member's" redrawing of an unfinished cartoon by Puvis de Chavannes; "cheap and snappy" rounding of picture corners; and the deletion of backgrounds of artists' pictures. Even so, during those same months, Swope dropped Watson genial notes commending him on his work. To one that read in its entirety, "I liked your art notes very much," Watson replied, in toto, "You don't like my art notes as much as I like your liking them."[5]

Watson attended hundreds of exhibits now, wrote thousands of words for his semiweekly and monthly commentaries, and traveled throughout the country to fulfill lecture engagements. Referred to by some as the H. L. Mencken of art, he had achieved the status of "art personality." Even in the annals of academia, he was "a somebody," included in a quiz question in the modern-art history course at Wellesley along with the likes of James Joyce and Oswald Spengler. One of fifty names Prof. Alfred H. Barr Jr. instructed students to relate to "modern artistic expression," the matching descriptor for Watson was: "Forbes Watson: Art critic of the *New York World* and editor of *The Arts* in which he maintains a standard of criticism and scholarship which is both conscious of the past and sensitive to the present."[6]

Writing came easily to him. Often he published his first draft with only minor emendations. Even his most important texts rarely exceeded three or four revisions, and, more often than not, those were to tone down excessively corrosive comments. To juggle all his professional commitments, Watson began his day at the *New York World* a little after dawn, leaving there before noon to attend to his other responsibilities. He shared a cubbyhole with Heywood Broun, the quintessentially liberal columnist and sometime drama critic, and Deems Taylor, world celebrated music commentator. His contact with them was limited, however. "We practically never meet except on such days as I am going to catch a train," Broun wrote of his colleague. "Mr. Watson has adjusted his life and his job so shrewdly that he never hears the noon whistle from this office. Some little while after dawn he reaches the office and does what he has to do. The rest of the day is his own and may be spent in such soul satisfying diversion as going from one art exhibit to another. . . . If he happens to like the pictures he may linger with them. And when there is nothing to his taste he may travel through the gallery like Nurin [*sic*] on the last lap. Nobody can come around and abuse him for leaving before the third act."[7]

He was not a member of Swope's inner circle or the celebrated Algonquin Round Table, to which some *World* writers belonged, but Watson was on cordial terms with several, most notably Frank Sullivan, Heywood Broun, and Quinn Martin. Early on, Watson persuaded Quinn to write film commentary for *The Arts.* The affable Broun, a self-described late riser, expressed admiration, if not awe, for Watson's energy. "I live in this office of mine with two musical critics and an art critic," Broun wrote soon after Watson began at the *World.* "Of course it isn't really my office, but the group has agreed for the sake of prestige, that each shall always refer to it as 'my private office.' So far there has been practically no friction. The art critic, in particular, is a delightful fellow. Art seems to be something which happens very early in the morning, for I have never seen Forbes Watson hereabouts later than 11 A.M. And so we seldom meet. But his charm remains persuasive, even during his absence, for he leaves his typewriter unlocked." Broun liked "to be able to throw references to Forbes Watson," he once wrote, "for they furnish internal evidence of industry."[8]

Watson occasionally reprinted one of his *New York World* columns in *The Arts,* and he was not reticent about promoting *The Arts* in the newspaper. Despite some duplication of material, however, his approach to the two periodicals differed. For a widely circulating metropolitan daily, he was obliged to be inclusive, with reports on the NAD, National Sculpture Society, and other conservative events. In *The Arts* his approach to academic art was political, and he handled it with broad strokes. Never one simply to go along, however, even in the *World* he managed to push modern art to the forefront, if only to criticize institutions and galleries for ignoring it. Headings remonstrated, "Modern Art Overlooked by Pennsylvania Academy," "Philadelphia Annual Show Is Safe and Sane," and "Winter Academy Exhibition Runs True to Type." To the delight of

New York World readers, Watson's unequivocating opinions came through as provocatively as they did in *The Arts,* more so in some respects, since a large general readership did not demand the same meticulousness as enlightened artists and art lovers did. Aptly pinpointing Watson's appeal, one *New York World* fan wrote: "With Watson, art is made sufficiently fundamental to be accepted as one of the large issues of life. He furnishes the bridge across. . . . I tell everyone that the best art education, outside the merely technical aspect, is found in the Sunday *World.* His Sunday editorial is the only sermon we bother with of a Sunday morning. The essentials are all there."[9]

By now, nearly all the principal New York daily newspapers had reputable critics on their staffs, although art commentary usually abutted the society pages rather than music or theater. For the artist, the relatively large number of newspapers compared to art galleries meant that "if you had an exhibition, and if you were at all fairly well known, . . . you were sure of having space somewhere in one of those papers."[10] In addition to Watson at the *World,* the most widely read critics were Henry McBride at the *New York Sun,* Royal Cortissoz at the *Herald Tribune,* Elizabeth Luther Cary at the *New York Times,* and William McCormick, a syndicated columnist. Watson and McBride were the most authoritative voices on the liberal side, often lumped together and often compared. Cook Glassgold, who following his stint with *The Arts* became McBride's associate editor at *Creative Art,* observed that whereas Henry McBride was closer to Stieglitz in his "excited inclination" toward the international avant-garde, Watson "was more the objective, dispassionate judge." McBride promoted the French modernists over Americans, artist Charles Sheeler recalled. "He was a snob in that regard, very much so; he was pretty much a snob too." McBride was also the more elegant writer, according to Lloyd Goodrich, "an essayist." But if McBride was the "extraordinarily genteel, . . . delicately cultivated wit of art criticism," as Thomas Hart Benton described him, Watson was surely the indelicately cultivated wit. Centered more in journalism than in the literary, Watson was the "activist in action and in writing, . . . much more *au courant* than Henry McBride," Goodrich believed. It was for Peggy Bacon, though, whose deliciously piercing caricatures skewered some of the mightiest celebrities of the day, to sum them up in an exhibition of caricatures of critics at the Downtown Galleries. The contrast between Watson's furiously contorted features and McBride's supremely polite mien spoke volumes.[11]

The young-minded artists liked to congregate in the Woodstock Colony in upstate New York during those years. It was situated in the Catskill Mountains, a convenient drive from the city, and artists were "the dominating element." Eugene Speicher spent summers in Woodstock. George Bellows built a home

Peggy Bacon, *Forbes Watson*, 1931. Pastel on canvas, 20⅛" x 15⅛". Saint Louis Art Museum, Saint Louis, Missouri. Gift of Wallace H. Smith.

next to Speicher's. Henry Lee McFee lived there, "seriously working out his studies of form in his still lifes." Andrew Dasburg first made his "discreet experiments in abstraction in Woodstock."[12] Hundreds of other artists lived or vacationed in the colony or attended summer sessions there. By the early 1920s a Woodstock school, or style, had evolved, characteristically a "middle course" between the nonobjective and figurative extremes that had warred in American art since the Armory Show.[13] It was Watson's kind of modernism, and many of those who came to be associated with the Woodstock style—Yasuo Kuniyoshi, Peggy Bacon, Alexander Brook, Ernest Fiene, and others—were his friends. They were modernists, he observed, but their experiments did not "dash out our eyes with their radicalism." Tourists loved to go to Woodstock to see the bohemians, and the colonists, who "had a great fondness . . . for not overdressing," did not disappoint. But while some of them took "the question of looking picturesque rather seriously," Watson noted, they were unpretentious and hard-working artists "who although they had plenty of jollifications, lived on the whole modestly. . . . And the wives entertained and cooked with equal distinction." It was "a genial spot to visit," and Juliana Force and Watson drove up frequently. She learned much from the Woodstock artists, Watson felt, and they, in turn, gained from her interest. Paintings done at Woodstock became the nucleus of the growing collection of the Whitney. So liberally did Force support Woodstock art that the inhabitants always made a great fuss over her when she visited. It was with only a touch of irony that the gifted sculptor John Flannagan, a beneficiary of Force's generous patronage and Watson's positive journalistic treatment, wrote in a letter from Woodstock, "Everyone is excited just now over an impending visit of the Dowager Queen and the Crown Prince, otherwise Mrs. Force and Forbes Watson."[14]

The dealer Frank K. M. Rehn, something of a counterpart to Watson and the Whitney group in his attachments to artists and collectors, was also partial to the moderate Woodstock style, so much so that his gallery came to be known as "the Woodstock Gallery."[15] Not surprising, *The Arts* covered Rehn Gallery shows quite faithfully.

Despite Watson's popularity among readers, the *New York World* terminated him in 1927. The paper's trustees, struggling with a deficit and attempting to offset a reduction in the price of the paper to two cents, had ordered heavy economies. "It was decided to apply the rule against those heads of departments who have been among the more recent to join the staff," Swope explained to Watson. "That is why your name is included." At the same time, he reaffirmed his admiration for the "intelligence," "discrimination," and "importance" of Watson's work and expressed the hope that a change in circumstances would soon warrant his return to active service.[16]

Occupied as he was with *The Arts,* more requests for speaking engagements than he could fulfill, exhibitions, and a host of other activities, Watson, nonetheless, was not one simply to settle for the proffered seven weeks severance pay and quietly depart. Nor would he deny himself a swipe at the trustees.

Quickly dispatching a handwritten reply to Swope, he demanded better terms. "You and Mr. Pulitzer know I am sure that I would not have left The World flat in mid-season. . . . I should hate to strain the finances of the trustees of The World but in my opinion morally The World is obligated to pay my salary for the season." Ralph Pulitzer himself responded: "Now that you have refreshed our recollection it goes without saying that the original seasonal understanding will be adhered to." Watson's final column for the *New York World* appeared in the issue of March 20, 1927. Swope left the *World* the following year. The paper never fully resolved its financial difficulties, however, and in February 1931 the Pulitzer family sold it to the Scripps-Howard chain, which merged the *World* with the *New York Telegram*.[17]

In the eleven years between Watson's appointments to the *New York Evening Post* and the *New York World,* modernism had become an acknowledged force in American art, controversial still but enticing to dealers, collectors, and museums. A migration of major art galleries to East Fifty-seventh Street had occurred during those years also, challenging Fifth Avenue as the preeminent art gallery thoroughfare. The Macbeth Galleries were there now, as were the Knoedler, Durand-Ruel, and Joseph Brummer. In 1924 alone, Parrish, Watson and Company, Feragil, and Frederick Keppel moved into new galleries on East Fifty-seventh, followed a little over a year later by Frederick Valentine Dudensing, who left "the more conservative atmosphere of his father's gallery" to join them. In time, East Fifty-seventh Street would become New York's signature stretch of galleries and swank shops. Referring to "the new avenue of aesthetics," Watson quipped, "It has been suggested that the dealers become so neighborly in order to save the tired critics' footsteps, for it's an old maxim among the dealers that a critic is only good as long as his feet hold out and sometimes not even then. . . . For my own part I have always felt that the ideal arrangement of galleries would be to place them exactly one cigarette's smoke apart. That gives an opportunity to overcome the benefits of fresh air while the mind recovers from one set of impressions sufficiently to register another."[18]

From his initial hostility toward the avant-garde through selective enthusiasms following the Armory Show, Watson reached his broadest affirmation of modernism during his years at *The Arts* and *New York World.* It had been a gradually warming embrace, but by the twenties, Henri Matisse, Max Weber, Alfred Maurer, and others whom he once dismissed as radical fashionmongers had supplanted Childe Hassam and J. Alden Weir in Watson's galaxy. Even Picasso gained in his esteem. He had also modernized his paradigm of the American artistic genius. Rejecting firmly the popular notion of "unharnessed vitality" as the essential note, he advanced a more comprehensive case for refinement as the special hallmark of American art—that is, the absence of "ebullient ornamentation," the "positive spirit of choice, and fastidious quality."[19] In his streamlined paradigm, the unique quality of refinement coalesced with abstraction and subsumed the other "American" traits of sanity and sincerity. Refinement, which now signified abstracted realism, had shifted subtly from intimations of good taste, polish, and delicacy to good taste, simplicity, and clarity. His quintessentially refined artists were Charles Demuth, Charles Sheeler, and John Marin. In his definitive essay on Sheeler, Watson delineated the prototypical American modernist: "It is easy to trace, through more than a century of American art, an inherent refinement, a definite quality of good taste which are part of a tradition to which the art of Charles Sheeler belongs." From a consciously arbitrary treatment of natural forms for purposes of abstract experimentation, Sheeler arrived at a filtered realism to express the permanent and essential character of the natural object. "We soon discover . . . that the realism is of a highly selected order, that choice, elimination, selection are dominating factors in the design." Once young American modernists abandoned the veil of "deliberate 'modernism,'" by which Watson meant Parisian imitativeness, they gained in distinctiveness and individuality. "Great beauty . . . and intelligent selection" keynoted the work of "the best living younger American artists," Watson observed. The one common feature that persisted and predominated was "characteristic American refinement."[20] Refinement. It was an interesting word choice for the inveterate mugwump.

He insisted on a spacious definition of modernism, effectively merging modernism with independence. The mark of the real artist, Watson told his audience at the Newark Art Club, was the ability to see the world with his own eyes and express what he saw in his own way. That made of every real artist "a modern of his time." Every great artist who broke from tradition was a "modern," he declared.[21]

More people paid attention to art now and to what Watson had to say about it. Articulated more sharply and apprehended within a more familiar context, his three-pronged campaign for independent American art—deflating competition, foreign and domestic; italicizing American genius; and fostering a discriminating American taste—achieved its greatest resonance during the twenties. Watson had become, in Lloyd Goodrich's words, "a messiah of the modern movement." Watson was less exclusive, and thus less prescient, than those of his contemporaries who trumpeted America's avant-garde. But more than they, he connected with the public, narrowing the gap between public taste and modern art. First, as a liberal democratic critic he widened Americans' exposure to the new forces, sharing his open-minded endorsement of the modern spirit in European and American styles. As an exhortative crusader and snappy fighter, he delivered the message of modern art pungently, deprecating its deprecators, galvanizing public interest. "He had an instinct for feeling strongly about issues that were important and making them vivid," a colleague remarked. "And, of course the reason was that he cared."[22]

Respected yet approachable, the urbane critic "gave the impression of being well educated and uppercrust, but not *very* uppercrust."[23] His delivery, personal and interactive, drew in readers and audiences. "'Would you mind explaining to me why modern artists make things so ugly?'" Watson quoted a member of his audience at a Carnegie Institute lecture. This prompted Watson "to waylay" people for their reactions to the "absurd" question. To his astonishment, "eighteen people out of twenty" not only did not consider the question silly but also wondered the same thing. The anecdote was the lead-in of an *Arts* editorial that challenged viewers' allegiance to conventional prettiness in art. A beautiful picture for them was "a more or less standardized object," Watson observed, based on "a more or less vague acquaintance with the starred pictures in the guide books." The standard did not recognize the artist as a personality. "Any thought . . . that acrid color may serve his purpose better than sweet color, or dissonance better than harmony . . . is outside the limits set by this standard. . . . When people ask why modern artists 'make things so ugly,' is it because they find too disturbing the work of a man who creates compositions and designs which cannot be tagged and measured and put away immediately, each in its proper pigeon hole?" To those who cared deeply for art as an expressive force, Watson insisted, the "new vision" was not ugly.[24] The article was widely quoted in the national press.

He could get especially personal in his attacks and "ridicule things like nobody's business." A column he wrote on distortion in modern art was a case in point. In it, Watson, reasonable and detached at first, observed that people naturally tend to derive pleasure from art in which they recognize ideas, subjects, and emotions they themselves experience. That premise established, however, he moved on to the intellect and lifestyles of those on each side of the distortion issue. By the end of the exposition, Watson left no doubt that conservatives were a boring lot, mentally dull and socially inferior to liberals. Those who enjoyed modern art did not constantly reread the old books from their youth and live on memories. They possessed "capacity and alertness." Compared to those who rejected modern art, "their visions have not been dried up."[25]

"Both plugged into, and critically detached from the art world," *The Arts* expressed nothing so much as Watson's own feisty independence. Lloyd Goodrich's description of Watson as "a very skeptical human being in many ways, . . .

agin' fashion," spoke to an independence honed to contrariness at times. For Watson, "réclame" was a term of derogation, and he used it often. He liked to "take the wind out of anything chichi," Goodrich observed. "As a matter of fact he would fight for what he believed in, but as soon as it was accepted, he'd go against the acceptance."[26] In his freewheeling commentary, Watson promoted the Society of Independent Artists, encouraged the Salons of America, and cheered on singular manifestations of artistic autonomy. Even as his associate editors on The Arts verged on exasperation with the frequently trivial talent in the Independents shows, Watson made allowances, convinced that the cause of independence made it all worthwhile.

His battle against the dominance of the National Academy of Design achieved its greatest potency during the twenties. Both in The Arts and in the New York World, he battered the manufacturers of "gray blond" pictures.[27] When the NAD announced a six-million-dollar fund-raising drive in 1925 "for an educational expansion program to make possible the fulfillment of the Academy's responsibility as a national institution," Watson fought it all the way. The academy was "not more national than the National Biscuit Company," he fumed.[28] He rallied liberals with a conspiracy scenario: If the NAD succeeded in raising the money they were so cleverly planning to raise, "the next thing we shall hear of is a Secretary of Art at Washington" with a member of the academy as secretary of art. Then there would be "a nationwide exhibition system, censored by the National Academy, and a College of Art censored by the National Academy."[29]

He sounded the alarm again following what he perceived to be a sly maneuver by the NAD to grab a portion of city land. In January 1927, in anticipation of its annual spring show, the academy offered to allocate one of its exhibition galleries to the moderns. After the moderns accepted—warily—the NAD sent out a circular letter pleading in typically "plaintive innuendoes" that its galleries were too small to accommodate its exhibitions and requesting that a section of Central Park land be turned over to them. Watson "raised the roof." If the city ever gave them a parcel of the public's land, it would be committing a wrong against the city and inflicting the greatest injury upon American artists in general. If the public felt inclined to give money to an artists' organization or to pay for a building, Watson argued, the deserving organization was not the NAD but the Society of Independent Artists, which never rejected a picture.[30] Watson and his allies beat back the academy's efforts at aggrandizement. The victory, which could not have tasted sweeter than the battle itself, marked the first tangible crack in the NAD stronghold.

Even though Watson had never been an admirer of the Rumanian modernist sculptor Constantin Brancusi, he hastened to his side in a notorious court case centering on the issue of artistic intent. It began in the fall of 1926, when photographer Edward Steichen, returning to New York from Paris, brought with him Brancusi's abstract bronze sculpture "*L'Oiseau*" (generally translated in English as "Bird in Flight" or "Bird in Space"). Rejecting Steichen's designation of the bronze as "art" and therefore duty-free, the customs-house official entered it under "kitchen utensils and hospital supplies," imposing a tariff of $240. Steichen appealed the ruling to the U.S. Customs Court.[31]

Ever eager for combat, especially in the cause of individual expression, Watson accompanied Marcel Duchamp, who was Brancusi's agent, and Henry McBride to the customs house to enter a protest. He also rallied his readers. "People who, like the present writer, feel that Brancusi is considerably overrated in America, are, nevertheless, infuriated by . . . the palpable ignorance which has brought about a tax on Mr. Brancusi's bronzes on the ground that they are not sculpture," he editorialized. "Everybody with a sense of fairness will turn gladly to the task of attempting to remedy a gross injustice."[32]

The popular press had a field day when Steichen's appeal came before the court. The *New York American* headlined one report, "How They Know It's 'A Bird' and Are Sure It is 'Art,'" printing excerpts of testimony by Watson and other expert witnesses along with illustrations of seven Brancusi sculptures, each with a tongue-in-cheek caption. Having denounced the officials, and especially the academic sculptors, for nearly two years, Watson heartily applauded the judge's finding, which reversed the customs officials' ruling in favor of Steichen. It was "a great service to art."[33]

Throughout the litigation Watson had suspected the academic stalwarts of pressuring the government to impose a tariff, a practice he vehemently opposed. His "Monroe Doctrine attitude toward art" may have seemed concordant with the prevailing mood of nationalism, but he had consistently repudiated its xenophobia and penchant for government intervention on behalf of American art.[34] A tariff on imported art would only put the American artist in the position of a "whining weakling," he argued, when the conservative American Artists Professional League appealed to Congress for an equalizing tariff on the importation of foreign art. American art could hold its own in the international market, he insisted. With the renaissance in American art in full swing, why "make a whimpering appeal to keep democracy safe for provincialism"?[35]

The fact was that for decades nearly every action the government took in the field of art, not to mention politics, favored the most conservative forces in the United States. "As soon as art and politics join hands something corroding happens to both," Watson warned, assailing a proposal by the American Federation of Arts to erect a seven-million-dollar national gallery of art in Washington. He scoffed at the projected vision of an American Louvre. Better to make the Metropolitan Museum a national museum, he countered, and use the seven million dollars to enhance collections and staff in existing museums. As for the works of art stored in the Smithsonian Institution for lack of space, they could be parceled out among museums around the country, which "would care to accept them."[36]

When Massachusetts representative George Tinkham introduced a bill in Congress to establish a cabinet-level department of fine arts, proof positive that the public had discovered art, Watson "blasted it to high heaven," Goodrich recalled. "Even art cannot escape from the present American hysteria for censorship and legislation," he railed. To those who believed that mediocrity could be sanctified through "the strong arm of the Government," he snapped, "why should Governmental supervision go only half way? Let us have a Department of Poetry. . . . Let the United States government add also a Department of Prose and a Department of Music. . . . Why not a Department of Dance and Jazz? Journalism . . . certainly should not escape."[37]

Not government, but museums and dealers were the appropriate agents for advancing American art, and Watson did not conceal his exasperation at their failure to do so. Private patrons too were vital enablers. A decade earlier, the Armory Show had spawned a small but influential group of American patrons who built pioneer collections of avant-garde art.[38] Following the world war, a surge of prosperity facilitated the rise of another group of collectors, bringing America's aggregate holdings of modern art to international prominence.

In the timid cultural climate of the early twenties, the character of those independent collectors and the special qualities of their acquisitions were critical, Watson believed, and he showcased them in extended, copiously illustrated articles, the only writer to do so in many instances. On sociable terms with a number of collectors, he visited with some in their homes and golfed with others. Some were investors in the Arts Corporation. Albert Barnes invited Watson and Nan down to Merion, Pennsylvania, from time to time for lunch or the weekend to view his acquisitions. Given Barnes's irascibility and Watson's combativeness, it was inevitable that the two would have a "knock-down-drag-out" in time, but while their association lasted, the public could glimpse the legendary collection in *The Arts,* which was the only publication allowed to reproduce pictures from the Barnes Foundation.[39] Three principal motifs emerged in Watson's essays on American collections. There was first Watson's own excitement, that of the connoisseur-critic, as he elucidated picture after picture, some the finest examples of art from abroad and the United States. He made much of collectors' personal pleasure in their art and their unconcern for official endorsement, meaning that American art was represented. He highlighted the special relationship between artists and the patrons who bought their works and the pivotal role artists played in patrons' choices, a point he returned to repeatedly. William Glackens advised Albert Barnes; Guy Pène du Bois guided many of Chester Dale's purchases; the Havemeyer collection would not have developed as it did had it not been for Mary Cassatt; nor would the Lizzie Bliss collection without Arthur B. Davies; Maurice Prendergast counseled a number of collectors.[40]

The most important collector of modern American art was Gertrude Vanderbilt Whitney, and *The Arts* was steadfastly attentive to her and her innumerable benefactions. But there were others as well. Not surprising, the first patron Watson featured in a special series entitled "American Collections" was Ferdinand Howald, who was second only to Gertrude Whitney in acquiring contemporary American art. Watson expressed admiration for the "adventurousness" of Howald's collection, noting with approval its lack of "confirmed academic politicians." In his piece on John T. Spaulding, he applauded his "firmness of point of view" in seeking out for himself the works of individuals not yet so widely known. The collection of financier philanthropist Adolph Lewisohn, which included certified masterpieces, was "a sound, conservative gathering of . . . orthodox art," although Watson regretted that little time had been "wasted on unknowns." Watson devoted a major essay to the collection of Frederick Clay Bartlett and his wife, Helen Birch-Bartlett, which they eventually donated to the Art Institute of Chicago. Together with the Ryerson gift, the Birch-Bartlett collection constituted "probably the most comprehensive group of paintings belonging to . . . the modern movement in art." Even so, Watson did not refrain from twitting Bartlett, "now that Mr. Bartlett has stated his preferences in French art . . . he may be led to make a collection of American paintings."[41]

The Arts featured other eminent collections as well, including those of Josef Stransky and Chester Dale. The most brilliant modern art collection in America, and the one that fascinated Watson the most, was that of John Quinn, "the noble buyer."[42] Quinn's incomparable holdings were the subject of several articles by Watson. He liked to point out that Quinn had acquired more than two thousand works by the most significant avant-garde artists of the twentieth century at a time when most American buyers scorned them. Characteristically, he also focused on "the human side of his collection and its broad-mindedness," observing that Quinn himself had told him that "his friendships with the artists were by no means the smallest part of his collection."[43]

As the twenties progressed and increasing numbers of dealers featured works by modern artists, Watson continued to encourage their anti-academic tendencies and lack of "froth" and "falsetto." The museums were another matter, however. That one the stature of the Carnegie Institute of Art, fearing it might arouse the public to a "questioning attitude," limited the number of modern works in its International Exhibition of 1926 to a maximum of 10–15 percent reflected the persistent antimodern bias among established museums. It was a dereliction of public responsibility, Watson bristled, a capitulation to the ignorant. Although exhibits of modern art were no longer uncommon in big-city museums, purchases were. Bold acquisitions such as those of Harvard's Fogg Museum and the Cleveland Museum of Art were singular exceptions to the typically "safe" accession practices of most institutions. In his many years of covering press conferences at the Metropolitan Museum, Watson never once heard Dr. Edward Robinson, the "dignified guardian of the sacred premises," mention a living American artist. Watson termed his criticism "just and interested" as he chided "reactionary" museums for timid holdings, lackluster shows, elitist programs, and for tolerating "ignorant ridicule of 'modern art'" in lecture courses.[44] American museums had had the same opportunity as Frederick Clay Bartlett, John Quinn, and other private collectors ten or fifteen years earlier to acquire Seurat's celebrated *Sunday Afternoon on the Island of La Grande Jatte* (1884–86) and equally important Picassos and Cézannes at modest prices, but because of die-hard purchasing committees, they had not. Now the cost would be multiplied.

When the Metropolitan Museum purchased John Singer Sargent's famous *The Wyndham Sisters* (1899), an inferior work in Watson's estimation and one that cost almost as much as Titian's illustrious *Portrait of Alfonso d'Este* (ca. 1523–34), he did not mute his contempt. First of all, the money, $90,000, had come from unspent Hearn funds, already a sore spot. In a scathing article in *New Yorker* magazine, he pointed a finger at the president of the NAD, a member in perpetuity of the Metropolitan's board of trustees, as mandated in the museum's charter. The foolish decision to add Sargent's *"Happiness Sisters"* to the Metropolitan's overstocked Sargent collection was not made by an expert, he declared. "It hangs there in all its vast dimensions, a glorious advertisement to popularity, a screaming warning to the Museum of the danger of employing too many stepfathers of art on its committees."[45]

As early as 1915, Watson began crusading for a museum devoted to modern art, "an experiment station, so to speak," rescued from politics, that would meet the contemporary painter's need for contact with the vital creative forces of his own period. A modern museum could purchase contemporary art for its own permanent collection, or it could act as a trial museum for the country's centrally situated museums, he suggested in January 1926. Financial support could come from other museums, and purchases could gradually be disseminated into their permanent collections. By spring he was pleading, "Heaven send [New York] a museum of modern art so that folks may see what is going on in the world."[46]

Attesting to Watson's considerable influence, the following year, when the American collector Albert E. Gallatin announced the establishment of the Gallery of Living Art at New York University, he credited Watson's editorial with giving him the idea. Gallatin planned to add to his outstanding collection of contemporary art only the work of living artists, "seeking out young men who have not yet been generally recognized." The gallery's location at the university would bring artists, many of whom lived nearby, and students into direct contact with the pictures and with one another, he hoped.[47]

Although generally enthusiastic about the Gallery of Living Art's opening exhibit, Watson nonetheless expressed regret that Gallatin had not shown "a little more daring" in his selections, by which he meant not radical, avant-garde works but contemporary American art. "It would be nice," he commented, "if the students of New York University were given, while they are studying, some idea of the fact that a great deal of living art is now being produced in America and that it is not limited to a few watercolor specialists or to a handful of artists who paint in oil."[48] Watson's use of the term "daring" was instructive not only for what it said about collectors' diffidence toward contemporary American art but also for its restatement of Watson's moderate position, that American modernism, tamer than that of Europe, was as extreme as he wished modernism to be.

The prophet of the European avant-garde in the United States was, of course, Alfred Stieglitz. Both he and Watson had been instrumental in introducing Americans to modernism, but where Watson was nationalist and resolutely democratic, Stieglitz was internationalist and elitist. Looking back, Goodrich believed certain of *The Arts*'s editorial positions were "a reaction in the first place against the very great weight given to European modernism as against new trends in American art and then against the exclusiveness of certain advanced modernists, the feeling that only they counted." The whole attitude of superiority in Stieglitz's coterie annoyed Watson and his associates. Of the Stieglitz painters, only John Marin and Charles Demuth received predominantly favorable reviews in *The Arts*. Then too there were personal factors. To Watson's well-bred sensibilities, Stieglitz seemed boorish, and his arrogant sermonizing and interminable talk grated. "I knew Alfred Stieglitz as slightly as circumstances would permit for many years," Watson reminisced in later life. "He was the only person who ever bored me to the raging point before I ever saw him. . . . But listening was not limited to friends alone. I was forced to listen to him for hours upon hours before I ever had a chance to notice how long was the hair in his ears. From some inner room his voice, unctuous, fatuous, in love with itself sent an endless chain of words into the exhibition galleries. I overcame this handicap by always going to 291 at lunchtime and asking the Negro elevator boy if Mr. Stieglitz had gone to lunch. When he said 'no' I left. When he said 'yes' I went up. But the elevator boy was evidently a disciple of Stieglitz and eventually refused to answer my questions. So eventually I did see the owner of that tireless voice."[49]

In time, the coolness between Watson and Stieglitz developed into an icy fissure. Inslee Hopper, Watson's assistant editor in 1932, recalled introducing himself to Stieglitz at a show at An American Place, Stieglitz's last gallery, and getting a "reception which would have chilled a polar bear." When Hopper mentioned the rebuff to Watson, Watson replied: "'It's not you. He and I are not exactly palsy. We don't see eye-to-eye on a lot of things.'" Inherently, Hopper observed, "Watson disliked anyone who was grandstanding, and trying to promote with an eye on the public and, of course, Stieglitz was primarily a promoter, and Forbes simply disapproved of a lot of the people that Stieglitz promoted." Stieglitz, in Watson's view, had devoted "a lifetime to this work of establishing an uncommercial status in a purely commercial venture." Watson "loved to fight with various people in the art world," Hopper recalled, and Stieglitz was one of those with whom "he had a knock-down-drag-out," following which Hopper was brought in "to pick up the pieces."[50]

The Arts years were the best of Watson's career, and the best of Nan's as well. During his first year as *Arts* editor, she exhibited at the prestigious Durand-Ruel Galleries in Paris in a group show with six important American artists, among them Charles Demuth and Charles Sheeler. In the United States, she was represented in major exhibitions in New York and elsewhere, including nearly every Whitney annual and biennial event. Certainly, Nan's paintings could and did stand on their own merit, but friends' comments about them seemed plumped by affection. Inslee Hopper declared them "absolutely delightful." Olin Dows, a close friend from the thirties, and Lloyd Goodrich were probably closer to the mark, however, when they described Nan's painting as "very good" and "very nice," respectively. Undoubtedly, Forbes's intimacy with Juliana Force had something to do with his wife's professional success. Nan was not one to create a row over his infidelities, and Juliana Force, without open acknowledgment, rewarded Nan's forbearance with exhibitions and purchases, acquiring several of Nan's still lifes for her homes and for the Whitney galleries. By the time the Whitney Museum of American Art opened in 1931, eight of Nan's oil paintings were in the museum's permanent collection, representing the institution's fourth-largest holdings for a single artist.[51]

Forbes had never perceived his own coverage of her shows to be a conflict of interest. In the early years, he made slight attempts to balance his complimentary notices with a criticism here and there such as "too limited in color range" or "incomplete canvas," inserting at the same time quotations from friends' well-disposed reviews. By the twenties, however, he was disarmingly open in his praise. Reviewing the group show, which had recently returned from Paris, he wrote, "Of the paintings of the seventh member of the group, Nan Watson, I have a very high opinion, which is rather fortunate since she is my wife." Inslee Hopper described Watson as "very, very even-handed" except toward Nan, whom "he did promote, very cutely. . . . She would have exhibitions at Kraushaar's and Forbes would always give a great boost to Nan Watson, and this, I think is quite justified in any world."[52]

Forbes and Nan's flourishing careers seemed to parallel the ascendancy of modern art in America. Interest in art had mushroomed by the end of the decade. On a speaking tour sponsored by various museums, colleges, and art associations in Iowa, Missouri, Illinois, Indiana, Michigan, and Ohio, Watson talked to large responsive audiences about modern art and the need to support local artists. He was gratified by the eagerness of Midwesterners to appreciate and create artworks. Optimism prevailed, and if there were signs of impending financial calamity, they were not apparent to the average American. The well-to-do were flocking to Europe as never before. Visiting galleries in Paris, London, and Berlin the summer of 1929, Watson found sales of modern art to be voluminous, with dozens of canvases, many celebrated works— Courbets, Renoirs, Cézannes—destined for collectors and museums in the United States. It was "enough to suggest a thrilling season," he told his readers. The whole world seemed to be competing for modern art, even the traditionally conservative galleries on Bond Street. Guy Pène du Bois, returning to America after five years' residence in France, was astonished at "the tremendous spread" of the New York art market. "In 1906 the exhibitions could be fairly thoroughly covered by one critic in one day," he observed. By 1924 when he left for France, "the increase in the number of galleries scarcely kept pace with the increase in the city's population." By 1930 "two critics must have had some difficulty in covering the galleries in three or four days."[53]

Those who celebrated the triumph of modernism in America also took sorrowful note of the recent deaths of two of its truest champions, Arthur Bowen Davies and Robert Henri. "What used to be called 'modern' art in America was a private tea party," Watson wrote in tribute to Davies, "with a few advanced artists, a few intelligent writers and a dealer or two singing 'Nearer my God to Thee' over it until Arthur B. Davies took the reins of the Armory exhibition into his hands and thereby completely turned over American painting and American appreciation."[54]

His introduction to a posthumous edition of Henri's popular book *The Art Spirit* summed up contributions very like his own: "He gave his followers complete respect for an American outlook," he wrote. "Yet for all the impulsion which he gave toward what might be called a native school, Henri was the first artist to spread in any broad way the news of the great French painters.... Henri was ... an inspired teacher with an extraordinary gift for verbal communication.... He came at a time when the officials were still in power, and had their heavy paws firmly on the neck of youth and originality. Henri fought for freedom and he gave to his students the courage to conquer officialdom."[55]

Without question, the most important event of the 1929 art season was the founding of the Museum of Modern Art, which opened on November 7 in galleries in the Heckscher Building at Fifty-seventh Street and Fifth Avenue. Alfred H. Barr Jr. was named director. The museum was palpable confirmation of the triumph of modernism in America, and a jubilant Watson took a bit of well-deserved credit for "the tilling of the soil." The actuality of the modern museum so buoyed him that he genially put aside years of diatribes against the Metropolitan Museum of Art, allowing that critics had treated the institution unfairly. True, its Hearn fund had been "atrociously mishandled"; its modern sculpture department was "pathetic"; it had sponsored some of the worst lecturers in the world as well as some of the best. Yet the Metropolitan had transformed itself from a provincial museum into one of the leading museums of the world. For its own part, the Metropolitan was pleased that the critics would now "have something else to knock besides us."[56]

Although slightly disappointed that the new museum's first exhibit had been devoted to French postimpressionists rather than Americans, its lack of extremism reassured Watson. He and other progressive critics were delighted with the quality of the show. They were not as pleased with the museum's second exhibition, however, the theme of which was "Nineteen Living Americans." Based on ballots from the museum's trustees, the directors selected nineteen artists believed to be "fairly representative of the principal tendencies in contemporary American painting": Charles Burchfield, Charles Demuth, Preston Dickinson, Lyonel Feininger, George Overbury "Pop" Hart, Edward Hopper, Bernard Karfiol, Rockwell Kent, Walt Kuhn, Yasuo Kuniyoshi, Ernest Lawson, John Marin, Kenneth Hayes Miller, Georgia O'Keeffe, Jules Pascin, John Sloan, Eugene Speicher, Maurice Sterne, and Max Weber.[57] Inevitably, the selection of nineteen contemporaries aroused animated debate among critics and the public. Henry McBride criticized the dearth of advanced artists;

Edward Alden Jewell, critic for the *New York Times,* questioned the inclusion of foreign-born artists. Readers of *The Arts* expressed a range of objections.

Watson certainly had his own ideas. First, Alfred Barr and Jere Abbott, director and assistant director, respectively, should have devoted as much attention to this exhibition as they had to the French postimpressionists the preceding month. Even though museum officials had been careful to emphasize that this was not intended as a show of the *best* living Americans, most viewers interpreted it as a ranking and thus took issue. What troubled Watson more than the museum's fallibilities, however, was the anti-foreign response.

"Sometimes, after reading my morning mail, I felt that someone wanted to start a race war and that bombs would be thrown through the windows of *The Arts* if it did not immediately join a kind of aesthetic Ku Klux Klan and go Methodist," he commented. A painter was American, he insisted, not because of his country of birth but because of his orientation and the tradition in which he worked. Of the Museum of Modern Art's choices for "Nineteen Living Americans," Watson argued that some belonged to the American school more than others. Yasuo Kuniyoshi, born in Japan, and Bernard Karfiol, from Hungary, contributed much more to the sum of American painting than Max Weber, whose development as an artist took no account of the American tradition but rather developed out of an immersion in the Parisian avant-garde art. By way of broadening perspective on the issue, Watson also pointed out that Lyonel Feininger, who was born in the United States, painted in the German tradition. "As a painter I should rank him in American art about two hundred and fourteenth."[58]

It seemed not just promotion, but a display of proprietary power when *The Arts* launched a contest offering a one-hundred-dollar prize to the reader who came up with the most ideal list of nineteen living American painters. "The object of this competition is not in any sense an effort on the part of *The Arts* to censure or to praise the Museum's selection," the announcement stated disingenuously, "but rather to give the art public at large an opportunity to express itself on a question which seems to have created nationwide controversy." The competition lasted two months, and at the end *The Arts* awarded duplicate prizes because the judges were unable to reach a unanimous decision. The two winning lists were not only similar to one another but also to the Museum of Modern Art's All-American Nineteen choices. Twelve of the top names were on all three lists. The largest number of votes went to Eugene Speicher, then in descending order, John Sloan, John Marin, Charles Burchfield, Edward Hopper, George Luks, Rockwell Kent, Bernard Karfiol, Kenneth Hayes Miller, Max Weber, Preston Dickinson, Charles Demuth, and Walt Kuhn. "The independent American painters won the race," Watson exulted. "The careful imitators of the latest fashions from Paris came in a poor second, and the so-called representational academicians were completely outdistanced." He was pleased to observe that "on the whole," Americans are interested in the subject in art. Pure intellectual theorizing doesn't appear yet to have hit them very hard.[59]

Those who represented the "outdistanced academicians" did not meekly accede to *The Arts*'s latest victory claim, however. At their annual meeting in May, the American Art Dealers Association, whose thirty members composed the "leading art galleries," unanimously passed a resolution condemning *The Arts* for "prejudicing public opinion in favor of so-called modern art and modern artists." Both sides knew that Watson had never been a dealer's critic, but the members believed this was going too far. According to their complaint, the contest was decided "through the instrumentality of 'a packed jury'" and was "merely another evidence of the dishonest nature of the modern art movement."[60] Watson would have relished a counteroffensive, but he was out of the country by then, bound for his summer tour of Europe. When he returned there would be other wars to wage.

5 THE DEMISE OF *THE ARTS,* 1930–1932

Although the stock market crash of October 1929 had a shattering effect on the art community, up to the time of the failure and for a brief period thereafter, American art held to its positive course. Most auspicious, perhaps, was the official acknowledgment of modernism and the public's receptiveness to its various permutations since the experiments of the second decade of the century. In retrospect, 1929 marked the apex of Americans' openness to diversity in art. Outwardly, *The Arts* appeared to be unscathed also, except that in the seven years of its existence it never broke even, much less turned a profit. Financial decline had threatened all along.

The way Guy Pène du Bois saw it, *The Arts* had always been too independent and honest to make money.[1] Despite Watson's hopes of eventual solvency, circumstances worsened by 1929 and retrenchment was unavoidable. All full-time editorial positions except Watson's were eliminated. Virgil Barker, Lloyd Goodrich, and Dorothy Lefferts Moore were reclassified to contributing editors, which meant that despite their yeoman work on the magazine, they were no longer salaried but rather reimbursed by the piece. C. Adolph Glassgold, whose name appeared on the masthead in September 1929 as the fourth contributing editor, had already left for *Creative Arts* magazine. As an economizing measure, *The Arts* was reduced from twelve to nine monthly issues, with a reduction in the annual subscription rate from five to four dollars.

Lloyd Goodrich had been distressed about financial operation for some time. In France the year before, he had been repeatedly embarrassed over delinquent reimbursements to European contributors, not to mention himself. Waldemar George had not yet received payment for his article on Georges

Roualt published nearly two years earlier. Jacques Mauny had not been paid for nearly a year and was "a little peeved about it." John Gould Fletcher and others complained as well. Owed for expenses and commissions himself, Goodrich had had to dip into personal savings to make ends meet. "In America the authors know they can send the bailiff around to collect at any time," Goodrich complained in one of his numerous reminders to the New York office, "but over here they are naturally suspicious if they don't get paid soon, and they can make it very unpleasant for me, let me state." Most of Goodrich's entreaties went unanswered, however, and finally annoyed Watson "a great deal." Watson responded with several "nasty," "dampening" letters. "It was the first break in our friendship," Goodrich recalled, "and it hurt me. . . . Forbes was a person who took things a little personally, . . . and it made a difference."[2]

Other factors now threatened the magazine's financial security. In October 1929, Gertrude Vanderbilt Whitney embarked on an ambitious new undertaking that required a heavy capital investment. Needing additional storage and display space for hundreds of works purchased during the days of the Whitney Studio and Whitney Studio Club, she decided to offer the collection, the largest of its kind in the country, to the Metropolitan Museum of Art, along with funding to sustain it, possibly even to build a wing for it. Juliana Force, deputed by Whitney, met with Edward Robinson, the conservative director of the Metropolitan, to present the offer. She had not gotten very far into the proposal, however, when Robinson responded "with a great sniff": "'My dear lady. What would we do with those pictures? We have a cellar full.'" Force "hit the ceiling." Returning to the Whitney Studio, where Whitney and Forbes were waiting, she recounted every detail of his "hauty refusal." "I shall never forget that morning," Watson wrote years later. "In a little less than two hours and one lunch," the three conceived the idea of the Whitney Museum of American Art; Watson persuaded Whitney to include the word "American" in the name. When he returned to *The Arts* office from lunch that October afternoon, Watson announced to Goodrich, "'there's going to be a museum of American art and we're going to be a great part of it,' meaning *The Arts*." Watson believed *The Arts* would be an unofficial voice for the new museum, and though he did not say it, he envisioned his own expanded influence in the museum itself. After all, he had played a role in its birth. "But it didn't turn out that way."[3]

Only a few weeks after Whitney's decision to establish the museum, the New York Stock Exchange crashed, ushering in the Great Depression. Although the project itself was not imperiled, the depression intensified in subsequent months, affecting all Americans. Concerned about the simultaneous burden of underwriting *The Arts* and opening a new museum, feeling the need to concentrate her resources on the museum during its first two years, Whitney asked Watson if he could raise money himself to support the magazine. Indeed, over the years Watson had made sporadic attempts to attract investors and reduce his dependence on the two women. But there had never been any urgency to do so. Now he went all out, contacting stockholders, wealthy friends, and patrons. From the Sachs banking family—Paul J. Sachs, director of the Fogg Museum at Harvard; his brother Walter; and his cousin Mrs. Howard Sachs—Watson obtained pledges of five hundred dollars per year for three years. Mrs. John D. Rockefeller bought five hundred dollars in stock and pledged one thousand dollars for 1930 and 1931. He received pledges from collector John T. Spaulding; from his good friend artist Allen Tucker and his wife Eufrasia (Frasita), both of whom were wealthy in their own right; and from others. But most investors were reluctant to put money into a publication operating on a deficit, especially during hard times. The collector Chester Dale, for example, turned down Watson altogether, despite his respect for *The Arts*. The new pledges fell considerably short of Whitney's annual contributions.

In September 1930 Watson moved *The Arts* offices to less expensive quarters at 232 East Fifty-fourth Street, where he also opened several rooms for the sale of color reproductions, portfolios, and books. Earlier that month Juliana Force had sent Watson a request through Anna Freeman, her secretary, for a summary of Whitney's donations to *The Arts*. Watson's report, dated September 8, 1930, confirmed what they already knew about the magazine's dependence on Whitney. Her contributions over the preceding eight years, together with those of Force, had amounted to $62,490, on average more than two-thirds of the total funding.

Had the deficit been the only issue, *The Arts* might have weathered the storm. But there was Watson's deteriorating relationship with Juliana Force. Their affair had endured for eleven years, surviving even occasional discreet dalliances on the part of each. That was a long spell for a "good-looking lady's man" like Watson.[4] But by late 1929, with his interest in Juliana fading, Watson became rather openly involved with another woman. As he troubled less and less to conceal the liaison, Juliana's humiliation and anger mounted. Lashing out, she inserted herself more high-handedly in the internal management of *The Arts*, a course that virtually guaranteed a collision between the temperamental lovers.

An editorial disagreement between Watson and Lloyd Goodrich precipitated a first notable clash. Goodrich had written a long article for *The Arts* about Thomas Hart Benton's murals, *America Today*, for the recently opened New School for Social Research. The murals, which depicted the impact of technology on modern life, exemplified the resurgent strain of realism in American art and along with José Clement Orozco's murals for the same building had generated considerable publicity, mostly positive. The entire idea—the concept of the New School, the modern architecture, and the contrasting liberal murals—was provocative in Goodrich's opinion. But Watson reacted negatively. "Well Forbes—he was a bit contrary," Goodrich observed, and "if a person was praised too much, he would begin to kind of downgrade them." In the winter of 1931 during a party hosted by Force at which both the Goodrichs and the Watsons were present, Forbes took him aside after dinner and told him he could not use the article, saying, "'Benton doesn't amount to anything'... and he began to derogate him as a publicity-seeker and all this kind of stuff," Goodrich recalled. "Well I was terribly hurt, and we argued for about half an hour.... Soon after rejoining the ladies we had a knock-down-drag-out argument." It was the first time in their long association that Watson had "refused" an article by Goodrich, though he had behaved discouragingly toward him during Goodrich's stint in Europe. After the party that night, Goodrich stayed up late and revised the article: "cut it down to size.... The particular point was that it was too long. The artist wasn't that important.... Well, I re-wrote it, sent it off to him the next day, but then he promptly published the original article! ... Mrs. Force was very annoyed. She said afterward she scolded Forbes.... She felt sorry for me.... When I came out of the room, I looked just stricken."[5]

The final rupture between Juliana Force and Forbes Watson occurred at another dinner party, this one given by Frank Rehn that winter, at which the guests included Forbes, Nan, and Juliana. As it was related to Goodrich, Watson had had a little too much to drink. "He was inclined that way. He never got obstreperous or unpleasant, but he could say things that were not very discreet. But some argument started between Mrs. Force and Forbes, and I understand that at the climax of the argument Forbes said 'I taught you everything you know.' That was not the thing to say!"[6] Force, hot tempered by nature, exploded, and a stormy exchange ensued, ending finally when Nan announced abruptly that she and Forbes were leaving. Juliana Force and Forbes Watson made their peace in time, but their former closeness was unrecoverable.

Everyone believed that Gertrude Whitney withdrew her support from *The Arts* because she needed to divert funding to the Whitney Museum. However, she and Juliana Force would probably have managed to keep *The Arts* afloat had not Force been so bitter over Watson's rejection. Following the confrontation at Rehn's dinner party, she was "obsessed with the whole idea of Forbes's ingratitude," talking about it incessantly to Goodrich, her good friend by then, and "threatening all kinds of retaliatory actions." But proof of the causal connection between Watson's faithlessness and the demise of *The Arts* came with Lloyd

Goodrich's disclosure some twenty years after Watson's death that Force had offered him the editorship in 1932 after Watson had been forced to suspend publication for lack of sufficient operating funds. Feeling some compunctions about Whitney's withdrawal of support, Force summoned Goodrich to her quarters and asked, "'if we revive *The Arts* would you take over the editorship?'" Goodrich declined. "I couldn't do that," he later explained, "not to my old friend. I told her I couldn't."[7]

In September 1931 Whitney sent word through Force of her decision to terminate her support of *The Arts*. Force was neither equivocal nor gentle in transmitting the message. William Robb, who was present when the end came, described the final scene: "'Mrs. Force called me and Watson down to her office. There was no mistaking her mood or what she meant. She started on a tirade, she knew where she was going and wouldn't be interrupted. She read the riot act to us, but she mostly ignored me. She said something, and then I disputed it. She told me to stop talking and not to interrupt her. She was angry and determined, and I realized that jealousy was involved. I don't remember what she said to us on that awful occasion, but she was hell-bent and we had to sit there and take it. Nothing was ever mentioned about the museum as the reason *The Arts* was folding.'" When Watson and William Robb left the meeting they were reeling from the blow.[8]

Over the next several weeks a desperate Watson, "wearing out shoe-leather and pleading for *The Arts*," sent out innumerable requests for backing, alluding wryly to his "begging" and the "beggees" he solicited. *The Arts* was threatening to become one more victim of the Depression, he wrote, unless he could replace Whitney's support. It would take ten thousand dollars to make it through the year, he estimated. He proposed to issue more stock to finance *The Arts* or to launch an alternative publication. Although his limited income precluded his contributing any additional money to the magazine, he was willing to work without salary. A note of optimism, unfounded, slipped in as he suggested to backers that if they could raise half or more of the ten thousand dollars, Whitney might subscribe the balance. "I have said nothing to her about this, but in the past her generosity to *The Arts* and her sympathy with its editorial aims warrant me in this belief."[9] His efforts were unavailing. The final number of *The Arts*, published late, was dated October 1931.

By mid-December Watson's hopes of reinstating the magazine had dimmed. Writing a friend about Nan's upcoming exhibition at the Kraushaar Galleries, he added ruefully, "perhaps by that time I shall be digging ditches nearby." To a sympathetic stockholder, collector Henry Shaefer, he despaired, "believe it or not, I talked with men and women whose combined capital amounts to over a billion and not one nickel toward the meeting of these deficits has been forthcoming." The prospect of an alternative publication came into sharper focus now. Should he fail in his efforts to revive *The Arts,* he could possibly launch a less-expensive publication, sustain it until the depression ended, and then resurrect *The Arts.*[10]

The loss of the women's friendship was ultimately devastating to Watson's career. He never discussed their altered relationships publicly, however, putting out the explanation, as they did, that Whitney's commitment to the museum made it impossible to finance the magazine. In the end, suppressing his anguish, he sent each woman a gracious letter. Force had explained to him "the other day at tea," he wrote Whitney, that unsettled financial conditions made it impossible for Whitney to continue to contribute to *The Arts.* He had not relinquished hope of bringing *The Arts* through its present ordeal, he assured her. "But even if it should be compelled, in this difficult year, to suspend publication, I should not feel, personally, that the work had been in vain or that your disinterested generosity had been for nothing." He briefly cataloged *The Arts*'s achievements and saluted the Whitney Museum of American Art.[11] The denouement differed sharply from Watson's expectations of power and influence in a Whitney Museum triumvirate.

Yet hope for eventual reconciliation and favor lingered. His behavior toward the women was, if anything, more ingratiating, his praise almost effusive. He would always believe in the Whitney's philosophy of patronage and purchase.[12] Too, that link between Watson and Juliana Force would never fully disappear. As late as the early 1940s, a colleague of Watson's in the Treasury Department observed how well Watson got on with Juliana Force. "He played up to Juliana; he played up to Mrs. Whitney too." Whitney did not come into the office, "but he spoke a lot about her."[13] He did not allow his resentment to surface until many years later, after both women had died. In an interview with a Whitney Studio historian, he described Gertrude Whitney's contribution to the arts as negligible until he appeared on the scene to advise her. As for Force, she never outgrew her roots as "a romantic little German girl from Hoboken." Watson's rancor was never public, however. The same year he vented his malice, he offered two of his most glowing tributes, one in a memorial exhibition catalog in honor of Juliana Force, and the other in an Art Students League lecture.[14]

Almost to the end, when advertising fell off sharply, *The Arts* showed little outward evidence of its mounting troubles. The editorial mood was ebullient as the magazine heralded gain after gain for independent American art, celebrating at the same time its own role in fostering liberal victories: The power of the National Academy of Design was waning. Noting the disquietude in academic ranks, Goodrich viewed the NAD and the National Institute of Arts and Letters winter shows as a last-stand effort to impress the public with the soundness and righteousness of their art. Then there was the auspicious demise of the School of Paris, pronounced dead by Jacques Mauny. The "great collective hallucination" was over, Mauny reported. The "putrefaction of the *École de Paris*" was very advanced. Paris exhibitions lately were scarcely worth visiting. "The best things are shown in New York first."[15]

By the issue of October 1931, *The Arts* had more or less summed up its legacy. Though there was no statement of cessation, Watson's final article, aptly titled "The Star-Spangled Banner," had all the earmarks of a valedictory. "On the eve of such a boom in American art that even that universal excuse, the Depression, may not be able to stop it, we, as good singers of The Star-Spangled Banner, good wavers of the Flag, or merely as poor citizens of The Land of the Dollar, might take a look about us—both backwards and forwards," he wrote. He eulogized the leaders in the struggle for recognition of contemporary American art: American artists, critics, and collectors. American artists were the first to fight for the modern style, he wrote, only to see the majority of the spoils of victory go into the pockets of the School of Paris. But they fought back. The American critics, "thank Heavens seldom agreeing, . . . worked with unremitting sincerity to bring to the attention of their extensive public the unbelievable fact that an American art exists." American collectors, the majority of whom, fortunately, "were not unbalanced by mere novelty," put their confidence in native artists. Whitney's studios were like "a garden of the Medicis," where the artist's "health was drunk, there was laughter and fun, living and art."[16]

Back in 1912, at the beginning of his career, Watson had examined the role of the critic vis-à-vis the artist, highlighting artists' responses to a survey he had conducted. He addressed the issue again in 1930 as part of a symposium in *Space* magazine. The critic, he stated, moved by a work of art, in turn moved the reader to experience it for himself. Now, in his final editorial for *The Arts*— in effect an apologia—Watson regarded once again the creative function the critic shared with the artist. Criticism was an art, not a science, he asserted, as he embraced the spark of contemporaneity over the "cold soup" of impartial distance. The loss of impartiality was a small price to pay for the warmer intimacy of sharing the life the artist used for source and interpretation. While the historian preferred the cooler atmosphere that the passage of time interposed between him and his subject, there would always be those lovers of their own time who cherished the confusion of closeness as a stimulant to keen discrimination and critical vigor. "They prefer the combat of forces through which, if they would be brave reviewers of the works of their contemporaries, they must follow the light of their vision wherever it points and whatever the obstacles." He was, of course, speaking of himself.[17]

Faced with the cessation of *The Arts* and a tenuous outlook for the Arts Publishing Corporation, Virgil Barker and Lloyd Goodrich left for more secure posts. Of the contributing editors, only Dorothy Lefferts Moore remained, along with William Robb and one clerk. Other clerical staff went to work at the Whitney Museum. Within a few months after *The Arts* folded, Barker joined the faculty of the University of Miami, where he distinguished himself as a teacher and scholar in art history. Since 1929, with Watson's blessing, Goodrich had supplemented his uncertain income from *The Arts* by being assistant art critic at the *New York Times* under Edward Alden Jewell. In 1931, thanks to a loan from his longtime friend Reginald Marsh and a generous grant from Gertrude Whitney, he left both *The Arts* and the *Times* to concentrate on a book he was writing about Thomas Eakins, beginning at the same time an illustrious career with the Whitney Museum.[18]

Goodrich expressed only admiration for the man who had given him his first big opportunity. Yet clearly there was ambivalence on his part, bearing as he often did the full weight of the magazine's operation, while Watson was off with the Whitney crowd. There was something more too: Watson's well-known womanizing, which did not exempt friends' wives. "My wife and he got on beautifully together," Goodrich commented in later years. "She was a very social person . . . , a person who was very friendly always, and loved people, and understood them. And she and he got on extremely well. . . . And I had rather a feeling he may have made love to her. He didn't get far. . . . I have a feeling that maybe he tried to do something that he did not succeed in doing. He was a bit promiscuous, you know . . . , and he was a very attractive man."[19]

After *The Arts,* Goodrich and Watson saw each other only occasionally. There was no real one-on-one contact for years, until around 1956 when Forbes and Nan met Goodrich for a drink at the hotel next door to the Whitney Museum on West Fifty-fourth Street. "It was very pleasant," Goodrich recalled. "We got on very well, and he was very complimentary to me, because by that time I had made something of a name for myself."[20]

The crucial stockholders meeting was held on January 11, 1932, its purpose being "to vote upon a proposition to amend the Certificate of Incorporation of the Corporation so as to provide for the increase of the amount of the capital stock of the Corporation by the issuance of a First Preferred Stock to consist of one thousand (1,000) shares having a par value of $50 per share." On the table also, but not acted upon, was an informal offer from the College Art Association to amalgamate *The Arts* with the association's magazine, *Parnassus.* The most important agenda item was a prospective new publication to be financed through the enabling amendment. "A rough dummy of the new publication was shown to the stockholders who agreed enthusiastically with my proposal," Watson wrote Mrs. John D. Rockefeller. "I have also shown the dummy to other publishers and to businessmen who have expressed, without exception, a firm belief in its practical financial possibilities. It will maintain the same liberal and uncompromising editorial standards that *The Arts* has always maintained." Failing to salvage *The Arts*, Watson did, however, receive sufficient proxies and pledges to move ahead with a successor.[21]

"Your courage is magnificent," Alfred Barr wrote Watson on the debut of the new magazine. Other friends from around the country proffered good wishes as well. *Arts Weekly: The News Magazine of the Arts* was introduced on March 11, 1932, with weekly issues planned from October through May and monthlies during the summer. Watson's hope of reinstating *The Arts* was apparent in the first number, which announced a forthcoming annual or semi-annual edition of *The Arts* in enlarged form. As further homage, each contents page contained the subtitle, "Successor to *The Arts*." The blue-bordered cover of *Arts Weekly* reminded readers of the signature blue of the original magazine, but flimsier paper stock, smaller type, a three-column format, and narrow margins reflected Watson's cost consciousness, evident also in his assumption of a greater proportion of the writing. At a presumably affordable price of fifteen cents a copy, *Arts Weekly* was a thin publication, less than one-third the size of *The Arts*, although its dimensions were larger, nearly nine inches by thirteen inches. As a weekly, it could carry "more and fresher news than a monthly," and, as Pène du Bois observed, it could "be run on a less dignified and more popular plane." In addition to broader treatment of events and personalities, there was regular coverage of the allied arts, with departments on architecture, books, dance, drama, film, and music.[22]

Watson served both as editor and managing editor of *Arts Weekly*, and William Robb continued as business manager. Reliable names from *The Arts* appeared on the masthead as "Associates," including Dorothy Lefferts Moore, Guy Pène du Bois, Henry Russell Hitchcock, and Jacques Mauny. Virgil Barker, Lloyd Goodrich, and Philip Johnson were also listed, though they had no involvement in the weekly. Watson added six new associates as well, most of them relative unknowns, evidence of his continuing generosity and keen eye for young talent. Twenty-four-year-old music critic Irving Kolodin would in time achieve international eminence as a music commentator. Lincoln Kirstein, twenty-five, chiefly responsible for film commentary, would become a prominent impresario, curator, and director of the New York City Ballet.[23] Catherine Bauer (later

Wurster), also in her twenties, would rise to the top in the field of urban housing and community planning, serving as adviser to Presidents Roosevelt, Eisenhower, and Johnson. Inslee Hopper, a recent Princeton graduate, came to Watson about the time *Arts Weekly* was getting underway with a letter of introduction from his former professor C. R. Morey, who had written for *The Arts*. Watson took Hopper right in "out of the cold," nearly bowling him over two weeks later when he made him assistant editor.[24]

Practicing artists contributed to *Arts Weekly*, as in the earlier publication. Along with the regulars, Harold Sterner, Henry Schnakenberg and other *Arts* alumni wrote exhibition and book reviews. Chicago's emergence as consequential art center was acknowledged with a regular column, "Chicago Letter," by C. J. Bulliet, art critic for the *Chicago Daily News*. Watson also introduced a series on progressive art dealers—N. E. Montross, the Macbeth family, and John Kraushaar—similar in approach to his *Arts* profiles of American collectors but considerably condensed. Gone were the extended critical essays that had distinguished *The Arts* and imparted luster. Nor were the handsome reproductions any longer feasible. Instead, there was a two-page picture section crammed with photos of art reproductions and newsmakers and some scattered small illustrations.

As before, Watson's trenchant, unreserved commentary set the tone of *Arts Weekly*. He admonished the Guggenheim Fellowship Award Committee to take risks and consider less established artists. He crowed over Edward Hopper's recent rejection of membership in the NAD. He chided the Museum of Modern Art for neglecting American painters and sculptors. The museum, he observed, had been "too fashionable; too interested in an artist's 'talking point,' too unheedful of the reticent."[25] He scoffed at American Scene painting even as the movement gained vocal adherents among artists and the public.

Despite its popular contents and healthy advertising sales, *Arts Weekly* could not endure in the depression-flattened market. "Each issue awaited donations before going to press," Pène du Bois recalled. "The donors grew scarce. There were delays in publication dates." Less than two months after Watson launched the weekly, he conferred with Henry Luce, who was considering purchasing the magazine's name. Negotiations fell through, however, and *Arts Weekly* ceased, its last issue dated May 7, 1932, after only nine weeks of publication.[26]

Watson had no immediate prospects when *Arts Weekly* ceased other than freelancing and lecturing. Unlike his longtime assistants Virgil Barker and Lloyd Goodrich, who moved from *The Arts* to careers as historians, Watson had little bent for scholarly research. In the final issue of *The Arts*, he had expressed interest in writing a history of the Whitney Museum collection, a subject, he commented, "that has long tempted me." He probably would not have followed through, however, as detailed, sustained exposition was not his forte.[27] His monograph *Mary Cassatt,* which the Whitney Museum of American Art published that year, typified his preferred format: nine pages of penetrating discussion of the artist and her art with around fifty pages devoted primarily to reproductions of her work. Watson's métier was that of art critic–cum–fighting journalist. He was most effective in sharp adversarial bursts.

Those who depreciated Watson's significance in the history of American art on grounds that he was more negative than constructive, however, missed the crusading thrust of his pugnacity. Indeed, as Goodrich observed, Watson probably enjoyed a good fight more than affirmative criticism.[28] But he would not have battled so long and so relentlessly had he not believed in the vitality of American art and the improvability of the public's taste. To confuse his zest for battle with misanthropy was to misread the essentially optimistic and evangelical energy of his campaigns.

The Arts had gone under, a casualty of the depression and to some extent Watson's nature as well. But the progressive warrior had won the major battles. His liberal voice had awakened interest and rallied support for contemporary American art. As important, through *The Arts* and the *New York World,* he illuminated the art issues of the twenties more frontally and engagingly than any of his fellow commentators.

6 FROM PROGRESSIVE CRITIC TO NEW DEAL CRITIC: THE PUBLIC WORKS OF ART PROJECT, 1933–1934

By the time *Arts Weekly* folded in May 1932, the Great Depression was firmly established. More than five thousand banks had closed between 1930 and 1932, and unemployment rose to more than thirteen million as a result of business failures. Thousands faced starvation. Olin Dows recalled: "Longshoremen would enter a grocery store, and I don't fault them for this. When you have a family that's hungry and you're able to work, but there's no work available, you enter an A&P store, take what you need to feed your family, protect your wife, and who's going to fool with a longshoreman as he stalks out the door?"[1] Communities of dilapidated, makeshift cardboard and rusted scrap-metal shelters known as Hoovervilles sprang up in cities across the nation, their dispossessed inhabitants subsisting on handouts and garbage. Hunger marches and demonstrations in cities around the country erupted in violence as Americans vented their frustrations and fears. Communism and other socialist agendas, which had held relatively little attraction for the public during the twenties, now seemed less extreme alternatives to some. A profound sense of demoralization enveloped the country.

Returning to the United States, many expatriates saw not the spiritual barrenness that had prompted their exodus to Europe but the nobility of the people and their suffering. Reconciliation with the common man and the American landscape took on new importance as they rediscovered the nation's heritage. Culturally, America was beyond the borrowing stage, literary intellectual Harold Stearns declared. What was important was "not how many elements of it were taken from European, but what—in the American scene and with the American social experience—we do with those elements."[2]

Pres. Herbert Hoover's cautious, deliberately paced efforts to stabilize the economy and restore confidence through increased loans and incentives to local relief agencies proved dismally inadequate. Left to address problems of mounting unemployment and hunger, municipal and state governments resorted to a range of measures, the most notable of which was work relief. Early programs concentrated on made-work for manual laborers, with little differentiation as to skills and with no provisions for white-collar workers or artists.[3] But local agencies, underfunded and unprepared to cope with a crisis of such magnitude, quickly exhausted their resources.

Fine art, a luxury in the minds of most Americans and traditionally associated with the genteel side of life, was all but forgotten in the bitter reality of bread lines. With few patrons to buy their work, artists shared the desolation of other citizens seeking food and shelter. A few wealthy collectors rescued favored painters from poverty with anonymous gifts, but the majority were ignored, except among themselves and a few dealers. Some estimated that in the vicinity of Washington Square and Greenwich Village alone, the depression halted the work of more than one thousand artists.[4] It was a "rough period" for the art community, Antoinette Kraushaar remembered. "Business was nothing" in the galleries. John Kraushaar, Antoinette's father and owner of the Kraushaar Galleries, returned from Europe with a large purchase of French pictures the week before the stock market crash. He exhibited them to appreciative critics and eager buyers, only to lose nearly all his sales a week later. Soon after, the Kraushaars joined the thousands on relief.[5] A number of galleries closed in the months that followed. That the leading museums were able to escape the most ruinous effects of the depression and do some purchasing did not mitigate the plight of American artists, since most museums accessioned European art.

American artists resented the continuing preference for foreign art, particularly in the face of their own poverty. At its spring 1930 meeting, the American Federation of Arts adopted a resolution urging citizens to oppose the practice of "calling outsiders to do work which artists nearer at hand were equally well qualified to perform." The American Artists Professional League recommended that federal commissions for official portraits and other art projects be awarded exclusively to Americans.[6]

Common adversity strengthened the bond among American artists, sharpening their politics and sparking their enterprise. Deprived of traditional channels, they joined together to vend their works directly to the consumer. Curbside art markets, which emulated the celebrated outdoor exhibits of Paris and the Luxembourg Gardens, became a popular means of establishing face-to-face contact with potential buyers. In Washington Square and other sites, artists offered their wares on the same streets as pushcart peddlers selling chestnuts and pretzels. Barter was also a means of securing the necessities of life, one that even the Society of Independent Artists adopted. It was a reasonable idea, in Forbes Watson's view. "I know of dentists who have given their services for a painting, of landlords who have accepted art in payment of rent, of restaurant keepers who, for a good landscape, have given many a solid meal," he commented. "And certainly all of us hope that when the forthcoming Independent exhibition . . . closes . . . , all of the painters and sculptors will find their teeth in perfect order, the larders stocked with food, their closets, if any, bountifully supplied with new suits, their hair well trimmed and their faces shaved."[7]

By now, the hard truth of bread lines and homelessness had diminished the allure of modernist novelties and art-for-art's-sake philosophies. Like the writers of the thirties, American artists sought inspiration in the spirit of the people and the land. Realism seemed the most appropriate genre for expressing the national character. Two branches of realism, not always distinct from one another, advanced to the forefront: socially conscious art, which portrayed contemporary human despair and suffering, and regionalist art, which depicted everyday life in cities and country.[8]

By the mid-thirties, American Scene art, a brand of Midwestern regionalism, had eclipsed all other art movements in popularity. Its homely images evoked the time-honored American values of hard work, self-reliance, love of country, and neighborliness. Originally termed the "American Wave," it consciously disavowed European models and glorified American styles. Thomas Hart Benton, Grant Wood, John Steuart Curry, and Reginald Marsh were its most celebrated practitioners, and Thomas Craven, earlier a proponent of modernism, was its ubiquitous spokesman. Craven, along with Thomas Hart Benton and several others, not only preached the rugged message of the American Scene but also infused it with some of its most stridently negative rhetoric—anti–big city, homophobic, anti-European. Their Americanism seemed almost a caricature of Watson's, which rejected obedience to dogmas and movements. For Watson, American art surpassed that of other nations because of its merit, not its subject matter. Nor did "the great strong, square-jawed American of poetic fancy . . . turn to art" in Watson's American paradigm. He turned to business.[9]

Like so many other victims of the depression, Watson had no immediate prospects when *The Arts* and *Arts Weekly* ceased publication. After ten years in the frontline of American art journalism, it was bitter to give up the editor's chair, worse still because little money was coming in. Two of Watson's monographs, *Mary Cassatt* and *Allen Tucker,* were published by the Whitney Museum of American Art in 1932. He also did an occasional book review for the *New York Herald Tribune*, but that hardly warded off insolvency. Nan had a one-person show at Kraushaar's in April 1932 and exhibited in the Whitney Biennial of 1932–33; she was also represented in the Museum of Modern Art "Fruit and Flowers" show in April 1933, but sales were meager. Jobless and facing a flat art market, their lives were bleak, and a dejected Watson took to drinking more seriously. Some slight help came through the good offices of Audrey McMahon, executive secretary of the College Art Association, whose organization advanced Watson funds for several articles, sustaining him through a difficult winter. Beginning in December 1932 and continuing for the next five years, he was a contributing editor to *Parnassus*, the College Art Association's magazine, which McMahon edited. Ironically, it had been only ten months since the College Art Association had proposed keeping *The Arts* afloat through an amalgamation with *Parnassus*.

That winter two programs for unemployed artists were initiated in Manhattan, legitimating for the first time artists' eligibility for work relief and, more significant, recognizing enrichment of citizens' lives as a worthy goal for madework. On the state level, at the suggestion of Harry Hopkins, chairman of New York's Temporary Emergency Relief Administration (TERA), the education department arranged for artists to teach adult art classes. In the private sector, responding to a petition from the College Art Association, the Gibson Committee, a charitable group, created a special department which employed artists to create murals for non-profit institutions and teach art in settlement houses. The plea of Audrey McMahon to "banish apathy and misunderstanding," to open minds to "an appreciation of the beautiful," and to "help the American artist to live" had begun to resound.[10]

If the opening paragraphs of Watson's first article for *Parnassus*, a favorable notice of the Whitney Museum's inaugural biennial exhibition, seemed an extension of his *Arts* commentary, his next topic, the Washington Square outdoor exhibition, signaled unmistakably that the depression had disrupted the sanguine course of American art. Watson praised the outdoor market as a viable approach to aiding the artist while preserving his independence. At the same time, he criticized both the sanctimonious dispensers of private charity and the "propaganda-artists" who called for municipal support for artists. He still believed in December 1932 that government should stay out of art. "The artist will look after the artists. This is as it should be."[11]

The following March, Franklin Delano Roosevelt was sworn in as president of the United States. Although voters knew little about him or his proposed "New Deal," they nonetheless called, by a margin of 22.8 million votes to 15.8 million, for a daring and energetic leader who would exercise every means at his command to end their distress. After reassuring a fearful public, the new president moved swiftly. Within the first hundred days of his administration, he initiated measures to deal with the banking and monetary crises, industrial inertia, farm failures, unemployment, and near-disasters in scores of related sectors.

Meanwhile, unpaid bills and letters from collection agencies had piled up on the Watsons' desk. Compounding their worries, Nan's aunt in Scotland became seriously ill, and when Nan hurriedly left to look after her overseas, Forbes accompanied her. It was as if they both dropped out of society that summer. "Laddie we have missed you," Allen Tucker wrote after finally receiving a letter from Watson in August. Tucker sympathized with his friends. But "it is good news that you are coming back. American art is sinking without your helping hand and mouth."[12] Following his return in the fall of 1933 (Nan stayed behind to look after her aunt), Watson began contributing to the recently inaugurated "Sunday Review" section of the *Brooklyn Daily Eagle,* where his old colleague Helen Appleton Read was art critic. There was still no dependable income, however.

The winter of 1933–34 was the most severe on record. Twenty million Americans, one out of every six, had "no means of obtaining fire or food, except from the public purse," *Time* magazine reported. "Thus," when Congress appropriated five hundred million dollars for relief under the Federal Emergency Relief Administration (FERA), "did the finger of God point at Harry Lloyd Hopkins," to administer it. Hopkins, a man whose economics "consisted largely of an urge 'to feed the hungry, and Goddam fast,'" got aid flowing to the states almost immediately.[13] Convinced that the dignity of work, no matter how lowly, was preferable to the dole, Hopkins also persuaded Roosevelt to establish an emergency unemployment relief program with himself as head. Funded with allocations from FERA and the recently created Public Works Administration (PWA), the Civil Works Administration (CWA) was established in November 1933 for the purpose of employing four million people in federal, state, and local make-work projects.

The idea of federally subsidizing work for artists was not new, but it had never been tried before in the United States. Roosevelt took an interest when artist George Biddle, a friend and fellow Groton alumnus, proposed it.[14] Despite resistance from the Fine Arts Commission, a strongly academic group of presidential advisers on art, Biddle pushed forward, enlisting the support of Assistant Secretary of the Treasury Lawrence W. Robert Jr. and a number of other officials.[15] Robert approached Edward Bruce, a recent appointee to the Treasury Department. Bruce was a successful New York lawyer, an entrepreneur with expertise in international monetary policy, and, beginning at age forty-four, a painter well regarded among critics. He "knew all his painter friends were having a hard time" and was definitely interested in the program.[16]

Renting a spacious home in Washington at 1227 Nineteenth Street Northwest, with a library for "close harmony" conferences and a ballroom for larger meetings, Ned, as friends called him, hosted a series of dinners at which he and influential Washington guests talked up the virtues of federal subsidization of the arts. If anyone could put it across it was Bruce. "He knew all the newspaper people and almost all the politicians, a very wide circle, and he was a wonderful talker himself and always got other people talking."[17] Once Americans had opportunities to experience quality art, Bruce believed, they would seek out beauty, and ugliness in the United States would disappear. Under the auspices of the federal government, talented American painters could engender a virtual renaissance in American art. He spent long hours formulating a plan before, in early November 1933, he and Biddle combined forces to gain the approval of Secretary of the Interior Harold Ickes for a project to employ artists in decorating public buildings. Ickes had little difficulty persuading Hopkins, whose experience as head of TERA in New York had demonstrated the reasonableness of work relief for artists.

The crash program, named the Public Works of Art Project (PWAP), was officially established on December 3, 1933, under a grant of $1,039,000 from the CWA to the Treasury Department. It was calculated that the allotment was sufficient to support sixteen hundred artists and five hundred laborers until February 15, 1934. Bruce was appointed chief of the project without salary. For the first time in American history, George Biddle observed, the government recognized the social necessity of art in life.[18]

It must have seemed serendipitous when Bruce ran into his old friend Forbes Watson on a busy street in New York City that fall. Watson was the ideal person to activate PWAP. Immediately, Bruce prevailed upon him to sign on, appealing to his patriotic duty to his country, to art, and to American artists. Bruce's arguments surely pulled powerfully at Watson, whose devotion to all three causes was deep and steadfast. Moreover, recently returned from Scotland, he was broke and dependent on erratic income from freelancing. Still, Bruce was talking about government patronage, a monster Watson had battled for twenty years. Watson wanted to think it over. A few days later, however, seated next to Juliana Force at a dinner party, "Watson was astounded to receive her congratulations upon an appointment that he had not yet finally decided to accept. Bruce always worked fast when he knew what he wanted!"[19]

Watson was appointed technical director of the Public Works of Art Project at three hundred dollars a month beginning December 8, 1933. With Nan away in Scotland, he took a small apartment in a rooming house at 818 Seventeenth Street Northwest, just a five-block walk from the Treasury Building, and plunged right in to his duties. The Friday of his appointment, Assistant Secretary Robert convened a luncheon meeting of the advisory committee at Bruce's home, inviting art leaders from all over the country to participate in the planning process. "Mrs. Roosevelt came to it and knitted all the way through the several hours-long meeting," visible evidence of the president's support.[20] After four hours of informal discussion, the Public Works of Art Project was mapped out, its stated purpose to employ artists in the embellishment of federal and other publicly owned buildings in Washington and throughout the country. The draft of the plan indicated that a portion of a fund which the PWA had set aside for special projects might also be made available to continue PWAP's work beyond the February expiration date.[21] Bruce was counting on it.

For purposes of administering the Public Works of Art Project, the country was organized into the sixteen regions previously demarcated by the CWA for its work relief programs, with a director and a volunteer committee in each division.[22] It would operate under CWA regulations. The regional chairmen and "their amazingly ample committees," approximately five hundred presumably impartial unsalaried volunteers composed largely of museum directors, collectors, and other art-minded citizens, advised the regional office concerning work to be undertaken and the artists to do it. The central committee, which appointed them, "did not want artists who were involved in cliques and rumpuses," Watson told one regional committee member, and they "also wanted some people on the committees who were technically equipped to pass on the work being done." The regional committees in turn selected subcommittees in individual states to promote local initiative and advise on art matters. The Advisory Committee on Fine Arts served as general adviser to Treasury concerning the program as a whole.[23]

Within four days of the meeting, artists were on the payroll, and by the fourth week wages were disbursed in every region. Since the Public Works of Art Project was financed with PWA money, artists' wages followed the PWA pay structure for skilled craftsmen, which translated to $42.50 per week for artists (Grade A), $26.50 per week for artists' assistants (Grade B), and $15.00 per week for laborers.[24]

Headquarters for the crash project were set up in room 168 of the Treasury Building, with four additional central-staff members—Cecil H. Jones, business manager; William J. Johnston, liaison officer; Ann Washington Craton, public relations coordinator; and Edward B. Rowan, assistant technical director—and ten clerks and stenographers. Speed was imperative in providing jobs and completing the artistic work before the February 15 termination date. Between

Edward Bruce, Eleanor Roosevelt, Lawrence W. Robert Jr., and Forbes Watson, examining a map of the sixteen regional districts of the Public Works of Art Project. The picture was taken at the White House on December 19, 1933, for distribution to newspapers around the country. Forbes Watson Papers.

December 10 and December 21, Watson and Bruce sent a series of telegrams and letters to the sixteen regional chairmen allocating employment quotas in each region, detailing procedures and guidelines, and transmitting a sense of their priorities and aspirations. "Cover preliminary work Monday as far as possible so that you can put men to work Tuesday morning," they instructed.

"Suggest the employment be week by week so that results can be checked and drones eliminated." "Only American citizens or those who have declared their intention of becoming citizens are eligible for employment." None of the money could be used for prizes or awards or for the purchase of work already completed. From each district a number of artists would be given roving commissions to make a pictorial record of Civilian Conservation Corps camps and public works such as Boulder Dam.[25]

They wanted to allow as much freedom as possible to the broadest range of artists. Murals, sculpture, easel pictures, paintings, drawings, watercolors, design, and crafts were acceptable if local and regional committees considered them appropriate. All art produced under PWAP became the property of the federal government. Detailed statistics were gathered on the numbers of artists employed in each region according to type of media and also according to sex and race. Photographs of completed works of art were collected to create a visual record of the Public Works of Art Project.

Just one year earlier, Watson had declared flatly that artists would look after their own, and that was the way it should be. Now, suddenly he was a believer, convinced that the Public Works of Art Project was "the greatest artist relief work ever undertaken by any government and absolutely vital to the American artists," and that there was "no finer more interesting or more patriotic work possible." Why the change of heart? Barely getting by himself, Watson had come to realize that neither individual artists nor the largest artists' organizations could redress the widespread indigence in the artist community. Bruce was certainly a major factor. He was the very personification of the sense of hope that the early New Deal days inspired. Watson and Bruce, born the same year, were both "men of deep convictions," passionate in their devotion to American art, and likeminded in their view of the world from the artist's perspective. In Bruce's conceptualization of the Public Works of Art Project, Watson could relate to an optimistic faith that exposure to fine art would elevate the public's taste. Watson also recognized that Bruce's "furious determination to help his fellow artists" was accompanied by an equal resolve to promote quality in art and resist the twin dangers of government patronage: standardization and mediocrity. It soon became apparent that Bruce also had the tactical skills to circumvent the pitfalls of both government politics and academic pressure without ruffling feathers, something Watson could not and did not particularly care to do.[26]

With the rush to put artists to work and the pressure to obtain results, a spirit of happy urgency prevailed at PWAP headquarters. Several weeks into the program, the Washington office alone was receiving some five hundred letters a day, each answered in due time. John Davis Hatch, a member of the New

England regional committee, recalled dropping by Bruce's office in the Treasury Building "and seeing on one side of the desk a pile of unanswered correspondence probably two and a half feet high. He [Bruce] was looking cheerfully from behind it all, beaming from ear to ear and saying this is just part of the problem we have to deal with." Back in New York for a few days of Christmas holiday, Watson had barely unpacked when a telegram arrived from Bruce notifying him that the work was "piling up" and, unless he had "definitely committed" himself, he should return to Washington early. During the entire six months of PWAP's existence, Rowan could not manage time for a trip home to Cedar Rapids to see his wife and three young boys. Nevertheless, everybody was good humored. "I think that you would get as much a thrill as I have out of seeing how splendidly and quickly this organization has been built up," Watson wrote George Biddle. "Ned Bruce did a marvelous job and everybody else here is on his toes. The business end is run by a bang-up man, Cecil H. Jones, and we are all working hard and on a most congenial basis."[27]

From their "untidy, distinctly inartistic office" in the Treasury Building, Bruce and Watson sustained the high momentum generated at the organizational meeting of December 8. The city of Washington itself was an exhilarating place to be during the early years of the New Deal, and the "dynamic team" inspired a special sense of drama among those involved in the project.[28] Even though the letterhead of the Public Works of Art Project contained only two names, L. W. Robert Jr. and Forbes Watson, and Bruce's official title was secretary to the Advisory Committee to the Treasury on Fine Arts, Bruce was everywhere, guiding the operation.

He and Watson monitored thousands of projects around the country. Olin Dows, a member of the Washington, D.C., regional committee, recalled that when any problem arose in the region, he went straight to the Treasury office and got Ned's and Forbes's advice. "They were interested, needless to say. It was the one region at hand, so they could see how the program was working."[29] Communication with the sixteen regional committees being a complex affair, Watson initiated a monthly bulletin, with Ed Rowan as news gatherer and Ann Craton as editor. Written in the informal style of a neighborhood gazette, six to seven mimeographed pages carried news of the various regions, announcements, updates from the central office, and encouraging messages from the higher administration. Only two issues were printed, February and March, but they established a precedent for the later, more significant organ of the Section of Fine Arts.

Watson, the named head, brought to the project a national reputation as editor of the "best and most vital art publication" in the United States, an

PWAP and Region no. 4 officials admiring a painting of the National Archives building by artist Dorsey Doniphan. *From left:* C. Law Watkins, W. L. Johnstone, C. Powell Minnigerode, Edward Bruce, Lawrence W. Robert Jr., Dorsey Doniphan, Forbes Watson, Julius F. Stone Jr., Cecil H. Jones, and Edward B. Rowan. Forbes Watson Papers.

insider's grasp of the art situation throughout the country, and, above all, scrupulous taste. "Ed, of course, was the spark plug of the whole thing," artist Henry Varnum Poor recalled, "the know-how in relation to the political set up to get things going, but Forbes was there as the real man with discrimination and judgment in relation to artists. He'd had a much more close contact with artists than Ed had." Watson's rapport extended to the smallest cities from coast to coast, even Europe. Everyone seemed to know him.[30]

Watson described the technical director's duties as essentially artist-oriented. The project required "a constant study of how to make use of the creative abilities of our artists" in such a manner as to "add to the beauty of America, and add to the powers of the artist," he wrote in a position description document. To achieve the goals of PWAP, it was necessary to travel extensively, to supervise the endlessly different undertakings in progress, and to advise and sympathetically criticize the artists at work. It was necessary to make speeches, "sometimes as many as three in one day, and to interview innumerable members of the press to win their sympathy for the Project, and their cooperation."[31]

The administrative side of his job interested him less. Official details bored him, and he found bureaucratic structure confining. Happily for him, Edward

Edward "Ned" Bruce in his "broad brimmed circular creased felt hat." Late 1920s. Forbes Watson Papers.

Rowan, the man he chose as assistant technical director, did not. Another in the long roster of talented young persons to whom Watson opened opportunities, Rowan had been the director of the Little Gallery in Cedar Rapids, Iowa, which had so impressed Watson during his Midwestern speaking tour in 1929.[32] "Eddie," like Bruce, was indefatigable.

Great fellowship prevailed at PWAP headquarters, yet temperamentally, and in specific matters of taste, Bruce, Watson, and Rowan were markedly unalike. Compared to Watson, who was suave, ironic, and full of "naughty" wit, Bruce's "earthy," "hardy" demeanor and large, powerful figure seemed all the more imposing. Swinging "hastily down the street in a broad brimmed circular creased felt hat and looking much more like a senator than a painter," he exuded vigor and enterprise. He worked eighteen-hour days and expected maximum performance from others, yet he was jovially informal, often packing "a critical wallop in a joke."[33] His habit of meticulous planning and detailed oversight compensated to a considerable extent for the organizational sprawl of the CWA regional layout and enabled him to maintain close control over the PWAP operation.[34] Rowan, the dark, slender young assistant with a gift for painting and a taste for poetry and theater, was a chain-smoking "bundle of nervous energy," warm and quick to enthuse, with a habit of earnest attentiveness that promised results. In contrast to the impeccably groomed, dapper Watson, Rowan's coats never seemed to fit or match his trousers. All three were modernist in outlook, but Watson was the most broadminded. Interestingly, among their differences in taste, Rowan disliked the work of one of Watson's favorite artists and dearest friends, William Glackens, and Watson deprecated Grant Wood, whom Rowan admired both personally and professionally. On the large issues, however, the three were entirely concordant. Alice Graeme Korff, who assisted Olin Dows on the Washington regional committee, remembered that everyone felt "the great possibilities of bringing art out of the very 'effete recherché' sort of atmosphere" to people who might have never come in contact with it before, "who wouldn't go into a gallery, but . . . would go into a post office and . . . would see it."[35]

Watson and Bruce instructed the regional directors: "The American scene should be regarded as a general field for subject matters for paintings with latitude for topical subjects appropriate to special projects." The assumption was that art depicting images from daily life was most likely to touch average citizens. They also believed that content as encompassing and nonspecific as the American scene was not likely to curtail artists' freedom of expression. To requests for clarification of "American scene," they responded in general terms, encouraging artists to draw from local life and lore. Watson, who could barely tolerate the "scholastic frumpery" of academic muralists, suggested that artists use contemporary rather than historical topics.[36]

But if the central office was reluctant to define precisely the subject matter of American scene art, it was not reticent about what was not American scene. After some weeks of reviewing artists' submissions, Rowan instructed regional chairmen to check up "very carefully" on the subject matter of each project and to insist that the American scene be stressed. "Any artist who feels that he can only find the picturesque and paintable and the imaginative in foreign subject matter had better be dropped and an opportunity given to the man or woman with enough imagination and vision to see the beauty and the possibility for aesthetic expression in the subject matter of his own country," he advised. Also, it was his personal feeling that any artist who painted a nude for the Public Works of Art Project "should have his head examined."[37]

How the American scene was presented varied not only according to geography and local culture but also to the modern or conservative impulses of the artists and the committees that reviewed their work. Presumably, the American-scene stipulation precluded abstract and other nonfigurative art, yet in the liberal New York region it was interpreted loosely enough to encompass works by Stuart Davis, Arshile Gorky, and even Burgoyne Diller, whose *Abstraction* had no subject matter as such. In the Southern California region, several PWAP artists produced totally abstract paintings. The Northern California committee, on the other hand, "'frowned upon imaginative and picturesque work which has seemed irrelevant to the American scene.'"[38] John S. Ankeney, chairman of the Texas-Oklahoma region, promised that "distorted forms of modernistic art won't adorn the walls of a single building. . . . They might send grammar school kids home to have nightmares or destroy the sense of proportion of some embryonic engineer." Nor would anything "communistic" be allowed. For the most part, those relatively few works that tended toward the abstract or expressionistic were "very polite" in their distortion, however, and "Bruce's tradition" of real-life subject matter and realistic treatment prevailed.[39]

Thanks to the sympathetic interest of Bruce and the zealous lobbying of Nina Perera Collier, the daughter-in-law of the Indian commissioner, American Indian art was a notable component of the Public Works of Art Project.[40] Watson himself, curiously limited in his appreciation of Indian arts and crafts, "not knowing a Zumi [Zuni] from a Hopi," was more than happy to defer to regional chairmen with substantial Indian artist populations. He did admonish those committees not to allow Collier to unduly sway them, however. She "would like to put the whole work of decorating the Indian buildings by Indian artists, over us like a tent. . . . From Mrs. Collier I gather that there is a great Indian artist behind every blade of grass in Arizona and New Mexico, but I personally am not sufficiently acquainted with the Indians to make so gorgeous an estimate of their gifts."[41]

Given the lack of precedents and the haste with which the program was implemented, some problems were bound to arise. Academicians, already "humiliated" at being excluded from the planning process and furious at the liberal composition of PWAP committees, challenged the right of officials to deliver taxpayers' money into the hands of one small art faction. They were also boiling mad, George Biddle observed, "because allowing needy artists to do mural work on public buildings at thirty-five dollars a week may cut into their swill." Four days after the Public Works of Art Project was launched, representatives of the National Academy of Design, the Municipal Art Society of New York, the American Artists Professional League, the Beaux-Arts Architects Society, and four other conservative organizations communicated their dismay at the meager wages PWAP offered. "It would be tragic," they wrote in a letter signed by all eight, "if the creating artist would be required to perform his work at the rate of $40 a week." Watson's response, oozing with ironic deference, respectfully emended their arithmetic (the wage was $42.50, not $40.00) and explained that higher, or normal, wages for artists would result in fewer commissions. He appealed to the signers, "occupying as you do positions of great influence and honor," to give wholehearted support "to an emergency program which has at heart not only the welfare of 2,500 of your fellow artists but also of 3,997,500 other members of our citizenry." Referring to their letter several months later, Watson did not veil his contempt for the presidents of eight "plum-picking club(s)" who had expressed their "morning-coated horror" at the PWAP plan. "Their eyes on the political ball," they only pretended concern for the welfare of the community, he charged. They and their confreres "still lifted their dry skinned, blue veined hands to grasp all the profits for themselves."[42]

Watson's attempt to put conservatives' fears to rest only raised other issues and precipitated another row, this time from the left. Insisting that the program was built on "impartial relief," Watson wrote George Elmer Browne, president of the Allied Artists of America, that PWAP was "not in the least concerned with critical estimates of esthetics" and wanted the government's money to go into the hands of the seriously unemployed artists. This was not Watson's own view, but policy he presumed came from Harry Hopkins, who sought work relief for the maximum number of needy artists. Four days later, a hasty wire from Bruce to the regional chairmen nullified Watson's statement and underscored the preeminence of artistic ability. "The word relief should be eliminated by you in all reference to the project and in any discussions with artists employed," he instructed. "We are going to be judged by class of work done and the quality of the artists employed is a most important factor in selection for this work."[43]

Personally, and in spite of his initial blunder, Watson could not have agreed more. Following a meeting with Francis Taylor and Julius F. Stone Jr., director of federal projects for the CWA, he delivered official reinforcement. "Mr. Stone was very explicit in stating that we are not concerned with relief," Watson reported to Bruce. "This was definite and absolute." As for what to do with the people they cut out, "Stone said to treat them exactly as a private organization would which fired its employees. Recommend them to see the local relief or their pastor, but do not take up their relief problems."[44]

Bruce had anticipated "a lot of 'yaps' from various parts of the country," and they materialized. But the "yappers" did not get very far. "The best crowd in Washington is back of us," he wrote a friend. In practice, it was difficult if not impossible to achieve an optimal reconciliation of talent and neediness. Applications from thousands of untalented unemployed amateurs who deemed themselves artists and mediocre artists who were indigent inundated regional committees. When PWAP committees bypassed them, many turned "agin the government," Peyton Boswell, editor of Art Digest, observed. PWAP was also criticized for employing financially secure artists such as William Zorach, John Sloan, Hayley Lever, and Stirling Calder. The reason for using them, of course, was not for providing relief but for quality assurance. They were dropped from the PWAP payroll very quickly, however.[45]

Challenges continued to come both from the left and the right. Unemployed artist groups picketed the Whitney Museum, charging Juliana Force with favoritism. Lloyd Goodrich, a member of the New York committee, remembered "riots outside and . . . leftist protests and threats." In Chicago, Wat Williams, president of the local chapter of the United Scenic Artists of the American Federation of Labor, demanded the "removal of Forbes Robinson [sic] and Edmund [sic] Bruce for establishing a dictatorship of the 'art' business without allowing artists the protection of . . . the N.R.A. 'to have the right to organize and bargain collectively.'" Unruffled, Watson observed that there were "always a few Wat Williams along the landscape. . . . Their brains are mostly in their feet which is, I suppose, why they are always kicking." When union members threatened to "tear down the buildings" if any nonunion artist's mural painting was installed, Bruce secured assurances from William Green, president of the American Federation of Labor, that he would take any action necessary to prevent it.[46]

In San Francisco, three of the twenty-five artists decorating the stairwell and lobbies of Coit Tower incorporated symbols into their murals "which might be interpreted as communistic propaganda." Defying outraged officials' demands that they change the offending images, the artists justified their pictures on the basis of the American-scene proviso.[47] Newspapers and magazines nationwide reported detail after detail of the standoff, causing Bruce prolonged embarrassment. The murals were not open to the public until October 1934.

The fact was that despite protestations of impartiality toward all artists and schools, Bruce and Watson scarcely concealed their disdain for both social protest art and academic art. It was not conservatives' imagination that they had been "slapped." Watson vowed that PWAP would not sponsor any of "that good old official stuff that the walls of America . . . had to bear on them in the past." When the ultraconservative Municipal Art League of Chicago unanimously passed a resolution to honor their "great Art Leader, Lorado Taft" with a commission to complete his *Fountain of Creation* sculpture under the auspices of the Public Works of Art Project, Watson promptly squelched it. "He is certainly the great-grandfather of mediocrity, and the PWAP will not aid and abet him without terrible screams emanating from me," he declared.[48]

A larger-scale controversy erupted when Bruce attempted to halt the installation of academic artist Gilbert White's classical-style mural in the Department of Agriculture Building. Bruce, who had dubbed the allegorical figures in White's pastoral mural "ladies draped in cheesecloth," preferred images of modern agriculture, perhaps agricultural machinery. As newspapers across the country picked up Bruce's catchy phrase, Watson backed him to the hilt, declaring White's painting "a scrapbook piece of work, something to fill in space." Bruce did not have his way, as it turned out, for Secretary of Agriculture Henry Wallace was an admirer of White's work.[49]

In most of the conflicts, whether labor problems in Chicago or the leftist standoff over Coit Tower, Watson was not so much the tactician—that was Bruce's forte—as the apologist, advancing the cause of the Public Works of Art Project and doing so with the zeal of a convert and the deftness of the seasoned journalist. The January 1934 issues of both *Parnassus* and *American Magazine of Art* contained lead articles by Watson in which he celebrated the democratic promise of the project. PWAP "believes that the artist is not the rare blossom that blooms once in a hundred years," he wrote, "and it also believes that the life of the spirit may quite well be carried on by men whose names will not go down permanently in history." A decade earlier he would not have made that statement, diluting as it did the artist's distinctiveness. He also touched on a theme he would expand later, that through a program of this kind the artist became a more integral part of the community. The government was not anticipating masterpieces for its money, but if one, two, or three genuinely imaginative mural talents emerged, and if in addition artists were inspired by their "new sense of vital association with their communities," who could doubt that an artistic record of permanent value would result?[50]

The campaign to sell PWAP to the American public and win over Washington had been in high gear from its inception. If the project was to be kept alive beyond the two-month mandate, success must be swift and conspicuous. "The great problem I have at heart is to carry on this work through the emergency stage into some permanent organization which shall be non-political," Watson wrote one of the regional directors. "You know how loathsome and fatal it is to have politics messing about in art." Not only were there Watson's articles and lectures, but Rowan, Olin Dows, and Bruce also published, and Bruce delivered speeches all over town, including at the White House. His address to the Cosmopolitan Club on the high caliber of PWAP artists and the stimulating impact government patronage was having on them and on American civilization was printed in the *Congressional Record*. Statistics were distributed furnishing evidence of the countrywide demand for PWAP art installations. Bruce urged artists to write their congressmen and senators telling them what the program meant to them, and he quoted passages from testimonials and tributes. Every member of Congress should have a painting by an artist from his state or district hanging in his office, he advised regional chairmen.[51]

Washington must also see how stringently the Public Works of Art Project managed its grant, and Bruce ran a tight operation indeed. Three days after giving regional chairmen authority to expend up to 10 percent of their gross payroll for artists' supplies, Bruce rescinded the allowance, notifying chairmen that artists would have to provide their own materials.[52] At the same time, he and Watson pressed suppliers to offer PWAP artists discounts. Fortunately, communities across the country, eager to decorate their schools, courthouses, and other public buildings with PWAP art, generously donated work space, equipment, and offices for the artists and officials engaged in local projects. During its entire existence, the project never spent money on rent. College art departments even gave students curriculum credit for assisting in local projects.

Watson faced the additional challenge of keeping his adversarial proclivities in check and getting along with government bureaucrats; at times it required all the restraint he could muster. Collaboration with navy brass on the design of a mural depicting the battle of Santiago for the Naval Academy's "hideously architectured" Memorial Hall at Annapolis was all the more trying for having to defer to a "peanut" like Adm. Thomas C. Hart.[53] Demanding technical and historical authenticity—and implicitly, oversight—in the *Battle of Santiago* mural, Admiral Hart was precisely the sort of self-important authority figure Watson would normally have annihilated with sarcasm. Instinctively, he resisted both Hart's literal ideas and his control, but under the circumstances, he resorted to evasion rather than confrontation. Even as he assured the overbearing admiral that a naval expert's advice would be followed for correctness of technical detail, Watson wrote Theodore Sizer, who organized the artists for the project, "the literalness demanded by the present Admiral of the Navy—this is all confidential—will not be carried out." Believing that Harry Roosevelt, assistant secretary of the navy, and other higher-ups were "all in favor of our point of view," he advised Sizer, "certain details like the position of the flags in battle, and the position of the guns, etc., should be correct, but not disagreeably so." His confidence in support was mistaken. Months after the Public Works of Art Project had been dismantled and a new government art program launched, Rowan, Bruce, and other PWAP officials were still appeasing naval officials, who rejected sketch after sketch because of incorrectness in the size of ships and guns, the position of the smoke clouds, the color of the bow wave, and countless other details. Finally, revisions completed, Naval Academy officials declined to install the *Santiago* mural in Memorial Hall because it did not harmonize with the existing mural on the opposite wall, the *Battle of the Constitution*. "Of course there is always the possibility of making a present of it to the Cuban government," an exasperated PWAP state supervisor offered after prolonged, fruitless efforts to locate an alternative space. Negotiations continued through the summer, but, in the end, the *Battle of Santiago* was never installed at the Naval Academy.[54]

In February, with much ballyhoo, Bruce invited the chairmen of the sixteen regional committees to Washington for a three-day meeting "to discuss ways and means of carrying forward the Public Works of Art Project, in the light of the experience of the past two months." The sessions, which ran February 19–21, included luncheon at Bruce's home and tea with Eleanor Roosevelt at the White House. There were progress reports, mostly optimistic, from the regional chairmen, and an evening slide lecture by Watson. Not only was the Public Works of Art Project producing an impressive number of paintings and sculptures, Watson stated, but through the project America was also "getting acquainted with itself, ... establishing a relationship between the points of view of the different parts of this country in a way that can only be done under the aegis of art." Bruce also announced that PWAP would follow CWA's policy of curtailing operations. Relaying Hopkins's target of a 50 percent reduction in the number of artists on PWAP payrolls from 2,500 to 1,250 by the beginning of May, Bruce projected, "we can gradually let the drones out and those who are proving that they can't do the work." He reminded chairmen of the dual test for cutting back, first, the applicant's qualification as an artist, and second, his need of employment.[55]

The culminating demonstration of PWAP's worthiness was the art itself, and that was to be displayed in the National Exhibition of the Public Works of Art Project held at the Corcoran Gallery from April 24 through May 20, 1934. It was the final campaign to win the program an extension. Watson put Rowan in charge of hanging the show, and with his and Bruce's assistance, they installed 511 items. There were seven galleries of oil paintings, one of watercolors, one of prints, another of American Indian arts and crafts, eight large murals, and a small number of sculptures. Watson prepared the catalog. Ideally, at least one example of each artist's work under the project should have been exhibited, Bruce commented in the foreword, but space in the Corcoran did not permit an all-inclusive show.[56] In truth, they were delighted not to display certain artists' works.

Exclusions and restrictions notwithstanding, within the designated subject of the American scene, PWAP artists had created widely varied images of families, their neighbors and animals, and laborers toiling in diverse occupations in factories, on farms, and in government projects. They portrayed local events and historic landmarks as well as ethnic and regional rituals and customs. Scenes were set in rural villages, small towns, suburbs, and big cities. They featured bridges, dams, oil wells, locomotives, steamships, and mechanical inventions. Still lifes and nature scenes were less common, offering fewer opportunities to convey the New Deal message of hope, vitality, and democracy. There were no nudes.

Watson oversaw a blitz of press releases, posters, and other publicity, and he and Bruce talked up the exhibition to groups ranging from local social clubs to national organizations as well as to each other in a nationally broadcast radio program. On the Friday afternoon preceding the opening, at a reception hosted by Undersecretary of State William Phillips and his wife, three hundred prominent Washingtonians heard Watson proclaim the National Exhibition to be "the greatest art event in this country since the Armory Show." President and Mrs. Roosevelt attended a special preview on Sunday, and the first lady selected thirty-two paintings for permanent exhibition in the lobbies of the White House Office Building. The president expressed his pleasure with the positive tone of the exhibit, noting that "not a single one of the . . . pictures . . . evidenced despair or despondency." Mrs. Roosevelt, who thought Julius Bloch's picture of an unemployed boy "almost the swellest thing in the exhibit," observed approvingly that even the expression on the boy's face appeared "more baffled than resentful." As one reviewer commented, artists in the National Exhibition had not chosen to see bread lines and strikes, perhaps thinking it "wisest not to do so while drawing government pay."[57]

More than 26,000 people attended the show, and requests for catalogs and pictures poured in from all over the United States and Europe. It was "full of vigor and honesty and fresh ideas," Watson wrote friends. It "opened people's eyes." At the same time, his keen critic's gaze could not gloss over some of the "honest, if uninspired efforts to turn a proffered wage" or ignore the regional unevenness in the exhibition. The Southeast was "definitely weaker than any other region," he noted privately. The Midwest was "definitely stronger than the average observer of New York exhibitions would have suspected." The Dakotas seemed to be "completely unproductive." The Northwest had some artists who were "definitely vigorous, and a lot who still belong to the 'Kiss Mama' school." The Pacific coast, though enthusiastic, "suffered somewhat from artiness." And the Northeast was "on the whole, conservative and . . . not particularly daring. . . . The most sophisticated work came from exactly where one would expect, namely the New York region."[58]

The critics generally reacted affirmatively, commending the show's geographic inclusiveness and the introduction of so many local talents; Howard Devree called it "a kind of national manifesto."[59] That the government could employ more than three thousand artists in a project of such magnitude was impressive, so much so that some critics probably tempered their professional disposition to dissect its weaknesses. The works were praised mainly for good intentions and amiableness. Not all the critics were inclined to make allowances based on the "biological" worthiness of the program, however. Lewis Mumford, for instance, found the prevailing note of the "devitalized" PWA art to be "one of hopeful banality."[60]

For Bruce, Watson, and Rowan, certification of the success of the exhibition, and, hence, of the project, came in comments urging continuation of federal arts patronage. "So impressed (was) President Roosevelt by the significance of the Public Works Art Exhibition," it was reported, "that little doubt remained yesterday that the Administration will establish, as a definite policy, the widespread employment of artists to embellish Government buildings."[61]

On April 28, 1934, four and a half months after the Public Works of Art Project began and four days after the opening of the National Exhibition, all artists were taken off the PWAP payroll. The program was cut off on May 20, 1934, with the termination of the Civil Works Administration. Artists whose projects were not completed were allowed to proceed without a means test under the newly created Emergency Work Relief Program of FERA, earning a "reasonable relief allowance," though somewhat less than PWAP had paid.[62] Those seeking new work were required to demonstrate need, just as required of white-collar relief workers. To facilitate the transfer, Ann Craton, whose title had been changed from coordinator to assistant technical director in charge of public relations, traveled the country to help integrate PWAP artists into state relief rolls.

Watson and Rowan, looking for ways to sustain the jobless artists, arranged temporary enrollment in Emergency Conservation Work camps and helped a small number obtain Guggenheim Fellowships. At the same time, they encouraged grassroots responsibility, urging communities to subsidize local artists' work. Watson also offered advice to the artists based on "the lesson" of the Public Works of Art Project: to bring their fellow citizens closer by lowering the prices of their work.[63]

Bruce was confident Roosevelt would approve another arts program, but until one was in place, he and Watson planned to keep alive the achievements of the Public Works of Art Project by circuiting the National Exhibition to museums, galleries, and art organizations in nineteen cities across the country. There was talk of setting aside a portion of the cost of new federal buildings for their embellishment. Also, he was optimistic about his recent proposal to the president to create a permanent division of fine arts, similar to the Public Works of Art Project but expanded to encompass music, literature, theater, crafts, and plastic arts.[64] Throughout the spring and summer, Ed Rowan, who would be named assistant director of the fine arts division, queried hundreds of writers, dramatists, musicians, critics, and commentators, gathering ideas about federal support in their fields, which Bruce passed on to the president.

In June, with Bruce at his summer home in Peru, Vermont, Watson preparing to leave for Scotland, and Ann Craton on tour, Rowan began dismantling the operation. A large number of art works were returned to their original regions. Others were transferred to the administration for display in public buildings, offices, and parks or lent to organizations such as the American Federation of Arts and the College Art Association for exhibitions. Bruce asked that work that was "not of such quality as to justify its use in the embellishment of public buildings" be shipped to Washington for final disposition.[65]

But everything ended abruptly in September, as CWA operating funds were recalled.[66] The circuiting National Exhibition, which was scheduled to travel from September 1934 through June 1935, only made it to the first stop of its itinerary. The division of fine arts failed to materialize.

FERA took charge of the remaining PWAP art when the public works project finally closed its doors. Thousands of works were liquidated between October 1934 and June 1935, sent to state universities and colleges, schools, libraries, and other tax-exempt sites. The worst of the "strange assortment" were destroyed, but there were still works "that were decidedly mediocre and poor, but about which one felt a little sentimental," Ann Craton reported. "It seemed too bad to destroy them when they possessed the merit of providing some color to many drab rooms and dull walls." Thus PWAP works, stripped of their brass tags and other identification, graced the walls of transient shelters, public assistance office waiting rooms, reception halls, and other public chambers around the country.[67]

In its five months of operation, the Public Works of Art Project expended $1,312,177.93, of which 90.3 percent was disbursed for artists' wages. It had employed 3,749 artists who created 15,663 works. It was a minor undertaking compared to later federal programs, but for its brief life, the Public Works of Art

Project was an intense, manifestly successful operation.[68] Had it not been, three succeeding federal arts programs would probably not have come into existence.

There had been flaws. Some officials were convinced that it was impossible to attain a high level of artistry under a government program of such magnitude. Artistically, its greatest weaknesses stemmed from the circumscribed approach to subject matter, which effectively discouraged experiment and modernist expressions.[69] While Watson himself did not address the consequences of PWAP's prescribed subject matter, during the war in Europe he had criticized a Friends of the Young Artists sculpture competition on grounds that its designation of a theme, "war," put restraints on the creative imagination.

In officially assigning the American scene as subject matter, the Public Works of Art Project also helped advance the American Scene movement.[70] It would be a mistake, however, to conclude that PWAP aligned itself with the "back-to-the-soil-sceners," as Watson contemptuously termed them, or subscribed to their philosophy. To Watson, the American Scene was only the latest in a long parade of fashionable movements, replete with its "own noisy publicity-man" and practitioners clad "in overalls and standing by the barnyard fence." Bruce and Watson's written communications regarding American scene subject matter consistently employed the lower case "s," emphasizing, symbolically at least, its separateness from the movement. The Public Works of Art Project was nationalistic but not negative, and it shunned extremism. Whereas Thomas Craven and other spokesmen for the American Scene movement "played to every prejudice which surfaced during the thirties," the Public Works of Art Project, for all its chauvinistic pronouncements, touted inclusiveness. The Treasury plan would be "no plan at all," Watson insisted, if it did not include "the Japs of California, the Scandinavians of Minnesota, the Negroes of Louisiana, the Jews of New York, the Biddles of Philadelphia, and the Cabots of Boston. . . . Certainly it would be almost too easy to become an American artist if the question depended merely on the choice of subject matter."[71]

There were artists who had disappointing experiences with PWAP, but, as the thousands of letters to the president and other officials testified, the vast majority were deeply appreciative.[72] Most regional committees observed a tangible rise in public interest in art, and local communities were pleased with their new PWAP decorations. Both as artifacts of the prevalent taste of the thirties and as evidence that notable work could result from the government's pilot effort to foster culture, PWAP art constituted an invaluable record. In this context, as a pioneer and prototype for future governmental art programs, PWAP made its most significant mark. The Public Works of Art Project inaugurated a new attitude on the part of the federal government in which "aesthetic goals became a part of official thinking and the public philosophy."[73]

Created "out of Mr. Bruce's brain," the Public Works of Art Project "developed with speed and health, bumping over, under, and otherwise past, a series of obstacles that would have smashed a less resilient and buoyant organization," Watson wrote at its conclusion. Bruce "was the chief motive force in saving about three thousand artists of pretty high average of accomplishment from a very hard winter." Without Watson's active commitment, however, most insiders felt, as Alice Graeme Korff did, that Bruce would not "ever have been able to put it across," not "without Forbes as the guiding light on it, as far as the aesthetic content of what was done." At the beginning, Bruce had hoped Watson would be an administrator, the one who would take charge. But he was not. "He was not punctual," Dows related. "He did not get things out on time." "Freewheeling" was how Korff described him, suspecting that colleagues kept him in line. Although the "whole group . . . looked to Forbes as their real most important critical judgment," following the experience of the Public Works of Art Project, he would not hold another administrative position.[74]

"I came to Washington with a Republican background," Watson wrote a fellow journalist, "and am entirely won over to the New Deal both on account of the brilliant, indefatigable workers I have met here, and on account of the spirit in which they are working. . . . This is certainly the time when all of us who want to accomplish something toward benefiting our art and our artists have our greatest opportunity." That statement, made after five months in Washington, summed up Watson's turnaround. Hard times had precipitated his conversion from intransigent foe to inspired proselytizer, as the federal government proffered the dignity of wages to suffering artists and facilitated the democratization of art. In a sense, the program represented for Watson an attack upon the privileged. It was the consummate Independent, offering audition, if not exhibition, possibilities to "new blood and fresh talents" nationwide, making possible "the development of talent on a wide and non-precious base." Too, regional decentralization of decision-making and local support of artists, built into PWAP, promoted the breakdown of the old power concentrations.[75]

With the New Deal, Watson focused more explicitly on the economics of democratization. Before the government put its hands in its pockets and dispensed wages to unemployed artists, he reflected, "costliness and quality were hopelessly mixed up." The average art dealer "carried on as if he were a combination of custom tailor and diamond merchant." Now, Watson forecasted a "just division of the treasures of the earth" in which artists would receive more balanced pay and also would charge the public more reasonable prices. Aside from the suffering the depression had caused, artists would one day look back on it as "a blessing," he predicted. "A moment's thought will show the difference, in the spirit of the worker, between producing on speculation and producing under the terms of the steady job." Assured an income without having to pander to fashion or compete with celebrity names, the artist, no longer a "misunderstood individualist," achieved greater independence.[76]

Still, Watson's endorsement was qualified. In the long run, he envisioned the federal government not as a patron of art but as a friendly promoter, a broker at most. He meant the artist's relationship with the community to be direct, without federal surrogacy or intermediation, although its terms were yet to be defined. "While the Government can be and has been of invaluable service to the artist," he wrote California artist Henri de Kruif at the conclusion of PWAP, "eventually the greatest service to the artists must come from their own communities. There is certainly room in the Government for an organization related in its purposes to the Public Works of Art Project, but it strikes me that the value of this organization would rest upon its stimulating powers rather than upon continuing material aid to the artists."[77] The government was only a temporary prop.

The depression had also brought slippage in Watson's critical standards. That he described PWAP artists optimistically as "of pretty high average of accomplishment" reflected his habitual candor merged now with realistically downsized expectations. The art that flourished under the Treasury program was not the ideal blend of democracy, independence, and artistry Watson had projected onto the pages of The Arts. In PWAP art, the democratic tended to overtake the individualistic, resulting in a reconfiguration, if not a perversion, of Watson's American paradigm. Much of it tended to be virile, rough grained, and machine oriented, conforming more to the art of Thomas Craven's "reckless, unrefined Yankee" than to Watson's refined and filtered prototype. American scene subject matter did not foster his vision of American uniqueness, it stalemated it by proscription.[78]

From the beginning Watson understood that the Public Works of Art Project was temporary. Neither he nor Rowan had established permanent residence when they came to Washington in December 1933. He had maintained his New York residency, although his rent on the Manhattan apartment was three months overdue. As bill collectors still plagued him, however, it seemed sensible to move from the Fifty-first Street apartment to more modest accommodations at 44 East Ninth Street, which would still provide Nan good light and space in which to paint. When the Public Works of Art Project officially ended in May with no definite word of a new program, Watson made plans to join Nan, who was "getting poised like a bird on limb ready to fly homeward," and accompany her back from Scotland.[79] It could not be too soon. Dalliances notwithstanding, he had missed her.

Resigning his position as of June 1, Watson tied up loose ends at the office, completed some writing and speaking commitments, and took vacation time to attend to some major dental work and other personal matters. Declining an invitation to judge the forthcoming Iowa Art Salon, he recommended Edward Rowan as "exactly the right person to do this job."[80] His plans for the future were uncertain.

Despite a steady paycheck for the past five months, money remained a problem, not only because his income was relatively modest but also because he was a free spender, impatient with the minutiae of budgets. "I don't mind paying bills when I have the money," he once commented, "but I loathe examining them and verifying them and being forced to indulge in nasty calculating material thoughts." The fact that the central office under Bruce was frugal did not curb Watson's penchant for high-end apparel nor his habit of treating friends and associates to drinks, lunches, and parties. Even as he assiduously hawked raffle tickets to aid George Picken, a destitute painter, he turned down a raffle ticket benefiting another worthy cause because he was "dreadfully hard up." His new partial dentures, which made him "somewhat irritable and nervous," also exacerbated his financial worries.[81]

The dentist having "completed his murder," and his affairs more or less in order, Watson sailed on Saturday, July 25, to join Nan in Scotland, planning to resettle in New York in the fall. Meanwhile in Washington, Ed Rowan, manfully addressing the Public Works of Art Project aftermath, had bought a home in Falls Church, Virginia, expecting to become assistant director of the projected fine arts division. His family had joined him. On August 15 Rowan officially replaced Watson, becoming acting technical director of the Public Works of Art Project at Watson's former salary. "Mr. Bruce is very anxious to hold Mr. Rowan in this organization in the event the new division is set up," Cecil Jones wrote in his official request for Rowan's reappointment.[82] Although the proposed division of fine arts did not go forward, plans for a new arts program would near completion around the time Watson returned to the United States.

7 THE SECTION OF PAINTING AND SCULPTURE, 1934–1938

A second Treasury art program, the Section of Painting and Sculpture, was established on October 16, 1934, four months after the termination of the Public Works of Art Project (PWAP). The Treasury Relief Art Project (TRAP) and the Works Progress Administration (WPA) Federal Art Project followed in quick succession. By August 1935, three new government art programs were in operation. The Section of Painting and Sculpture, a nonrelief program, employed artists to decorate new federal buildings. The Treasury Relief Art Project employed artists both on relief and off to decorate existing as well as new federal buildings. The WPA Federal Art Project, strictly a relief program, employed needy artists, writers, musicians, dramatists, and performers.

Vacationing in Vermont the summer PWAP was dismantled, Bruce spent his days painting and planning for its successor. He kept in touch with Secretary of the Treasury Henry Morgenthau Jr. and others close to Roosevelt and consulted with his dedicated lieutenants from PWAP, Ed Rowan and Olin Dows. By fall, when he returned to Washington, Bruce had a program outlined. With President Roosevelt's blessing, Secretary Morgenthau issued an administrative order on October 16, 1934, establishing the Section of Painting and Sculpture within the Public Buildings Branch of the Procurement Division. Bruce was chief, accepting an annual salary for the first time; Rowan was superintendent, sometimes referred to as "assistant chief"; and Dows was assistant superintendent. Their mission was "to take charge of and carry out, under the direction and regulations of the Procurement Division, Treasury Department, the work of embellishment of public buildings constructed by the Treasury Department with paintings and sculpture." Under the terms of Morgenthau's order, 1 percent of the total cost of new federal buildings was earmarked for embellishment if there were funds left over when construction was completed. In practice about one-third of newly constructed federal buildings ended with a surplus. Most were post offices.[1]

Bruce had learned much from his experience with the Public Works of Art Project. Supervising three thousand artists within a five-month employment period had been too unwieldy, resulting, despite "extraordinary enthusiasm," in lowered standards.[2] Under the Section, there would be no equivocation on the issue of quality. The program was intentionally small and not set up to handle relief; control was centralized in Washington. A system of open, anonymous competitions was put in place to assure that artists would be selected strictly on the basis of quality.

The PWAP experience had also confirmed for Bruce the importance of positive public relations. Less than a month after the Section of Painting and Sculpture was established, he proposed to Adm. Christian Joy Peoples, director of procurement, that a regular bulletin be issued to inform artists and others about the section's activities. He recommended Forbes Watson for the job of preparing the bulletins and handling general publicity.[3] Watson rejoined his cohorts in Washington in December 1934, not as director this time but as sectional public information advisor, a part-time position. Nan remained in Manhattan, where she was preparing to exhibit at the Whitney Biennial.

Bruce needed Watson for more than half-time editing, however. By summer 1935 he persuaded Peoples to assign Watson additional writing duties and upgrade his position to full-time adviser. With "a gratifying raise in salary" from $2,600 to $4,600 annually, Watson decided to give up the New York apartment and move to Washington.[4] Nan, who had once again been called to Scotland to nurse her failing aunt, was due back in the States in September—"*Gott sei dank!*"—and Forbes hoped they could move to a permanent residence by winter. Meanwhile, he took an apartment he had rented once before in the Ugly Duckling Tea House at 115 B Street Southeast, very small but comfortable quarters near an excellent little inn. When Nan arrived, she made herself a working studio out of a pleasant north room. "The landlord was a little shocked at her having the carpets and the other odds and ends removed," Watson wrote a friend, but decided that her desire to have a bare room was "just one of those peculiarities that all artists indulge in."[5]

Watson's responsibilities at the Section included editing, writing, lecturing, reviewing competition decisions, inspecting project sites, overseeing exhibitions, and advising on a wide range of art matters. His reputation for outspokenness and confrontation having been only too well established, he had pledged to stay in line and "not . . . touch anything controversial." "Every single thing" he put out was to be shown to Admiral Peoples. "So," he assured Bruce, "I am sure he will protect me from making any breaks."[6]

Rowan and Dows were the administrators, which was fortunate, for early in June 1935, less than eight months after the section was established, Bruce suffered a debilitating stroke. In mind, enthusiasm, and drive, he was "absolutely undiminished" and continued to come to the office, but he was paralyzed on the left side and required frequent treatment and rest. He spent part of every year in Key West, Florida, to replenish his strength. Regardless of where he was, Vermont or Florida, summonses, telegrams, long-distance phone calls, and letters, sometimes at the rate of three per day per recipient, issued forth to the Washington office. Rowan ran the office, and he and Dows were the troubleshooters. Maria K. Ealand, a niece of Bruce's wife, served as senior administrative assistant to the directors. A Vassar graduate and "good amateur painter," according to Watson, Ealand managed the welter of projects and paper work that government contracts generated, moving the hectic operation along with cheery efficiency. In time, she also participated in art selection sessions with Watson and the others.[7]

Bruce, Dows, and Rowan had worked out detailed procedures for selecting murals, easel art, and sculpture through competitions. First, members of the Section of Painting and Sculpture studied architectural plans for new federal buildings having surplus funds and consulted with the architects to identify suitable spaces for embellishment. Then, when money became available, the section invited an artist who did not wish to enter the competition, a museum director, the head of a nearby art association, or some other "expert with taste and discrimination" to head a committee to run the competition.[8] The chairman in turn appointed board members consisting of the architect of the building and one or two other qualified people. Any artist who was a citizen of the United States was eligible to enter a competition, which could be national, regional, state, or local. Competitions were announced in the Section *Bulletin* and in the local press, and committees also notified artists individually. Bulletin announcements described the building and space available, suggested the general subject matter, and specified contractual obligations and pay, which usually ranged from ten to twenty dollars per square foot. To preserve anonymity, all entries were unsigned. Only after the local jury submitted its recommendations to Washington, and Section staff reviewed and forwarded them to the director of procurement, was the envelope containing the artist's name unsealed and a contract drawn up.

Although Section officials rarely reversed a local competition decision, they did recommend modifications in designs. They also invited artists who had submitted outstanding entries that did not win to design for another specific building without further competition. The idea behind the combination of competition and appointment, Dows explained, was to attract talent through the competition and at the same time make it clear to artists that "they were not wasting their efforts in a one-shot raffle."[9] In certain cases, particularly allotments of less than seven or eight hundred dollars, the section was permitted to purchase paintings or sculpture outright rather than commissioning special work. National competitions awarded the largest contracts, attracting prominent artists such as William Zorach, George Biddle, Ben Shahn, Henry Varnum Poor, Grant Wood, and John Steuart Curry. The more numerous local competitions often brought forward relatively unknown artists.

When Congress created the Works Progress Administration for national work relief in April 1935, Bruce had been invited to head its new arts program. He declined, but, ever resourceful, he applied for and received a grant from the WPA to hire unemployed artists to decorate existing buildings, since Treasury funds were restricted to new construction.[10] To administer the $530,784 grant, the Treasury Department established the Treasury Relief Art Project (TRAP) on July 15, 1935. Under Bruce's general direction, TRAP worked hand in hand with the Section of Painting and Sculpture. Olin Dows was named chief; Henry LaFarge, Dows's old friend known for his scholarly ways and quiet competence, was his assistant; Watson was technical adviser; and Cecil Jones was business manager.

Dows, who had, in George Biddle's words, "the best blood in the state," was a Dutchess County, New York, neighbor and old family friend of the Roosevelts and the Morgenthaus, and although he did not use his high-level connections to advance himself, the sense of belonging was always there. He had not experienced the desperation many artists suffered in the depression, yet he was deeply committed to giving artists "a break." Teetotaling, self-effacing, and a person who tended to see mostly good in people, Dows had none of the cocktail-hour adroitness or honed skepticism of Watson, but from the beginning, the two had a special rapport, stemming perhaps from similarly privileged backgrounds.[11]

TRAP was the most flexible of the four federal art programs, as it was less circumscribed by stipulations concerning the buildings and spaces it could decorate.[12] In addition to post office and courthouse murals and sculptures, TRAP artists made decorative hangings, painted screens, copied historic portraits, and executed a variety of other art products. Their work was installed in sites as diverse as the leper colony at Carville, Louisiana; overseas embassies; and a reformatory in Chillicothe, Ohio.

When Dows left the Section to head TRAP, Watson brought his former assistant editor, Inslee Hopper, down from New York to replace him as assistant superintendent. Hopper had accrued considerable experience since the demise of

Arts Weekly, inspecting sculptures for the Whitney Museum. Still, he found he "had quite an educational job to do" in his new role, reconciling a competitively determined sculptor's work with the architectural conception, as most architects were very conservative.[13]

For decades, the generally accepted practice was to use a portion of the construction funding for embellishments in federal buildings, but under the Section, artists rather than architects selected the designs. The architects had not gladly relinquished control of art commissions, and they were generally not enthusiastic about the Section's projects. Nevertheless, unlike painters, Dows observed, "who get very excited and take a strong moral attitude on things," architects did not argue beyond a certain point. Louis Simon, supervising architect for the Section, authorized all contracts with artists and forwarded his recommendations to Admiral Peoples for final approval. This worked out relatively well, according to Dows, because even though Peoples had "no interest whatsoever" in the art program, "he realized it was well done and he liked us all."[14]

As with PWAP, informality prevailed at the Section's specially remodeled quarters in the Procurement Division's Federal Warehouse Building at Seventh and D Streets Southwest. Staff members were housed in a row of four unpretentiously bare partitioned rooms, "cubbies" as Watson referred to them, easily available to one another. A spacious room down the hall accommodated the hundreds of designs arriving daily from around the country. Large wall placards mounted alphabetically by state identified tall stacks of sketches and hung works, making it convenient for staff and jurists to wander in and out and examine them over a period of time.[15]

With Watson, Dows, Rowan, Hopper, and visiting artists who were called in at times, sessions on new design entries were animated, outrageously candid, and, despite wide diversities in taste, highly productive. Very few "duds" made it through those meetings, Hopper remembered. They were pretty much winnowed out. There was a continuous stream of visitors, artists, museum directors, critics, government officials, and even an occasional foreign dignitary. Eleanor Roosevelt visited from time to time, and Elinor Morgenthau, wife of Secretary Morgenthau, was a frequent guest. Working at the Section was a round-the-clock commitment. "The amount of energy expended above and beyond nine to five was tremendous," Dows recalled. "Talking shop, thinking shop, often having dinner and seeing people for business reasons. . . . You get very involved in it." Bruce entertained at dinner in his home at least five nights a week, Hopper estimated. "It was a lobbying job."[16]

And they had "a marvelous time at the office," Hopper remembered. Luncheon parties were "the usual thing." Bruce would prevail upon the cafeteria manager to let him see daily menus to order sandwiches and soft drinks, Ealand recalled. "A long table was pulled out into the corridor. There were many times when visiting jury members . . . would take a break and eat a sandwich. Everyone would contribute with the latest news of the art world." After selections had been made, and between sessions, Watson "helped out with the entertaining of the juries, . . . and taking care of them." He always "enjoyed going out for a long lunch with a couple of cocktails."[17]

If Bruce was the master strategist, Watson was the master aesthetician. "When it came to really seeing things and understanding, they all looked to Forbes as being the number one man in a sense," Henry Varnum Poor observed. "He went way out ahead with his ideas," Alice Graeme Korff recalled. Watson was the undisputed authority on and principal contact with the art world. Ask him, and he could refer you to the person most experienced with pigments; the expert on antiques, tapestries, and furniture; the man for restorations; the person who best understood auction methods; or the honest dealer. He was the deftest at arranging exhibitions. With a lecture schedule that would have depleted one less knowledgeable and gregarious, he appeared at the most prestigious museums, art schools, colleges, and professional associations in the country.[18]

Whereas the most inspiring man in the section was Bruce , Watson was the most scintillating. "Oh he was . . . an *enfant terrible,* he was," Korff remembered. "He used to say anything." Nobody seemed to mind that his disposition "was up and down." "He was a person that we had great fun with," Dows recalled. "It was never just pure funny fun. It was ironic and witty. . . . He . . . reminisced beautifully, knew everybody—a vast number of people—and remembered things about them. Very frank talker too. . . . Quite often you'd have to work on Saturday. For instance, a document would come and have to be answered immediately. After we'd done the job Forbes would start reminiscing and you'd linger on for hours, jawing. . . . His was a very well-stocked mind."[19]

Watson was the Section wordsmith. If a document was targeted for a significant readership, it was certain that Watson had a major hand in it. His were the phrases people remembered and loved to quote. Bruce missed him "like the devil" when he was not there to oversee final preparation of a bulletin. So fluent, yet, according to Ealand, he would sometimes spend hours searching for the perfect word. His secretary, Gladys Watson (no relation), "a wonderful old girl," efficient and precise with pince-nez perched just so, occasionally startled and amused Watson, interrupting his dictation when a big word such as "architectonic" came up. Leaning forward and in a loud voice, she would command: "Spell it."[20]

Dedicated as he was to the Treasury art programs, however, the substance of it never engaged him as fully as *The Arts* had, nor ignited his fervor to the flashpoint. Cook Glassgold for one believed that "much of the edge and sharpness seemed to have worn off. He appeared not to be as penetrating as he had formerly been." Some of Watson's colleagues at the Treasury Department too, those who had not known the Forbes Watson of *Arts* days, saw a figure quite different from the lacerating commentator and peerless raconteur Olin Dows and friends from the twenties admired. Even in the eyes of as sisterly an associate as Maria Ealand, Watson was a "loquacious" gossip who "spent hours over a scotch and soda describing and dissecting the artists he knew, and many he didn't." While his standing among peers in the art world remained high, new acquaintances remarked first his penchant for alcohol, parties, and women. Charlotte Partridge, for example, director of Layton Art School in Milwaukee and a former regional director of PWAP, "liked him very much, aside from the fact he drank too much. That was too bad," she observed. "but oh could he write!"[21]

The wives of some of his colleagues, quite probably objects at one time or another of his "roving eye," also held a different view.[22] Ed Rowan's pretty wife, Leata, deflated Watson's trial balloon early on. To his ostensibly generic letter to her concerning a magazine article, which began "Dear Leata," and ended, "I am more than ever anxious to see you again. Love and Kisses," she replied with a gracious bread-and-butter note to her husband's boss. "Dear Mr. Watson," it began, and closed with a courteous "Most cordially yours."[23]

When Watson started the *Bulletin of the Section of Painting and Sculpture* on March 1, 1935, distribution was limited to three thousand copies, he and the others having decided not to send it to those "who would only be disappointed if they applied for painting or sculpture jobs."[24] Circulation eventually reached ten thousand, however, as the periodical became a demonstrably effective organ for broadening interest in the Treasury art programs.

At the height of Section activity, issues of the *Bulletin,* which appeared irregularly, averaged eighteen to twenty pages, though some exceeded thirty. The introduction of photographic reproductions in September 1938 added interest, but the *Bulletin* intentionally remained a relatively low-budget, no-frills publication. Watson was the principal writer and ghostwriter. Dows was actively involved, and Rowan, Hopper, and other Section and TRAP members contributed items and ideas. It tracked all Section competitions and reported on major TRAP activities. It contained news about competition winners and appointees, biographies, notices about exhibitions of section art, updates on legislation, excerpts from official statements and current periodicals, and artists' comments. Reginald Marsh and Henry Varnum Poor were among the prominent artists who contributed.

While the *Bulletin's* purpose was to offer "straightforward, unbiased and clear information about each and every project," it was not the "small dignified . . .

Frank Long, *Indiana Agriculture*. Oil on canvas. Mural in Crawfordsville, Indiana, post office, 1942. Section of Fine Arts, Public Buildings Administration, Federal Works Agency, Washington, D.C. Forbes Watson Papers.

publication" Watson originally had in mind. Bruce, concerned that the average artist might not quickly grasp the opportunities presented or might confuse Section projects with those of the WPA (a persistent problem), insisted on a concrete, popular level of communication. By the end of the first year, all issues contained step-by-step expositions and plenty of recapitulation.[25] There would have been more "chatty material" too, if Bruce had had his way. In all, twenty-four issues of the *Bulletin* appeared, from March 1935 through May 1941. Read in sequence, they provide an account of the projects themselves, which included art for buildings and monuments, ships, posters, postage stamps, and coins, and running testimonials to the general benefactions of the Treasury art programs. By the forties, another theme emerged, the decencies of government art during a time of global indecencies, reflecting the Section's struggle to remain significant in the midst of the international crisis of World War II.[26]

Admiral Peoples set the tone in the inaugural issue, suggesting to artists: "Take advantage of the advice of those people who are not only experienced in matters

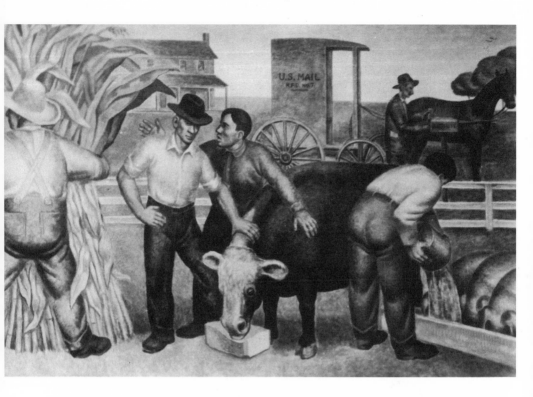

of art, but, through their residence in the place where the particular building is, have a special interest in the artists and in the life of that region." So advising, SPS officials indicated at the outset their emphasis on localism. As with PWAP art earlier, familiarity was considered to be the key to public acceptance. All agreed with Henry Varnum Poor that complicated or highly intellectual ideas were "something to surmount rather than a real help." Louis Simon "heartily" endorsed a sample issue of the new illustrated *Bulletin* but cautioned Watson, "in selecting these illustrations may I suggest the exercise of a brand of conservatism that is not *too* liberal and beyond the reach of ordinary intellects."[27]

By then, Watson, too, acknowledged the precedence of veracity over aesthetics in engaging the average citizen. His response to Milton Avery's design for the Rockville, Indiana, post office mural suggested he had all but abandoned his long-standing regard for distortion in artistic expression. Avery would gain recognition as one of America's outstanding modernists during the succeeding decades, but for the Section, those very qualities which distinguished him later were problematic now. Watson was dismayed during a progress visit to Avery's studio. "He is very poor, with an anxious wife and a charming kid," Watson noted in his trip report. "All three of them sat down with me to hear just what I had to say about a mural which, to put it mildly, is something. . . . I explained as gently as I could, with clarity, that I couldn't help feeling that the landscape which he had painted had so little of the character of the place that I doubted if it would be a satisfactory mural." Never having seen Indiana and too poor to travel, Avery's wife had collected photos. "While I should like to give a favorable opinion of the mural to save their distress, I feel that Mr. Avery has not understood the problem. He has painted a landscape with a single very badly drawn cow. . . . Mr. Avery has a distinguished sense of color and a great fear of realism. The result is that he has painted a mural which in spite of some fine passages, is rather soft and unconvincing."[28]

In a similar vein, Watson offered a tip to John Sloan concerning his design for the Bronxville, New York, post office: "I thought you would like to know that mural paintings, by going into post offices and court rooms in different parts of the country, are beginning to build up a body of natural criticism— not the affected stuff that so many of our scribes indulge in. From this criticism we are learning that the people in general are particularly interested in scale and in drawing. They always notice whether a horse, for example, is completely convincing; they always notice hands and the relative sizes of figures." Indeed, letters from local citizens and comments from sidewalk spectators attested to their wariness of aberrations.[29] Even though Washington controlled the money and commissions, administrators had a frank fear of public controversy and went to great lengths to accommodate local aesthetics.

The Section's attempts to think locally and act centrally were illustrated most hyperbolically in the "48-State Competition" held in 1939, the most far-reaching, heavily publicized program they attempted. Artists from anywhere in the country could submit designs for any or several of forty-eight mural commissions, one for a designated post office in each state of the union. The mammoth competition attracted 1,476 submissions, and the jury took five days to select winners. Artists had been strongly urged to visit post offices for which they submitted designs, but not all of them did. Moreover, some artists were awarded commissions to decorate post offices they had not designed for. Even where artists visited the site and conferred with locals, however, their renditions did not necessarily meet with hometown approbation. Measured in terms of community reception, the forty-eight murals ranged in success from friendly acclaim to noisy fiasco, but one thing was certain, neighborhood critics kept Section officials hustling.[30]

With administrators in Washington and projects dispersed throughout the country, supervision was carried out largely through the mail. Whenever feasible, Rowan, Watson, Dows, or Hopper visited artists and installation sites and conferred with local officials to assess progress, determine the need for modifications, and decide whether payments were due the artists.[31] Bruce relished their trip reports, the more detailed and gossipy the better. Their candid insights not only apprised him of the course of a project but also gave him a feel for the local political situation, which he relied on for strategies.

Site trips were usually a day or two but sometimes a week if several proximate inspections were combined. Watson made one memorable two-month-long countrywide tour in 1937. For the veteran of the public relations–lecture circuit, it was more than an inspection tour: it was an opportunity. The central office set up so many lectures along the way that Ealand feared the schedule might drain him, but the Watsons were keen travelers, exhilarated by the hectic pace and diverse contacts. In addition to inspection rounds, Watson lectured at every stop, sometimes several times a day. He gave interviews to the local press and talked on the radio. He visited the studios of "a great many artists," observed art classes, and sold copies of the book he and Bruce had recently written, *Art in Federal Buildings*. With Nan accompanying him and maintaining a daily journal, Watson visited twenty-two cities between April 3 and May 24, lectured to approximately six thousand people, and examined not only the work being done under the Treasury Department but that under the WPA as well.[32] He also managed to take in local landmarks and cultural attractions and renew acquaintances with hundreds of old friends while making countless new ones at luncheons, dinners, receptions, and parties arranged in his honor. The old "bacchanalian and epicurean cognoscente" relished the tour so much and felt it so worthwhile that he was all for embarking on another almost immediately upon his return to Washington.[33]

Watson's reports, the most spirited and entertaining of any, were typically merciless toward the "dodo," the "moron," the "brainless old ass," and the "astoundingly bad" picture. Elise Seeds's *Airmail* panel of an airplane in flight for the Oceanside Post Office looked to Watson "a bit like a huge dead herring suspended over an equally dead world." Omaha was "a place to make you feel like a snob and like it." Favorable observations far outweighed the negative, however, as Watson believed most of the artists were giving "the very best that was in them."[34]

While affirming his confidence in the program and his gratification with the widespread enthusiasm it had engendered, several of the recommendations in Watson's fifty-one-page final report hinted at disappointment in the overall artistic production. The Section of Painting and Sculpture should make a greater effort to know the artists personally, he advised, and "concentrate on securing . . . only work of a very high standard." He urged greater cooperation between architects and the Section to secure more propitious spaces and lighting for art. He further recommended that the spirit of rivalry between the

Section and WPA artists be discouraged. The Section could only lose if WPA artists were polarized and did not enter its competitions.[35]

"Art that Belongs to the People" was the title of the prepared lecture he delivered at each stop, and it was also the title of a White House talk he presented in February 1938. Perpetually in need of money, Watson accepted speaking engagements of all kinds, from a "lay" presentation at the Tuckahoe Woman's Club to formal lectures at Harvard, Yale, and the Universities of California and Chicago. Many, but not all, dealt with the government art programs. If he traveled to a particular town on Section business, the lecture was free, since the government prohibited employees from collecting fees if they received travel expenses and a per diem allowance ($5 in lieu of subsistence). Otherwise, he charged an honorarium, usually $100, though later $150 and expenses. Despite his experience as a speaker, and as much as he enjoyed the public contact, Watson "was always in a state of extreme nervousness beforehand," according to Ealand. Nan's journal of the inspection tours did not suggest nervousness on his part so much as unusually disciplined preparation and meticulous attention to slide selection.[36]

Up until the creation of the Section of Painting and Sculpture, Watson effectually wrote off American mural painting as tamely pretentious, "untouched by the fervor" of imagination. With the exception of John LaFarge and a handful of other nineteenth-century artists, traditional American muralists were "imbued with a kind of vapid hysteria of idealism." He also dismissed the cooperative muralists, who would have benefited from "the cooperation of a little talent with their obvious good faith," and American versions of the "recent dowdy pomposities of the overrated Mexican sociologists." Compounding the sorry state of mural art in the United States were the "reactionary" architects, who favored "the gentle sanities of scrap-book painting" for their buildings.[37]

Even as he assumed the directorship of the Public Works of Art Project in 1933, Watson believed that "if most of the American murals, past and present, were removed and a few good pictures hung in their places the walls would look much better." More than one thousand fresco and mural projects later, he remained unimpressed. In response to Theodore Sizer's complaint that murals were underrepresented in PWAP's National Exhibition, Watson pointed to the difficulty of exhibiting them, adding, "since we are a nation of easel painters more than a nation of mural painters, I feel that there is still some justice in the world."[38]

Pomposity and pretentiousness notwithstanding, murals were the main work of the Section of Painting and Sculpture, and Watson was ipso facto their chief exponent. Faced with the challenge of converting his disrespect to respect, he looked to the democratic imperative. Of all artists, the muralist had the greatest community responsibility, Watson reasoned, inasmuch as that person was commissioned to create location-specific images that would tell the average citizen a story he could understand. Unlike the easel painter, the muralist did not create for himself and then sell his work as a product. He served the community first.[39]

Among Watson's most enduring contributions to the government's mural programs was a book he coauthored with Bruce, *Art in Federal Buildings*. The idea for it had begun to crystallize by early 1936, as Watson and the others became convinced that the works themselves had the greatest power to persuade artists of the validity of the Treasury programs. Dows and Hopper discovered early on that it was worthwhile to lug cumbersome folios of photographs of Section art along on inspection tours, as the murals had an "amazing" effect on those who were currently involved in projects. "They feel entirely differently about the Project after they have seen them," Hopper noted in a trip report.[40]

The book was projected to be a multivolume set, of which volume one, *Mural Designs, 1934-1936*, was to be "a complete reference book" of the preliminary studies and designs for murals in federal buildings. Volume two was to cover sculpture, and a later volume would illustrate the completed murals and other decorative work. The goal was to "bring out a good-looking book that doesn't cost too much money." It was Watson's kind of undertaking. "Naturally, I am madly excited about getting up this book as it is right down my alley," he wrote Bruce. "It is a book that will convince the skeptical." With assistance from Dows and the Section and TRAP staffs, Watson tackled the project with the enthusiasm and sureness of the old *Arts* days.[41]

Since there was no legally authorized government funding, the book, a non-profit venture, was financed privately through an incorporation agreement. Dows was president, Watson was vice president, and Cecil Jones was secretary-treasurer.[42] The editors volunteered their services. Dows personally provided the initial capitalization of $3,000 and secured financing up to $6,500. He had hoped to pass on revenues from book sales to the artists, but it was decided to use the income to defray costs and finance a second volume.

Uptown in a small room on the tenth floor of the Barr Building, Watson and Dows set up the Art in Federal Buildings operation, hiring a young woman, Jane Watson (no relation to Forbes), to assemble the material for the book and handle the paperwork. The office was two floors up from the American Federation of Arts suite, which housed the *American Magazine of Art*. Jane Watson, a cousin-in-law of Henry LaFarge and the sister of an old schoolmate of Olin Dows, had come down from New York City to visit her friend Alice Graeme Korff and was "quite bowled over." The air in Washington was so filled with optimism compared to the depression gloom of New York that she stayed on.[43] She later became an assistant editor at the *American Magazine of Art* and an art editor at the *Washington Post.*

Art in Federal Buildings, volume one, appeared in November 1936 in two editions, an artists' edition and a limited library edition at $4.50 and $10.00, respectively.[44] It was a well-produced, handsome book, wide enough (13.5 inches) to do justice to mural illustrations. There were 490 reproductions of Section and TRAP mural designs, 380 line cuts of architectural drawings showing their positions in the buildings, and 29 quality half-tone reproductions of earlier American murals. The arrangement of reproductions alphabetically by artist's name rather than geographically underscored their centrality, as did the biographical index of the 125 artists represented. Bruce wrote a preface and described the purpose and procedures of the Treasury Department Art Program. Watson wrote an introductory essay, "A Perspective of American Murals."

Artists and critics received the book enthusiastically, and sales were brisk, though not brisk enough. "Even in those days, I do not see how volume one could have sold at $5.00 to begin with without loss," Jane Watson reflected. Publication had been "a very expensive proposition because of the quality of the reproductions and the paper on which it was printed." Costs far exceeded original estimates, "and there seemed at the outset no very practical way to handle the distribution."[45] By December it was clear that the operation was in financial trouble. Dows and Bruce turned to the American Federation of Arts, which took over distribution of the book. Soon afterward, the "artists' edition" became the "regular edition" with a price increase of $2.00. Still, several thousand unsold copies remained in storage, for which Dows paid rent for nearly ten years.

A small number of copies of *Art in Federal Buildings* were sold through the Art in Federal Buildings Corporation, which also published guides and distributed Watson's monograph on Aaron Sopher in 1940. For the most part, however, the corporation remained more or less inactive, not unlike the Arts Publishing Corporation after the cessation of *The Arts.* In April 1938, the Carnegie Corporation, under the enlightened presidency of Frederick Keppel, a sympathetic friend and steadfast supporter of Bruce and the Section, donated six thousand dollars toward the publication of the second volume. Helen Appleton Read was tentatively scheduled to carry out the work, but the book never materialized. Although *Art in Federal Buildings* did not become the comprehensive multivolume set Watson first envisioned, the single volume, *Mural Designs, 1934-1936,* endures today as the most informative pictorial source on Treasury murals of that period in federal arts history.

As notable as the images, Watson's introduction pointed up more lucidly than any contemporary document the nexus for the Treasury programs, the advance of American mural art, and the social benefits of that alliance. Its three principal themes were: First, mural art was in a state of decline until the advent of the Section, which forged a more harmonious union between the architect and the artist. More precisely, the Section removed decision-making power from the architect and gave it to the artist. Second, as a consequence of timely governmental stimulation, a more "courageous" mural art flourished in America. Third, thanks to the Treasury art programs, Americans throughout the country could visit their local post office and courthouse and enjoy "good contemporary art."[46]

Encouraged by readers' responses to, if not by the revenue from, *Art in Federal Buildings,* Watson embarked on a series of illustrated art guides in 1938. The first, self-guided tour books to the murals and sculptures in Justice Department and Post Office buildings, were handy, brightly colored paperbacks containing brief descriptive material, illustrations, biographies, and a convenient map. They cost twenty-five cents a copy. Like *Art in Federal Buildings,* the guides were published privately under the auspices of the Art in Federal Buildings Corporation. Watson had hopes that the series would eventually turn into "a real publishing thing," pay its own way, and even expand into nongovernmental art.[47] Unfortunately, there were no facilities on the premises for vending the guides, since government concessions then were granted only to the physically handicapped to sell snacks and soft drinks. Later, when the country was at war, security guards were posted at all entrances, discouraging the public from entering, just to view art. So this publishing project too did not advance.

The "real publishing thing" did not materialize, but Watson continued to contribute to several magazines. Also, he had been appointed to the Columbia University Department of Fine Arts summer faculty, where he taught American painting from 1900 to the present. The weeklong course, which was offered every summer for five years, consisted of four lectures with slides. At forty dollars per lecture, he could quickly pick up extra income and still make it to Harbor Springs for most of the season.[48] "There is a lot you could teach them," his friend Allen Tucker observed encouragingly.[49] And Watson did. It was another opportunity to spread the word.

Clearly, though, his options were dwindling. His own financial distress, together with that of countless American artists, had brought him to his present situation, "front man" for the Treasury art programs. In the opinion of George Biddle, he had become "just a mouthpiece for the Section." Although his colleagues insisted Watson was "genuine," a man of "rock bottom integrity," there was no denying that the "objective, dispassionate judgment" that Cook Glass-gold had observed in him earlier had receded behind a showy one-sidedness.[50] Expedience offered a compelling explanation for Watson's recently relaxed critical attitude, but there was something else as well. The persistently uninspiring level of much of the Treasury art he was obliged to promote was something for which even the more pedestrian entries in the Society for Independent Artists shows had not prepared him. Could its general sameness have dulled his customary critical edge? Whether it was opportunism on his part or the mediocrity of the art itself, Watson's potent gift for words seemed increasingly rechanneled from critical mode to campaign mode, and from art to art personalities.

8 CONFIRMED NEW DEALER, 1936–1942

The year Watson published the first volume of *Art in Federal Buildings,* 1936, was also the year he and Nan finally found a place that suited them. In the fall they moved to 1400 Fairmont Street Northwest, the twenty-three-year-old Fontanet Court. It was a large apartment, ideal for their kind of entertaining, with a good room for Nan's studio. As in their New York residence, they filled the walls with paintings by artist friends. It had taken a while, but Nan had adjusted to Washington, joining the Washington Artists' Guild and becoming acquainted with local artists' circles. She had exhibited in the Corcoran Biennial that spring and there were upcoming shows. By the time they settled in at the Fontanet Court, she was "very happy," Watson wrote Edward Bruce, "working regularly and comfortably, and now that she has added her sales to the number of seven, she thinks that she is pretty hot stuff. At least, I think she does. You know the Scotch always hide their enthusiasm about themselves."[1]

Though a little farther away now, Forbes and Nan still managed to see Watson's sister, Mary, from time to time. A portrait of Mary, *The Artist's Wife,* which her late husband, Alfred Quinton Collins, had painted nearly forty years earlier, was featured on the cover of *Coronet* magazine in April 1937. The original work was in the permanent collection of the Metropolitan Museum of Art. It was easy to see Forbes's resemblance to the young woman in the well-mannered portrait, gazing straight out at the world with cool, composed assurance. There was the same slightly long face and smooth, high forehead and the same distinctively arched eyebrows, though hers had a fine, imperial curve. Mary seldom visited Forbes's Washington office, but each time she did, Maria Ealand was impressed with the "handsome," "carefully dressed," and "charming"

CORONET

"INFINITE RICHES IN A LITTLE ROOM"

APRIL, 1937

THIRTY-FIVE CENTS

IN GREAT BRITAIN 2/6

Forbes Watson's sister

Cover of *Coronet* magazine, April 1937. *The Artist's Wife,* Mary Collins, Watson's sister.

"proper Bostonian." "There was an air of distinction about her," Lloyd Goodrich observed, "which showed the kind of background Forbes came from. . . . And you had a feeling of her aristocracy, of mind, of a quality." Except for Mary, Forbes and Nan had only occasional contact with the Watson side of the family, mostly the nieces and nephews. They saw more of Nan's brothers' families and a good deal of Alice Paterson, Nan's younger sister, a high-school chemistry teacher who lived on West Fourth Street in New York City. "Forbes couldn't stand her," Ealand recalled. "She was very Republican." Watson's letters to mutual friends made frequent mention of Alice, usually in exasperated or teasing tones, but there was unmistakable affection there. The fact was that the entire Paterson clan, except Nan, was devoutly Republican.[2]

For his part, Watson had become a confirmed "New Dealer," both in politics and art, and he carried his crusade over to nongovernment enterprises as well. He included a heavy component on federal art in the course he taught at Columbia. "The more tired school teachers who hear me," he wrote Bruce, "the more in their weary way they will spread the gospel to those corners of the earth from which Columbia University takes up its summer attendance."[3]

A lecture he delivered at the Metropolitan Museum of Art in 1935 demonstrated the sly tactician's brazen bent for stacking the deck. "I got slides of all the very worst things in the Library of Congress," he confided to Bruce, "including . . . a terribly weak sentimental nothing by Blashfield called 'Human Understanding' . . . , and some other atrocities. . . . I said to the audience that I . . . wanted them to come to their own conclusions and that what I intended to do was to show them what the government had done by the old method and what the government was doing under the new method. Through the selection of slides I made everything we had done look like a masterpiece. And I didn't set up any counter irritation by over praise."[4]

In addition to official documents—issues of the *Bulletin,* reports, exhibition catalogs, and press releases—Watson published two books and nine major magazine articles devoted exclusively to the Treasury art programs. Occasionally eloquent, at times strained and circumlocutory, each preached a variation of the same message: That government patronage was good for the American artist and the artist was good for America. By 1939, most read like inspired tracts. "Could there be a stronger force than the knowledge of the artist that he can live in his own community, develop his ideas out of a well rooted existence and sell his art to a client who buys it without ulterior motive?" Watson asked in an article in the new *Kenyon Review* magazine. Indeed, he concluded, it was fair "to characterize it [the government] as a powerful new force in American art."[5]

Watson further described the "powerful new force" in an introduction to *American Painting Today,* which the American Federation of Arts published that same year. F. Allen Whiting Jr., editor of *American Magazine of Art,* assembled the book of paintings by 184 living artists who represented, in Watson's words, the "new order" in American art. The "new order" being a direct outcome of the federal art programs, he focused not on the painters or reproductions but on their rescue by the government from the dealer-created mire of artificial luxury.[6]

Watson's conversion seemed complete. The old artist-centered aesthetic had given way to a community-centered vision. A decade earlier he had rhapsodized over the "capricious spirit" of an artist such as Jules Pascin and the wayward unconventionality of his "willful, fantastic, intransigent" work.[7] Now the indomitable artist of Watson's paradigm had become a regular citizen, indistinguishable from others in the community except as his artistry emerged through government projects.

Abandoning his twenty-year crusade for artistic independence, Watson had transformed the term "individualism" into one of derogation, equating it with egocentrism, extremes of abstractionism, and the recent shenanigans of publicity-minded artists seeking "new ways of scorning the facts." The artist had become "a law unto himself," gloating over the average citizen's inability to understand his production. In moving from "soloist" in the days of "hyperindividualism" to "a member of the orchestra" under the government's mural program, the artist graduated from "a lonely and isolated life" into one in which "a sturdier, healthier and stronger school of artists" would develop. "I believe that the great new advance in the art of today is going to come out of, or evolve from, a less individual and more cooperative theme," Watson told his friends at Woodstock. It was a measure of his conversion that he had even come to endorse a notion he once loved to belittle, the "educational" possibilities of art. The coincidence of Watson's own course from free-speaking editor of *The Arts* to civil team-player was compelling.[8]

Vestiges of his earlier positions endured, not advanced confrontationally as in the past but still there, occasionally in tandem with promotional output. While Section of Painting and Sculpture administrators, including himself, urged more lifelike portrayals, Watson continued to insist that "facts . . . remain subservient to design." "Are our eyes becoming so accustomed to colloquial subject matter that the story is the thing and we no longer see abstract quality?" he complained.[9]

Particularly in his independent writing was Watson's aesthetic bifocalism apparent. His comments on art outside the aegis of government suggested at times an uncompromised critical rigor and a more-or-less uninterrupted progression of his ideas from *The Arts* years. He applauded the inventiveness of Dunoyer de Segonzac, whose works were "never copies—always creations." He paid tribute to the "arbitrary, personal, and abstract" color of Max Weber, the master of American abstract artists, and endorsed Weber's statement: "Art dies when naturalism dominates."[10]

In one particularly nonconforming essay, Watson took aim at those who enshrined the average in art, arguing for a return to elegance. "When men and women are crying for bread it may be slightly perverse to come to the defense of so old-fashioned an attribute, so grandmotherly an ideal, as elegance," he wrote. "It implies an unawareness of our descent into necessitous realisms. Yet refinement and symmetry which are inherent in elegance are qualities that continue to beckon us in the midst of the battle for more tangible needs." Elegance signified "distinction of expression" and the refinement he had once pinpointed as uniquely American in American art. It "is never born of compromise," he declared. Elegance was achieved when both the artist and his audience were "deeply civilized." Linking elegant art to the socially secure artist esteemed by the socially secure patron, the unregenerate mugwump looked not to government but to art schools and colleges to create a new public. Citizens emerging from their training would support art and demand from the artist a civilized product.[11]

Americans would have to part ways with "the shirt-sleeved and suspendered," "the gum chewers," and "the boobish and uncultivated mortals" whom the "go-getters of regionalism" held up as the noblest products of democracy if they were to discover "such light symbols of elegance as gaiety, social charm, delicate manners and refinement." They would have to relinquish the notion "that all urban life is carried on . . . in the slums and that all country life goes on amidst a conglomeration of shacks and barns which long since lost their level lines." Nor was it necessary for the civilized painter to be strident. "Tact, reticence, discretion and clearness are the native heritage of such an artist," he declared, "as many worlds removed from the vulgar lackeyism of the flattering portrait painter as . . . from crass and muddle-headed imitation sociology."[12] So much for "the people" and "democracy."

If Watson saw no need to reconcile his dissonant approaches to uncommissioned art and federally sponsored art, it was because at bottom he viewed the latter as predominantly social. To encourage the artist to create within the mainstream and to value his artistic contribution, these were the goals that powered Section and Treasury Relief Art Project programs. Even though he and Bruce sought quality art, not relief, there was implicit acknowledgment that in forging a widely receptive audience for art, aesthetic expectations would inevitably be lowered. Assuming social goals to be paramount, artistic standards could be tacitly slanted and compromised in their pursuit. Thus, with the onset of the Great Depression and the compassionate response of the New Deal arts programs, Watson moved from the tenuous accommodation he had once achieved between aesthetic and democratic values toward a more encompassing quest for democracy. A wide gap had opened since the decade when he praised the Arts Club of Chicago for its refusal to "cajole and appeal to undeveloped taste" or compromise for the "popular vote."[13]

At the same time, Watson's anti-elitist instincts took on a sharper economic thrust. Even as he sought to integrate the artist into the community, he accentuated the polarities between the artist and the establishment: wealthy versus poor artists, collectors versus artists, museums versus artists, sanctimonious benefactors versus government employers of artists. Powerful forces "out there" were exploiting the American artist, perpetuating his underdog status, Watson asserted. In a review of the Pittsburgh International show, he denigrated the city's "possessively nationalistic and conservative" millionaires, noting, "one of their Andrews [Carnegie] could endow our greatest annual international art exhibits while another of their Andrews [Mellon] can buy the costliest old masters. And far beneath the palaces on the hill the hunkies sweat."[14]

Such remarks, though faintly suggestive of socialist dogma, did not signify political radicalism. Watson had little tolerance for those who looked at the Soviet Union "through rose-colored glasses" and "cry like babies for communism." Even during the severest years of economic hardship, when artists' organizations moved left, Watson not only did not embrace socialism, he actively scorned it. "Gentlemen in brown shirts with a 5 o'clock shadow threatening . . . control of U.S. culture" only increased his disdain. Nor did propaganda art gain legitimacy in his eyes because times were hard.[15]

He nicely differentiated between the literary and the ideological in the Artist Union's magazine, *Art Front,* advising readers that however unsympathetic one might be toward *Art Front*'s economic program, "only the rather stupidly prejudiced" could resist the "wit, sincerity and purpose," of many of its pieces.[16] But kudos notwithstanding, friction between Stuart Davis, its editor, and Watson erupted in hostile discourse throughout the thirties, with Davis vociferously assaulting the Section, TRAP, and the Works Progress Administration for their exclusionary practices, and Watson countering with civilized irony.

Shortly after the publication of Watson's paeanistic article "The Chance in a Thousand" in August 1935, Davis published a belligerent rejoinder, "Some Chance," in which he accused Watson and other Section "functionaries" of rigging the so-called open anonymous competitions. By appointing businessmen, museum directors, and other elitists to do the initial screening, he charged, and then packing the artist juries, the Section excluded modern, abstract, and proletarian artists. Secretly, the officials also knew the identity of the anonymous competitors. Watson came in for the worst drubbing, as Davis cited parallels between statements by Watson and those of Thomas Craven and Fred McCormick, linking him indirectly to the "fascist Hearst." Small wonder Davis was one of the few exclusions from Watson's commodious galaxy of American stars.[17]

But attacks from the left were not as big a headache as opposition from the right, particularly within the program. Over the years, the Commission of Fine Arts, whose members George Biddle referred to as "nine old geese," had repeatedly derailed Treasury projects. In addition, there were the architects, whose resistance was subtler and more pervasive. Even after years of collaborating, and despite expressions of mutual cooperation, neither the architects nor the artists were won over to the other's view. As late as 1938, Watson was still struggling "to get the hideously reactionary architects ... to arrange for spaces in the buildings that may be called fairly mural spaces." An exasperated Bruce was more explicit. "The small murals in the little type post offices make one sick to the stomach as the greatest picture in the world would [look] like hell in these nasty little spaces which these architects provide for use. ... When I get back I am going to declare war on that damn little squirt Louis Simon, who has no interest in art and who will never give us a suitable space. ... As it is now I am almost in a frame of mind to suggest that we discontinue doing any of these murals in the little type post offices. They are at best hardly more than little pill boxes, and perhaps a better description would be unattractive, untidy little privies."[18]

Adversaries notwithstanding, the Section of Painting and Sculpture gained support throughout the 1930s. Its competitions attracted artists nationwide, and the public grew increasingly receptive to art, having come to embrace cultural enrichment as part of the New Deal's social-reform program. Given the patent success of the Section and the WPA, it was not surprising that calls for a permanent federal art agency proliferated. Watson's own experience had convinced him of the government's efficaciousness in alleviating artists' despair, but it had also solidified his distrust of the bureaucracy. There was a vast difference between the Section, with its clearly defined purposes, and a permanent government department so inclusive "that no single human being could possibly grasp its scope." Then there was the problem of politics. How could the country be assured that such an agency would be directed by an appointee who arrived at his high position "without the testing of a single political wire?"[19] As Congress proposed a succession of permanent offices of fine arts between 1934 and the early 1950s, Watson attacked each one.

Two from Representative William I. Sirovich (Democrat, New York) drew his heaviest fire. The first, offered in March 1935 (H.R. 220), provided for the establishment of a department of science, art, and literature with a cabinet-level director and three undersecretaries. While Adm. Christian Joy Peoples, Simon, and Bruce testified with apparent equanimity before the House Committee on Patents, Watson decimated both the resolution and the congressmen who drafted it, citing not only the bill's potentiality for "political chicanery" and "tricks and travesties" but also the authors' dubious mental capacity. As evidence, he quoted passages from the resolution, "facts wrapped up in tripe," and urged readers to voice their opposition, which they did.[20] The bill died in committee.

Sirovich's second major bill, coauthored with Representative John M. Coffee (Democrat, Washington) in August 1937 and introduced in the Senate by Claude E. Pepper (Democrat, Florida), contained more specific provisions, one of which would transfer the Section and the WPA to the authority of the Bureau of Fine Arts. That aroused even more passionate debate, which raged for nearly a year before that proposal too was defeated.[21]

The failure of the Coffee-Pepper bill was a victory for both government arts programs, and came in a year of further promise. In October 1938, Secretary of the Treasury Henry Morgenthau made the Section of Painting and Sculpture a permanent unit of the Treasury Department, known thereafter as the Section of Fine Arts, thus bringing greater certainty to the 1 percent allocation for building embellishment. Thanks to Bruce's resourcefulness, the Section had managed to maintain amiable relations with other federal units and at the same time hold the line against the kind of political pressure congressmen, with "their little projects," and even art organizations exerted. It helped, of course, having the full backing of the president. Franklin Roosevelt was very proud of the arts program, according to Henry Morgenthau, who had heard him remark, "one hundred years from now my administration will be known for its art, not its relief." Morgenthau himself was a close friend as well. "The Bruces must have eaten in his house at least once a week in Washington." The support of these men was "the great, great open Sesame," Hopper remembered, "and it saved our necks so many times." Elinor Morgenthau, who more than her husband and more than Eleanor Roosevelt had the interest and time to get personally involved with the cause, was especially helpful in resolving a few difficult administrative matters. Both she and Mrs. Roosevelt had very conservative taste in art, Hopper thought, but both were benevolent and sincerely interested in doing something for artists.[22]

Unfortunately, the situation changed in April 1939 with the passage of the Administrative Reorganization Act. Formulated to simplify the innumerable boards, commissions, and agencies of the federal government and thereby increase efficiency, the act consolidated unit after unit, including the Public Buildings Branch of the Treasury, which was converted to the Public Buildings Administration of the Public Works Agency. Under presidential order, the Section of Fine Arts was transferred from the Treasury Department to the Federal Works Agency. Instead of Henry Morgenthau and Admiral Peoples, the Section thereafter reported to John M. Carmody, federal works administrator, and W. E. (Burt) Reynolds, commissioner of public buildings. In moving out of Morgenthau's jurisdiction, the Section lost the sympathetic support of the man who was perhaps closer than anyone in the cabinet to Roosevelt, and one of the very few with both power and an interest in art.[23]

Procedures remained the same, and the Section continued to occupy offices in the Procurement Division Building for the time being, but the old sense of security and a comfortable relationship with administrative superiors were gone. "You may tell Ned Bruce he has lost none of his old friends and gained some new ones as a result of reorganization," Carmody wrote the president reassuringly. Morgenthau had spoken with Carmody and conveyed "his special interest in the art project and the special interest you and Mrs. Roosevelt and Mrs. Morgenthau had taken in it." Indeed, Carmody believed, "a practical working agreement along the lines of his one percent suggestion" was "entirely possible."[24] Unfortunately, he could not deliver on his assurances.

Following the transfer, Edward Bruce made several unsuccessful efforts to get out from under the Federal Works Agency. His final attempt, incorporation with the proposed Smithsonian Gallery of Art, would have ensured a sympathetic home and a base from which to expand the Section's operation. But because of conservative resistance to Eliel Saarinen's architectural design for the gallery, though primarily because of preoccupation with the war in Europe, plans did not go forward.

Up until the beginning of World War II, Americans had concentrated on domestic matters, despite growing anxiety over the spread of fascism abroad. Between 1935 and 1937, the president and Congress reacted to the aggressions of Hitler and Mussolini in Europe, Japan in Asia, and civil war in Spain with a series of neutrality acts. But when Hitler invaded Poland in September 1939, provoking Great Britain and France to declare war on Germany, strict neutrality became difficult. As the Germans systematically crushed first Poland, then Denmark, Norway, the Netherlands, Belgium, and France, an interventionist mood gradually supplanted the isolationism of the 1930s. The first peacetime conscription act was passed in September 1940, creating an atmosphere of war preparedness as more than a million men were drafted into the service. When Japan officially joined the Axis that September, relations between that nation and the United States, already strained, became precarious. Lend-Lease, the arming of merchant ships, and the shipment of war material across the Atlantic to Britain brought the United States as close to war as it could get without an official declaration.

It was impossible not to think about war. Watson sympathized with Bruce, who was distracted from his painting. "Nan is having a tough time too," he wrote, "and artist after artist tells me how difficult it is to keep the mind on the paint brush under the curse of Hitler."[25] Bruce, Watson, and the others watched as Hitler's relentless advance through Europe brought an accompanying recession in art interest in the United States. Much as Roosevelt sympathized with Bruce's aims, America's security and military preparedness had to take precedence. By the end of 1940, Congress had severely cut appropriations for building programs, and the Public Buildings Administration was ordered to stop all new construction.

Alone in the apartment in July 1940, fighting off discouragement, Watson radically revised his Columbia University lectures, making the main theme "the importance of keeping American art going at this time and to that end keeping the Section of Fine Arts going." The old apartment was lonely without Nan, "but," he wrote Bruce, "I have to work evenings and Sundays to get my lectures ready so I manage to get by all right."[26] Two of his oldest and dearest friends had died recently, William Glackens in 1938 and Allen Tucker in 1939, both major losses to the American art community and to Watson personally; he wrote movingly of each in memorial exhibition catalogs. Not surprising, the upcoming election was also on his mind that summer, especially after he joined Nan in conservative Harbor Springs. He was resolved to remain optimistic. "I have a hunch that even if Willkie is elected we shall go on with the Section of Fine Arts," he wrote Bruce. "That is due in part to the fan mail I have received from my editorials dwelling on the necessity of keeping the art movement going at this time and partly due to the response to my lectures."[27]

Left with relatively meager funds from earlier allocations and unsuccessful in raising private funds, Bruce tried to finish as many existing contracts as possible, instructing artists to complete designs and cartoons only and postpone installation. All new and circuiting exhibitions were deferred. There were still a few competitions, designs for the new War Department building (the future Pentagon) and also for cargo and passenger vessels in the Maritime Commission's American President Lines. But with a cap on new construction and little interest on the part of the Maritime Commission in additional ship decorations, the Section's embellishment program was stymied. Bruce also looked to the possibility of financing Section projects out of allotments for the renovation of public buildings, but in this sphere Congress had the final authority and seized the opportunity to block the effort.[28]

As Bruce doggedly searched for funding, Watson argued the case for art in wartime. "We shall have collectors who will say that they cannot do anything about art in this hour of calamity," Watson wrote in October 1939, and "newspapers who can't be bothered with art news just now," and "sculptors and poets and musicians who will use the great excuse." "Slackers," he charged. Now was the time for artists and those who backed them to hold together. "Every good sculpture, painting, book, poem, composition that we now produce is a direct shot at barbarism." As military preparations accelerated, his metaphors of war intensified. The artist was a "soldier" who showed his fiber in the courageous pursuit of the truth and in his loathing of aggression. "Fortunately for the world," he wrote, "artists have ever been the defenders of ideas, the warriors for civilization. . . . Their work is their weapon."[29]

Reminiscent of his inspirational writings from France during the First World War, Watson's editorials revealed again the enduringly moral, patriotic side of his heritage. In "The Enemy Sees You," he defined the enemy not as those who attacked with dive-bombers and flame-throwers but as those who attacked "our hearts and minds with panic and defeatism. . . . To overcome an otherwise increasing army of the invisible enemy we need more, not less, creative initiative." He exhorted artists not called to active service to prove their courage "by keeping art alive." When price controls on art materials were proposed, precipitating alarm over shortages and high prices, Watson called upon artists to remember their real priorities. "The artist can fight," he admonished, "not to lower the price of canvas or paint or copper or zinc—but for something more important. His fight is to keep before his people the spirit of liberty in its unpretentious purity. This he can only do by means of art that rings the bell." The article was reprinted in the *Washington Post* on Sunday, December 7, 1941, the day of the Japanese attack on Pearl Harbor. Once the United States declared war, Watson warned: "The time will come of course . . . when patriotism will demand dull jobs, lettering, mechanical drawing, ordinary labor, when some artists will be favored with opportunities for fame while others do humble everyday work. . . . An inspiring service faces the artist whether destiny leads him to a minor or a major job."[30]

Not only did the war sap funds that might have financed Section projects, but, worse still, sentiment was growing "that art should be eliminated and particularly if it costs anything." The Section's announcement of the winner in the Yakima, Washington, post office and courthouse competition in December 1941 set off a torrent of angry letters from Yakima civic groups and private citizens. The Broadway Grange of Yakima passed a resolution protesting the "expenditure of any funds whatsoever for the placing of mural decorations in the Post Office." Responding righteously that such judgments overlooked the value of art in elevating national morale, the Section staunchly reaffirmed its commitment to the winning artist, but then postponed the project indefinitely.[31]

Fortunately, Watson had continued to supplement his income during his Treasury Department tenure with lecturing and writing.[32] Publishing and *The Arts* were never far from his thoughts, and, as his mail testified, his readers had not forgotten him. Even Ann Craton, who recognized from the first that he stood above the others, had nonetheless been amazed during her nationwide tour to discover the breadth of esteem in which he was held. "While here in Washington and the East the publicity about the Project centered around Ned, as was to be expected," she wrote Watson, "I was delighted and somewhat surprised to find that in the West that the interest centered around yourself. . . . Everyone asked about Forbes Watson, and your name meant much more to them than anyone's. I hope that you can either revive The Arts, or start a new magazine, and I am sure from the response that I got that it would be a success."[33] Watson's flourishing relationship with the editors of the *American Magazine of Art* offered an opportunity to get actively involved in publishing once again.

Only a few years earlier, he had regularly battered the magazine for its reactionary editorial policy and berated its parent organization, the American Federation of Arts, for abetting the National Academy of Design. Now, under the editorship of F. Allen Whiting Jr. and his wife, Philippa, Watson was convinced the *American Magazine of Art* had abandoned the "uplift bunkum" of "that great-grandmother of mediocrity Miss Leila Mechlin."[34] He began writing "The Innocent Bystander" column and occasional articles in January 1934. But his presence inevitably grew larger. How could the most distinguished editor in the field of art, a man "older, and stronger in enthusiasm," fail to influence the young editor? In March Watson assumed the position of advisory editor without salary and in October, associate editor. Looking back, Lloyd Goodrich thought Allen Whiting grew "a little bit too dependent on Forbes." The decisions to change the name of the magazine to *Magazine of Art* in 1937 and revise the format to utilize "every possible square inch of paper page to the benefit of the illustrations" reflected Watson's touch. So did the appointment of Jane Watson as assistant editor in January 1938.[35]

By late 1938 Watson was "putting a wee bit more dynamite in the magazine." The *Magazine of Art* would "henceforth publish much more material on painters and sculptors who are at work today," he wrote sculptor Louis Slobodkin and other artists from whom he solicited articles. "The character of the articles has been left in my hands," he explained, and involved "a rather complete collaboration between the artist and myself." He would have none of the "paean with a dash of blah" that characterized the "customary article by the artist's best friend." No longer would issues be "full of stuff stuck in at the last moment because there was not more stuff to stick in." "I must say that the *Magazine of Art* had them all skun a mile in looks," a pleased Watson wrote Olin Dows after he and Jane Watson compared all the domestic and foreign art magazines in the Library of Congress. Beginning in January 1939, Watson took over the editorials on a regular basis. He had also become more involved in the American Federation of Arts. In the unsalaried position of art director, he and Dows selected works for the federation's traveling shows; Watson often served as a speaker and panelist at federation-sponsored events. In December 1940 he became a member of the board of trustees.[36]

Allen Whiting had "never been the man for the job" in Olin Dows's opinion, and when Whiting talked about resigning as editor in late 1940, Dows, a second vice president in the American Federation of Arts, recommended Watson as a replacement. "I believe it is essential to make the Magazine considerably better than it now is," he wrote Robert Woods Bliss, president of the federation, "and I think this can only be done by having an editor with a point of view." Watson was "by far the most distinguished writer in the art field at the moment," he believed, and *The Arts* "still the most lively magazine that has yet been done." Whiting changed his mind about leaving, but even if he had resigned, Watson probably would not have succeeded him, as many trustees on the board of the American Federation of Arts considered him too democratic and "too much of a power in the policies" of the magazine.[37]

Board members' reservations about him turned to belligerence, and Watson himself became an issue as a result of an editorial he wrote in March 1941 about Andrew Mellon and the National Gallery. The new fifteen-million-dollar building, scheduled to open that month, had been built with money Mellon donated to the federal government to house the impressive collection of European art he had presented the nation earlier. "I find the picture of President Roosevelt accepting the key to the National Gallery, as it were, on an aluminum plate, a piquant formality," Watson wrote in his editorial. Belittling Mellon—and the Morgans, the Wideners, and the Fricks at the same time—whose "excess profits" had bought carloads of old masters at splendid prices, Watson noted that they had done little or nothing for their contemporary artists. Yet these millionaires found in art "the surest road" to immortality. As for the palatial-style building itself, John Russell Pope's "feat of archaeological memory," Watson dubbed it "the last Papal bull."[38]

The editorial not only deepened schisms on the board of trustees, it also precipitated a shake-up in the magazine's operation and effectively ended Watson's career in art journalism. A furious David Finley, director of the new National Gallery, hardly needed to complain to George Hewitt Myers, first vice president of the American Federation of Arts. No friend of Watson's, Myers went after him with score-settling relentlessness. Watson had undermined the federation's ability to attract donors, he charged, and "raising hell" with Tom Parker, director and secretary of the federation, he demanded that Watson's "article—editorial or whatever you wish to call it" be removed from the front section of the magazine. Among the letters to the editor following Watson's editorial, one from Myers, pointedly titled "Mr. Watson's Day," expressed the outrage that ultimately spurred the trustees to take action. Myers assailed Watson's "bad taste," his "slurs," and "innuendo[s]" and also challenged his artistic assumptions. His final sentence, "I hope never to be obliged again to comment upon 'Mr. Watson's Day,'" was prophetic.[39]

By the time of the annual trustees and members meeting on May 26, Watson's removal was a foregone conclusion. He anticipated it, having recently rented an office at 808 Seventeenth Street to carry on his projects. "I hope that it has been a lesson to Forbes," Bliss wrote Dows, "though I hae ma douts." Watson had not learned a lesson. That was obvious in his reaction to a letter Dows had drafted in an attempt to defuse the controversy.[40] The letter was a model of evenhandedness, but in Watson's view, Dows had "misjudged the spirit and purpose" of his editorial. In retrospect, the editorial had been "too mild," Watson concluded. Had he made comparable remarks about "some poor WPA venture, situated on the wrong side of the tracks, none of our Republican boy friends would have lifted an eyebrow," he wrote Dows. It should at least be made clear to the country that Mellon's gifts were not those of a noble generous creature, he persisted, but "the gifts of a vain old pirate." The paintings had been publicized to the public as being fine, not because of their intrinsic quality but because of the high prices that the rich old man paid for them. "Until you reduce him to his natural level, the pictures will not be looked at for themselves as they should be.... Anyway, lots of other artists have been very complimentary about the editorial."[41]

Dows's letter, which he never sent, made four essential points: No matter what Mellon's motives, the many vital pictures in the Mellon collection would benefit the nation. Despite its "massive columns and some of the other Roxy-like details," the new gallery showed the art works to better advantage than most museums. People like Mellon, who were brought up with "so-called cultural advantages," were very slow to realize the cultural implications of a living art. The tradition of the great American collectors was still too strong, and Watson's criticism of their relationship to modern art was more than justified. The excellent criticism of perfectionists such as Watson or Dean Hudnut should not be offensive to the National Gallery and its well wishers. "Except for several witty digs which I am malicious enough to have thoroughly enjoyed," Dows added, "I can see very little in Mr. Watson's article or Dean Hudnut's either for that matter, that is not obviously true and does not harm to be said."[42]

Watson left the magazine in February 1942, following the dismissal of Jane Watson, whose termination was part of the decision to oust Forbes and silence his adherents. An article critical of the Mellon gallery, which she had published in the same issue as Watson's editorial, precipitated the action against her. Looking back, Jane Watson was "sure" that she had been "influenced by Ned and Forbes." Nevertheless, more than fifty years later she continued to believe in the reasonableness of their position. "Mellon had been so impressed with the National Gallery in London, and he had no interest in the American artists, or particularly in art," she recalled. "That place opened, and there wasn't any American art in it. . . . And then they had that famous clause that was devised by David Finley, . . . and that clause precluded admission of any work by an American artist until after he had been dead for [twenty years]. And this was ridiculous, because you've got a man like George Bellows who died in his forties and there was John Sloan who died in his late seventies, I think. That was the feeling, . . . they [Watson and Bruce] felt that this was a shame. Here was a National Gallery of Art opening in our own country without any American art in it."[43]

The February 1942 issue of Magazine of Art was Watson's last. "I am no longer connected in any way with the American Federation of Arts or with the Magazine of Art," he wrote Max Weber. "They treated one of my fellow workers with great unfairness and I accordingly resigned. The country needs a good magazine of art and we must talk about it when we get together." Dows resigned from the second vice presidency and the board of trustees in March 1942, and Whiting left in May to work in the newly established Office of War Information.[44] The next issue of the Magazine of Art, which appeared in October 1942, introduced the new editor, John D. Morse, the new editorial board, and the new editorial policy. As justice would have it, Lloyd Goodrich was named chairman of the editorial board, a position he retained for eight years. In December the editorial offices moved from Washington to New York City. It would be ten years before Watson contributed to the magazine again.

Looking back on Watson's break with the magazine, Goodrich pointed to the same old character trait. "Forbes was always agin' the powers that be."[45] Indeed, there appeared to be a correlation between Watson's ouster from the

Magazine of Art and the incident thirty years earlier when Frank Munsey had fired him from the *Scrap Book* for "rudeness." That combination of very strong convictions and a habit of outspokenness revealed Watson as all too human. It also heightened his readability. But, combined with an abiding anti-authority streak and a gift for ridicule, it had cost him two major journalist positions, one at the *Scrap Book* and now the *Magazine of Art.* To a certain degree it had also led to his loss of *The Arts.*

Ralph Flint, former editor of *Art News,* published a cheering tribute the month following Watson's fateful editorial. It came as a timely kudos. "Long before *A Ballad for Americans* was composed," Flint wrote, "Watson was chanting 'Be American' and 'Buy American' at the top of his capacious lungs." Tracing the course of Watson's "rugged Americanism" from his first published art criticism in 1912 through the federal arts programs, Flint beamingly observed: "His earlier slogans have become imperative commands, paving the way for what he believes (and we surely have the power to make it come true) will be the greatest artistic renascence the world has ever known." Paraphrasing the popular musical comedy *Show Boat,* Flint concluded, "I can hear him shouting like Captain Andy, 'It's only the beginning, folks!' He is certainly in the right place with a big job ahead of him."[46]

9 MAKING ART RELEVANT DURING
WAR, 1942–1946

Their involvement in community and country having been encouraged over seven years of government solicitude, American artists were readily engrossed in the issues of World War II, considerably more so than in 1917, when artistic experimentation mattered more than world affairs. The international crisis had weakened the ideological power of the American Artists' Congress and other leftist organizations, so the question was no longer where to stand but how to help in the war effort and keep art alive in wartime. A number of Watson's colleagues and friends joined the military or related services. Olin Dows, who had become a consultant in the Office of Civilian Defense in January 1942, joined the army the following August. Although well beyond draft age and in a position to wrangle a commission, he completed rigorous engineering training, became a technical sergeant, and later distinguished himself in battle. Inslee Hopper enlisted in the U.S. Army Air Force in 1942, "actually glad to be in uniform." It had "been one sad goodbye . . . after another all summer long," sculptor Heinz Warneke wrote Watson.[1]

Artists who did not join up tried to do their bit. Edward Rowan planted a garden at Red Cross House at St. Elizabeth's Hospital for victims of war neuroses. Warneke raised beef. Maurice Sterne, one of many who applied for and was denied a commission, was thrilled when offered an opportunity to contribute to the war effort through art. Ugly acts of hate and discrimination against Japanese and German Americans outraged Watson and others, who spoke out in their defense. "It's good to have a friend," Yasuo Kuniyoshi thanked Watson. "I will always try to keep my head up." Kuniyoshi turned to writing scripts for short-wave broadcasts to Japan and enlisted others from the Committee for Democratic Treatment for Japanese Residents in Eastern States to do the same.[2]

In January 1942, thousands of artists in New York City and vicinity merged with delegates from twenty-one art societies to form the Artists Council for Victory, a nonprofit organization whose purpose was to "make fully effective the talents and abilities of the artistic professions in the prosecution of the war and in the protection of the country." It was the largest artist-sponsored undertaking to date. Hailing the merger, the *New York Times* noted, "10,000 American artists have organized to help win the war against an ex-Austrian ex-painter and his Axis partners."[3]

War-related art projects proliferated across the country, some generated by artists, others by civic or business organizations. Private industry took the lead, the New Deal programs having demonstrated dramatically the social utility of art in American life. Abbott Laboratories of Chicago, Standard Oil, the Chrysler Corporation, and *Life* magazine all sponsored competitions and exhibitions and also commissioned civilian artists to record various aspects of the war.[4]

Government agencies—the Office of Facts and Figures, the Office of War Information, the War Production Board, the Treasury Department, and the Army and Navy Departments—utilized civilian artists to design training manuals, visual aids, and camouflage as well as to make pictorial records of the warfront. Soldier-artists got together during off-duty hours and, using materials paid for by interested friends and institutions, created murals and other works for recreation halls, battalion dayrooms, and service clubs in more than fifty military bases around the country.[5]

So widespread was public interest in art with war themes that the Section of Fine Arts could not fill all the circuit requests coming in from museums, local governments, and civic organizations and offered to mix in landscapes and still lifes.[6] A wartime mentality charged the Section's daily routines, with punctilious reporting of consultants' citizenship status, bombproof storage arrangements, and new official identification cards, not to mention shortages, stringencies, and multiplied paperwork associated with the requirements of the Joint Committee on Reduction of Nonessential Federal Expenditures. Unfortunately, the Section's workload did not reflect a commensurate level of involvement in the war effort.

Eight days after Pearl Harbor, the Section joined with the Division of Information of the Office for Emergency Management (OEM) in a project to portray civilian defense in the United States. It was a two-part endeavor comprising both national competition and commissioned art, the best of which was exhibited at the National Gallery of Art and then sent on a nationwide tour.

Watson's catalog for the show giddily predicted the advent of "the post–Pearl Harbor period of American art." A similar competition in March 1942, organized in collaboration with the American Red Cross, interpreted Red Cross activities "by means of significant posters [and] realistic visual records." The winners also exhibited their works at the National Gallery followed by three traveling shows around the country. But the Red Cross competition was the Section's final joint enterprise. If it was to survive, the Section had to play an operational role in producing war-related art.[7]

Though no longer officially connected with the Section, Olin Dows had devised such a program, the Pictorial War Correspondents Project, which, if approved, would bring a $255,000 allocation to the Section and situate it at the center of war-art production. Under the plan, the Section would organize and coordinate a group of pictorial war correspondents to create a record of the war, "pictures of the armed forces in action, pictures of war training and production, and of the significant changes which war is bringing about in American life."[8] The rationale was outlined in detail in the prospectus submitted to President Roosevelt.

Unfortunately, however, the man Roosevelt assigned to review the proposal, Wayne Coy, acting director of the Bureau of the Budget, recommended against approval, citing redundancy with army and navy activities current and projected. Dows, indignant that Coy had presented the program "unflatteringly," appealed to members of the Fine Arts Commission and to Elinor Morgenthau. He even called on Mrs. Roosevelt in her Hyde Park home, something he would normally consider unthinkable. It was no use, however. The president remained convinced that adequate provision had been made. Bruce was too ill by then to lobby for Dows's plan, although it is doubtful that even he could have salvaged it.[9]

Disappointment was palpable at the Section. This latest rejection virtually guaranteed the Section's eventual dissolution. Striving for optimism, Watson wrote Dows, "I think you will be glad to know that while we were of course deeply disappointed yesterday afternoon when we first heard the news, we are now coming back strongly with the idea that as a group we can find a place where our experience will not be lost and where we can best plant the seeds from which may grow the full fledged program as you have developed it." He went on, determinedly cheerful: "I did not thank you for the most welcome presents which you left behind. . . . I hurried home with the wine and the brandy and kept them for a celebration of the expected good news. They cannot be used for that, alas, but they can be used as delicious consolation and it is proposed by Mr. and Mrs. Forbes Watson that Maria and Neilson and the Watsons shall partake of them this evening at 7 P.M. We will drink to your health." The final paragraph of a letter Dows wrote Reynolds before leaving for the army urged, "I hope you will be able to place Forbes Watson in a job suitable to his distinguished service, as well as the other members of the Section who have done such an extraordinarily faithful, intelligent and enthusiastic job. . . . It is a very important achievement and one which in the future will increasingly be recognized as such."[10]

Earlier that month Watson had been appointed to a committee of the Treasury Department, along with Elinor Morgenthau, Julian Street, a representative of Abbott Laboratories, and others, whose mission was to promote the sale of war bonds. With little work left for him in the Section, Watson officially transferred to the War Savings Staff effective July 25, 1942, as senior advertising specialist, a consultant's position. He continued to work out of the Section of Fine Arts office in Room G-342 of the North Interior Building.

Edward Bruce died six months later, on January 26, 1943, having literally given his life for the federal arts programs. Recognition, from honorary degrees to presidential tributes, had come to him during his lifetime. After his death, Bruce's stature only grew, as the legacies of PWAP and the Section imprinted the course of American art. He had demonstrated most powerfully "that art and democracy are not only compatible but vital to each other," as Watson wrote in a memorial catalog.[11]

The section "just petered out," Dows recalled. Rowan, named director after Bruce's death, presided over its demise, finishing up what had been underway before Roosevelt's 1940 budget eliminated all extra spending.[12] The *Bulletin* had ceased unofficially with the May 1941 issue, there being no new competitions. A few contracts for murals that were still in the design phase when the Section closed were extended until after the war to enable artists to complete their commissions.[13] Congress officially terminated the Section of Fine Arts on August 31, 1943, the same time it "killed" the Art Advisory Committee of the War Department and the Graphic Division of the Office of War Information.[14]

The key to the Section's success, according to the majority of those involved, had been the open competition, which recognized unknown talent. "This influx of new blood, though involving a relatively small number of artists, . . . definitely raised the vitality and quality of our public art," sculptor Robert Cronbach declared. Artists such as Philip Evergood and Paul Cadmus first gained serious recognition through their Section and PWAP work. Thanks to "that wonderful intervention of the federal government," Peter Hurd was able to become a mural painter, and artists such as Ben Shahn, Philip Guston, and Jack Levine could continue as full-time artists during the depression. Also, as Secretary Morgenthau noted, increasing numbers of women secured mural commissions through the open anonymous competitions. Under the old system, there had been considerable prejudice against them.[15]

At the same time, Section art was criticized for its generally conservative character, which critics blamed on Bruce's tight control. Dows insisted that there had been room in the Section for every kind of style. "The only thing we didn't have was abstract murals. We probably were all slightly prejudiced against it," he admitted nearly thirty years later. But "sketches were not submitted. I don't remember any competition with an abstract solution sent in." Erica Rubenstein posited the explanation that a number of artists accommodated their art to what they perceived to be Section preferences, toning down or abandoning experimental styles and radical subject matter as they moved from the Federal Arts Project to the Section. This group, they believed, operated on the assumption that publicly funded art should satisfy the public, which meant less artistic leeway. Many gave a name to their efforts to comply with this aim of harmonizing mural art with public taste: "to paint Section." Nonetheless, Section artists ranged from traditionalists such as Gifford Beal and Eugene Savage to modernists Peter Blume, Max Weber, and Marsden Hartley, and from impressionist landscape artists such as Ernest Lawson to social realists such as Stefan Hirsch and Philip Evergood.[16]

There were complaints, particularly from the Artists Union, that the program employed too few artists. Indeed, employment under Section auspices was limited, particularly compared to the Federal Arts Project and even the Public Works of Art Project. But then, Juliana Force and others who disliked the whole idea of government-subsidized art favored Treasury Department projects for that very reason. "They seemed upper level," Lloyd Goodrich recalled. Also, "Forbes was involved, and . . . they were not so democratic." Force even put on a series of exhibitions at the Whitney for the Treasury Department. Dows believed the artists themselves preferred the Treasury because they were dealing with fewer people and there was less red tape.[17]

In social terms, few disputed the Section of Fine Arts' accomplishments. "The wonderful thing about all these men was their real love and respect for the artist involved," Henry Varnum Poor commented. "They made you feel as though you were an extremely useful citizen." And the government "actually did cough up cash at a very important time, in a very modest but substantial way, to a great many artists," Dows mentioned, "and it was administered almost everywhere with real understanding, sympathy and knowledge." Too, through working together for the Section, TRAP, or the WPA and building a sense of artistic community, a milieu was created out of which the abstract expressionist movement later developed.[18]

That the preponderance of Section murals were executed not for the monumental buildings of the nation's capital but for countless post offices and courthouses across the country guaranteed the popularization of art on a national scale. This broke up the old geographic monopoly of art interest and spread a general art consciousness across the United States. "Government support of art has gone a long way to create a real audience for art in America," sculptor William Zorach remarked in 1938, "even if as yet not a buying public which I'm sure will develop later if the government keeps up its support and interest." Annual museum attendance rose to over twenty million people when the government art projects were operating, according to George Biddle, and an exhibition of Old Masters in New York attracted nearly three hundred thousand spectators. Thanks to Section art, years after the programs ended, Americans could gain a deeper awareness of their country as it had not been defined before.[19]

Watson was sixty-three years old when he transferred to the War Savings Staff of the Treasury Department. "Slightly rotund" now and gray, he wore glasses most of the time and suffered an occasional bout of lumbago, but he remained exceptionally vigorous and engaged.[20] He still arose at 5 A.M., enjoyed his daily cocktails, and got in rounds of golf when possible, especially during Harbor Springs summers. And Watson had lost none of his appetite for the ladies. He still made frequent trips to Manhattan and other cities for shows, to attend friends' openings, to jury and consult, and to lecture. His and Nan's long-standing graciousness toward young artists was amplified during the war, as they extended their liberal hospitality to those stationed near Washington or passing through the city.

He assumed his new duties as war bond promoter with customary gusto. The bond campaign, launched in May 1941, was the most ambitious in Treasury Department history, touting the patriotic and financial benefits of savings bonds and stamps through a wide assortment of media.[21] The department put out pamphlets and handbooks for trade unions, women's clubs, and other social and vocational organizations. There were posters, investment guides, and documentary films, even original plays and songs for schools. The department organized tours for movie stars such as Clark Gable, Marlene Dietrich, and Lana Turner, who sold kisses for fifty thousand dollars. Secretary Morgenthau's appeal to "buy a share in America" resonated with every segment of society.[22]

Of all the methods of bond promotion, posters were the most effective, being "the most visible reminder of the war on the home front." And posters were Watson's bailiwick. Within days of his appointment, he sent off hundreds of letters "to the artists whom I admire," advising them of the "great patriotic opportunity" to create pictures and posters to stimulate the sale of war bonds.

The Treasury would pay the artist twenty-five dollars if his idea was accepted in rough sketch and two hundred fifty dollars if it asked him to develop it. Earlier, the Section had failed to persuade the Office of Facts and Figures of the superiority of creative art over graphics in interpreting the war program, and Watson was determined now to have real artists produce work that was "not designed for morons but for the intelligent and understanding audience." From a large pool of submissions he selected for immediate production thirty-six paintings, drawings, and sketches by twenty-nine artists of national reputation, including Reginald Marsh, Thomas Hart Benton, and John Steuart Curry. Abbott Laboratories, "in a deed of generosity which sets a fine example," paid the artists and turned the pictures over to the Treasury Department.[23]

The poster designs were featured in a heavily publicized "Art for Bonds" exhibition that opened at the Brooklyn Museum on April 9, 1943, Bataan Day, to promote the second war-bond drive. The price of admission was a bond, which 2,500 people purchased for a total of $330,000. Favorite designs included Alexander Brook's *Remember Me? I Was at Bataan,* a picture of an emaciated prisoner of war appealing to the viewer to purchase war bonds, and Joseph Hirsch's *Till We Meet Again,* which depicted a soldier waving from the port-hole of a transport. Hirsch's design was reproduced on five million postcards and, blown up to an eighty-foot image, on a building in New Orleans. Pictures from the exhibit were reproduced in a variety of locations: on the sides of vans, in stores and factories, in train stations, and in other public places all around the country.[24]

From the Brooklyn Museum, the "Art for Bonds" show traveled to Washington, Baltimore, Boston, and other major cities. The Washington opening, September 12, 1943, helped kick off the third war-loan drive, which began with the army's mighty "Back the Attack" extravaganza on the grounds of the Washington Monument. At the Baltimore venue Eleanor Roosevelt attended a special preview with Watson, where she was serenaded via radio with a lively rendition of the song "Pistol Packin' Mamma." Her appearance brought $52,000 in war bond purchases.[25]

Meanwhile, less than a year after the president had turned down Olin Dows's pictorial war correspondents proposal, George Biddle gained approval for a similar plan. Roosevelt ordered a pictorial record of war scenes, but made by the Army Corps of Engineers and administered, not by the Section, but by the War Department Art Advisory Committee, a civilian committee that Biddle headed.[26] Biddle and his group selected forty-two "outstanding American artists" to go to active war theaters, "and there to obtain a graphic record of the war."[27] Within six months, however, the Art Advisory Committee was unceremoniously obliterated and its artist-correspondents stranded when conservative congress-men eliminated its funding from the War Department budget.[28] At that point, Watson recounted, *Life* magazine and Gen. Edward Greenbaum, husband of the sculptor Dorothea Greenbaum, mounted a rescue operation. *Life* put a num-ber of the abandoned army artist-correspondents on its staff, enabling them to continue their projects, and, thanks to his friend General Greenbaum, Watson was allowed to step in. He matted and framed a selection from the steady stream of pictures arriving from almost every battle front. Army personnel had been rolling them up "in a rough and ready manner" and tossing them into a room at the Pentagon, where they lay neglected on the floor. Watson got them "look-ing their best" and then took them to Secretary Morgenthau's home. "I sug-gested to Secretary Morgenthau and Mrs. Morgenthau that there were many more pictures where these came from and that if I prepared an exhibition and took them through the country it would stimulate the sale of bonds tremen-dously. They liked the work and agreed instantly."[29]

"I am in an excited state of mind," he wrote Dows that November, "because of the expected opportunity to catalogue the entire Artist War Corps output." Moving in December 1943 to a sunny office on the top floor of the Treasury Building, Watson, with one secretary, and painter Edward Rosenfeld, who had been with him at the Section, happily handled all correspondence, catalog ed-iting, framing, matting, and packing.[30]

The first big "Army at War" exhibition opened at the National Gallery on February 20, 1944. "Every bigwig in Washington, including the entire Supreme Court," was on the National Committee of Sponsors, with Eleanor Roosevelt as honorary chairman, Watson recalled. "What with our impressive national committee even the smart Republicans came." Nineteen painters were repre-sented, among them George Biddle, Reginald Marsh, Henry Varnum Poor, Sgt. Jack Levine, and Sgt. Olin Dows, who was stationed in England. *Life* magazine, which had begun its own project earlier, photographed all the material, pub-lishing pictorial spreads over the next two years. Secretaries Morgenthau and Henry L. Stimson wrote prefaces to the catalog, and Elinor Morgenthau, who with Dorothea Greenbaum, Edward Rosenfeld, and Watson spearheaded the exhibit, supplied the foreword. "These artists have depicted the greatest Army that our country has ever assembled as it truly is, minus strut and parade," she stated, sounding remarkably like Watson. The exhibition attracted enormous crowds, and John Walker, chief curator of the National Gallery, rated it the best contemporary show they had ever assembled in the museum.[31]

The project shifted into high gear, Hollywood style, following the National Gallery exhibition, as Ted R. Gamble, "Secretary Morgenthau's very able right hand man and head of War Finance, . . . ponied [their] forces." By then, the War Finance Division had swelled into a vast agency, with Gamble as its national director, and was responsible for sales of all government securities to the public. Gamble, who had been an executive in the theater business, brought in Charles P. "Ike" Skouras, a Twentieth Century Fox executive, and Skouras's "man Friday," R. V. Sturdivant, "who did his boss's bidding with positively tempestuous fury." The National Gallery show had a "good gate," Skouras allowed, but he was a man who "counted his audiences in millions" or did not consider them audiences. "So," recalled Watson, "into our little office . . . entered the echoes and adherents of the fabulous world" of Skouras. While Watson managed the show, "Skouras et al. were to manage the publicity and bring in the millions." "'I am going to make a household word of every painter in the show,'" one movie magnate promised. Skouras's team lined up advance men in each city, engaged famed war correspondent Quentin Reynolds to narrate film trailers, and supplied Technicolor moving pictures.[32]

For the touring "Army at War" exhibition, Watson selected 167 pictures by twenty-three artists. The exhibition catalog reflected the polish the new art-for-bonds production had acquired in the four months since the first one, including biographies (by Watson) and photographs of the artists and their work. The revised roster of the National Committee of Sponsors contained the names of sixty-one dignitaries, more than twice as many as originally. There was also a National Executive Committee now, headed by Skouras, which included ten major generals and some big-name movie moguls.[33]

Working with Skouras was an adventure. "For the full details of what I think of the moving picture industry you will have to wait until we are having a cool drink together," a sardonic Watson wrote Dows several months into the "fast and furious" nationwide swing. For all his irony, however, Watson was beguiled, particularly with the possibilities Hollywood know-how offered. He admired, for instance, the wonderful system of screens the moving-picture people built, which could be lashed together to make two small rooms, two hollow squares, one big room, or run zigzag down the sides or middle of a narrow room. They were set up at each stop, and the pictures looked "simply stunning" on them.[34]

Skouras had the idea that "museums were passé as crowds went. . . . The happy dream was that if the exhibition were shown in movie picture houses it would be seen by many more millions and many more millions of dollars of bonds would be sold." Thus, on October 11, 1944, "in a dazzling halo of publicity," the show opened for a three-week engagement at the Roxy Theater in New York City. Between New York and Seattle, however, there were only two movie houses that could display paintings before the public entered the theater, and government exhibitions had to be free. So Skouras's "great dream did not come true" exactly as planned. "We turned to the more congenial museums," Watson recounted. "And, oddly enough the crowds were much bigger." From the Roxy they took the show west, with stops in twenty-eight major cities through June 1945. The exhibition did "a record breaking business," Watson related, "if you'll pardon the word in connection with art."[35] It was installed not only in museums but also in hotels and other commercial establishments, wherever local committees identified feasible spaces. In Rochester, New York, the show was hung in the gas and electric company building, and in Buffalo on the mezzanine floor of the Statler Hotel. In each city, Watson talked on the radio, met with the local press, gave lectures, and presented fifteen-minute gallery talks, twice in the morning and twice in the afternoon.

In each city there was enormous media backing. Billboards displayed enlargements of the paintings; radio stations promoted the show; there were trailers in the movies and posters in shop windows; newspapers were friendly and attentive. There were bond-selling committees in every city and every big businessman was proud to be a member. The night they closed at the Chicago Art Institute, the army moved in with its trucks and transported them to the Layton Art Gallery in Milwaukee. For the first time in its history, the gallery was floodlit, the name of the show was emblazoned in electric lights above the door, "and again some big bow wow cut the ribbon that opened the show and the crowd jammed in once more breaking attendance records."[36]

"These were not desultory visitors," Watson insisted regarding the 208,100 people who came to see the "Army at War" show during its first eight weeks. "I have watched the people looking at the pictures and they show great interest, probably for the most part in subject matter. But if you can get people who never went to museums before to look at good pictures through their interest in the subject matter, that at least is a start toward a larger appreciation of what the artist is doing." On the whole, critics accepted the art more or less on its own terms, finding it "thought-provoking," "stirring," and "picturesque." Nonetheless, while applauding *Life* magazine and other agencies that sponsored artists' war pictures, particularly following Congress's ignominious withdrawal of support, some regarded them as no more aesthetic than tinted photographs. One critic wondered that museums were so willing to exhibit such works, which had "nothing to do with art."[37]

It was a measure of Watson's congenitally positive outlook that he appeared to muster as much enthusiasm for war art as he had for the creative production of Glackens or Demuth several decades earlier. At times, though, he was wistful for the stimulation of artists' company and serious art dialogue. He wished he

Nan gazing with pride at Forbes, late 1930s. Forbes Watson Papers.

"could go to Rockport for a visit and renew all the old friendships," he wrote his friend, art expert and artist Max Kuehne, but there seemed little chance of any vacation. "Wouldn't it be nice if we could all get together some day and really talk things over?"[38]

World events moved so rapidly that it was a struggle merely to stay current. "I might send an article to The New York Times mentioning D-Day in France and the forthcoming climax of victory only to find that victory had arrived before the article is printed," he complained. The whirlwind tour left no time for his normal schedule of freelancing and lectures, and he was away from Washington so much he fully expected his office in the Treasury Building to be assigned to someone else. It was. Nan and he had little time together, but fortunately, her art kept her busy.[39]

She had come a long way since the initially reluctant move from New York to become a fully integrated member of the Washington art scene. Her paintings were shown at the best galleries, including the Corcoran and the Phillips.

She also exhibited at the Pennsylvania Academy, the Denver Art Museum, and in New York at the Whitney and at Marie Sterner's. One of her paintings, *Modern Puritan,* was included in the forty-eight-state IBM Collection Exhibit at the World's Fair of 1939. The following year, the Metropolitan Museum of Art purchased her watercolor *Little Bouquet* for its permanent collection. The critics who reviewed her shows were often friends, who praised her paintings for qualities Nan herself possessed, "graceful sanity and fine taste," for instance. Alice Graeme Korff, *Washington Post* critic, characterized Nan's work as "quiet," "sound," "unobvious," and "restful." "Flowers were made for Nan Watson to paint," a *Minneapolis Tribune* writer gushed, for Nan was "a demure unassuming flower-like person herself."[40] With few exceptions, notices of Nan's shows included references to her husband, Forbes.

The great success of the "Army at War" show attracted attention overseas as well, and Watson was invited to arrange an exhibition of American pictures for the National Gallery in London in the fall of 1944. It was Maria Ealand, with her "customary energy and ability," who did most of the work, however, as Watson was immersed in the U.S. tour. She had begun working at the Office of War Information that April "for just such purposes." Nevertheless, Watson had to assure a nervous Dows in England that he would have "one to three fingers" in the pie and that Maria would send over "only good stuff." The show, which opened on September 29, was the first of its kind in England and very welcome, particularly considering British unfamiliarity with American pictures "in other than the celluloid sense of the phrase." Like American critics, the *London Times* reviewer found the works to be largely "illustrative in purpose" and "easily grasped."[41]

Undoubtedly, the "Army at War" would have continued to break attendance records, but in April 1945, as victory in Europe appeared imminent, the War Department decided to suspend the tour with the Denver venue and concentrate on the war against Japan. Watson immediately left for New York, where he spent the week of April 12 visiting artists' studios and searching the files of *Life* magazine, Associated American Artists, and *Fortune* magazine for suitable paintings for the new project, inelegantly titled "Fighting the Japs." President Roosevelt had died that week and Harry S Truman had been sworn in as the new president. Watson, saddened and vaguely out of sorts, noted toward the conclusion of his report that "in New York, as everywhere else, there was only one topic of conversation—Roosevelt."[42]

On the eighteenth, the "Fighting the Japs" committee, comprised of Watson, Dorothea Greenbaum, Eddie Rosenfeld (now with the title of advertising consultant), and Capt. Hermann Williams, held its first meeting in Watson's reassigned office in Room 5224 of the Treasury Building. A core collection was already on hand, since Aaron Bohrod and Howard Cook had produced a number of pictures in the Pacific for the "Army at War" circuit. The navy and marines were also lending pictures. Renamed the "War against Japan," the show, which comprised 134 pictures by seventeen artists, ran from May 27 through June 19, 1945, at the National Gallery in Washington before moving out to the Metropolitan Museum of Art on July 4. From there it was scheduled to tour the country, ending up at Indianapolis in March 1946.

Compared to the elaborate forty-four-page catalog for the touring "Army at War" exhibit, the "War against Japan" catalog was little more than a leaflet, spare, unillustrated, and printed on flimsy paper. Paper was scarce, Watson explained in the initial draft. It was "not through lack of appreciation of the courage of our war painters or of the distinction of their work." The message, signed by Ted Gamble but written by Watson, had the usual punch, however.[43]

Like the popular "Army at War," the "War against Japan" exhibit also went overseas, this time to cities in Australia. There too the press was enthusiastic, describing the pictures as "frankly shocking" and "utterly brutal." The *Brisbane Courier Mail* compared them favorably with Australian war art, which "too often sacrificed realism for decorativeness."[44]

"True as art and revealing as information" was how Watson described the first OEM show of war art in 1942. The 1944 "Army at War" exhibition was "a happy combination of art and patriotism." By 1945, Watson declared the "War against Japan" exhibition "an authentic record in painting." War artists "could not deal in abstract calculations or non-objective inventions," Watson explained several years later. "They could not be purely subjective. They could not indulge in any statement which the large public could not read. The test they had to meet was the test of making a record, which not only the layman of today can read, but the layman of future generations. The record was the predominating factor." Thus, as Watson's promotion of PWAP and Section art had underscored his philosophical ambivalence—the democrat on one side versus the fastidious critic on the other—resulting finally in a critical double standard, his approach to war art represented the end of the spectrum.[45]

Patriotism redefined art. Art that depicted the war had to be propaganda art, a form of sociological art, which during the twenties and even the thirties, Watson had dismissed outright as inimical to the aesthetic function of art. But the forties were another matter. "I am sorry this word ["propaganda"] has come to mean something evil," the foreword to the first *Art for Bonds* catalog stated, "because the idea of propagating faith in our country and in the aspirations of the American people is to me a beautiful idea. That is what every artist represented in this exhibition has attempted to do—to propagate patriotism."[46] The critical hierarchy was reordered once again, merging at the top two lifelong themes, Watson's devotion to country and his dedication to American art. Not that the war-art exhibits did not feature some of America's most able painters, but for all intents and purposes, critical rigor was suspended for the duration.

World War II bonds were "the most successful consumer product ever sold in history." Thus, when the French government organized the Interallied Exhibition of Savings to stimulate the sale of French bonds following the European war, the U.S. Treasury Department graciously sent an exhibit. Thanks to the friendly intercession of Henry and Elinor Morgenthau, an elated Watson took leave from his "War against Japan" duties to accompany the European show as consultant to the American section, responsible for promotion and exhibition management.[47]

Watson left on July 2, 1945, admittedly nervous about his first flight overseas but thrilled to be renewing his "long acquaintance with Paris."[48] The show, which featured different countries' techniques for bond promotion, opened on July 10 at the Palais de Glace with much pomp and celebration. Once the American exhibit was installed, Charles W. Adams and Turner Shelton, the other two members of the American delegation, returned to the United States, leaving Watson in charge.

Some 315,000 visitors attended the exposition. The American section alone averaged 11,000–13,000 per day.[49] Of all the countries, America's exhibit was "the most serious," Watson believed. Even the U.S. Army participated, bringing in three powerful searchlights from Germany to illuminate the front of the Palais de Glace and a specialist to run their movie. Watson himself spoke in French on the radio and at ceremonial affairs, so steadily, in fact, that by the time he left France he had "become daring if not grammatical." "Bons de la Liberté," the slick catalog of the American section, was filled with striking color photographs of the Statue of Liberty, war-bond posters, Norman Rockwell favorites, and other popular American images. The text, in French, proclaimed the success of democracy, the war effort, and bond selling in the United States; it had little to do with art.[50]

In his summary report to Gamble, Watson wrote, "although I have spent several years in France, I never received so much courtesy and so many friendly invitations as I did during this visit. It seems to me that this may indicate in a small way how much the French want, especially at this time, to be on good terms with Americans." Good terms, indeed. Life was decidedly "duller" for his many new friends after Watson left. "We have not had a party all month which could compare with any we had together," his friend George Wolfenson wrote.

His co-consultant, Charles Adams, already back in the States, teased Watson that the girls in the office had "not learned the truth from me so that if you get yourself in trouble when you return I'm not to blame."[51]

The old haunts were irresistible. "Each day something exciting, charming or merely agreeable happens," he wrote Nan in one of his long daily letters. "Monday morning . . . I took one of those Paris walks that cannot be duplicated anywhere. . . . It was a morning like a cool lipped kiss. It was singing to walk along"[52] He managed to get together with Olin Dows, now Technical Sergeant Dows, several times before Dows was shipped back to the States.

Sprinkled ever more liberally with French phrases, his letters rhapsodized over fabulous private art collections little known outside France and fascinating art figures he encountered. In one letter he announced that he was visiting the "ACTUAL STUDIO OF DELACROIX." A visit with Georges Braque in his home "was a real delight." Braque, Despiau, and André de Segonzac were rumored to have been collaborators during the war, he learned, adding, "a Frenchman defined a *collaborateur* to me as 'one who collaborated more than I did.'"[53] Conversations with Segonzac left a powerful impression, and he returned to them in letter after letter, relating Segonzac's version of what really happened with the Nazis, describing Segonzac's unique ideas about color application, about Picasso, and other art issues.[54] No impression was wasted: furniture and window treatments in the sumptuous homes he visited; the twelve-course meals, wines, aperitifs, and scotch he was served; studios "you might dream about"; and the "unsurpassed" hospitality conferred on him.[55]

He became "very sentimental about the French" and lamented Americans' failure to take advantage of the opportunity to understand them better. The growing anti-French, pro-German sentiment among American soldiers distressed him deeply. "It was only when I met someone who cared about painting that I found genuine sympathy for the French," he wrote Elinor Morgenthau.[56]

One night in late July, Watson attended a Franco-American fete at the opera at which the popular American opera singer–movie star Grace Moore performed. He was disappointed in her "gross affectation," but that same evening he saw two films, *The Fighting Lady* and *Iwo Jima*, narrated by Charles Boyer, shown in France for the first time. At the conclusion of the performance, "they showed Roosevelt on the screen between the tri-color and the stars and stripes giving that famous part of his speech in French. The audience stood and taps were played for Roosevelt. Very moving!"[57]

Four days before Japan surrendered, French papers reported the war was over. Almost afraid to hope and without official word, Watson tried in vain to verify the news. "I would give anything if we were sitting together by the radio having some drinks," he wrote Nan. "There are planes flying across dropping leaflets and I am wondering if they are about V-J or V-M day, world victory or whatever they call it. Probably they are about a new play, as the French love to advertise events by dropping leaflets from planes. . . . God, how I miss our radio at a time like this."[58]

Even if the reports were premature, however, peace was imminent. Watson was thrilled, yet he could not ignore the prospect of his own uncertain future, especially since Henry Morgenthau had resigned as secretary of the Treasury on the very day Watson had arrived in Paris. He had heard from Charles Adams that Ted Gamble positively would stay with the War Finance Division until the end of the war. "Does that mean the end of this week or the end of next?" he wrote Nan. "I hope it means at least until I get back. But with the war ended there will be such a rush of liquidation and wild haste back to civilian production that none can guess what government jobs will vanish and what remain. Will people, for instance, still care whether the War Against Japan Exhibition continues its tour or not? Well, as I said before, I'm not the least bit worried about all that. We can just thank God that the war is over and that no more kids will be killed. . . . This is a time for the whole world to celebrate right up to the hilt."[59]

In any event, the French odyssey was ending. "Altogether, instead of being an easygoing walking propagandist and a sightseer I'll have to begin getting things tied up against the day of departure." The American exhibit closed on September 2, and Watson flew home two days later. Job insecurity notwithstanding, before he left Paris, Watson gave all the clothes he had brought with him, "except the ones on my back," to the young French architect of the exhibition. Upon his return to the United States, he sent five packages of tea, coffee, and other edibles to his friends back in France. For his work in Paris, the French government decorated Watson.[60]

Demobilization was on everyone's mind when Watson arrived in the United States on September 6. "To have the boys home" was suddenly the all-important thing, Watson wrote a friend in France, "and whole groups are having fits over the slowness of discharging the soldiers." The army, which earlier had received nothing but praise, was criticized now, "because it does not practically throw the soldiers out of the boats into the arms of their families."[61]

The "War against Japan" tour had been canceled on September 3, when it closed at the Metropolitan Museum. But preparations were already underway for a new bond drive, the eighth, renamed the Victory Loan Drive, and Watson and the other staff members worked on it "day and night." By the time the drive was launched on October 29, however, the new secretary of the Treasury, Fred M. Vinson, had decided to cut the War Finance Division "to the bone" within three months. Unsure of his status with the government, Watson began moving his belongings out of the Treasury Building and into the private office he had rented since 1941. That was where he had conducted the residual business of Art in Federal Buildings and handled his other publishing and freelance commitments. "I am very happy to be going back to my own office," he wrote friends in Paris, "because it is an odd little nook in a quiet building right next door to the Tally-ho Restaurant on 17th Street and I have the walls crowded with all sorts of pictures of artists and other people and it is arranged just to suit my own personal eccentricities and it is a very sympathetic place to work and write in."[62]

Among the projects pending was a traveling exhibition of Allen Tucker's works, which in the end did not take place. But Watson had a far more ambitious venture in mind: to bring back the Section of Fine Arts. George Howe, deputy commissioner for design and construction in the Public Buildings Administration, had discouraged Watson, convinced that the program could not succeed without a Ned Bruce. Truman and his entourage were "without an aesthetic glimmer," Howe cautioned. Postmaster General Robert E. Hannegan, for one, had declared that the post office was "no place to discuss art. It's a place to buy stamps."[63] Nonetheless, Watson refused to be discouraged. "George is no fighter," he wrote Dows, "and I can think of lots of ways of fighting for the revival of the Section." In November 1945 Watson and Maria Ealand lunched with W. E. "Burt" Reynolds, commissioner of public buildings, who had been a sympathetic ally during the struggle to keep the Section alive in 1943. Burt "was certain that the Section would become active again. In fact, that it would have a great deal to do, but he thought it would be several months before financial matters would be sufficiently settled." The Section was never revived.[64]

There were other possibilities to explore. This was the time to preserve the valuable art that had been produced for war projects. Currently, it was casually stored in boxes and left, with no assigned responsibility for its safekeeping. Watson had earlier tried to have Dows transferred back home to work on "certain hush-hush and confidential museum plans," but Dows preferred to remain with his unit as it moved into Germany, so Watson "pulled no wires."[65] Later that year, when the army appointed a committee of high-ranking officials from several branches of the service to consider a war museum, Watson was among the few civilians included. His vision of the museum as a memorial to President Roosevelt was rejected early on, but he still wanted to ensure that the museum would "not confuse art and souvenirs." In October 1945 the committee drafted a letter to President Truman proposing that he appoint a small commission to develop plans for a war museum of national scope. Prompt action was needed, the letter urged, because of the potential loss of material. The official art world was actively behind the move.[66]

A draft of the prospectus for the National War Museum bore Watson's unmistakable stamp, particularly the section on war art. Pictures whose appeal came solely from their representation of war subjects belonged in the science and history division of the war museum, the document stated, while those whose appeal derived from the quality of their art should be housed in the art section. "The important point to be harped upon unceasingly is that the art collection of a war museum should be judged as art and not according to subject matter," Watson declared, reverting to his prewar position that aesthetics superseded facts. Under the final section, subtitled "Warning," was his familiar caveat: "Unless a proposed war museum is organized in a way which liberates it forever from political pressure nothing can stop it from becoming a dismal hodge-podge."[67] The war museum did not materialize either.

Still upbeat as he prepared to leave the Treasury Department despite the collapse of one prospect after another, Watson planned to try New York City, where he had a "somewhat promising publishing line out, but otherwise no definite plans." He had never abandoned hope of starting a new publication. Back in the spring of 1942, at the time of his break with the *Magazine of Art,* he had been approached about directing a new "quality," "trust-busting" publication, but after more than a year of on-again, off-again discussions, the venture sputtered out.[68]

Guy Pène du Bois contacted him in late 1944 about a new quarterly to be launched by Sam Golden, publisher of art books and Christmas cards. Each number would be devoted to a single subject—realism, romanticism, classicism, and others—and edited by a different person. Watson was to edit the series on regionalism, Pène du Bois the number on realism, and Frank Jewett Mather Jr. on either romanticism or classicism.[69] But that project did not go forward either.

The New York publishing line "boiled down to a comfortable writing contract," Watson told Dows. "I do not know the man who has given me this advance intimately but I know several close friends of his and they tell me that he is an extremely generous straight shooter and a very able man."[70] The man was Samuel Golden, who earlier had considered, then abandoned, the idea of the new magazine. But this publishing opportunity also came to nothing.

Watson did discuss with Golden the possibility of taking over *Art in Federal Buildings.* There was a slow, steady demand for the first volume *(Mural Designs),* he noted, and as a historical document it should be available to schools, museums, and libraries. "While I have had some expense—storage, rent, a little promotion, etc.," he wrote, "the main expense has been Mr. Dows and he owns all the stock in the corporation. I am pretty sure he will be as happy as I am to dispose of the books on any terms that would be agreeable to you." Golden referred Watson to the Harlem Book Company, which finally offered $1.75 per copy for the regular edition and $2.00 for the library edition, of which there were 965 copies and 265 copies, respectively. Fifty years later, the regular edition would sell for $175.[71]

Although he had not planned to retire then, by early 1946 Watson had reached the end of his career. The government was definitely out of the art business, and by one route or another he had depleted the options for regular employment in the publishing and editorial fields. When the City of New York took over the warehouse in which he had stored the last three or four thousand copies of *The Arts*, Watson sold those too. "I have no further financial interest in them," he wrote Dows, "but I hope they will fall into the hands of artists before they are sold for pulp."[72]

That spring, Forbes and Nan went to Harbor Springs, packed up their accumulations of thirty years, and sold the house, furniture and all. They returned to Washington, still with no prospects. When the Skowhegan School of Painting and Sculpture contacted Watson several weeks later, offering him a house in Lakewood practically rent-free in return for lecturing at the school, he "hustled up to Maine." But although he liked Willard Cummings, the head of the school, and the layout, he and Nan found the living accommodations "quite impossible. The cottages at Lakewood positively dripped with trees. That wouldn't do at all for us," he wrote Dows. "I hate dark rooms and there is no tree so beautiful that it can make me enjoy half lighted windows." At any rate, they "wedged in a most delightful family visit," having taken Mary along on the trip for a visit with their brother Carroll and his family in Bath, Maine.[73]

Fortunately, Nan's aunt in Scotland had left her a modest inheritance, which would now support the couple in retirement. Having sold their summer cottage, they asked friends and relatives to be on the lookout for a place for them. There was no particular hurry, but they had definite ideas about where they would settle. They wanted "a small country town or village house with enough ground around it for a small garden and a studio. . . . We want it on a good railroad line beyond commuting distance but not more than three or four hours away from the great city. We want it within walking distance of the stores and the station as we shall not have a car." Initially, they had hoped to settle in Dutchess County, in either Dows's hometown of Rhinebeck or the Morgenthau's neighborhood, but both areas were probably out of their financial reach. Besides, as Elinor Morgenthau pointed out, Hopewell Junction and Fishkill, where she lived, had no railroad connections to New York.[74]

In August, "after forty discouraging sights and after ten days in the trains and automobiles," they found the right house, "a nice little working place built for couples without cars. It is in the village of Gaylordsville, which is near the New York boundary line in Connecticut on the Housatonic River in a beautiful valley with lovely painting country, which is something that Nan wants very much because she is going to take a turn again at landscape painting. There is a barn crying for a north window, a good vegetable garden, a pleasant little pasture and altogether it is just the right kind of 'last house in the village' for a writer and a painter to live in," he wrote Dows. Even though they had hoped to live closer, Watson noted that they were "not too far away for a hustling driver" like Dows and urged him to come by as soon as they were settled. It was also only a half to three-quarters of an hour from Fishkill Farms, Elinor Morgenthau wrote them, and she extended an open invitation to come for a meal. Their artist-friend Henry Schnakenberg also lived nearby. The Watsons were scheduled to move on September 21, and getting ready would be "a terrible time." They not only had to move their belongings from the house on Fairmont Street, where they had lived for ten years, but also from his office on Seventeenth Street.[75]

In the midst of packing and last minute moving preparations, Watson received word of Edward Rowan's death on August 31, 1946. Rowan had been on leave from the Public Buildings Administration the preceding year, serving as an art instructor at the Army University in Biarritz, France. Upon completing his assignment with the War Department in March, the forty-eight-year-old Rowan returned to the United States, already ill with cancer, and never regained his health. The Section of Fine Arts had ceased three years earlier, ending the era of government art patronage. With Rowan's death and Watson's move to Connecticut, the last of the pioneers in federal arts administration departed Washington.

10 GAYLORDSVILLE, 1946–1960

Watson's Paris fling was his farewell hurrah. The war's end had not only obviated the need for his positions over the past three years but also altered the climate that had conduced to his employment. Americans' jubilation over the armistice briefly deferred concerns about long-term peace, but once the celebration ended, the implications of the atomic bomb coupled with power shifts in Europe seemed daunting. Truman's attitude toward Russia was not conciliatory, and differences over control of Eastern Europe and atomic energy steadily eroded the wartime spirit of cooperation between the United States and the Soviet Union. Ultraconservative politicians, playing on Americans' anxieties about security from communism, intervened in spheres of everyday life. To the House Committee on Un-American Activities, the real threat was domestic communism; disloyalty among public figures in all fields, particularly politics, journalism, and arts and entertainment, posed a greater security risk than Russia itself. Artists were definitely suspect. "When people began to talk about the Atomic era I had no idea it would be what it seems to be now—an era of fear," Watson wrote friends in France. "The un-American Activities Committee is just as bad as the old Dies Committee and possibly a little more stupid."[1]

On his return from Paris, Watson had been dismayed to find little residual warmth toward America's allies and a general unwillingness to help Europe. Everywhere, he sensed a mood of conservatism. President Truman, hailed as a hero when he brought World War II to a decisive conclusion, could not garner congressional support for his initiatives in civil rights, health insurance, agricultural price supports, or price controls. Strikes erupted around the country as labor unions, freed from their wartime nonstrike agreements, were demanding "catch-up" wage increases. Although Watson was concerned that the strikes might interfere with the shipment of goods to France, his sympathies, none-theless, happened "to be with labor."[2] Not so for many Americans, however, who believed labor was growing too big and powerful and needed to be curbed.

Artists' prospects were not encouraging. Public interest in art had declined to a state of lethargy. "Fifty-seventh Street is in the midst of its worst slump in years," a fellow artist wrote Concetta Scaravaglione. "Leon Kroll, big business man that he is, sold only a little $200 picture at his show; while the great Max Beckman's show had sold nothing when I last heard." Few artists could support themselves by selling their work. Nationalist art was on the wane, sym-bolized perhaps by the deaths of two leading painters of the American Scene, Grant Wood in 1942 and John Steuart Curry in 1946. That concern to express the roots of America's character, so prevalent during the 1930s, no longer seemed relevant. In fact, a new internationalism was emerging. "The artist has always been an internationalist," a sympathetic Watson had declared during the war years. "It's a big world and there's room for lots of different kinds of art in it. . . . Nothing in art is quite as bad as jingoism, unless it is snobbish fear."[3]

After more than a decade of dominance, realism had receded in popularity, yielding in some quarters to a revived interest in abstraction. By the mid-1940s, stunning experiments were taking place in the studios of Jackson Pollock, Mark Rothko, Robert Motherwell, and Hans Hofmann, establishing the first corpus of a new abstract art in America. Unnamed and unheralded, abstract expres-sionism, the most powerful and original movement in the history of Ameri-can art, drew inspiration largely from surrealism, the abstract expressionism of Kandinsky, the later works of Picasso, and a group of American abstract pioneers, among them Arthur Dove, Arshile Gorky, and Max Weber. Although well underway when Watson returned to the United States in September 1945, the general public was not yet aware, and museums were not taking it seri-ously. Nor did Watson's resurgent internationalism encompass the new non-objective art.

From the floor of the House of Representatives political conservatives ha-rangued and attacked even moderately modern art as communistic, and dema-gogues such as Michigan congressman George Dondero "made a crusade" out of digging into artists' past affiliations with front organizations. President Truman was no help. His tastes in art ran to western scenes and Missouri sub-ject matter, and he let the world know he disliked modern art. When the State Department canceled a five-year European and Latin American tour of con-temporary American paintings because of pressure from the Hearst papers, conservative art organizations, and ultimately Congress, President Truman's criticisms only amplified the chorus of scorn. *Time* magazine quoted his assessment of the "ham and egg art" in the exhibition as "the vaporings of half-baked lazy people." One direct result of the brouhaha over the State Department exhibit was the founding of the Artists Equity, whose principal purpose was to combat such actions and lobby for artists' rights.[4]

Had Watson had a forum during those years, the compulsive "firebrand" would have joyously lampooned the presidential pronouncements and lashed the demagogues. Certainly, he wanted to do so. He missed being in the thick of controversy. Writing and art had always energized him, and his financial situation was chronically precarious. But the climate was not propitious in 1946, and there appeared to be no suitable niche for him. Still, despite retirement to Gaylordsville, Watson remained actively connected to the art world. Not only were there frequent commutes to New York, he was also an avid letter writer, and both he and Nan had "advanced cases of telephonitis," so there was no lack of communication.[5]

Now there was time to write the book he had planned, a blend of memoir and commentary for which he had been assembling notes, jotting down reminiscences, and selecting photographs. In initial drafts he recalled the beginning of his career and early associations with Leon Kroll, Gutzon Borglum, Ben Foster, Thomas Moran, William Ritschel, Alfred Stieglitz, and other art figures. He recalled Frank Munsey and the encounter with President Theodore Roosevelt. Personal and gossipy, his vignettes and viewpoints would have captivated some readers and infuriated others, much as his unconstrained remarks had done earlier, although the streak of malice, discernible only occasionally during the 1920s, was more pronounced now.[6] Watson reported "slow but fair progress" on the book in 1948 and thought he was "in sight of the end." Still working on it in 1952, Watson thanked Peggy Bruce for sending him a photograph he intended to use in the chapter on Ned. For his chapter on *The Arts,* he was "combing out the pearls from back numbers" with which to make "a diadem" for his story, he told Pène du Bois in 1953. He turned down Ernest Fiene's invitation to serve on an upcoming jury because his book contained "a long, harsh chapter attacking our museums. . . . If I should serve on a jury now it would refute what I have written and make me appear slightly ridiculous." Ira Glackens urged him on. "I keep hearing from Antoinette Kraushaar about your book and how I wish you would finish it," he wrote Watson in late 1955. But Watson never did. Fragmentary typescripts and manuscripts only hint at the withering insights and snappy anecdotes that would have filled its pages.[7]

Nan and Forbes had been in Connecticut less than a year when his beloved sister, Mary, died on April 9, 1947. She had been afflicted with cancer and a heart condition. "One hates to be parted from so sensitive and beautiful a woman," he wrote Esther Williams, "but she wanted to die suddenly and she escaped the intensive agony of cancer for which the doctor said there was nothing constructive to be done." Under the terms of her will, Forbes was executor and sole beneficiary of her estate. Characteristically, however, despite his meager circumstances, he refused to accept the all-out bequest. "I do not believe in such wills and am dividing her small estate with the other members of the family," he wrote Dows. He commuted to Boston well into June to arrange for the division of property, trying to direct her bequest to his brother's children rather than to his brother Carroll, who did not need the money. Watson removed a rose bush from Mary's apartment when she died and transplanted it in his garden, where he tended it devotedly, covering it on frosty nights and uncovering it when the sun shone. His "cherished rose bush" flourished. On December 20 of the following year, Carroll, Forbes's last surviving sibling, died in Bath, Maine. Although saddened, Watson had never been close to the "handsome bull-like" man "who loved to fight and play football, loved hard labor, liquor and women and was nauseated by the sight of a book."[8]

As soon as they were settled, Nan built a good working studio for herself. Forbes put together a makeshift office until he could convert the barn into a satisfactory workspace. "If you have ever lived in the country you, or at least your wife knows that it requires about three times as much organization as it does to live in the city," he wrote painter Edward Millman. Fix-up projects dominated their time at first. "My painting has been confined to the kitchen floor," he wrote Olin Dows. "I find that I am a super Mondrian because to realize what sensitive linear relationships I establish you have to have enough imagination to imagine the lines."[9]

An early riser still, Watson awoke at five o'clock every morning, attended to writing and correspondence, then removed to the kitchen, where he sat with a huge cup of café au lait into which he broke "many hunks of bread," enjoying himself "like a French peasant girl warming her insides before the family begins to rattle round the house." He cooked breakfast for Nan then, and took it up to her, later doing the dishes. "Lovely spring in the country is of all the seasons the big chore time," Watson wrote his current lover, Isabella Howland, "and although I have been a bad boy this morning and am chatting to you when I should be working I refuse to even glance in the direction of a chore until my day's allotment of writing is over. The country place is either your master or you are its.... The leaves can stay unraked, the lilacs untrimmed, the garden unplowed, the lawn unseeded, the barn and cellar in a mess but I won't go near them until after four o'clock."[10]

Nan and Forbes standing beside their yellow Victorian house with "doo dabs" dripping from the roof, in Gaylordsville, 1952. Photograph courtesy of Maria Ealand.

They enjoyed living "simply and car-lessly." A convenient commuter train, just a short taxi ride from their house, enabled them to make the ninety-mile trip into New York City with little trouble. Nan's sister, Alice, was happy to come to Gaylordsville to pick them up and take them to the Bonnard show and other events, as were their many friends. The local grocery store, which was "excellent," delivered to their door. And their house, though built in 1840, had all the necessary machinery. "As a matter of fact," he wrote Leon Kroll, "I had to come to the country before I learned how extraordinarily romantic machinery is." His "sweetest little loves" were the oil furnace, an electric water heater, the gas range, and an automatic electric pump. He also had "two top-notch servants," he wrote Millman, "a good houseman named Forbes Watson and a splendid cook named Nan Watson. . . . We give precedence to our office and studio hours respectively and the little house seems [to] get on all right without too much spoiling."[11]

"A Room of One's Own." Watson in his loft study in Gaylordsville, 1952. A photograph of Juliana Force is prominently displayed on the wall behind him. Photograph courtesy of Maria Ealand.

Forbes quickly learned to become a "decent villager." He was a volunteer fireman, voted in all the local elections, and he and Nan entertained the village children with apples, cookies, and candy at Halloween. Even so, among some of the more conservative members of the community, the Watsons were slightly suspect, as the neighbors on their left warned those across the street to "'look out for those Watsons; they had been in the Government.'"[12]

They loved the rolling land and the seasonal bloom of flowers all about. They never lost interest in the vegetable garden or in the simple routines. Every afternoon around five o'clock, Forbes sat on the back steps with his cigarette and highball while Tommy, the neighbor's cat, crouched beside him drinking a dish of milk. "Can you think of a picture further removed from the Coplon trial, the Lilienthal Hearings and the various hysterics of a congress overrun with charlatans?" he wrote Maria Ealand. Each night they sipped a whiskey and listened to the radio before retiring.[13]

Their little Victorian house on Route 7, painted yellow with green blinds and dripping "doo-dabs from the roof" pleased them enormously. When a new house went up across the road "with a horrid little gifty shoppe right in front," Watson noted that "for their sins in having no taste whatever," they were having "nothing but bad luck since they arrived here." There were endless improvements and additions to consider. For months Watson was immersed in converting the hayloft into a workroom for himself, a "Room of One's Own," as he referred to it, and his letters were filled with details, including hand-drawn sketches, of carpentry, colors, and materials. The renovations laid them "flat on our financial backs" to the extent that they needed a second mortgage, but the room brought Forbes the "cheeriest contentment" imaginable, and Nan thought it "a triumph of imagination and the spitting image" of Forbes. As the years passed, convenience and ease assumed greater importance, and they looked into a downstairs basin and toilet. Following one particularly dry spring, they put in an artesian well.[14]

The quiet rural existence was good, but sometimes they missed their old social life, mingling and talking art. Watson was even sorry when a neighboring couple, whom he did not particularly like, decided to move abroad, "because they do have a place in our exceedingly sparse social life." Harsh winters especially tended to intensify their isolation. And they were expensive. It cost eighty dollars a month to keep the house warm during severe winters, due to increased consumption of bottled gas and electric power, extra tasks for the chore boy, and repairs when pipes froze. For a time, they contemplated renting a small, furnished studio apartment in New York from December through March, but cost eliminated that option. When Forbes and Nan decided to spend a month in New York during the Christmas holidays in 1949, Alice was "very glad . . . because it will give Nan a let-up from house work and from the bad weather they have there in winter," she wrote their mutual friend Concetta Scaravaglione.[15]

Watson's interest in the art scene, and particularly in the Whitney, had not slackened. Back in 1943, the year following Gertrude Whitney's death, hearing a rumor that the Whitney heirs, who were "all cordially bored by art," were turning the Whitney Museum collection over to the Metropolitan Museum and liquidating the Eighth Street buildings, Watson was horrified. "The poor Whitneys, if they save enough on art, can still pay their income taxes and keep a few horses on the side," he snarled. "It's as if a friend had been murdered," he wrote Juliana Force. "You have given your life to this work. You know the collection, . . . what it has meant to the American artist and how it has educated the American public. So the final tragic decision is made by those who neither know nor care. . . . There's still a lot to do for art. And the thing for you is to conquer again as you did before. . . . Up and at 'em!"[16] As late as 1953, he could still become irate that the Whitney featured George Grosz instead of an authentically American painter in a final show before moving from the old Eighth Street address. "Ain't that a Yankee trick?" he wrote Pène du Bois.[17]

The Watsons were by no means forgotten in Connecticut. Visits from friends who appreciated Forbes's counsel and were "dazed and dazzled" by the royal hospitality he and Nan conferred kept them abreast of news and remembered elsewhere.[18] Nan still exhibited occasionally. Her group watercolor show at Marie Sterner's with Max Weber and William Zorach, among others, made Forbes especially proud. Artists were still eager to have Forbes in attendance at their shows. Henry Varnum Poor wanted him to do an article about a recent project of his, and Ward Lockwood asked him to write a foreword. Young artists still solicited letters of recommendation. The editors of a new artist-writer-owned publication *The Magazine of the Year,* invited him to contribute an article. The piece, "Belief and Painting," reaffirmed Watson's old vision of the centrality of the artist; its thesis emphasized that the faith of the artist himself, unguided and unconscious, not ecclesiastical subject matter, made a painting religious.[19] Charlotte Devree, art editor of *Look* magazine, invited him to serve on a panel of sixty-seven critics and museum officials to select the ten best living painters in America. Noting that there was not a single artist among the authorities and viewing the whole thing as a stunt, Watson turned down *Look*'s invitation with a "snooty" reply. "If we are ever to be cured of our timidity and name-chasing," the old democrat chided, "it will not be through an attempt to confer taste by authority. . . . Here you have a magazine fortunate enough to be named *Look* saying to its 15,000,000 readers: 'Don't look, just listen, and especially don't look at art; we'll tell you authoritatively what's what.' For me it is an utterly repellent plan."[20]

Freelancing, arranging exhibitions, and lecturing continued to be vital activities in Watson's life, not only for social and professional reasons but also from an economic standpoint. Trips, even to New York, could be a financial drain if he did not "sell some lectures." The traveling Allen Tucker exhibition he had worked on in 1946 did not come off, but the following October the Macbeth Gallery held an exhibit of Tucker's works, for which Watson wrote the catalog. Two weeks after the show closed, Watson resumed a more or less regular association with the Art Students League, beginning with a series of six lectures on nineteenth-century art. Commuting to New York once a week in November and December, he found the league significantly changed from twenty-five years earlier, when he had been on the faculty. The school had grown much larger, occupying all of the Fine Arts Galleries. Some fifteen hundred students were enrolled now. The halls swarmed with them, and the evening classrooms were "far too crowded." That did not diminish his pleasure in returning to the podium and basking in the veneration of former students, however.[21]

The weekly lectures also offered Watson convenient opportunities for assignations with artist Isabella Howland, with whom he carried on a three-year affair. In between trysts, managed through complex commuter arrangements, Watson romanced his "doveoflove" with a steady flow of tamely raunchy, verse-embellished love letters.[22] "The League sent its check today," he wrote his "très chère warmer-upper," "and I couldn't help laughing to myself, for the League will never know that I have been rewarded beyond their power to pay."[23] Howland was another reason Watson was eager to winter in New York.

In March 1949 Watson presented a series of four lectures in conjunction with talks by John Sloan, Walter Pach, and Harry Wickey. His talks pleased the league so much, he "boasted" to Maria Ealand, that he was invited to give ten the next winter. The lectures, presented between October and December 1949, covered some of his pet topics: government and art, museums and artists, taste, Juliana Force and Gertrude Whitney, artists and publicity, and war art. For the league's seventy-fifth-birthday exhibition at the Metropolitan Museum of Art, which featured seventy-five notable alumni and former faculty members, he contributed ten of the catalog essays, ranging from academician Kenyon Cox to abstractionist Andrew Dasburg.[24]

As he was preparing a speech for a testimonial dinner in honor of Yasuo Kuniyoshi in March 1948, Watson suffered a painful attack of lumbago, now termed "sacroiliac displacement," which forced him to do his writing in bed. "I'm not used to pain and doctors and having someone else put on my stockings and shoes," he complained in a letter to Concetta Scaravaglione. Happily, though, the doctors pronounced him remarkably healthy and ordered him only to reduce his weight and liquor consumption. The dinner, given by Artists Equity in New York, followed a retrospective show of Kuniyoshi's works at the Whitney and drew some four hundred artists. Watson was "ashamed to be seen" because he could not stand straight and walked as if he were "a hundred and eighty." But he had a marvelous time. The tribute was "magnificent," he wrote Scaravaglione. He was "flabbergasted" to see Juliana Force at the opening, as he had heard she was very ill with cancer. But "there she was smiling, weak and dignified." He overflowed with admiration for her courage.[25]

Juliana Force died five months later, on August 28, 1948. For her ally of thirty-two years, her death could only underscore the displacement of moderate modernism, the Woodstock variety, from the epicenter of contemporary American art. He noted ruefully that a number of artists who should have been at the funeral, "even if benefactions had been followed by fights," were not. When the Whitney Museum held a memorial exhibition the following year, Watson wrote one of four forewords to the catalog. In it he described affectionately the unique collaboration of Juliana Force and Gertrude Whitney and the remarkable results their combined energies produced. His working draft, aptly titled "The Achievement of Two Ladies," also formed the core of a slide lecture at the Art Students League the following month, which he illustrated with a sampling of work by the innumerable artists Juliana Force had promoted, including Nan.[26]

By 1950, when Watson delivered a series of three Sunday afternoon lectures at the Metropolitan Museum of Art on the topic of twentieth-century American painting, he no longer found it necessary to deflate the established artists to advance the moderns. This was especially apparent in his discussion of John Singer Sargent, whom he had once loved to vilify as the greatest painter of "mundane portraits" in America and England. Now he put aside his splendid sarcasm, highlighting Sargent's mastery—not sneeringly, but respectfully—and acknowledging with equanimity that history would resolve the widely disparate assessments of the famed portraitist. That Watson had not lost his caustic touch, however, was evident in his statements about Kenyon Cox, whose integrity he praised, but whose compositions he described as "symmetrically static to a stupefying degree."[27]

In the final lecture of the Metropolitan series, Watson returned to the old controversy about the meaning of modernism. "Today," he observed, "if [the painter] works in certain ways his head will be surrounded with the halo of modernity. If he works in certain other ways the sacred gates of modernity will be closed against him. But that does not matter, for in the end only the independent spirits will be accepted in Heaven." The term "modern" now denoted for Watson the artist's "complete freedom to use or not to use man-made objects, or nature seen through the naked eye or the microscope and to create in his own way a work of art which depends on its own logic and not on natural resemblances." Significantly, in pinpointing the victory of individualism as the paramount achievement of modernism, Watson repudiated his most overdrawn pronouncements of the late 1930s, in which he condemned the "wayward and fruitless experiment[s]" of individualism.[28]

That same year, 1950, Bruce Bliven, editorial director of New Republic magazine, published a symposium on American culture since the turn of the century in which various writers took stock in the fields of politics, medicine, national affairs, morals, business, music, education, and other areas.[29] Watson wrote the chapter on art. Mellower at seventy-one, his essay was one of the most sorted out and evenhanded of his career, almost textbook-like in its aim to be comprehensive while concise and dispassionate.

His style still tended toward the personal, as for example when he discussed the Armory Show: "From the moment I woke up in the morning I looked forward to my daily visit. I do not remember seeing a docent or hearing a lecture. The eyes had it." He still made his points. Both artists and public were too willing to embrace the latest novelties in art. Too many modernists were interested solely in what was going on in their "insides." Now his sting was lighter, however. Contrasted with his scathing attacks on the School of Paris during the twenties, he predicted, with only a touch of sarcasm, that "not so many American artists in the second half of the twentieth century will keep their ears close to the transatlantic telephone as did in the first half."[30]

His tone was sanguine as he noted the expansion of museums of all types and sizes and the trend toward better management, improved choice of materials, and encouragement of local artists. Watson even pardoned them for an offense he had long denounced, their failure to purchase contemporary work. "Museums are not as hesitant as they were," he noted, but "when they did hesitate it was to avoid being stampeded by the vogue of the moment into getting things that might soon be outmoded." He was optimistic about art education, as administrators and teachers had at last realized "that history minus art simply was not history," and he applauded the tremendous growth in programs at the collegiate level.[31]

While his belief in federal art support had not wavered, he had grown less intense about it. Government patronage was no longer all-embracing, but one among several agents for progress in American art. Reasonably, he credited the New Deal arts programs with putting artists to work "from one end of the country to the other" and with initiating "a decentralizing process . . . which awakened the entire country to the actualities of the working artist." He justified the realistic character of New Deal art as well as army and navy war art. "The subject matter . . . had to be understood, to put it bluntly, by the taxpayers. They were the ones who paid for all of this work." In the case of private, noncommissioned works, the artist had the right to do exactly what he wanted to do.[32]

Watson had not only retained most of his earlier ideas, he borrowed heavily from past articles and lectures. Certain phrases expressed his views so aptly there was no reason not to recycle them. One, an aphorism Watson had used countless times and would repeat all his life, was that of the old ninth-century Chinese philosopher "who said that most people see paintings through their ears."[33] What could express more pithily Watson's longtime harangue against fashion artists and Americans' timid taste?

Having settled upon a definition of modernism, he concluded: "The dogma, so often heard in France in the early days when to be modern was a religion, was that the one sure way to be truly modern was to be yourself, to make your own statement. I am inclined to supplement this dogma with the further dogma that the only way to see modern is to see it in your own way with your own eyes."[34] Independence and individuality had returned to the forefront.

If ever there was an appropriate forum in which to comment on new trends, it was an anthological survey such as *Twentieth Century Unlimited,* in which contributors not only summed up the past but also assessed prospects for the future. Clearly, though, Watson was not going to acknowledge the abstract expressionist movement fermenting in New York by 1950. He probably hoped it would just go away. In his Metropolitan Museum talk that April, he made only passing references to Pollock, Motherwell, Tobey, and Stamos. Here, he ignored the abstract expressionists altogether. It was true, as Dows remarked, that Watson kept abreast of the latest developments in the field of art "right up to the end." But he did not like them. Arshile Gorky's paintings were "stupid and neurotic and always exhibition size," he complained. The abstract expressionists' mixed-media productions were nothing more than "tricks." William Baziotes's *Primeval Landscape* looked "like an illustration for a child's book on the first age of the world."[35]

He may have seemed out of touch, but for Watson, modern art ended with the 1920s, and his admirers respected his viewpoint no less than they had two decades earlier. During one of his visits to Manhattan in the fall of 1952, Watson dropped in on a free lecture by Philip Evergood. The artist interrupted his talk to announce to the class that "the great American critic" Forbes Watson was present. "I knew what that meant," Watson related to Peggy Bruce, "and was not in the least surprised when Mr. Evergood continued: 'The class would be very happy Mr. Watson if you would give us the benefit of hearing your thoughts on our subject.' Well, the subject, if there was one, was The Impasse of Abstract Art. Free lecture nothing."[36]

Cook Glassgold thought Watson had begun "to deteriorate somewhat" by the time *The Arts* ceased in 1932. "And I think this was purely physical," Glassgold observed: "He was an ailing man." Glassgold may have been referring to Watson's drinking, a habit George Biddle and others viewed as extreme. "He drank heavily all his life," according to Biddle, "and he was a disappointed man and he was penniless." He remembered Watson as "drifting on to a disillusioned, bitter end." But Maria Ealand, who observed no such side, pointed out that "Forbes didn't like Biddle, and the people that he didn't like he didn't make too much effort to hide. . . . He disliked people who were insincere . . . and he thought

Biddle was insincere."[37] (Interestingly, Biddle also described Ned Bruce as a "bitter, angry man.")[38] More than ever, Watson despised "highfalutin'" pronouncements about art, and if his attacks on Aldous Huxley as a "windbag" and Meyer Schapiro as "that masterly aesthetic diarhealist" seemed more personal than analytical, that was no startling change.[39]

Still, that characteristic ripple of maliciousness, more permeative now, sometimes drowned out the old irony, betraying a residue of resentment. Rosalind Irvine, secretary of the American Art Research Council, who compiled a history of the Whitney Studio, refused to transcribe some of Watson's remarks concerning Juliana Force and Gertrude Vanderbilt Whitney in her 1949 interview with him because "they were of a highly personal nature and in my opinion come under the heading of 'malicious gossip.'"[40]

Writing Concetta Scaravaglione, who was returning to the United States after a fellowship in Italy, Watson mourned the changes that had occurred since she left, specifically, the ascendancy of abstract art. "Even in the three years (or was it centuries) of your absence the world of art has greatly changed or at least gone further along the road on which it had started. Motherwell and Pollock [spelled "Pollach"] are the favorite painters of the Whitney, now industriously following in the footsteps of the Modern. In sculpture Rozak (if that's the way you spell it) is very much à la mode, with Zorach looked upon as old master of another period." It was a time of trends, he observed, "a time when museum people especially are afraid that they might be called reactionary." Even the Metropolitan was embracing the abstract, "something in the manner of a baby playing with a puppy that it is half afraid of."[41]

Nor was he reconciled by 1958, when the spectacular ascendancy of abstract expressionism had propelled New York to the summit of the international art world. Its blatant disengagement from observable life only intensified Watson's appreciation of his favorite moderate modernists. He wrote painter Leon Hartl: "You know how much we love and admire your painting. It has an inherent quality of affection, a quality which I find a great relief especially today when so many people are painting through their ears."[42]

It was "a confused period." He had seen about twenty-five shows during the month of November 1953, Watson wrote Pène du Bois, "and heard on every side that, to quote an uncultivated dealer, 'if it ain't dipped in modern you can scream your life away and you can't sell it.'" Another dealer had told him "of our daring public: 'They either want literalism or modernism. They want to see every detail or something that they don't understand.'" The two most successful painters that season were Ogden Pleissner, a realist, and Andrew Wyeth, "another meticulous objectivist." "You explain it. I can't," he wrote Dows, referring to their sellout shows. So "how explain that even the Metropolitan Museum is scared to death not to be 'avant-garde'?" Hoisting more resolutely the banner of independence against the onrush of abstractionism, Watson observed, "I think we can agree . . . that the artist who wishes to be himself, like you, must stick to his religion, must have faith. The bandwagon is overcrowded. On the other hand this is supposed to be a free country. So let us paint as we each want to paint."[43]

In 1952, ten years after they severed their professional association, the *Magazine of Art* published two articles by Watson, one about John Sloan, the other about Arthur Bowen Davies. Watson was ironic as he traced Davies's rise and decline in the context of modernism. Even though Davies had been the dominant force behind the watershed Armory Show and a percipient advisor to modern-art collectors in the United States, he himself never satisfactorily assimilated modernism into his own work. "What would Miss Lillie Bliss, to cite one of those who revered Davies, have thought if she had lived to see that the critic captains of 1952 could not find a berth for the 'designer of dreams' on their ship of art?" Watson mused.[44]

As with much of his later writing, Watson's article on John Sloan, which coincided with a retrospective of his work at the Whitney, was reminiscent in flavor. Sloan possessed the journalist's ability to observe, Watson noted, and an "acid and wit, that kept his art "out of the dull precincts of self-righteous social consciousness." Examining the source of Sloan's originality, Watson pinpointed the "arrant independent" at the core of the successful artist, teacher, and leader.[45]

After a lapse of five or six years—during the Great Depression—when he abjured artistic individuality and independence in favor of subordination to the community, Watson had restored independence to the fulcrum of his aesthetic credo. "I've often wondered," he wrote in 1955, "why the word independence is such a favorite of mine. It may be that being born within the shadow of the Washington elm in Cambridge and being taken as a child to such landmarks as Bunker Hill and Concord, I unconsciously developed romantic notions of the War of Independence—notions which went with me when I was taken into the world of independent art. . . . Other worlds have come into being since then—modern art, advanced art, abstract art, avant-garde art, worlds without number, but my favorites still remain the independent and revolutionary worlds. I don't ask anyone else to make these worlds their favorites. I merely ask permission that I may belong to them, that I may be an independent revolutionary."[46]

That was the opening statement in a draft of an article about Maurice Prendergast, whom Watson admired for his courage and independent eye. "Even an independent has his theories," he wrote in another draft, "but they are *his* theories and do not belong to the word. . . . The artist can be academically modern, advanced, abstract, but an academic independent is a contradiction in terms. Independent then, though even in art, it seems a middle-aged word, and in other fields as old as revolution, is the right term. . . . The kind of independence which I am attempting to describe combines the spirit of the pioneer with the spirit of the revolutionary."[47] Despite certain material dependencies in later life, Watson himself personified the independent revolutionary he described in that 1955 manuscript.

Appropriately, Watson's final publication was devoted to William Glackens, the subject of so many earlier tributes. The occasion was the Pennsylvania Academy of Fine Art's 150th Anniversary Exhibition, held in 1955, honoring the academy's twenty-five most famous students of the past. The list included distinguished names such as George Caleb Bingham, Mary Cassatt, William Merritt Chase, Robert Henri, Thomas Eakins, Charles Demuth, John Marin, and Benjamin West. For the catalog, Joseph Fraser, the director of the academy, wanted "personal appreciation and evaluations," not a mere listing of "cold biographical material." He had the right man. Watson's essay, affectionate and knowing, celebrated Glackens's glorious, hardy independence, the same qualities Watson had praised in his first article about him in 1920.[48]

To verify a few facts and request the loan of several of Glackens's paintings for the show, Watson wrote the painter's son Ira, who was working on a book about his father at the time. Over two years of correspondence, Watson and Ira's friendship grew as they exchanged bits of information and advice as well as candid opinions of mutual acquaintances. Searching for details about his father's early years, Glackens wrote Watson, "You alone in your monograph have recorded some, and are the sole repository of those facts." Ira condoled with Watson, still craving cigarettes after more than a year of physician-imposed abstinence.[49] And Watson sympathized with Ira, furious over Van Wyck Brooks's comments about his father in a recently published biography of John Sloan. "The dunce" had stated, among other things, that Glackens was prone to tantrums. "Nothing could be further from the truth," Ira complained. In response to a commiserative letter from Watson, he commented that it was "depressing to learn that even in ninth century China they had their Van Wyck Brookses!" Watson quoted Ira in his catalog essay, and Ira profited from the older professional's encouraging comments about his manuscript.[50] Ira and his wife visited the Watsons in Gaylordsville in May 1956, their first get-together since Ira was in his twenties. It was not their last. Watson always had a special interest in and appeal for young people, which was probably one reason he remained youthful all his life.

That year, the Allen Tucker Memorial, of which Watson was a trustee, trans-ferred fifty thousand dollars to the Art Students League for the establishment of four annual Allen Tucker scholarships for painting.[51] In time, administra-tion of the trust was transferred to the league entirely. Watson chaired the memorial trust, faithfully attending board meetings each year until 1957, when Nan became ill.

Forbes and Nan were houseguests of their old friend Peggy Bruce in Wash-ington that spring. A week's visit with Peggy, Watson liked to say, was "equal to a month's visit to anyone else because her California hospitality is literally over-whelming." The weather turned unexpectedly wintry and wet, however, and Nan caught a terrible cold. Rushed to the hospital with lung and blood com-plications, she was near death. Forbes, Alice, and Nan's brother John sat in the hospital for weeks following her emergency surgery, while she passed the crisis and gradually began to recover. "Nan has a sister who adores her and a gener-ous and prosperous and also adoring brother," he wrote Jane Jones, the widow of his artist-friend Wendell Jones. "Were it not for them I should be in jail now for nonpayment of medical dues." Worried and frustrated when he was away from Nan's bedside, and with no typewriter to keep him occupied, Forbes be-gan his scotch and soda at 10:00 A.M. It was a "trying situation" for both Forbes and Peggy, who was no longer used to having a man around in the daytime.[52]

Nan, who was nearly eighty-one years old, and Forbes, seventy-eight, showed their age for the first time that April. Up until then, their seemingly boundless vitality and fascination with life belied a gradual deterioration in health and physical vigor, he because of a bad heart, which required daily digitalis medi-cation, and she from a malfunctioning thyroid. How frail the couple must have appeared that morning on April 25 as Peggy Bruce helped them settle into a drawing room on the 11:00 A.M. train to New York. It had been one month since they had arrived in Washington for a week of warmth and diver-sion. "When we were finally alone, Nan and I,—no nurses, no doctors, no hos-pital smells, no sympathizers, we looked at each other, breathed deeply and smiled. . . . Nan lay down on the couch and slept until Newark. I sat looking out of the window, oh! so happy to be homeward bound!" he wrote Jane Jones. "Of course one cannot go through such a black ordeal without learning some-thing. I learned a lesson, strange to say, in the psychology of money. I was be-ginning to feel the weight of the nurses' and hospital bills when Nan's family, having been warned that she might not live, arrived in Washington and her brother handed me a fat check, one of those 3 figure ones, and said: 'Now stop worrying. I can pay all the bills without the slightest inconvenience to me.' It was just like having the Rock of Gibraltar get off your chest and the good financial news lifted Nan's spirits up, up, UP!"[53] Forbes drafted his final will and testament that spring.

Steady decline marked the years that followed. Nan and Forbes required regular help in the house now in addition to the chore boy. "Our lovely giantess comes on Wednesdays and takes the house apart," he wrote Jane Jones, urging her to come for a visit. They also had "another lady about a foot shorter who is Chairman of the Committee on Spiritual Affairs at the Church and the luckiest Bingo Player in the village." Nan had not been robust since her illness in 1957, and Forbes's heart condition had worsened. The cosmopolitan couple who once thrived on travel now hardly left their yard, though they still relished company. They had wanted to visit their friend Pène du Bois during his final illness in 1958, but Nan's knees buckled without warning now, preventing her from traveling. Over a ten-month period, they made only two trips, both to the town of New Milford, of which Gaylordsville was a district, six miles from home. Nan's sister, Alice, died on Christmas Eve 1958 following a massive stroke, throwing them into "the deepest depression they had known in their long life together." Then two months later, while still sorrowing over the loss of darling Alice and wrestling with her apartment's contents, which they had moved to Gaylordsville, Nan's older brother Will died. Nearly paralyzed with grief by these losses, they "opened the White Horse and let her go down the hatch. When this endearing stimulant began to overcome the numbness in our bodies and souls we rolled up our sleeves and went at it and they have been rolled up ever since. . . . We decided that, without forgetting, we must end our mourning. We must . . . lead the artist's life: create, create, create and enjoy, enjoy, enjoy." It was the artist's spirit reemergent, the motivating force of Watson's life.[54]

Their resolve to remain positive was increasingly tested, however, as Watson's heart continued to weaken. "You ask how the winter treated us," Nan wrote Jane Jones in May 1960, "and I can only report that the treatment we got was lousy. Poor Forbes has been sick all winter and spring most of the time in bed and is now extremely ill in the New Milford Hospital. . . . He cannot walk at all and has to have nurses around the clock. . . . Sometimes his mind is clear and sometimes it is very confused. When it is clear he seems at times like the old Forbes . . . , but the prospect is not good. . . . It would be still harder for me but for the help I have had from my niece and my nephew who come when they can and are very good to me."[55] Sick as he was, Watson wanted to know everything that was going on with his friends. He wanted to know about Eugene Speicher, whose wife, Elsie, had died recently. He had Nan answer friends' letters and bring him all the news. Up to the end he talked of going home, not realizing the seriousness of his condition. Forbes Watson died on Tuesday, May 31, of heart failure. The funeral was held the following Friday in the Lillis Funeral Home in Gaylordsville with the pastor of the Gaylordsville Methodist Church officiating. He was buried in Morningside Cemetery, just a mile and a half from his home of fourteen years. Obituaries in the major New York City newspapers, the *Washington Post,* and national art magazines reviewed his distinguished career as critic, lecturer, editor of *The Arts,* and federal arts administrator.

George Biddle, whose observations about acquaintances seemed to gain in malice, if not in reliability, as time passed, speculated that Watson "lived in extreme poverty" toward the end and that "they had to collect funds after he died for his wife."[56] In fact, Nan continued to receive a modest income from her aunt's bequest, but the main purpose of a loan exhibition of her paintings that November was to raise money for the widow. Held at the Wadsworth Atheneum in Hartford, Connecticut, the show, in memory of Forbes Watson, consisted of nineteen of Nan's still lifes, two lent by the Whitney Museum of American Art, one by the Metropolitan Museum of Art, two by Olin Dows, and the remainder (which were for sale) by Nan. It was a fitting memorial. Henry Schnakenberg prepared the exhibition, and Dows wrote the introduction to the catalog. Together, fifty-seven patrons purchased a painting by Nan to be added to the Atheneum's permanent collection. The list of contributors included Eleanor Roosevelt, organizations such as the Art Students League, artists, friends, colleagues, critics, and museum officials. It would have contained countless more names had not so many of Forbes's dearest friends preceded him in death.

In his catalog introduction, Dows described Nan's paintings as "the best of daily companions, . . . friendly, unassuming, . . . charming and modest," much as he might have described her. Forbes Watson, he noted, would have taken delight in the fact "that one of the country's oldest, most experimental and courageous museums had the perspicacity to put on this exhibition of his wife's paintings." Dows paid tribute to *The Arts* and to Watson the man: "Above all he enjoyed life and especially painting, writing about it and talking about it too; enjoyed the fights that flared up around it and enjoyed using his magnificent weapons in these encounters, his trenchant wit and personal integrity."[57]

Following Forbes's death, Nan's niece and nephew, who had come during Forbes's illness, arranged for full-time help in the Gaylordsville home. Friends and family were attentive and visited when they could, but Nan's failing vision was a problem. In 1962, thanking Leon Hartl for his New Year's greetings and wishing him success with his forthcoming show, Nan wrote, "I am unfortunately unable to paint now as my eyes are not good enough and it is difficult for me to get around." Without Forbes's companionship and the absorption of her painting, Nan moved back to Washington the following year, selling the

Gaylordsville house and taking an apartment at 4114 Davis Place Northwest near her niece, Elizabeth Quick. Alice Graeme Korff visited her several times a year, and as late as Nan's eighty-ninth year found her still "delightful" and "very articulate, . . . always glad to talk about the days when Forbes was so prominent." Thanks to "Talking Books," she spent long hours listening to the classics she had read in her younger days.[58] But she was growing physically frail and easily susceptible to the illnesses of old age. Nan Watson died of pneumonia on September 26, 1966.

In the end, Forbes Watson was remembered chiefly for *The Arts*. Even during the New Deal, when he was the prominent technical director of the Public Works of Art Project and publicist for the Section of Painting and Sculpture (and its successor, the Section of Fine Arts), his editorship continued to bring him the greatest celebrity. In the spring of 1967, more than thirty-five years after *The Arts* had ceased publication, the Adams, Davidson Gallery in Washington mounted an exhibition entitled *Homage to Forbes Watson and* The Arts, offering works from the Ashcan Group, the Whitney Studio Club, and other New York painters of the 1920s and 1930s who appeared in the pages of *The Arts*. It was like old home week. Some thirty works by Glackens, Henri, Sloan, Arthur B. Davies, Allen Tucker, Reginald Marsh, and others were shown, most of them from the walls of Forbes and Nan's home. They ranged in price from $125 to $6,500.[59]

What made *The Arts* the foremost magazine of a whole generation of American artists was the unique integrity of Watson's voice—authoritative, independent, keenly combative, and human. Indeed, that spirit of "humanitarian liberalism" that he hailed in Van Wyck Brooks's *The Writer in America* characterized his own life. His openness to new art and fresh ideas, his discriminating vision, and his passionate support of contemporary American art powered *The Arts*'s editorial excitement and inspired a long roster of talented assistants and contributors. Because he approached issues head-on and expressed his positions so entertainingly, the art world paid attention. When they picked up a copy of *The Arts*, readers knew they would find no equivocating. His countless campaigns, sincere and intense, delineated the aesthetic battle lines and escalated the level of artistic combat, rallying them to independent artists' causes, illuminating all the while the condition of American modernism.

At its most extreme, Watson's undeflectable independence also worked against him, marking the difference perhaps between an important legacy and an outstanding one. He "didn't care what he said," Goodrich observed. He was "agin' réclame, . . . no respecter of persons or of money, and occasionally he offended powerful people." Watson was "the most important" critic of his period, in Olin Dows's estimation, but he made enemies among rich trustees and museum people so that his reputation was "nothing like what it should be."[60]

Watson was viewed by art historians of the twenties as a champion of modernism and by New Deal historians as a conservative. He was both. Not an out-and-out modernist at the beginning and not a conservative at the end, he was a mugwump, a liberal simultaneously hailing the new generation of American artists and valuing their heritage. The renowned American modernist Max Weber saw clearly the genius and biases that animated Watson's work. He wrote to him: "You have watched with almost eagle-eye sharpness, discernment and exceptional intelligence the development of the modern art movement from its very inception elsewhere, and with what patriotic and cultural concern you have watched its unfolding and development in our own country."[61]

Watson's career began as European modernism made its historic debut at the Armory Show in 1913. It ended as American modernism approached its apogee in the abstract-expressionist movement. He never accepted the new expressionism, but then he had not fully embraced abstract art thirty years earlier. Yet all along, Watson, a personal liberal, had been a rousing force for the advancement of modern American art. The accents, inflections, and thrust of his potently expressed ideas remained provocative and influential for three decades.

APPENDIX

CHRONOLOGY OF EDITORIAL POSITIONS ON *THE ARTS,* JANUARY 1923–OCTOBER 1931

January 1923	Forbes Watson appointed editor
August 1923	Virgil Barker appointed associate editor
October 1924	Virgil Barker steps down as associate editor
October 1924–March 1925	Robert Allerton Parker appointed associate editor
April 1925–July 1925	Virgil Barker returns as associate editor
July 1925–December 1926	Virgil Barker appointed European editor
December 1925–October 1927	Lloyd Goodrich appointed associate editor
January 1927–September 1927	Virgil Barker appointed contributing editor
November 1927–October 1928	Lloyd Goodrich appointed European editor
November 1927–October 1928	Virgil Barker appointed associate editor
April 1928	C. Adolph Glassgold appointed contributing editor
November 1928	Lloyd Goodrich returns as associate editor
November 1928	Virgil Barker appointed contributing editor
December 1928	Dorothy Lefferts Moore appointed assistant editor
September 1929	Lloyd Goodrich and Dorothy Lefferts Moore appointed contributing editors
September 1929	C. Adolph Glassgold leaves; goes to *Creative Arts* under Henry McBride

EDITORIAL POSITIONS ON *ARTS WEEKLY,* MARCH 11,1932–MAY 7, 1932

March 11, 1932	Forbes Watson, Editor
April 30, 1932	Inslee Hopper, Assistant Editor

ABBREVIATIONS

AAA	Archives of American Art, Smithsonian Institution
AMA	*American Magazine of Art*
BCP	Belisario Contreras Papers
CORTRAPFAS	Central Office Records of the Treasury Relief Art Project and the Fine Arts Section of the Public Buildings Administration 1934–43, National Archives Record Group 121, Archives of American Art (DC 38–DC 42)
CSP	Concetta Scaravaglione Papers
DFP	David Fredenthal Papers
EFP	Ernest Fiene Papers
ERP	Edward Beatty Rowan Papers
EWP	Esther Williams Papers
FW	Forbes Watson
FWP	Forbes Watson Papers
GBP	George Biddle Papers
GPBP	Guy Pène du Bois Papers
GVWP	Gertrude Vanderbilt Whitney Papers
IHP	Isabella Howland Papers
JLP	Julian E. Levi Papers
LHP	Leon Hartl Papers
LKP	Leon Kroll Papers
MA	*Magazine of Art*
MWP	Max Weber Papers
NA	National Archives (Numbers indicate Record Group followed by Preliminary Inventory)
NYEP	*New York Evening Post*
NYEPSM	*New York Evening Post Saturday Magazine*
NYW	*New York World*
ODL	Olin Dows Letters
PHP	Peter Hurd Papers
PWAPFR	Public Works of Art Project Final Reports, Report Materials, and Project Issuances, 1933–1936, National Archives Record Group 121, Archives of American Art (DC 12)
SRPWAP	Selected Records of the Public Works of Art Project, 1933–1935, National Archives Record Group 121, Archives of American Art (DC 1–DC 4, DC 8)

SRTRAP	Selected Records of the Treasury Relief Art Project 1935–1938, National Archives Record Group 121, Archives of American Art (DC 14)
WJP	Wendell Jones Papers
WMAAA	Whitney Museum of American Art Archives

NOTES

INTRODUCTION

1. By and large, historians of American art of the twenties place FW squarely among the pro–modern art critics. For example, see: Barbara Rose, *Readings in American Art, 1900–1975* (New York: Praeger, 1975); Peninah R. Y. Petruck, "American Art Criticism: 1910–1939" (Ph.D. diss., New York Univ., 1979); George H. Roeder Jr., *Forum of Uncertainty: Confrontations with Modern Painting in Twentieth-Century American Thought* (Ann Arbor, Mich.: UMI Research Press, 1980); and Susan Noyes Platt, *Modernism in the 1920s: Interpretations of Modern Art in New York from Expressionism to Conservatism* (Ann Arbor, Mich.: UMI Research Press, 1985).

During the thirties, several American modernist painters criticized FW for his conservative bias. For example, see: Stuart Davis, "Some Chance," *Art Front* 1 (Nov. 1935): 4; and Davis, "What about Modern Art and Democracy?" *Harper's* 188 (Dec. 1943): 16–23. Art historian Karal Ann Marling portrayed FW as resistant to the more modernist tendencies in mural painting during the New Deal. See Marling, *Wall-to-Wall America: A Cultural History of Post-Office Murals in the Great Depression* (Minneapolis: Univ. of Minnesota Press, 1982). Dore Ashton referred to him as "the conservative critic Forbes Watson." Ashton, *The New York School: A Cultural Reckoning* (New York: Viking, 1972), 148.

1. BACKGROUND AND EARLY YEARS

1. Van Wyck Brooks, *The Writer in America* (New York: E. P. Dutton, 1953), 109, 112; FW to Van Wyck Brooks, May 26, 1953, FWP AAA.

2. Thomas H. Eliot, *Two Schools in Cambridge: The Story of Browne & Nichols and Buckingham* (Cambridge, Mass.: Windflower Press, 1982), ix; Maria Ealand, interview with author, telephone tape recording, Mar. 31, 1994.

3. FW to Elinor Morgenthau, June 19, 1945, FWP AAA.

4. FW to Isabella Howland, Jan. 3, 1949, IHP AAA.

5. FW, "Preliminary Fragment of Note on Alfred Quinton Collins," Mar. 6, 1954, MS., [p. 1], FWP AAA; FW to Olin Dows, May 19, 1947, ODL AAA; FW, "Forbes Watson," undated typescript, FWP AAA.

6. "A School for Boys in Cambridge," announcement of opening of Browne and Nichols, in Eliot, *Two Schools in Cambridge*, 4.

7. FW, "Caw, Caw, Caw," undated typescript, p. 2, FWP AAA; FW, "A Matter of Experience," undated manuscript, [p. 3], FWP AAA.

8. FW, "Denis and I," *The Bellman* 3 (Oct. 5, 1907): 383.

9. FW, "Caw, Caw, Caw," 2; *Harvard Class of 1902: Fiftieth Anniversary Report* (Cambridge, Mass.: Privately printed, 1952), 654; FW, "At the House of the Countess," *Harvard Advocate* 69 (Mar. 24, 1900): 25; FW, "A Spool of Thread," *Harvard Advocate* 70 (Oct. 3, 1900): 7.

10. *Harvard College Class of 1902: Twenty-Fifth Anniversary Report 1902–1927* (Cambridge Mass.: Harvard Univ. Press, n.d.), 670.

11. FW, "The Bet," *The Scrap Book* 5 (May 1908): 827–30.

12. FW, "Thomas W. Dewing," in *The Metropolitan Museum of Art Presents the 75th Anniversary Exhibition of Painting and Sculpture by 75 Artists Associated with the Art Students League of New York* (New York: Art Students League of New York, 1951), [8].

13. William Innes Homer, *Robert Henri and His Circle* (Ithaca, N.Y.: Cornell Univ. Press, 1969), 145; FW, "New Forces in American Art," *Kenyon Review* 1 (spring 1939): 124; The Gilder, "Palette and Brush," *Town Topics,* Feb. 6, 1908. In this widely read weekly, the critic, "the Gilder," attacked the exhibition of The Eight at the Macbeth Gallery, noting "vulgarity smites one in the face, . . . the whole thing creates a distinct feeling of nausea." He denounced most of the work of The Eight as coarse, vulgar, unadulterated slop.

14. FW, "The Achievement of Two Ladies," Art Students League Talk No. 6, Nov. 18, 1949, typescript, p. 6, FWP AAA.

15. Antoinette Kraushaar, interview with author, tape recording, July 15, 1985.

16. Thomas Hart Benton, *An American in Art: A Professional and Technical Autobiography* (Lawrence: Univ. Press of Kansas, 1969), 16.

17. FW to Mrs. Edward Bruce, Dec. 19, 1935, 121/125 NA.

18. Lloyd Goodrich, interview with author, tape recording, Mar. 16, 1985; Jane Watson Crane, interview with author, telephone tape recording, Apr. 25, 1994; Maria Ealand, "Recollections of Nan and Forbes Watson," Jan. 17, 1988, typescript, p. 2; Kraushaar interview, July 15, 1985; Inslee Hopper, interview with Robert Brown, tape recording, July 28, 1981, AAA; Allen Tucker to FW, Jan. 8, 1938, FWP AAA.

19. FW, "Reminiscences," Jan. 17, 1946, typescript, p. 1, FWP AAA.

20. FW, "Reminiscences," Jan. 17, 1946, 1.

21. FW, "George Bellows—The Boy Wonder of American Painting," lecture given at the National Gallery, May 27, 1945, typescript, pp. 2–3, FWP AAA; FW, [Reminiscences], Jan. 18, 1946, typescript, p. 3, FWP AAA.

22. FW, "The Making of Tennis Champions," *Outing Magazine* 58 (June 1911): 371–76; FW, "Athletic Stars of the Year," *Outing Magazine* 59 (Dec. 1911): 354–64. In a letter to Isabella Howland, FW referred to a "small book" he had written about sports. "I explained how all sports developed from the original ball games played against the castle wall and using the buttresses for angle shots." FW's book apparently was lost, as there is no physical or bibliographic record of it. FW to Howland, Mar. 25, 1949, IHP AAA.

23. FW, "Reminiscences," Jan. 17, 1946, 1; FW, "Caw, Caw, Caw," 1.

24. FW, "Reminiscences," Jan. 17, 1946, 1; FW, "Eugene Speicher—A New Arrival," *International Studio Supplement* 46 (Mar. 1912): xix–xx.

25. FW, "Artists become Critics: Letters on Art Reviews from Painters and Sculptors," NYEP, Oct. 4, 1913.

26. Rose, *Readings in American Art,* 3–36.

2. NEW YORK EVENING POST YEARS

1. Oswald Garrison Villard, *Fighting Years: Memoirs of a Liberal Editor* (New York: Harcourt Brace, 1939), 169, 168; FW, "Caw, Caw, Caw," undated typescript, p. 2, FWP AAA.

2. '*Tis Love that Makes the World Go Round*, NYEPSM, Feb. 7, 1914.

3. FW, "At the Art Galleries," NYEPSM, Mar. 11, 1916; FW, "At the Art Galleries," NYEPSM, Mar. 10, 1917.

4. FW, "Art Notes," NYEP, Nov. 23, 1912; FW, "Art in Philadelphia," NYEP, Feb. 13, 1915; FW, "The National Academy," NYEP, Mar. 30, 1917; FW, "Art Notes," NYEP, Oct. 16, 1915.

5. FW, "The American Art Exhibition in Venice," *Arts & Decoration* 13 (Aug. 1920): 213; FW, "Art Notes," NYEP, Nov. 9, 1912; FW, "Art Notes," NYEP, Nov. 7, 1914.

6. For a detailed account of the Armory Show, see Milton W. Brown, *The Story of the Armory Show*, 2d ed. (New York: Abbeville Press, 1988).

7. FW, "Modern Art," NYEP, Feb. 17, 1913.

8. FW, "International Art . . . First Notice," NYEP, Feb. 20, 1913.

9. FW, "International Art . . . Second Notice," NYEP, Feb. 22, 1913.

10. Stuart Davis, *Stuart Davis*. (New York: American Artists Group, 1945), [8]. For a comprehensive study of American art of this period, see Milton W. Brown, *American Painting from the Armory Show to the Depression* (Princeton, N.J.: Princeton Univ. Press, 1955). Abraham Davidson provides a detailed examination of American modernists of this period in *Early American Modernist Painting, 1910–1935* (New York: Harper and Row, 1981). For a detailed examination of the progress of vanguard art and theory in America from 1913 through 1918, see Judith Katy Zilczer, "The Aesthetic Struggle in America, 1913–1918: Abstract Art and Theory in the Stieglitz Circle" (Ph.D. diss., Univ. of Delaware, 1975).

11. FW, "Art Notes," NYEP, Dec. 20, 1913.

12. Arthur Miller quoted in Jean Nathan, "Within the Walls of the Chelsea," *New York Times*, Feb. 7, 1993. Listed on the National Register of Historic Places, the Chelsea Hotel served celebrated tenants such as Mark Twain, Thomas Wolfe, Arthur Miller, Dylan Thomas, Tennessee Williams, O. Henry, William Dean Howells, Eugene O'Neill, Sarah Bernhardt, John Sloan, Virgil Thomson, Willem de Kooning, and Jackson Pollock. Frank Rehn, who later established the Rehn Gallery, was born there.

13. FW to Edward Bruce, Sept. 1, 1937, 121/122 NA; FW to Bruce, Aug. 18, 1938, 121/122 NA; FW to Bruce, Aug. 20, 1940, 121/122 NA; FW to Bruce, Sept. 19, 1940, 121/122 NA; FW to Bruce, July 2, 1937, 121/122 NA.

14. FW, *Mary Cassatt* (New York: Whitney Museum of American Art, 1932), 12.

15. Lloyd Goodrich reminiscences, as recorded in talks with Harlan B. Phillips, 1963, AAA. For a history of the National Academy of Design drawn from its own official files, see Lois Marie Fink and Joshua C. Taylor, *Academy: The Academic Tradition in American Art* (Washington, D.C.: Smithsonian Institution Press, 1975).

16. FW, "The National Academy," NYEP, Dec. 18, 1915; FW, "Reminiscences," Jan. 17, 1946, typescript, p. 2, FWP AAA; FW, "Reminiscences," Jan. 23, 1946. In his earlier reminiscence of Jan. 17, 1946, FW had written concerning this episode, "for some weeks afterwards Gardner Symons could not even see me in the elevator without flushing and shedding some tears of rage." FW apparently meant Mrs. Symons.

17. FW, "Academy Exhibition . . . First Notice," *NYEP*, Dec. 18, 1912; FW, "National Academy . . . Second Notice," *NYEP*, Mar. 18, 1913.

18. Goodrich reminiscences, 1963; FW, "The National Academy . . . First Notice," *NYEP*, Dec. 20, 1913.

19. FW, "At the Art Galleries," *NYEPSM*, Nov. 18, 1916; FW, "Art Notes," *NYEP*, Apr. 24, 1915; FW, "First Day of Academy," *NYEP*, Dec. 14, 1912.

20. FW, "Art Notes," *NYEP*, Feb. 5, 1917; John Sloan, *Gist of Art* (New York: American Artists Group, 1939), 14.

21. Although FW never stated the equation explicitly, he often implied it. For example, in a letter to Nan in which he described a "nice" young bureaucrat he worked with in France, "a fine American type from Georgia, very methodical, very hard-working, very efficient, very inartistic." [FW to Nan Watson], July 12, 1945, FWP AAA.

22. FW, "Caw, Caw, Caw," 2. Lloyd Goodrich, Antoinette Kraushaar, and Jane Watson in their interviews of Mar. 16, 1985, July 19, 1985, and Apr. 25, 1994, respectively, made special mention of this distinguishing characteristic about FW, commenting on his "tremendous" circle of artist friends both in the United States and abroad.

23. Ralph Flint, "Quick, Watson—The American Way," *Art News* 40 (Apr. 15, 1941): 13; FW, *Allen Tucker* (New York: Whitney Museum of American Art, 1932), 7–8.

24. Frank Jewett Mather Jr., for example, a contemporary of FW's and a conservative, viewed art as the artist's emotional response to nature.

25. In his book *Art*, published in 1914, and in subsequent writings, Clive Bell set forth the thesis that the formal qualities in a work of art—line and color—and the relationship of these qualities elicit an aesthetic experience. This relationship he named "significant form." To appreciate significant form, the perceiver needed to bring to the artwork nothing from life. The experience involved the perceiver and the work exclusively. The term "significant form" became a byword of formalist critics.

26. FW, "Art Notes," *NYEP*, Oct. 26, 1912. Under Henri's scheme, the MacDowell Club of New York, established in memory of American composer Edward MacDowell and devoted mainly to music, mounted in its small art gallery a jury-free, biweekly rotating exhibition for different groups of visual artists.

27. "There is a weakness in the plan of having exhibitions which are not supervised," Watson wrote a week after his first congratulatory review. "They may be composed of pictures which do not impel the visitor to make a second visit." He made much of the large number of "healthy, growing talents" in a 1914 show, but then dismissed a group the following year as "somewhat amateurish as a whole." In 1916 FW reported with pleasure, "those interested in the ideal democracy of the MacDowell Club plan will be glad to know that the gallery has had its best year artistically and practically. It has introduced and reintroduced artists whose work has not found a way to the public's attention through the ordinary channels and who, thanks to the MacDowell Club, have greatly extended their audience." But he oscillated again the next year, observing, "the fine MacDowell Club movement has been discounted by the inundation of beginners' works." FW, "Art Notes," *NYEP*, Nov. 2, 1912; FW, "Art Notes," *NYEP*, Jan. 24, 1914; FW, "Art Notes," *NYEP*, Jan. 30, 1915; FW, "At the Art Galleries," *NYEPSM*, Apr. 29, 1916; FW, "At the Art Galleries," *NYEPSM*, Apr. 14, 1917.

28. FW to Edward Bruce, Mar. 21, 1938, 121/122 NA; FW, "Art Notes," *NYEP*, Dec. 7, 1912;

FW, "Art Notes," *NYEP,* Mar. 15, 1915. In an article written in 1934, FW delved into some of the more insidious sources of discrimination against women artists, noting that it required "a woman of stronger will that is required of a man to make progress in her profession." Other women's jealousies and timidities were a major reason. Women were "made for love and not for professions," in their view, and therefore all women artists were "really misguided beings."

Some "women-obstacles . . . to the advancement of their stronger-willed sisters" believed that matrimony conferred on them "the right to be didactic judges." As judges they echoed their husbands, praising women's paintings as "gay" and "great fun," never "profound" or "vital." In essence, they were "pretty good for a woman." But the greatest obstacles were the lady amateurs who maintained "their little studios and kitchenettes," with financial support from home, and wandered in sprightly fashion from tea to meeting pretending to believe they were professional artists. These "dilettante parasite[s] on art" set a superficial standard. FW, "The Vicissitudes of Women in Art," *Brooklyn Daily Eagle Sunday Review,* Feb. 25, 1934.

29. FW, "Art Notes," *NYEP,* Oct. 16, 1915.

30. FW, "Art Notes," *NYEP,* Nov. 27, 1915. Doctor Weichsel, a mathematician, social theorist, and critic, was "well known in 'radical' circles of New York," according to Thomas Hart Benton. Benton, *An Artist in America,* 4th ed. (Columbia: Univ. of Missouri Press, 1983), 379.

31. FW, "Preliminary Fragment of Note on Alfred Quinton Collins," Mar. 6, 1954, [p. 1], FWP AAA.

32. George Mowry, a noted historian of the Progressive Era, observed, "most progressives set themselves apart from the crowd. Mankind was basically good and capable of progress, but benign change scarcely issued from the masses. Rather it was only accomplished through the instrumentality of a few great and good men." George Mowry, *The Era of Theodore Roosevelt and the Birth of Modern America* (New York: Harper and Row, 1962), 89.

33. FW, "Art Notes," *NYEP,* Nov. 1, 1913.

34. The public's image of FW emerged in an unexpected way in 1917 when *Arts & Decoration* ran an unattributed series of columns, "Confidences of an Errant Artist," in which an anonymous writer, affecting "a gossipy but engagingly naive conversational style, . . . made sharp and witty comments on current figures and events in the art world." The amusing series aroused considerable speculation as to the identity of the author, who was actually Jerome Myers posing as a woman painter. "Sounds like Forbes Watson," one of the readers commented. Betsy Lee Fahlman, "Guy Pène du Bois: Painter, Critic, Teacher" (Ph.D. diss., Univ. of Delaware, 1981), 79, 96.

35. "Eight Critics of Art without Whom No Artistic 'Movement' Can Be Launched in New York," *Vanity Fair* 4 (June 1915): 34.

36. Zilczer, "Aesthetic Struggle," 29. Several historians of the period use the term "avant-garde" rather than "modern" to signify vanguard art. Arlene Olson in her discussion of theory and criticism during the period 1900–1913 distinguishes between conservative and avant-garde thought. Arlene Rita Olson, *Art Critics and the Avant-Garde: New York, 1900–1913* (Ann Arbor, Mich.: UMI Research Press, 1980). Virginia Mecklenburg also focuses on conservative versus avant-garde thought in her dissertation, "American Aes-

thetic Theory, 1908–1917: Issues in Conservative and Avant-Garde Thought" (Ph.D. diss., Univ. of Maryland, 1983).

37. FW, "Allen Tucker: A Painter with a Fresh Vision," *International Studio Supplement* 52 (Mar. 1914): 20. In his dissertation on American critical reaction to European modernism between 1908 and 1917, Howard Risatti takes his definition of modernism from critics writing in America between 1908 and 1917. "Using the term in this respect, Cézanne, van Gogh, and Gauguin will be considered the major artists of the modern movement as will artists such as Matisse, the Fauves, the German Expressionists, the Cubists, and the Futurists." Howard Anthony Risatti, "American Critical Reaction to European Modernism, 1908 to 1917" (Ph.D. diss., Univ. of Illinois, 1977), 5.

38. Zilczer's term "symptoms" seems particularly apt. Zilczer, "Aesthetic Struggle," ix; Brown, *American Painting*, 66. Also see note 41 below. H. Wayne Morgan points out, as does Mecklenburg, that some conservatives also held artist-centered views of art. Where the modernists and conservatives parted ways, though, was in the conservatives' emphasis on comprehensibility. "Traditionalists agreed with modernists on the artist's special nature and role in society. But they insisted more strongly than ever that these must be logical and understandable to the world at large. The artist could be in advance of what most sensitive people thought they wanted from art, but not so unusual that patrons could not catch up. The artist spoke a special language, but it *was* a language." H. Wayne Morgan, *Keepers of Culture: The Art-Thought of Kenyon Cox, Royal Cortissoz, and Frank Jewett Mather Jr.* (Kent, Ohio: Kent State Univ. Press, 1989), 10.

39. See note 25 above.

40. Arthur Wesley Dow, "Modernism in Art," AMA 8 (Jan. 1917): 116; Zilczer, "Aesthetic Struggle," 32.

41. Mecklenburg identifies two strains of conservative thought relating to artistic expression: the "traditionalist" view, represented principally by Kenyon Cox, Frank Jewett Mather Jr., and Edwin Blashfield, and the "expressionist" view, represented by Royal Cortissoz, Robert Henri, and William Merritt Chase. Cox "deplored the idea of the 'insanity of genius,' believing that 'universal ideals' demanded sane and disciplined expression." For Cortissoz, Chase, Henri, and other expressionists, the most fundamental issue was "that artists feel free to express their 'genius' and their unique perception of the world ('the bidding of their own temperaments') within rather loosely applied limits of style and decorum. . . . For them the artist's emotional and visual experiences provided the real substance of a painting, and artistic interpretation involved much less mental sifting and intellectual ordering than it did for the traditionalists. . . . Following a Tainian understanding of the artist's master faculty, Cortissoz described paintings as revelations of the character or experiences of their creators." Mecklenburg, "American Aesthetic Theory," 80–85.

42. FW, "Modern Art," NYEP, Feb. 17, 1913; FW, "At the Art Galleries," NYEPSM, Nov. 11, 1916; FW, "International Art," NYEP, Feb. 20, 1913; FW, "Art Notes," NYEP, Feb. 7, 1914; FW, "J. Alden Weir," NYEPSM, Mar. 28, 1914.

43. FW, "Art Notes," NYEP, Mar. 29, 1913; FW, "International Art," NYEP, Feb. 20, 1913; FW, "Art at Philadelphia," NYEP, Feb. 14, 1914; FW, "At the Art Galleries," NYEPSM, Mar. 24, 1917.

44. FW, "American Art Exhibition in Venice," *Arts & Decoration* 13 (Aug. 1920): 213; FW, "At the Galleries," NYEPSM, Apr. 28, 1917; FW, "The National Academy," NYEP, Mar.

21, 1914; FW, "Art Notes," *NYEP*, Mar. 20, 1915; FW, "Art Notes," *NYEP*, Feb. 8, 1913; FW, "Paintings in Washington," *NYEP*, Dec. 17, 1914.

45. FW, "The National Academy," *NYEP*, Dec. 19, 1914; FW, "At the Art Galleries," *NYEPSM*, Apr. 1, 1916.

46. FW, "William Glackens," *NYEPSM*, Mar. 7, 1914; FW, "At the Art Galleries," *NYEPSM*, Oct. 14, 1916; FW, "At the Art Galleries," *NYEPSM*, Jan. 20, 1917; FW, "Art Notes," *NYEP*, Dec. 20, 1913; FW, "Art Notes," *NYEP*, Mar. 29, 1913.

47. FW, "Art Notes," *NYEP*, Apr. 3, 1915; FW, "Art Notes," *NYEP*, Nov. 21, 1914.

48. For a detailed examination of the aesthetic thought of conservative and avant-garde critics during the period 1908–17, see Mecklenburg, "American Aesthetic Theory." In her discussion of the conservative aesthetic, she notes: "To communicate an ideal to the viewer required the artist to use a visual vocabulary that was widely understood. For conservatives this meant depicting natural forms." (69)

49. *Harvard Fiftieth Anniversary Report*, 654; FW, "Art Notes," *NYEP*, Jan. 23, 1915; FW, "Art Notes," *NYEP*, Nov. 20, 1915.

50. FW, "Art Notes," *NYEP*, Nov. 14, 1914.

51. FW, "Art Notes," *NYEP*, Apr. 11, 1914; FW, "At the Art Galleries," *NYEPSM*, Nov. 4, 1916; FW, "The National Academy," *NYEP*, Mar. 23, 1914; FW, "Art Notes," *NYEP*, Oct. 17, 1914; FW, "At the Art Galleries," *NYEPSM*, Mar. 18, 1916.

52. Goodrich reminiscences, 1963; FW, "Art Notes," *NYEP*, Nov. 13, 1915; FW, "At the Art Galleries," *NYEPSM*, Apr. 8, 1916.

53. FW, "Art Notes," *NYEP*, Jan. 23, 1915; FW, "Modern Art," *NYEP*, Feb. 17, 1913; FW, "Art Notes," *NYEP*, Dec. 26, 1914; FW, "Art Notes," *NYEP*, Feb. 20, 1915.

54. Jerome Myers, *Artist in Manhattan* (New York: American Artists Group, 1940), 66; Lloyd Goodrich, interview with author, tape recording, Mar. 16, 1985.

55. Members of the committee were: critic and lecturer Christian Brinton; John Weichsel, president of the People's Art Guild; W. H. de B. Nelson, editor of *International Studio;* Willard Huntington Wright, author and editor of *Forum* magazine; Robert Henri; and Alfred Stieglitz. Seventeen artists were actually represented in the Forum Exhibition. Painter Marguerite Zorach, wife of William Zorach, was also invited to exhibit.

56. Forum *Exhibition of Modern American Painters, Mar. 13 to Mar. 25, 1916, on View at the Anderson Galleries, New York* (New York: Mitchell Kennerley, 1916), 5; FW, "At the Art Galleries," *NYEPSM*, Mar. 18, 1916.

57. FW, "At the Art Galleries," *NYEPSM*, Apr. 14, 1917; Davidson, *Early American Modernist Painting*, 179; FW, "Independent Art," *NYEP*, Apr. 10, 1917.

58. FW, "At the Art Galleries," *NYEPSM*, Apr. 14, 1917.

59. FW, "Whitney Museum Talk," Nov. 12, 1931, typescript, pp. [1]–2, FWP AAA.

60. Goodrich interview, Mar. 16, 1985.

61. Ibid.; FW, summary of interview with Rosalind Irvine, Feb. 18, 1949, WMAAA, H.1/ f38; FW, "At the Art Galleries," *NYEPSM*, Jan. 15, 1916.

62. The women not only promoted American artists, they also took a personal interest in them, funding study abroad and, when needed, underwriting living costs for their families. For a detailed biography of Juliana Force, including accounts of her relationships with Gertrude Vanderbilt Whitney, FW, and other art personalities, see Avis

Berman, *Rebels on Eighth Street: Juliana Force and the Whitney Museum of American Art* (New York: Atheneum, 1990).

63. FW, "The Achievement of Two Ladies," Art Students League Lecture No. 6, Nov. 18, 1949, typescript, pp. 3, 10, FWP AAA; [Rosalind Irvine], "The Whitney Studio Club and American Art, 1900–1932," undated typescript, p. 5, WMAAA, H.1/32.

64. FW, "Art Notes," NYEP, Nov. 20, 1915; FW, "Art Notes," NYEP, Oct. 24, 1914; FW, "Art Notes," NYEP, May 1, 1915.

65. FW, "Cartoons of Raemaekers Shown," NYEP, Nov. 20, 1916; "FW," "To the Editor of the *Evening Post*," NYEP, May 23, 1916.

66. Janet Scudder, *Modeling My Life* (New York: Harcourt, Brace, 1925), 283–84.

67. Pène du Bois to Whom It May Concern, July 19, 1917, FWP AAA.

68. "The Evening Post Introduces Mr. Forbes Watson," NYEPSM, Mar. 31, 1917. Typically, an ambulance section of the American Field Service included a French lieutenant who served as liaison, an American chef, one or two sous-chefs, twenty volunteer drivers, an odd number of assistant drivers, an American-paid mechanic, and a varying number of French mechanics, cooks, and clerks. Charles A. Fenton, "Ambulance Drivers in France and Italy, 1914–1918," *American Quarterly* 3 (winter 1951): 332–33.

69. Alumni and students from Harvard represented the largest contingent of American Field Service volunteers, with which the Norton-Harjes Corps sometimes worked, followed by Yale, Princeton, Dartmouth, and Cornell. Fenton, "Ambulance Drivers," 326–43.

70. FW, "Fragments from France," NYEPSM, Oct. 13, 1917.

71. FW, "Serving 10,000 Meals a Day," *Red Cross Magazine*, Mar. 18, 1918, 29–34.

72. [Rosalind Irvine], "The Whitney Studio Club and American Art, 1900–1932," undated typescript, p. 3, WMAAA, H.1/32.

73. In 1945, while on a mission for the Treasury Department, FW revisited their old house and studio at 20, rue Jacob. "To my sorrow the romantic little house in the garden had been replaced by a modern quite homely apartment house which goes from the street next door . . . right through to the end of the garden," he wrote Nan. "But your studio is just the same from the outside. The concierge I did not see, so I don't know if she is the same but probably not, since she was no chicken in the last war." [FW to Nan Watson], Aug. 10, 1945, FWP AAA.

74. [FW to Nan Watson], July 19, 1945, FWP AAA.

75. FW, "Lemordant—Painter, Soldier," NYEPSM, Apr. 5, 1919.

3. LAUNCHING *THE ARTS*

1. In FW's time, the name "School of Paris," or *L'École de Paris*, was loosely applied to the modern-art movements—cubist, fauvist, surrealist, and such—centered in Paris before and after the First World War.

2. FW, "Playing the Game," *Arts & Decoration* 12 (Feb. 1920): 239; Brown, *American Painting*, 93.

3. Ruth L. Bohan, *The Société Anonyme's Brooklyn Exhibition: Katherine Dreier and Modernism in America* (Ann Arbor, Mich.: UMI Research Press, 1982), 29–30; Henry McBride, "News and Reviews of Art," *New York Herald*, Mar. 27, 1921.

4. Lloyd Goodrich reminiscences, as recorded in talks with Harlan B. Phillips, 1963, AAA.

5. Villard's outspoken opposition to America's entry into the war had resulted in a drop in the NYEP's circulation. Consequently, he sold the newspaper and concentrated his attention on the paper's weekly periodical, *The Nation;* Flint, "Quick, Watson," 13.

6. Fittingly, in a 1933 painting, *Nightclub,* Pène du Bois used FW and himself as background figures. Even though in time Pène du Bois grew less tolerant of modern trends as FW grew more amenable, their empathetic friendship endured all their lives.

Pène du Bois, had given up the editorship of *Arts & Decoration* several times during the years 1912–1921 in order to devote more time to his art, only to return to the magazine to ensure a regular income. For a brief time in 1916, Condé Nast, owner of *Arts & Decoration,* replaced Pène du Bois with Thomas Ashwall, who served as both publisher and editor. However, Condé Nast sold the magazine soon thereafter and Pène du Bois returned. In Dec. 1917, having left *Arts & Decoration* again, and again finding himself in need of a salary, Pène du Bois took FW's old job at the *New York Evening Post,* where he remained until Apr. 1919, when, "sick of writing," he quit. Within two months he was back at *Arts & Decoration.* Pène du Bois Diary, Apr. 12, 1919, quoted in Fahlman, "Guy Pène du Bois," 83.

7. FW, "Unreasoned Awards at Winter Academy," *Detroit News,* Dec. 28, 1919; FW, "Playing the Game," 239.

8. Lloyd Goodrich, interview with author, tape recording, Mar. 16, 1985.

9. Xavier J. Barile, interview with Mrs. John Sloan, transcribed from Sloan's notes by Rosalind Irvine, [1949], WMAAA, H.1/38; Blendon Campbell, interview with Rosalind Irvine, Mar. 22, 1949, WMAAA, H.1/38; Carl Zigrosser, *My Own Shall Come to Me: A Personal Memoir and Picture Chronicle* (Philadelphia: Casa Laura, 1971), 173.

10. Goodrich interview, Mar. 16, 1985. Perhaps as a form of flattery, FW occasionally made catty remarks to artists about their fellow artists. In a note complimenting Gertrude Vanderbilt Whitney on her exhibit, he portrayed their mutual friend and respected sculptor Janet Scudder as a jealous competitor. "'Dear Janet looked a bit like an onion that had spent the night on an ant hill,'" he wrote Whitney. B. H. Friedman, *Gertrude Vanderbilt Whitney: A Biography* (New York: Doubleday, 1978), 611. To his young friend sculptor Concetta Scaravaglione, he teasingly referred to their mutual friend sculptor Dorothea Greenbaum as "your rival" and implied that Greenbaum was envious of Scaravaglione. FW to Concetta Scaravaglione, Nov. 27, 1946, CSP AAA.

11. Guy Pène du Bois, *Artists Say the Silliest Things* (New York: American Artists Group, 1940), 212; Friedman, *Gertrude Vanderbilt Whitney,* 420; FW, "Art Golf Tourney a Smashing Success," *Art News* 23 (May 1925): 6.

12. FW, "American Art Exhibition in Venice," 153, 214, 152–53; FW, "Prince, Bourgeois, and Bolshevist," *Arts & Decoration* 13 (Sept. 1920): 228. Then seventy-four, infirm, and nearly blind, Cassatt talked incessantly, "with a kind of hungry violence," about art and politics. "Her political prejudices were appalling," FW recalled. It seemed uncanny to him that "this wreck of a great intelligence, this old lady who did not hesitate to use language, . . . which was profane and scandalous, could have devoted so many hours of her life to a tender, though always unsentimental study of a subject at once so difficult and dangerous as the contrast in form, in tone, and in expression between the baby and the mother in whose arms it is held." FW, "Mary Cassatt," undated typescript, p. 3, FWP AAA; FW to George Biddle, June 25, 1926, FWP AAA.

13. Berman, *Rebels on Eighth Street*, 163; FW, interview with Rosalind Irvine, Feb. 18, 1949, WMAAA H.11/f38; Maria Ealand, interview with author, telephone tape recording, Mar. 31, 1994. FW's letters to a lover, artist Isabella Howland, which contain numerous husbandly references to Nan, illustrate his casual attitude toward extramarital relationships. Describing the new study he had recently added to his home, FW wrote Howland: "I am installed in my room of one's own and never shall be satisfied until it echoes with your beautiful voice and sees your lovely self. As for you, you are going to fall in love with it. I didn't let Nan see it until Jan. 1st. I brought a nice cold bottle of Chablis and let Nan in. Says she: 'It is a triumph of imagination and the spitting image of you.'" FW's letter went on to effuse over a "thrilling" show coming up for Nan. FW to Isabella Howland, Jan. 3, 1949, IHP AAA.

14. Goodrich interview, Mar. 16, 1985; Campbell interview, Mar. 22, 1949; Goodrich reminiscences, 1963.

15. Raphael Soyer, interview with Milton Brown, tape recording, May 28, 1981, AAA. The advertisement for the Art Students League stated, "The League gives freedom of expression while providing a thorough fundamental training." *The Arts* 15 (Jan. 1929): 72; Allen Tucker, "The Art Students' League—An Experiment in Democracy," *The Arts* 6 (Nov. 1924): 264–66.

16. The following statement appeared in the Art Students League 1923 course descriptions: "The Board feels that this course, in which history will be considered from the viewpoint of the organic development of Art, is so important to the student, that it has been eager to give all students free attendance to these lectures. This has now been made possible, and it is hoped that the students will avail themselves of the opportunity." "Art Students League of New York Course Listings: Lectures Held at the Art Students League of New York," 1923, p. 3, FWP AAA.

17. Goodrich, "'The Arts' Magazine, 1920–1931," *American Art Journal* 5 (May 1978): 80; Henry McBride, "Hamilton Easter Field's Career," *The Arts* 3 (Jan. 1923): 3.

18. Hamilton Easter Field, "Editorial," *The Arts* 1 (Dec. 1920): [7]. In that same issue, Field disclosed in his commentary that FW would no longer be writing for *Arts & Decoration,* nor would the editor, Guy Pène du Bois. "*Arts & Decoration* has sent ashore the two men who were piloting the craft through the shoals of art," Field wrote. "So large a craft needs skillful direction and the art world is wondering who will take the helm. Rumor has it that the control has passed into the hands of a sculptor. Another report is that Mr. Judd has hired Madison Square Garden in order to give a dinner to the ex-editors. I shall accept." Field, "Comment on the Arts," *The Arts* 1 (Feb.–Mar. 1921): 35.

19. FW, "The Innocent Bystander," AMA 27 (Nov. 1934): 607; Goodrich reminiscences, 1963; FW, "The Dallas Exhibition," *The Arts* 1 (Apr. 1921): 30–31. The article for *The Arts* was excerpted from the catalog of the Dallas exhibition, which FW had written.

20. "Editorial," *The Arts* 2 (Feb. 1922): [257].

21. "Plan for Incorporating Company to Acquire and Continue the Publication of 'The Arts'" and "Agreement," 1922, FWP AAA.

22. Goodrich reminiscences, 1963; Flint, "Quick, Watson," 36; Goodrich interview, Mar. 16, 1985. Lloyd Goodrich noted that earlier, "a whole younger generation of liberal and radical artists which was emerging, had little opportunity to reach the public, and no forum for their ideas." Goodrich, "'The Arts' Magazine," 79.

23. Goodrich reminiscences, 1963. Lloyd Goodrich commented about William Robb: "He was quite unaesthetic. But he was just a very nice young man who took care of the business matters." Goodrich interview, Mar. 16, 1985; FW, "The Adventure of Two Ladies," Art Students League Talk No. 6, Nov. 18, 1949, typescript, p. 10, FWP AAA.

24. FW, "Editorial," *The Arts* 3 (Jan. 1923): 2.

25. FW, "The Barnes Foundation," *The Arts* 3 (Jan. 1923): 9. In fact, the Barnes Foundation was not established as a public museum. See Howard Greenfeld, *The Devil and Dr. Barnes* (New York: Viking, 1987).

26. FW, "Charles Demuth," *The Arts* 3 (Jan. 1923): 77.

27. "Forbes Watson Named Editor," *New York Times,* Jan. 14, 1923; Goodrich, "'The Arts' Magazine," 79.

28. Eugene Speicher to FW, May 25, 1923, FWP AAA; Pène du Bois to FW, undated, FWP AAA; Allen Tucker to FW, Aug. 2, 1926, FWP AAA; Albert E. Gallatin to FW, Jan. 17, 1923, FWP AAA.

29. FW, "Editorial," *The Arts* 6 (Dec. 1924): 299; FW, "The Skylight," *The Arts* 3 (Jan. 1923): 81.

30. FW to Dows, Nov. 12, 1948, FWP AAA.

31. See Virgil Barker, *A Critical Introduction to American Painting* (New York: William Edwin Rudge for the Whitney Museum of American Art, 1931); Virgil Barker, *Henry Lee McFee* (New York: Whitney Museum of American Art, 1931); and Virgil Barker, *American Painting: History and Interpretation* (New York: Macmillan, 1950).

32. Goodrich reminiscences, 1963; Goodrich interview, Mar. 16, 1985. Goodrich authored, coauthored, or edited more than eighty-one monographs, exhibition catalogs, and other books on art and artists.

33. Flint, "Quick, Watson," 13; Goodrich, "Lloyd Goodrich Reminisces, Part I," 12; Goodrich reminiscences, 1963.

34. Edward Hopper to FW, Apr. 21, 1927, FWP AAA; Hopper to FW, Dec. 10, 1926, FWP AAA; Goodrich, "'The Arts' Magazine," 83; Hopper, "Charles Burchfield: American," *The Arts* 14 (July 1928): 5, 12; Pablo Picasso, "Picasso Speaks: A Statement of the Artist," *The Arts* 3 (May 1923): 315–29. A unique exhibition, "Homage to Forbes Watson and The Arts," held at the Adams, Davidson Gallery in Washington, D.C., in 1967, seven years after FW's death, featured works by New York painters of the twenties and thirties who had written for *The Arts* or appeared on its pages. The show featured names such as John Sloan, William Glackens, Robert Henri, and Reginald Marsh. But the central figure was FW and his *Arts* magazine.

35. Igor Stravinsky, "Some Ideas about My Octuor," *The Arts* 5 (Jan. 1924): 5–6; Virginia Woolf, "The Cinema," *The Arts* 9 (June 1926): 314–16. The identical article was published again two months later in the *New Republic* under the title "The Movies and Reality" (vol. 47, Aug. 4, 1926, 308–10), apparently as the result of a misunderstanding. In a letter to Virgil Barker, Woolf apologized and blamed the breach on an agreement between the *Nation* and the *New Republic,* which enabled the latter to publish the article without her knowledge. She proposed to submit additional articles of a more literary nature, beginning in Oct. with a 1,500-word piece on the diaries of the historical painter Benjamin Haydon. Her fee was twenty pounds. Virginia Woolf to Virgil Barker, Sept. 27, 1926, FWP AAA. The proposed article never appeared in *The Arts.*

36. Charles Downing Lay, "The Hearn Fund," *The Arts* 11 (Mar. 1927): 139–42.

37. William Sizer, "William M. Ivins, Jr. (1881–1961), 'FOG DISPELLER,'" *Yale University Library Gazette* 36 (Apr. 1962): 172; William M. Ivins Jr., "A Note on Aesthetic Theory," *The Arts* 8 (Dec. 1925): 303–10.

38. Meyer Schapiro, "Rendering of Nature in Early Greek Art," *The Arts* 8 (Sept. 1925): 170–72. *Les Six,* or The French Group of Six, was the name given to a loosely associated group of young French composers consisting of Durey, Georges Auric, Arthur Honegger, Darius Milhaud, Francis Poulenc, and Germaine Tailleferre. Their music and philosophy represented a reaction against the impressionism of Debussy and the romanticism of Franck.

39. Andrew Dasburg, "Cubism—Its Rise and Influence," *The Arts* 4 (Nov. 1923): 284; Oliver S. Tonks, "The Creed of Abstract Art," *The Arts* 7 (Apr. 1925): 215–18; Leo Stein, "Tradition and Art," *The Arts* 7 (May 1925): 265–69; Leo Stein, "Renoir," *The Arts* 12 (Dec. 1927): 311–13. Lloyd Goodrich recalled contacting Royal Cortissoz in 1927 to ask him to write an article on a London show of Flemish masters. Cortissoz, personally very likable, agreed to write the article but said he could not get to it until the following Friday. "Well, when could you have it for us with this difficulty?" Goodrich asked. "Well, I guess about Monday," was his reply. "An old oracle! He was a pro," Goodrich marveled. Goodrich interview, Mar. 16, 1985. Cortissoz's article, "Flemish Art in London," was published in the Mar. 1927 issue of *The Arts* (vol. 11, 115–33).

40. FW referred to Kenyon Cox, who died in 1919, as "the last of the loyal and fearless reactionaries . . . not merely a prejudiced reactionary, but a sincere believer in his own ideas, with just claims to scholarship. To be attacked by him was a pleasure." FW, "Editorial," *The Arts* 8 (Sept. 1925): 121–23.

41. Alfred H. Barr Jr. to FW, Feb. 9, 1927, FWP AAA.

42. Olin Dows, interview with Harlan B. Phillips, tape recording, Oct. 31, 1963, AAA; Barker, "Preface," *American Painting: History and Interpretation,* vi. For FW's influence on the acceptance of American Indian art, see Henry Varnum Poor, "Anonymous American Art," *The Arts* 10 (July 1926): 5–14.

43. FW, "The Rise of Edward Hopper," *Brooklyn Daily Eagle Sunday Review,* Nov. 5, 1933; FW, "Art Notes," *NYEP,* Oct. 17, 1914; FW, "Art Notes," *NYEP,* Nov. 20, 1915; FW, "A Note on Edward Hopper," *Vanity Fair* 32 (Feb. 1929): 64, 98, 107; Jo Hopper quoted from a 1954 diary entry, in Gail Levin, *Edward Hopper: An Intimate Biography* (New York: Knopf, 1995), 477. For examples of *The Arts*'s coverage of Hopper, see: Barker, "The Etchings of Edward Hopper" (June 1924): 323–27; Goodrich, "New York Exhibitions," 9 (Feb. 1926): 98; Goodrich, "The Paintings of Edward Hopper," 11 (Mar. 1927): 134–38; FW, "In the Galleries," 16 (May 1930): 626–27; and FW, "A Note on Edward Hopper," in *The Arts: Portfolio Series* (New York: Arts, 1930).

44. FW, "Art Notes," *NYEP,* Nov. 14, 1914.

45. See Thomas H. Benton, "Mechanics of Form Organization in Painting," *The Arts* 10 (Nov. 1926): 285–89; 10 (Dec. 1926): 340–42; 11 (Jan. 1927): 43–44; 11 (Feb. 1927): 95–96, 11 (Mar. 1927): 145–48.

46. Henry Adams, *Thomas Hart Benton: An American Original* (New York: Knopf, 1989), 110. Benton's influence on his pupil Jackson Pollock established a major conduit from the modernized figuration of his regionalism to the improvisational abstraction

of Pollock's work, abstract expressionism. For a detailed examination of the social, political, and stylistic link between Benton's regionalism and Pollock's abstract expressionism, see Erika Doss, *Benton, Pollock, and the Politics of Modernism: From Regionalism to Abstract Art* (Chicago: Univ. of Chicago Press, 1991).

47. Raymond Escholier, "A Delacroix Exhibition in Paris," *The Arts* 13 (Apr. 1928): 211–20; Raymond Régamey, "A Corot Exhibition," *The Arts* 14 (Sept. 1928): 143–53; Claude Roger-Marx, "The Courbet Exhibition in Paris," *The Arts* 16 (Sept. 1929): 9–18.

48. Goodrich interview, Mar. 16, 1985; Goodrich reminiscences, 1963; Goodrich, "Lloyd Goodrich Reminisces: Part I," 12.

49. Goodrich, "'The Arts' Magazine," 84.

50. C. Adolph "Cook" Glassgold, interview with Harlan B. Phillips, tape recording, Dec. 9, 1964, AAA; Goodrich reminiscences, 1963; Inslee Hopper, interview with Robert Brown, tape recording, July 28, 1981, AAA; Goodrich interview, Mar. 16, 1985. "I wrote a piece about Picasso's pictures of Antique," Goodrich recalled, "a piece which I'm ashamed of now. I'm ashamed of it, because it was very . . . anti, and didn't show any interest in what he was doing at all, the new development in Picasso's art. I think maybe this was a little bit [the] influence of Forbes, you know. I was always influenced by him. No question." Goodrich interview, Mar. 16, 1985. See Goodrich, "In the Galleries," *The Arts* 16 (Feb. 1930): 410–16. Goodrich was thirty-two years old at the time he wrote the piece; FW was fifty.

51. Goodrich interview, Mar. 16, 1985; William Robb to Barbara Goldsmith, Aug. 9, 1982, WMAAA H.1/44. Robb made this comment in a letter to Goldsmith regarding her book *Little Gloria . . . Happy At Last* (New York: Knopf, 1980), in which the author discussed the Whitney Studio and FW. Robb chided Goldsmith for describing FW as "the misanthropic art critic." Although his tone was cordial, Robb clearly felt the opposite was true.

52. FW, "American Art in Paris," *The Arts* 6 (Aug. 1924): 102–7.

53. FW to Gertrude Vanderbilt Whitney, 1924, GVWP AAA.

54. A decade later, when the American Scene movement had reached the pinnacle of its popularity, FW responded to an *American Magazine of Art* reader who accused him of being a "provincial New Yorker": "These are somewhat harsh words to use against a reviewer who wrote about Iowa and other regional centers before the now famous artists of Cedar Rapids, Fort Dodge, Stone City and other points along the corn belt, had even won a prize in a state fair; before the Art Institute of Chicago had ever heard of those self-appointed and slightly tardy leaders of regionalism." FW, "The Innocent Bystander," AMA 28 (June 1935): 371.

55. FW, "The Cleveland Museum," *The Arts* 13 (Feb. 1928): 73; FW, "Editorial," *The Arts* 7 (Apr. 1925): 187; FW, "Mid-Western Optimism," *The Arts* 16 (Dec. 1929): 215.

56. FW, "Fresh Paint," *The Arts* 13 (June 1928): 390. (Originally printed in NYW, May 18, 1928.)

57. FW, foreword to *Georges Seurat*, by Walter Pach (New York: Duffield, 1923).

58. Pach, *Georges Seurat*; FW, *William Glackens* (New York: Duffield and *The Arts*, 1923). The preliminary paging of the two published monographs in the Arts Monograph series, *Georges Seurat* and *William Glackens*, listed additional Arts Monographs titles as follows: *George Seurat*, by Walter Pach; *William Glackens*, by FW, *Aikens* [sic], by

Bryson Burroughs; *Arthur B. Davies,* by FW; and *Toulouse-Lautrec,* by Alexander Brook. There is no physical or bibliographic record or secondary reference to the latter three monographs. An editorial footnote to Daniel Catton Rich's article on Toulouse-Lautrec in *The Arts* for Feb. 1931 cites Brook's article on Toulouse-Lautrec, which appeared in the *Arts* issue of Sept. 1923, but there is no mention of a book.

59. Tucker's book, *Design and the Idea,* consisted of essays that appeared in *The Arts* Jan.–Apr. 1930.

60. Lists from William M. Milliken, Harley Perkins, Erwin Barrie, J. S. Carpenter et al., and FW form letter, Feb. 1926, FWP AAA.

61. "Your Client's Good Taste," *The Arts* 9 (Feb. 1926): v. As with the Arts Monograph series, there is no bibliographic or physical evidence to document that the remainder of the advertised portfolios were published. The fact that after May 1929 Arts Portfolio advertisements listed only three, and finally nine, folios supports the assumption that the other forty-six were never issued.

62. Robb to Barbara Goldsmith, Aug. 9, 1982, WMAAA H.1/44. Berman, who interviewed William Robb for *Rebels on Eighth Street,* elaborates on the above meeting between Juliana Force and William Robb. "Since it rankled Forbes to have to report to Juliana on the financial status of *The Arts,* he began sending Robb to meet with her once a month to inspect the previous month's operating statement. *The Arts* always lost money, and because of all that red ink, Robb had expected these meetings to be solemn, cringing occasions. But Juliana's door was open to him, and she was ever the amiable hostess. At the beginning of one glorious month, Juliana inquired, 'Mr. Robb, how much do you pay Mr. Watson and how much do you draw yourself?' When he told her that he got $40 a week and Forbes made $75, Juliana replied, 'I am shocked. How can you possibly get along on that? Double both of your salaries immediately!' Berman, *Rebels on Eighth Street,* 240.

63. Gertrude Vanderbilt Whitney to FW, undated, FWP AAA.

4. ILLUMINATING THE TWENTIES ART SCENE

1. From 1930 to 1932, the *New York Sun* art critic Henry McBride took on two similar responsibilities when he became editor of the magazine *Creative Art.* However, according to Daniel Cotton Rich, "he was forced to resign at the end of the second year from sheer exhaustion." Henry McBride, *The Flow of Art: Essays and Criticisms of Henry McBride,* ed. Daniel Catton Rich (New York: Atheneum, 1975), 26.

2. The move away from Eighth Street in Greenwich Village also made way for another Whitney expansion. By now the Whitney Studio Club exceeded three hundred members. Its annual show was so large it could not be held in the existing galleries. When the new club opened at the Watsons' former address, the Whitney Club and Studio occupied numbers 8, 10, and 14 West Eighth Street. Daniel Chester French owned number 12.

3. Philip Pearl, "The World Passes," *Saturday Review of Literature* 7 (Mar. 14, 1931): 663.

4. Arnold T. Schwab, *James Gibbons Huneker: Critic of the Seven Arts* (Stanford, Calif.: Stanford Univ. Press, 1963), 274–75; E. J. Kahn Jr., *The World of Swope* (New York: Simon and Schuster, 1965), 260; James W. Barrett, *The World, the Flesh and Messrs. Pulitzer* (New York: Vanguard Press, 1931), 82. Some contemporaries whose columns also appeared in

the "Metropolitan Section" were Ring Lardner, Frank Sullivan, Robert Benchley, Carl Van Dorn, Finley Peter Dunne, Granville Hicks, and Franklin P. Adams. Adams attracted other luminaries to his column, "The Conning Tower," without compensation. Dorothy Parker, Marc Connelly, E. B. White, George S. Kaufman, Edna Ferber, and Gellett Burgess were among his guest contributors. On the Op-Ed page, FW was featured along with Alexander Woollcott, Heywood Broun, Franklin P. Adams, Deems Taylor, H. L. Mencken, and others.

5. FW to Herbert Bayard Swope and Louis Weitzenkorn; Weitzenkorn and Swope to FW, Feb. 5, 1925–Mar. 20, 1925, FWP AAA.

6. Alfred H. Barr Jr., "A Modern Art Questionnaire," in *Defining Modern Art: Selected Writings of Alfred H. Barr Jr.,* ed. Irving Sandler and Amy Newman (New York: Harry N. Abrams, 1986), 56–59. Sophisticated readers of *Vanity Fair* also had an opportunity to test their proficiency when the quiz was reprinted in the Aug. 1927 issue. Alfred H. Barr, "A Modern Art Questionnaire," *Vanity Fair* 28 (Aug. 1927): 85, 96, 98.

7. Heywood Broun, "It Seems to Me," *NYW*, Feb. 28, 1925. Paavo Nurmi, known as "the marvel of Finland," was considered the greatest runner in history.

8. Broun, "It Seems to Me," *NYW*, Dec. 27, 1923; Broun, "It Seems to Me," *NYW*, Feb. 28, 1925.

9. FW, "Modern Art Overlooked by Pennsylvania Academy," *NYW*, Feb. 22, 1925; FW, "Philadelphia Show is Safe and Sane," *NYW*, Feb. 21, 1926; FW, "Winter Academy Exhibition Runs True to Type," *NYW*, Nov. 16, 1924; J. Nivison to the Managing Editor, *NYW*, [1926?], FWP AAA.

10. Alexander Brook, interview with Paul Cummings, tape recording, July 7, 1977, AAA.

11. C. Adolph "Cook" Glassgold, interview with Harlan B. Phillips, tape recording, Dec. 9, 1964, AAA; Charles Sheeler, interview with Bartlett Cowdrey, tape recording, Dec. 9, 1958, AAA; Lloyd Goodrich, interview with author, tape recording, Mar. 16, 1985; Benton, *An Artist in America,* 47. An amused McBride joined into the spirit of the roast. Assuming a mock psychoanalytical approach, he wrote: "If there has been any one that the critics have been systematically kind to, it is Peggy Bacon.... Yet now, suddenly, and out of a clear sky, as it were, she turns and bites the hands that feed her.... What she does to Forbes Watson is something terrible.... She steps, in fact, so far beyond the confines of propriety in this caricature, that I think that the medicos who may be called in to study this case, will get all the data they need from it.... This is an example of the emotional school of caricature.... As for me, *moi qui vous parle,* Miss Bacon makes me look like a broken-down actor, thus confirming what Virgil Barker once said about me. ... But every one agrees I came out luckily from this affair." Henry McBride, "Some Caricatures of Critics," *New York Sun,* Apr. 26, 1931.

12. FW, "The Achievement of Two Ladies," Art Students League Lecture No. 6, Nov. 18, 1949, typescript, pp. 6–7, FWP AAA. For a detailed history of the Woodstock Colony, see *Woodstock: An American Art Colony, 1902–1977; Vassar College Art Gallery Jan. 23–Mar. 4, 1977* (Poughkeepsie, N.Y.: Hamilton Reproductions, 1977). Alexander Brook described the thriving artists' community thus: "There are at least three groups of illustrators, bad, good and indifferent.... There are two groups of 'Moderns,'—those who are and those who are not. There are four groups of academicians; those who are and are proud of it, those who are and scorn it, those who would like to be and some day

will be, and those who wish to be and will never be." Alexander Brook, "The Woodstock Whirl," *The Arts* 3 (June 1923): 418.

13. Karal Ann Marling, "Introduction," *Woodstock*. In her introduction, Marling depicts the Woodstock school as a synthesis of the nonobjective style of the "Rock City radicals" and the representational style of the "Woodstock Academy." The "date of the stylistic coalescence" was marked as 1923.

14. FW, "Achievement of Two Ladies," 6–7; FW, "The Happy Valley," *The Arts* 10 (Aug. 1926): 119; Berman, *Rebels on Eighth Street*, 230; John B. Flannagan to Carl Zigrosser, 1929, in Flannagan, ed., *Letters of John B. Flannagan* (New York: Curt Valentin, 1942), 20.

15. John Casey, interview with Paul Cummings, tape recording, July 10, 1970, AAA.

16. Swope to FW, Dec. 30, 1926, FWP AAA.

17. FW to Swope, Jan. 5, 1927, FWP AAA; Ralph Pulitzer to FW, Jan. 6, 1927, FWP AAA.

18. FW, "New York Exhibitions," *The Arts* 9 (Mar. 1926): 160; FW, "New Galleries and Other Notes," *The Arts* 6 (Oct. 1924): 225–28.

19. FW, "Editorial," *The Arts* 7 (Feb. 1925): 59–60.

20. FW, "Charles Sheeler," *The Arts* 3 (May 1923): 334–44; FW, "American Collections: No. I—The Ferdinand Howald Collection," *The Arts* 8 (Aug. 1925): 91–92.

21. "Every Vital Artist Essentially 'Modern' Editor-Critic Says," *Newark Evening News*, Jan. 17, 1925.

22. Lloyd Goodrich reminiscences, as recorded in talks with Harlan B. Phillips, 1963, AAA; Olin Dows, interview with Harlan B. Phillips, tape recording, Oct. 31, 1963, AAA.

23. Goodrich interview, Mar. 16, 1985.

24. FW, "Editorial" *The Arts* 3 (June 1923): 373.

25. Goodrich interview, Mar. 16, 1985; Goodrich reminiscences, 1963; FW, "Pleasures of Recognition," NYW, Jan. 24, 1926.

26. Willard Clopton Jr., "Gallery Honors Famed Critic Watson," *Washington Post*, May 8, 1967; Goodrich interview, Mar. 16, 1985.

27. FW, "Art News of the Week," NYW, Mar. 23, 1924.

28. FW, "Reviews and Notes of Current Events in Art," NYW, Mar. 15, 1925. The comparison of the NAD to the National Biscuit Company also appears in Sloan, *Gist of Art*, 28. Neither FW nor Sloan attributed the remark to the other. But it is likely that the jibe originated with FW, since it appeared in the *World* two years before Helen Farr (later Helen Farr Sloan) began attending Sloan's lectures and taking the notes that make up the core of his book, which was published fourteen years after FW's remark.

29. FW, "Editorial," *The Arts* 7 (Apr. 1925): 183–87.

30. FW, "Hospitality's Dividends," *The Arts* 11 (Apr. 1927): 167; Goodrich reminiscences, 1963.

31. "Bird in Flight" was exhibited in Nov. as part of a major Brancusi show at the Brummer Gallery, where, thanks to the flurry of publicity, more than ten thousand dollars' worth of Brancusi's works were sold. *The Arts* reviewer, Thomas Hart Benton, found the bronzes sterile and precious despite Brancusi's perfect technique and sincere craftsmanship. Thomas Hart Benton, "New York Exhibitions," *The Arts* 10 (Dec. 1926): 344. More noteworthy than the critics' response, however, was that of the customs appraiser who categorized all the works as utensils and assessed a 40 percent tariff, four thousand dollars, on the pieces sold.

32. FW, "Editorial," *The Arts* 11 (Mar. 1927): 113.

33. "How They Know It's 'A Bird' and Are Sure It Is 'Art,'" *New York American*, Dec. 25, 1927; FW, "Fresh Paint: A Just Decision," *The Arts* 14 (Dec. 1928): 337. Other expert witnesses were Frank Crowninshield, editor of *Vanity Fair;* William H. Fox, director of the Brooklyn Museum; renowned sculptor Jacob Epstein; and Henry McBride. For a transcript of the trial, see *Brancusi vs. United States: The Historic Trial, 1928,* English ed. (Paris: Societé nouvelle Adam Biro, 1999).

34. In a 1929 article, FW related that a French journal had accused him "of having a Monroe Doctrine attitude toward art" because he did not consider "every clever painting maneuver by Picasso" a masterpiece or every "pot boiling head by Derain" a serious work. FW, "To Our New Museum," *The Arts* 16 (Sept. 1929): 49. It was not only Parisian arrogance that rankled FW. When the distinguished German critic Julius Meier-Graefe proposed a cooperative project to bring a group of German paintings to the United States in 1928, FW's objections had a familiar ring. The sum total of American liberality toward German art had far exceeded German generosity toward American art, he asserted, citing Walt Kuhn, who had reported the number of Germans who availed themselves of the opportunity to see a three-week-long exhibition of American paintings in Berlin at exactly twenty-five. "He had counted them." FW warned, "America is not going on forever accepting the prejudiced viewpoint toward her art which has been fostered in Germany and France." Germany would be wise to invite a serious American exhibition selected by Americans, he admonished. FW, "Shifting Valuations," *The Arts* 13 (Apr. 1928): 209–10.

35. FW, "The Proposed Tariff on Art," *The Arts* 15 (Feb. 1929): 78.

36. FW, "Art News of the Week," *NYW,* Jan. 27, 1924.

37. Goodrich reminiscences, 1963; FW, "Art News of the Week," *NYW,* Feb. 17, 1924.

38. For a succinct discussion of American collectors following the Armory Show, see Brown, *American Painting,* 92–99.

39. Inslee Hopper, interview with Robert Brown, tape recording, July 28, 1981, AAA. Leon Kroll described one such visit, recalling that early one afternoon in 1921 or 1922, Dr. Barnes picked up FW and Nan, Eugene Speicher, and himself at the North Philadelphia Station and drove them to his home in Merion for lunch and a look at his collection. Thrilled with the pieces, Kroll was, however, notably disappointed in the pauper's lunch of scrapple. Leon Kroll, *A Spoken Memoir,* ed. Nancy Hale and Fredson Bowers (Charlottesville: Univ. Press of Virginia, 1983), 65–66. For other contemporary accounts of Albert Barnes, see Benton, *An Artist in America,* 61; and Maurice Sterne, *Shadow and Light: The Life, Friends and Opinions of Maurice Sterne,* ed. Charlotte Leon Mayerson (New York: Harcourt, Brace, and World, 1952), 153. It was not easy to sustain a friendship with the strong-headed millionaire. Barnes was rude, quick to anger, and prone to hold lifelong grudges. Even after he established the Barnes Foundation, strict admission policies severely limited the flow of visitors to the gallery. Permission to view the collection came only from Barnes himself, and he could be very petty in granting it. For a biography of Barnes and a history of the Barnes Foundation, see Howard Greenfeld, *The Devil and Dr. Barnes* (New York: Viking, 1987).

40. FW related in later life that Barnes "hated the Renoirs and Cézannes that Glackens got for him until he realized that they were making him, Barnes, famous." FW to Ira Glackens, Mar. 19, 1955, FWP AAA.

41. FW, "American Collections: No. I," 64–95; FW, "American Collections: No. II—The John T. Spaulding Collection," *The Arts* 8 (Dec. 1925): 321–44; FW, "American Collections: No. III—The Adolph Lewisohn Collection," *The Arts* 10 (July 1926): 15–48; FW, "A Note on the Birch-Bartlett Collection," *The Arts* 9 (June 1926): 303–13.

42. Judith Zilczer relates that the Irish painter Jack Yeats bestowed the fitting title on Quinn, "who deserved to be remembered chiefly for the way in which he spent his money. . . . When he died in New York at the age of fifty-four after a successful legal career, Quinn left not a fortune but a vast and unparalleled collection of modern art." Zilczer, *"The Noble Buyer": John Quinn: Patron of the Avant-Garde* (Washington, D.C.: Smithsonian Institution Press, 1978), 9.

43. FW, foreword to *John Quinn 1870–1925 [sic]: Collection of Paintings, Water Colors, Drawings, and Sculpture* (Huntington, N.Y.: Pidgeon Hill Press, [1926]), [6]. Nearly twenty-two years after Quinn's death, FW, with the whiff of malice that permeated his reminiscences in later years, disclosed just how critically Arthur B. Davies and Walt Kuhn had affected Quinn's collection:

> When the late John Quinn financed the short lived Carroll Galleries on East 44th Street he was a great friend of Arthur B. Davies and Walter Kuhn, and the exhibitions which followed each other at the Carroll Galleries showed that there were artists in the background. Among these exhibitions was the first one-man show by Picasso. . . . Before the paintings could be returned to Paris, war had been declared and shipment of the work became impossible. Arthur B. Davies suggested to John Quinn that he could buy the whole Picasso collection very cheap because of the war and because at that time Picasso was not the international public figure which he has since become. Quinn told Davies that he didn't want the Picassos, that he didn't like them. Davies retorted that he was very foolish not to take advantage of such a wonderful opportunity. Thereupon Quinn did buy the collection and it wasn't so very long before this purchase established in the minds of the public the idea that John Quinn was a great and far-sighted collector. After the war one saw pictures of him with Picasso, the great modern collector and the great modern artist. This process of becoming a modern collector has often been repeated here and abroad. In other words, the nigger in the woodpile is frequently an artist and not the man who signs the checks.

FW, "Incidents—No. 2," Apr. 26, 1946, typescript, [p. 1], FWP AAA.

44. FW to Antoinette [Kraushaar], Dec. 17, 1946, FWP AAA; FW, "The Carnegie International," *The Arts* 10 (Nov. 1926): 252–54; FW, "The Achievement of Two Ladies," [1949] typescript, pp. 4, 5, Frances Mulhall Achilles Library Archives, Whitney Museum of American Art; FW, "The Museum Guarantee," NYW, Mar. 21, 1926.

45. FW, "A Reporter at Large: Stepfathers of Art," *New Yorker* 3 (May 14, 1927): 32–38. Sargent's *The Wyndham Sisters: Lady Elcho, Mrs. Adeane, and Mrs. Tennant*, popularly known as "Three Graces," was facetiously nicknamed "The Happiness Sisters" by less reverent viewers.

46. FW, "Art Notes," NYEP, Apr. 17, 1915; FW, "Art Notes," NYEP, May 8, 1915; FW, "Editorial," *The Arts* 9 (Jan. 1926): 3–4; FW, "Editorial," *The Arts* 9 (May 1926): 240.

47. "Modern Art for New York Univ.," *Art News* 26 (Nov. 5, 1927): 1–2; Albert E. Gallatin, "The Gallery of Living Art, New York Univ.," *Creative Art* 4 (Mar. 1929): xl–xli.

48. FW, "Recent Exhibitions," *The Arts* 13 (Jan. 1928): 37.

49. Goodrich reminiscences, 1963; FW, "Caw, Caw, Caw," undated typescript, [p. 1], FWP AAA. During the twenties, Stieglitz's stable of artists consisted principally of five Americans: John Marin, Georgia O'Keeffe, Arthur G. Dove, Marsden Hartley, and Paul Strand. For a study of Alfred Stieglitz and American modernism, see William Innes Homer, *Alfred Stieglitz and the American Avant-Garde* (Boston: New York Graphic Society, 1977).

50. Hopper interview, July 28, 1981; FW, "Incidents—No. 1," Apr. 26, 1946, typescript, pp. 3–4, FWP AAA. FW wrote in this reminiscence, "In all his years of selling paintings Stieglitz has taken the position that he is the one and only Pope in the religion of art.... Apparently many people like his sermons which in late years have been devoted to less than a handful of artists and feel that in purchasing a Marin, O'Keeffe or a Dove that they are acquiring a very special virtue."

In another reminiscence, FW described Stieglitz's promotional excesses: "The last conversation I had with him was at an exhibition of the work of Georgia O'Keeffe. She was in the room at the time and heard all of the conversation. She heard Stieglitz place her upon a pedestal and occasionally as he continued his flow of words, I glanced at Miss O'Keeffe, then Mrs. Stieglitz, to see if she showed any signs of embarrassment. But apparently I was the only person embarrassed by the talk.... Some years later I was reminded of this conversation and of my wonder at seeing Miss O'Keeffe show no signs of embarrassment over the maundering praise by her husband when I met her.... It was ... she who brought up the subject of Mr. Stieglitz and who told me that her family had nicknamed him Caw Caw because he crowed so much.... I couldn't help wondering whether it was her way of telling me that she had been embarrassed or whether in a subtle, feminine manner she was now having her laughing revenge." FW, "Incidents—No. 1," [1]–2.

51. Hopper interview, July 28, 1981; Dows interview, Oct. 31, 1963; Goodrich interview, Mar. 16, 1985. Berman notes that Nan "remained silent and benefited professionally from her position as tolerant spouse." According to Berman, Nan Watson holdings in the permanent Whitney collection ranked ahead of John Sloan, George Luks, Arthur B. Davies, George Bellows, Yasuo Kuniyoshi, Reginald Marsh, and Charles Sheeler, represented by three oils each; Thomas Hart Benton, Oscar Bluemner, and Maurice Prendergast, represented by two; and Georgia O'Keeffe, Charles Demuth, Marsden Hartley, Max Weber, and Edward Hopper, who were only represented by one painting apiece in 1931. Berman noted also that after Juliana Force's death, Nan Watson's canvases were gradually reduced from eight to four. Berman, *Rebels on Eighth Street*, 166.

Nan apparently had the final say on the Juliana Force affair, however. FW's papers, which she donated to the AAA after his death, contain no personal correspondence between him and Force and few references to her except in lectures and public documents. For the record, at least, Nan effectively expurgated Juliana Force from FW's life.

52. FW, "The National Academy," *NYEP*, Dec. 18, 1915; FW, "The National Academy," *NYEP*, Dec. 16, 1916; FW, "Paintings by Seven Artists Return from Paris Invasion," *NYW*, Jan. 27, 1924; Hopper interview, July 28, 1981.

53. Ira Glackens, *William Glackens and The Eight* (New York: Horizon Press, 1983), 239; FW, "New Arrivals in America," *The Arts* 16 (Sept. 1929): 49; Pène du Bois, *Artists Say the Silliest Things*, 258.

54. FW, "Vanishing Influences," *The Arts* 15 (Jan. 1929): 3.

55. FW, "Robert Henri: Introduction," in *The Art Spirit,* by Robert Henri (Philadelphia: J. B. Lippincott, 1930), 5–10. FW's introduction was a slightly revised version of an editorial from 1929. FW, "Robert Henri," *The Arts* 16 (Sept. 1929): 2–8.

56. FW, "To Our New Museum," *The Arts* 16 (Sept. 1929): 46; Goodrich, "The Opening Season," *The Arts* 16 (Oct. 1929): 142.

57. Alfred H. Barr Jr., foreword to *Paintings by Nineteen Living Americans: Dec. 13, 1929 to Jan. 12, 1930* (New York: Museum of Modern Art, 1929), 9.

58. FW, "The All American Nineteen," *The Arts* 16 (Jan. 1930): 301–11.

59. "Play the Game of the Month," (advertisement) *The Arts* 16 (Jan. 1930): 359; FW, "The Winning Lists," *The Arts* 16 (Apr. 1930): 519.

60. "Modernists Use Unfair Tactics, Say Art Dealers," *New York Herald Tribune,* May 15, 1930.

5. THE DEMISE OF *THE ARTS*

1. Pène du Bois, *Artists Say the Silliest Things,* 255.

2. Goodrich to Barker, Apr. 12, 1928, Lloyd Goodrich Papers, WMAAA, H. 18/d45; Lloyd Goodrich, interview with author, tape recording, Mar. 16, 1985.

3. FW, "The Achievement of Two Ladies," Art Students League Talk No. 6, Nov. 18, 1949, typescript, p. 7, FWP; Goodrich interview, Mar. 16, 1985; FW, "The Achievement of Two Ladies," Art Students League Talk No. 6, Nov. 18, 1949, typescript, p. 7, FWP; FW recalled in a 1949 draft of an essay for a memorial volume, *Juliana Force and American Art,* "The idea of a museum did not come up until some time after lunch. Then it was tossed back and forth between us like a bean bag and each time that one of us caught it we put another bean in it. Before we parted in the late afternoon the idea had jelled and become serious. We were all excited for this seemed to be a historic event in American art. It was, we now know." FW, "The Achievement of Two Ladies [1949], typescript, p. 4, Frances Mulhall Achilles Library Archives, Whitney Museum of American Art; FW, "The Achievement of Two Ladies," Art Students League Talk No. 6, Nov. 18, 1949, typesript, p. 7, FWP; Maria Ealand, interview with author, telephone tape recording, Mar. 31, 1994; Goodrich interview, Mar. 16, 1985.

4. "Good-looking" and "lady's man" were Goodrich's terms. Goodrich interview, Mar. 16, 1985.

5. Goodrich, "The Murals of the New School," *The Arts* 17 (Mar. 1931): 399–403; Goodrich interview, Mar. 16, 1985.

6. Goodrich interview, Mar. 16, 1985.

7. Goodrich interview, Mar. 16, 1985.

8. Berman, *Rebels on Eighth Street,* 295. Berman offers a more complete account of Whitney's withdrawal of support from *The Arts* (292–95).

9. FW to Stephen C. Clark, Nov. 25, 1931, FWP AAA.

10. FW to Evelyn Blunt Ficke, Dec. 17, 1931, FWP AAA; FW to Henry Shaefer, Dec. 17, 1931, FWP AAA.

11. FW to Gertrude Vanderbilt Whitney, Sept. 30, 1931, GVWP AAA.

12. In 1937, in an otherwise favorable review of Thomas Hart Benton's book *An Artist in America,* FW chastised Benton for his "inaccurate and undignified attack on the

Whitney," the museum which had "done more for him in particular and for American art in general than any other." FW, "A Portrait of the Artist by Thomas Hart Benton," *New York Times Book Review,* Nov. 28, 1937.

13. Ealand interview, Mar. 31, 1994. Among the pictures displayed on the wall of FW's study years after he retired was a large photograph of Juliana Force.

14. FW, interview with Rosalind Irvine, Feb. 18, 1949, WMAAA, H.1/f38; *Juliana Force and American Art: A Memorial Exhibition, Sept. 24–Oct. 30, 1949* (New York: Whitney Museum of American Art, 1949), 54–63; FW, "The Achievement of Two Ladies," Art Students League Talk No. 6, Nov. 18, 1949, typescript, FWP AAA. In his interview with Irvine for her history of the Whitney Studio Club, FW spoke of Juliana Force's generosity to artists and their families, though at the same time describing her as "a romantic little German girl from Hoboken" who "continued to be one until the end." He insisted that up until the opening of the Whitney Museum, her position was that of secretary to Gertrude Whitney. As for Whitney, "he intimated that she had made no genuine contribution to the arts up to the time he met her." At the end of her transcript of the interview, Irvine wrote: "I have omitted making any record of other stories from Watson about Mrs. Whitney and Mrs. Force. They were of a highly personal nature and in my opinion come under the heading of 'malicious gossip.'"

15. Goodrich, "Exhibitions," *The Arts* 17 (Dec. 1930): 173; Jacques Mauny, "Paris Letter," *The Arts* 18 (Oct. 1931): 21.

16. FW, "The Star-Spangled Banner," *The Arts* 18 (Oct. 1931): 50–56.

17. FW, "All the World's a Critic," *Space* 1 (Jan. 1930): 6–7; FW, "The Gain and the Loss," *The Arts* 18 (Oct. 1931): 3–4.

18. Goodrich was listed as a director of the Arts Publishing Corporation when the corporation changes were transacted in 1932, with FW as president and Robb as secretary-treasurer. Actually, he did not participate, staying on in name only long enough to see FW through the ordeal of reorganization. In 1958 he was appointed director of the Whitney Museum of American Art and served in that position until 1968.

19. Goodrich interview, Mar. 16, 1985.

20. Ibid. Goodrich was associate director of the Whitney Museum at the time of the meeting.

21. "Notice to the Preferred and Common Stockholders of the Arts Publishing Corporation," [Jan. 1932], FWP AAA; FW to Mrs. John D. Rockefeller, Jan. 14, 1932, FWP AAA.

22. Alfred H. Barr to FW, Mar. 12, 1932, FWP AAA; FW, "*Arts Weekly* and *The Arts,*" *Arts Weekly* 1 (Mar. 11, 1932): 4; Pène du Bois, *Artists Say the Silliest Things,* 255.

23. For a detailed account of Kirstein's role in bringing the contemporary arts to the attention of the American public, see Nicholas Fox Weber, *Patron Saints: Five Rebels Who Opened America to a New Art, 1928–1943* (New York: Knopf, 1992).

24. Inslee Hopper, interview with Robert Brown, tape recording, July 28, 1981, AAA.

25. FW, "The Museum of Modern Art," *Arts Weekly* 1 (Apr. 23, 1932): 143.

26. Pène du Bois, *Artists Say the Silliest Things,* 255; Hopper interview, July 28, 1981.

27. FW, "Star-Spangled Banner," 52.

28. Lloyd Goodrich reminiscences, as recorded in talks with Harlan B. Phillips, 1963, AAA; Goodrich interview, Mar. 16, 1985.

6. FROM PROGRESSIVE CRITIC TO NEW DEAL CRITIC

1. Olin Dows, interview with Harlan B. Phillips, tape recording, Oct. 31, 1963, AAA.

2. Harold E. Stearns, *Rediscovering America* (New York: Liveright, 1934), 221.

3. William F. McDonald, *Federal Relief Administration and the Arts* (Columbus: Ohio State Univ. Press, 1969), 16–18, 348.

4. "Want Art Market on Washington Sq.," *New York Times,* Apr. 12, 1932.

5. Antoinette Kraushaar, interview with author, tape recording, July 15, 1985.

6. "Art Federation Asks Distribution of Work," *New York Times,* May 17, 1930; "Wants Americans to Paint Our Officials: A. T. Reid Sees Foreign Artists Favored," *New York Times,* Jan. 18, 1931.

7. FW, "Publicity, Independence, and Barter," *Arts Weekly* 1 (Apr. 2, 1932): 71.

8. Nancy Heller and Julia Williams in their book, *The Regionalists,* loosely distinguish the following categories of regionalist style: landscape; small-town America; urban America; and mythical, historical, and social commentary. Nancy Heller and Julia Williams, *The Regionalists* (New York: Watson-Guptill, 1976).

9. FW, "American Collections: No. 1—The Ferdinand Howald Collection," *The Arts* 8 (Aug. 1925): 91–92. For a broad examination of the American Scene movement, see Matthew Baigell, *The American Scene: American Painting of the 1930s* (New York: Praeger, 1974). While emphasizing the lack of a single definition or philosophy, Baigell pinpoints several major characteristics of the American Scene movement: It was a movement of "optimism" and "self-glorification." There was an attempt to detach American art from foreign entanglements and to look to America's "own traditions and aspirations." Rejecting modernism as it had evolved in Europe, the American Scene relied on realistic painting to develop a democratic art readily accessible to the ordinary person by means of easily recognizable images. Personal sensibility was rejected as a dominant avenue of communication in favor of concrete images. (18–21)

10. Audrey McMahon, "May the Artist Live?" *Parnassus* 5 (Oct. 1933): [1]–4. For a detailed account of artists' relief, see McDonald, *Federal Relief Administration and the Arts,* 349–53.

11. FW, "Gallery Explorations," *Parnassus* 4 (Dec. 1932): 3, 4.

12. Allen Tucker to FW, Aug. 19, 1933, FWP AAA.

13. "Relief," *Time,* Feb. 19, 1934, 11; Harold Ickes quoted in Eric Frederick Goldman, *Rendezvous with Destiny* (New York: Knopf, 1966), 331–32.

14. For an account of the development of Biddle's plan, see George Biddle, *An American Artist's Story* (Boston: Little, Brown, 1939), 261–76. Biddle had been inspired by the Mexican experiment of the 1920s, in which young artists, given a living wage, frescoed government buildings with images of Mexican socialism. He envisioned young American artists similarly expressing "in living monuments" the social ideals that Roosevelt was struggling to achieve. The president liked the idea.

15. The Fine Arts Commission, or Commission of Fine Arts, was created by an act of Congress in 1910. Composed of seven "well-qualified judges of the fine arts," members were appointed by the president to serve four-year terms. For detailed accounts of the beginnings of the Public Works of Art Project, see: Richard D. McKinzie, *The New Deal for Artists* (Princeton, N.J.: Princeton Univ. Press, 1973), 5–11; and McDonald, *Federal Relief Administration and the Arts,* 357–63.

16. Dows interview, Oct. 31, 1963.

17. FW, "Edward Bruce," 1940, typescript, p. 2, FWP AAA; Dows interview, Oct. 31, 1963.

18. George Biddle, "An Art Renascence under Federal Patronage," *Scribner's Magazine* 95 (June 1934): 430.

19. Erica Beckh Rubenstein, "Tax Payers' Murals" (Ph.D. diss., Harvard Univ., 1944), 21. FW related this incident to Rubenstein in an interview or interviews (dates not specified) for her dissertation.

20. Dows interview, Oct. 31, 1963. Present in addition to Bruce, FW, Mrs. Roosevelt, and members of the advisory committee were museum directors William M. Milliken of the Cleveland Museum of Art, Juliana Force of the Whitney, Homer Saint-Gaudens of the Carnegie Institute of Art, Louis LaBeaume of the St. Louis Museum of Art, Francis Henry Taylor of the Worcester Museum of Art, C. Powell Minnegrode of the Corcoran, Duncan Phillips of the Phillips Memorial Art Gallery, Fiske Kimball of the Pennsylvania Museum of Art, Ellsworth Woodward of the Isaac Delgado Museum, and Alfred Barr of the Museum of Modern Art. Others who attended were Edward Warburg, a trustee of the Museum of Modern Art; Louis Simon, supervising architect for the Treasury Department; Dr. William Mann, director of Washington's National Zoological Park; Harry Lindeberg, architect; Alfred Granger of the American Institute of Architects; Dr. W. Carson Ryan Jr., director of education, Indian Service, Department of Interior; artists Olin Dows and George Biddle; and FERA officials Jacob Baker, Oliver Griswold, and F. Bartlett. Belisario Ramon Contreras, "The New Deal Treasury Department Art Programs and the American Artist: 1933 to 1943" (Ph.D. diss., American Univ., 1967), 23.

21. Public Works of Art Project, *Report of the Assistant Secretary of the Treasury to Federal Emergency Relief Administrator, Dec. 8, 1933–June 30, 1934* (Washington, D.C.: GPO, 1934), 2–4; "Preliminary Plan on Public Works of Art Project," undated, pp. 2–3, 121/105 NA.

22. "Preliminary Plan on Public Works of Art Project," undated, pp. [1]–2, 121/105 NA. Chairs of the sixteen regional PWAP committees were appointed as follows: Region no. 1—New England states: Francis H. Taylor; Region no. 2—New York state and metropolitan commuting zones of Connecticut and New Jersey: Juliana Force; Region no. 3—Pennsylvania east of the Susquehanna River, Delaware, and New Jersey (exclusive of metropolitan New York area): Fiske Kimball; Region no. 4—District of Columbia, Maryland, and Virginia: Duncan Phillips; Region no. 5—Georgia, North and South Carolina, Tennessee, and Florida: J. J. Haverty; Region no. 6—Mississippi, Louisiana, Arkansas, and Alabama: Ellsworth Woodward; Region no. 7—Missouri, Kansas, Nebraska, and Iowa: Louis La Beaume; Region no. 8—Pennsylvania west of the Susquehanna River and West Virginia: Homer Saint-Gaudens; Region no. 9—Ohio, Indiana, Kentucky, and Michigan: William Milliken; Region no. 10—Illinois, Wisconsin, and Minnesota: Walter Brewster; Region no. 11—Colorado, Wyoming, North and South Dakota: George L. Williamson; Region no. 12—Texas and Oklahoma: John S. Ankeney; Region no. 13—New Mexico and Arizona: Jesse Nusbaum; Region no. 14—Southern California south of and including Paso Robles Hot Springs: Merle Armitage; Region no. 15—Northern California north of Paso Robles Hot Springs, Nevada, and Utah: Walter Heil; Region no. 16—Oregon, Washington, Idaho, and Montana: Burt Brown Barker.

Public Works of Art Project, *Report of the Assistant Secretary of the Treasury to Federal Emergency Relief Administrator*, 3–4.

23. Edward B. Rowan, "Will Plumber's Wages Turn the Trick?" AMA 27 (Feb. 1934): 81; Memorandum, FW to Mr. L. W. Robert Jr., Dec. 20, 1933, 121/106 NA; FW to Theodore Sizer, Jan. 20, 1934, 121/109 NA; "Preliminary Plan on Public Works of Art Project," undated, p. 2, 121/105 NA. The members of the Advisory Committee to the Treasury on Fine Arts were Frederick A. Delano (President Roosevelt's uncle), chairman; Rexford Tugwell; Henry T. Hunt; Harry Hopkins; and Charles Moore. Edward Bruce was acting secretary.

24. In New York City, Juliana Force and Lloyd Goodrich, who assisted her on the regional committee, objected strenuously to the notion of grading artists by their abilities. As a result, in New York the difference between the two higher categories was split, and a uniform $34.00 a week was paid. Lloyd Goodrich reminiscences, as recorded in talks with Harlan B. Phillips, 1963, AAA.

25. Night letter, FW and Bruce to Francis H. Taylor, Dec. 10, 1933, 121/106 NA; night letter, FW and Bruce to Merle Armitage, Dec. 14, 1933, 121/109 NA; night letter, FW and Bruce to Duncan Phillips, Dec. 12, 1933, 121/114 NA; night letter, FW and Bruce, "Blanket Communication," Dec. 14, 1933, 121/106 NA; telegram, FW to Walter S. Brewster, Dec. 21, 1933, 121/109 NA.

26. FW, "Gallery Explorations," *Parnassus* 4 (Dec. 1932): 3; telegram, FW to Edward B. Rowan, Dec. 10, 1933, 121/105 NA; Olin Dows, "The New Deal's Treasury Art Programs: A Memoir," *Arts in Society* 2 ([1963]): 56; FW, "The Innocent Bystander," AMA 27 (Nov. 1934): 605.

27. Bruce to Arthur Millier, Jan. 9, 1934, 121/106 NA; John Davis Hatch, interview with H. Wade White, tape recording, June 8, 1964, AAA; telegram, Bruce to FW, Dec. 22, 1933, SRPWAP AAA DC 3; FW to George Biddle, Dec. 20, 1933, 121/105 NA.

28. Dows, "The New Deal's Treasury Art Programs," 55. Describing the Public Works of Art Project, a *Washington Post* reporter wrote, "the nerve center of the whole far-flung undertaking . . . is the untidy, distinctly inartistic office in the Treasury Building of Edward Bruce, who is serving voluntarily as Secretary to the Treasury's advisory committee on fine arts." "Roosevelt Plans to Put Artists to Work Decorating Buildings," *Washington Post*, Apr. 26, 1934.

29. Dows interview, Oct. 31, 1963.

30. Dows, "Nan and Forbes Watson," in *Still-Lifes by Nan Watson: Loan Exhibition, Nov. 10–Dec. 4, 1960, Wadsworth Atheneum, Hartford* ([Hartford, Conn.: Wadsworth Atheneum, 1960]); Henry Varnum Poor, interview with Harlan B. Phillips, tape recording, 1964, AAA.

31. [FW], "In re: Forbes Watson, Technical Director of the Public Works of Art Project," undated, typescript, 121/106 NA.

32. FW devoted the major portion of an *Arts* editorial to Rowan at that time. In it he praised the "unpretentiousness," "practicality," and "undaunted enthusiasm" with which Rowan made the Little Gallery "useful to the people and helpful to the creative artists." FW, "Mid-Western Optimism," *The Arts* 16 (Dec. 1929): 215. Testimony to the considerable weight of FW's approbation came from Frances D. Keppel, president of the Carnegie Corporation, who congratulated Rowan: "As you know, Forbes Watson is not very easy

to please and an expression of appreciation on his part is of more than ordinary significance." Frances D. Keppel to Rowan, Jan. 21, 1930, ERP AAA.

33. Alice Graeme Korff, interview with Harlan B. Phillips, tape recording, Oct. 7, 1965, AAA; Maria Ealand, interview with author, telephone tape recording, Mar. 31, 1994; Jane Watson Crane, interview with author, telephone tape recording, Apr. 25, 1994; FW, "Edward Bruce," 1940, typescript, p. 2, FWP AAA; Dows, "The New Deal's Treasury Art Programs, 56; "Ed Rowan's Column," *Public Works of Art Project Bulletin* 1 (Feb. 1934): 5.

34. Marling and others suggest that Bruce exercised very tight control over the operation of PWAP, imposing his own philosophical aversions to avant-garde and rearguard art on the entire program. Discussing a brouhaha over "radical" symbols depicted in murals in Coit Tower in San Francisco, Marling commented, "by 1934 it had already become obvious that no program with which Edward Bruce was associated would tolerate the slack supervisory procedures that courted such dismaying surprises." Marling, *Wall-to-Wall America*, 44, 48.

35. Maria Ealand to Jane Watson Crane, Mar. 9, 1992; Alice Graeme Korff interview, Oct. 7, 1965. Commenting on a recent exhibit at the Art Institute of Chicago, Rowan remarked, "I never liked Glackens and while I found it interesting to see a number of his works in the original I note that my opinions concerning his art have not changed." Rowan to Dudley Crafts Watson, June 19, 1934, SRPWAP AAA DC 4. Discussing the demise of the American Scene movement, FW commented, "a movement which can bring about the elevation to fame of such a tenth rate painter as Grant Wood has already swallowed the poison which is bound to bring about its death." FW, "Art in the Storm," Nov. 1, 1945, typescript, p. 2, FWP AAA. In a letter to the author dated Apr. 18, 1994, Maria Ealand commented, "Forbes admired many American artists and never lost an opportunity to praise them for qualities of intelligence and generosity and willingness to help others, with the exception of Grant Wood and Stuart Davis."

36. Telegram, FW and Bruce to Juliana Force, [Dec. 10, 1933], 121/106 NA; FW, "Americanism Unalloyed—A Defense of Alloys," *Brooklyn Daily Eagle Sunday Review*, Dec. 17, 1933.

37. Edward B. Rowan to Homer St. Gaudens, Mar. 5, 1934, 121/105 NA.

38. Quoted in McKinzie, *The New Deal for Artists*, 23–24. For a comprehensive description of the various styles of art produced under the Public Works of Art Project, see Contreras, *Tradition and Innovation in New Deal Art*, 67–101.

39. "No Distorted Modernistic Murals for School Walls; Must Reflect True America," *Dallas Morning News*, Dec. 23, 1933, 121/116 NA; Dows interview, Oct. 31, 1963. Contreras notes that Bruce's aesthetic tradition, which derived from Maurice Sterne, included the elements of "good drawing, careful observation of nature, and the development of instinct to assure an individual approach." Contreras, *Tradition and Innovation in New Deal Art*, 101.

40. Alice Graeme Korff noted that Bruce actively promoted Indian representation, believing "that this was a way of preserving their art too and helping them." Korff interview, Oct. 7, 1965.

41. FW to Jesse Nusbaum, Jan. 4, 1934, 121/106 NA; FW to John S. Ankeney, Jan. 3, 1934, 121/116 NA. FW wrote to Nusbaum: "Mrs. Collier seems anxious to know whether the Zumi [*sic*], Navajo and Hopi Indians, as well as the Indians of Southern Arizona, are to

be given any employment. I merely pass on this question, not knowing a Zumi [sic] from a Hopi."

42. "Art Conservatives Attack CWA Plan," *New York Times,* Dec. 13, 1933; George Biddle, diary, Dec. 11, 1933, GBP AAA; FW, "The Affiliated Plum Pickers Attack the Public Works of Art Project," undated typescript, p. 1, 121/109 NA; FW to Electus D. Litchfield, Dec. 20, 1933, 121/109 NA; FW, "The Affiliated Plum Pickers Attack CWA Project," *Washington Daily News,* Apr. 14, 1934; FW, "The Dignity of Wages," undated typescript, p. 2, FWP AAA.

43. FW to George Elmer Browne, Dec. 13, 1933, 121/105 NA; Bruce, "Telegram to be Sent to all Regional Chairmen," Dec. 17, 1933, 121/106 NA.

44. Memorandum, FW to Bruce, Feb. 2, 1934, 121/105 NA. It is interesting to note that in Assistant Secretary Robert's final report to Harry Hopkins, the issue of quality versus relief was delivered less emphatically. The introduction stated: "While the primary purpose of the project was to give employment to needy artists, a dual test was set up in the selection of those employed: first, that they were actually in need of the employment and, second, that they were qualified as artists to produce work which would be an embellishment to public property." The "Business Report" section added: "The primary aim of the Public Works of Art Project was relief to artists. It was the duty of the business office to keep down the overhead in order that this goal might be attained." *Report of the Assistant Secretary,* 2, 5.

45. Bruce to Arthur Millier, Jan. 9, 1934, 121/106 NA; [Peyton Boswell], "Tragedy," *Art Digest* 8 (Apr. 1, 1934): 3–4, 11.

46. Lloyd Goodrich, interview with author, tape recording, Mar. 16, 1985; Wat Williams to Ivan Albright, Jan. 12, 1934, 121/109 NA; FW to Brewster, Jan. 22, 1934, 121/109 NA; telegram, Brewster to FW, Jan. 9, 1934, 121/116 NA; Brewster to FW, Jan. 17, 1934, 121/109 NA; Brewster to Bruce, Mar. 20, 1934, 121/109 NA; Bruce to William Green, Jan. 11, 1934, 121/109 NA; Green to Bruce, Jan. 16, 1934, 121/109 NA. At the Feb. meeting of regional directors in Washington, the various directors gave brief, predominantly glowing reports on progress in their districts. Walter S. Brewster, however, reported "many troubles, . . . politics of art in Chicago, trouble with labor unions, and communistic groups." Summary of meeting of regional directors, Feb. 19, 1934, [p. 3], 121/105 NA.

47. Telegram, Walter Heil to Bruce, June 28, 1934, 121/114 NA. For detailed accounts of the Coit Tower controversy, see McKinzie, *The New Deal for Artists,* 24–26; and Marling, *Wall-to-Wall America,* 45–48.

48. "Art Conservatives Attack CWA Plan," *New York Times,* Dec. 13, 1933; FW to Merle Armitage, Feb. 1, 1934, 121/109 NA; FW to Brewster, Jan. 23, 1934, 121/109 NA.

49. Bruce to William M. Milliken, Mar. 28, 1934, 121/109 NA; "PWAP Chief Assails White's Farm Picture," *Washington Post,* May 16, 1934.

50. FW, "The U.S.A. Challenges the Artists," *Parnassus* 6 (Jan. 1934): 1–2; FW, "The Public Works of Art Project: Federal, Republican, or Democratic?" *AMA* 27 (Jan. 1934): 8.

51. FW to Ellsworth Woodward, Feb. 5, 1934, 121/109 NA; Bruce, "Public Works of Art Project—Address by Edward Bruce," *Congressional Record,* 73d Cong., 2d sess., 1934, vol. 78, pt. 1:765–67; Bruce to Julian E. Levi, Jan. 18, 1934, JLP AAA; "Minutes of Meeting of Regional Chairmen of the Public Works of Art Project," Feb. 20, 1934, [p. 4], 121/106 NA.

52. FW and Bruce to regional chairmen, undated, 121/106 NA.

53. FW to Theodore Sizer, Feb. 8, 1934, 121/106 NA. Attempting to arrange for artists to

visit the Annapolis site following their Santiago tour, FW wrote Sizer, "Confidentially, you might tell your friend Mr. Schmalz that Admiral Hart in my humble opinion is a peanut, and not to worry about what he says." FW to Theodore Sizer, May 4, 1934, 121/106 NA.

54. FW to Adm. Thomas C. Hart, Mar. 14, 1934, 121/106 NA; FW to Sizer, Feb. 8, 1934, 121/106 NA; FW to Sizer, Mar. 2, 1934, 121/106 NA; Cecil H. Jones to Arthur Schmalz, Aug. 25, 1934, 121/114 NA; Paul W. Cooley to Bruce, May 28, 1935, box 2, folder 10, ms. 145, New Haven Colony Historical Society. Jim Cheever, senior curator, U.S. Naval Academy, insisted that the *Battle of Santiago* mural was never hung in the Naval Academy, nor is the mural on the premises. Jim Cheever, telephone conversation with author, Oct. 13, 1994.

55. "For Release Monday, Feb. 5, 1934," 121/106 NA; "For Immediate Release," Feb. 20, 1934, 121/106 NA; "Minutes of Meeting of Regional Chairmen of the Public Works of Art Project," Feb. 20, 1934, [p. 7], 121/106 NA.

56. Public Works of Art Project, *Report of the Assistant Secretary of the Treasury to Federal Emergency Relief Administrator, Dec. 8, 1933–June 30, 1934* (Washington, D.C.: GPO, 1934), 6; Bruce, foreword to *National Exhibition of Art by the Public Works of Art Project, Apr. 24, 1934 to May 20, 1934* (Washington, D.C.: GPO, 1934), 3.

57. "PWAP Exhibit Lauded as Step Forward in Art," *Washington Post*, Apr. 21, 1934; "For Release," undated, p. 1, DC 1, SRPWAP AAA; "Roosevelt Likes C.W.A. Art," *Philadelphia Record*, Apr. 26, 1934, File of Publicity Materials, DC 8, SRPWAP AAA; "A Mirror to America," *Washington Daily News*, Apr. 20, 1934; Helen Buchalter, "Uncle Sam's Art Show," *New Republic* 79 (May 23, 1934): 43. The painting of the unemployed boy was *Young Worker* by Julius Bloch.

58. FW to Mrs. Jeanette Fiene, June 8, 1934, 121/105 NA; FW to Sizer, May 1, 1934, 121/104 NA; FW, "The Innocent Bystander," *AMA* 27 (Nov. 1934): 601; FW to John Gaw Meem, May 25, 1934, 121/105 NA.

59. Leila Mechlin, "Notes of Art and Artists," *Washington Sunday Star*, Apr. 29, 1934; Buchalter, "Uncle Sam's Art Show," 43–44; Howard Devree, "Public Works Art Shown at Exhibit," *New York Times*, Sept. 18, 1934.

60. Buchalter, "Uncle Sam's Art Show," 43; Mechlin, "Notes of Art and Artists"; Mary Morsell, "Selected Works of PWAP Project at the Corcoran," *Art News* 32 (May 5, 1934): 14; Edward Alden Jewell, "Public Works Art Shown at Capital," *New York Times*, Apr. 24, 1934; Lewis Mumford, "The Art Galleries," *New Yorker* 10 (June 2, 1934): 38, 40, 42.

61. Quoted without attribution in Bruce, "Public Works of Art Project: To the Chairmen and Members of Regional and State Committees," May 2, 1934, p. 2, 121/114 NA.

62. "For release Thursday, Apr. 26, 1934," 121/110 NA.

63. Memorandum, FW to Bruce, June 3, 1934, 121/106 NA.

64. "Schedule of Traveling National Exhibition," undated, DC 4, SRPWAP AAA; Bruce to Jonas Lie, June 7, 1934, DC 4, SRPWAP AAA; Bruce to Grace Overmyer, July 21, 1934, DC 4, SRPWAP AAA.

65. Bruce, "Public Works of Art Project: To the Chairmen and Members of Regional and State Committees," May 2, 1934, [p. 1], 121/114 NA; Bruce, "Bulletin, Public Works of Art Project: Disposition of Rejected and Preliminary Work," May 23, 1934, DC12, PWAPFR.

66. In a letter to Beatrice Winser, director of the Newark Museum, who had been pressing Rowan to send the National Exhibition there, Rowan wrote: "The C.W.A. funds

under which we have been operating have been recalled so that this particular office is to close shortly and the Division of Fine Arts, which Mr. Bruce has been working for as a permanent institution in the Government, has not been set up. The appropriation for funds to carry on until such time as an adequate program was outlined which the President expressly signed before leaving for Hawaii has been held up by a governmental technicality, with the result that we in this office do not know if we are coming or going. It is mighty embarrassing I can assure you." Rowan to Beatrice Winser, Sept. 5, 1934, DC 4, SRPWAP AAA.

67. Ann Craton, "Public Works of Art Project Report Covering Its Activities and Liquidation," [1935], typescript, [p. 23], 121/105 NA.

68. *Report of the Assistant Secretary of the Treasury to Federal Emergency Relief Administrator,* 5. Of the four federal arts programs during the 1930s, PWAP expenditures were the lowest, except for the Treasury Relief Art Project. It employed the largest number of artists, apart from the Federal Arts Project of the WPA. Dows, "The New Deal's Treasury Art Programs," 52.

69. Dows interview, Oct. 31, 1963; Merle Armitage to Rowan, Oct. 22, 1934, 121/123 NA, quoted in McKinzie, *The New Deal for Artists,* 31. Karal Ann Marling underscores Bruce's covert exclusionary policy, noting, "the effect of the seemingly innocent American Scene proviso was to harness public patronage, from the outset, to a nebulous species of realism, defined by the extremes Bruce chose to shun. Painting the American Scene excluded radical types of abstract art because the artist, in effect, was required to limit his or her creative activity to matching up some visible element of the environment with a picture that recapitulated the same." *Wall-to-Wall America,* 44–45.

70. Matthew Baigell observes that the American scene was chosen as the project's guiding theme "to give the PWAP coherence, and to allow artists freedom of expression as well. In effect, this gave the American Scene an official imprimatur and it acknowledged, as the summary report of the program indicated, the pre-eminence of the nationalistic movement in American art." *The American Scene,* 46. Karal Ann Marling cites the *Report of the Assistant Secretary of the Treasury to Federal Emergency Relief Administrator* to document the close alliance between the Public Works of Art Project and the American Scene movement. "Federal Patronage and the Woodstock Colony" (Ph.D. diss., Bryn Mawr College, 1971), 39, 40, 62.

71. FW, "Hustling 'Em Off the Stage," undated typescript, pp. [1]–2, FWP AAA; FW, "Americanism Unalloyed—A Defense of Alloys," *Brooklyn Daily Eagle Sunday Review,* Dec. 17, 1934. George H. Roeder Jr., discussing the American Scene movement's challenge to modern painting, notes, "Craven, who played to every prejudice which surfaced during the Thirties, expressed deepest contempt for American modernists, who by imitating foreign painting rejected their own cultural experience." *Forum of Uncertainty,* 120.

72. The celebrated sculptor Isamu Noguchi was one of those whose experiences with PWAP were unsatisfactory. The New York regional committee initially rejected his designs for a children's play mountain because they were considered too abstract. Later, he was suspended from the PWAP payroll because of a series of misunderstandings with the regional office. Replying to an inquiry from Belisario Contreras in 1964, Noguchi wrote, "I do not particularly believe in government in art," adding, "I did try to get on but they refused me and that was that." Isamu Noguchi to Contreras, Sept. 15, 1964, BCP AAA.

73. Arthur A. Ekirch Jr., *Ideologies and Utopias: The Impact of the New Deal on American Thought* (Chicago: Quadrangle, 1969), 141. See also Erica Beckh, "Government Art in the Roosevelt Era: An Appraisal of Federal Art Patronage in the Light of Present Needs," *Art Journal* 20 (fall 1960): 3, 5.

74. FW, "The Innocent Bystander," AMA 27 (Nov. 1934): 605–6; Korff interview, Oct. 7, 1965; Dows interview, Oct. 31, 1963; Poor interview, 1964, AAA. Korff was referring to both the Public Works of Art Project and the Section of Painting and Sculpture, which Bruce headed.

75. FW to Frances Wayne, June 4, 1934, 121/105 NA; FW to Homer St. Gaudens, Jan. 2, 1934, 121/109 NA; FW, "Whitney Talk," [1941 or 1942], typescript, p. 6, FWP AAA.

76. FW, "Speaking of Art, No. II," [June 1934], typescript, pp. 2–3, 121/105 NA; FW, "The Artist Recognizes the Community" (address before College Art Association), undated but Apr. 1934, typescript, pp. 5–12, 121/105 NA; FW, "A Steady Job," AMA 27 (Apr. 1934): 168.

77. FW to Henri de Kruif, June 27, 1934, 121/108 NA.

78. FW, "The Innocent Bystander," AMA 27 (Nov. 1934): 606; Thomas Craven, "Men of Art: American Style," *American Mercury* 6 (Dec. 1925): 432.

79. FW to Mrs. Ernest Fiene, June 8, 1934, 121/105 NA.

80. FW to Henry Ness, July 10, 1934, 121/105 NA.

81. FW to Howland, Mar. 11, 1948, IHP AAA; Thomas Donnelly to FW, undated, 121/105 NA; FW to Donnelly, May 10, 1934, 121/105 NA; FW to Bruce, July 2, 1934, 121/122 NA. Updating Bruce on the PWAP report he was writing and several other matters, FW added: "The eight teeth which were dug out of my handsome countenance at great pain to my soul and body, have been replaced so I feel as if I had just inherited a china factory. Not being accustomed to this inheritance yet it renders me somewhat irritable and nervous. Besides, every day I have to interrupt myself once or twice to go to the dentist and be fiddled around with. The blow to my finances has been something appalling, and I am thinking very seriously of embracing the faith so heartily that I can start walking to Scotland. I resigned from the payroll last Saturday, and am making up the many hours presented to the dentist this week."

82. FW to Bruce, June 16, 1934, 121/122 NA; memorandum, Cecil Jones to Assistant Secretary Robert, Aug. 26, 1934, 121/114 NA.

7. THE SECTION OF PAINTING AND SCULPTURE

1. "Treasury Department Order PWB No. 2-0," Oct. 16, 1934, ERP AAA.

2. Olin Dows, interview with Harlan B. Phillips, tape recording, Oct. 31, 1963, AAA.

3. Memorandum, Bruce to Admiral Peoples, Nov. 14, 1934, 121/122 NA.

4. FW to Bruce, Dec. 19, 1935, 121/125 NA; FW to Bruce, July 23, 1935, 121/125 NA. FW was assigned three successive titles in the first year: sectional public information advisor, assistant, and, finally, editor.

5. FW to Bruce, Aug. 28, 1935, 121/122 NA; Ealand to Ned and Peggy Bruce, Sept. 19, 1935, DC 40, CORTRAPFAS; FW to Max Kuehne, Oct. 8, 1935, 121/125 NA. As it turned out, FW rented the New York apartment to his sister, Mary, who resided there during her many trips to the city. FW and Nan also stayed there when they were in town. Spending Christmas week in New York in 1935 while Mary was in Boston, FW wrote friends that they would have their "own apartment to ourselves" and expect "to have a wonderful time." FW to Mrs. Edward Bruce, Dec. 19, 1935, 121/125 NA.

6. FW to Bruce, Dec. 19, 1935, 121/125 NA.

7. Inslee Hopper, interview with Robert Brown, tape recording, July 28, 1981, AAA; Maria Ealand, interview with author, telephone tape recording, Mar. 31, 1994; FW to Jane (Mrs. Wendell) Jones, Mar. 19, 1957, WJP AAA.

8. Edward Bruce, "The Treasury Department Art Program," in *Mural Designs, 1934–1936*, by FW and Edward Bruce, vol. 1 in *Art in Federal Buildings: An Illustrated Record of the Treasury Department's New Program in Painting and Sculpture* (Washington, D.C.: Art in Federal Buildings Corporation, 1936), 283.

9. Dows, "The New Deal's Treasury Art Programs," 65.

10. The program included music, drama, and writing as well as plastic arts. Neither Bruce nor Secretary Morgenthau wanted to undertake a strictly relief program, particularly one of such massive scale. Consequently, the WPA initiated its own arts program, the Federal Arts Project; Holger Cahill was appointed national director. Dows, "The New Deal's Treasury Art Programs," 68–70.

11. George Biddle, interview with Harlan B. Phillips, tape recording, 1963, AAA; Olin Dows, interview with Emily Williams, July 7, 1978, typescript, p. 11, Franklin D. Roosevelt Library, Hyde Park, N.Y.; Dows interview, Oct. 31, 1963. On only one occasion did Dows use his social connections to further a cause. After TRAP had been in operation for about a year, the WPA decided it would no longer allocate funds to projects outside its jurisdiction and would withdraw all unspent funds. Concerned that this would cause TRAP to breech certain commitments to individual artists, Dows paid President Roosevelt a professional call "for the first and only time." Not only were the TRAP jobs completed as planned and the program permitted to retain its unspent funds as a result of the visit, but TRAP later received two supplementary appropriations.

12. Dows, "The New Deal's Treasury Art Programs," 68.

13. Hopper interview, July 28, 1981. Hopper's title was later changed to consultant to the chief.

14. Dows interview, Oct. 31, 1963.

15. Ealand interview, Mar. 31, 1994; FW, "Woodstock Talk," undated typescript, p. 8, FWP AAA. "Small but important proof of Bruce's efficiency is that out of thousands of designs sent to him, none was ever mislaid or lost," one magazine writer noted admiringly. "America Sees Itself in New Government Murals," *Life*, Jan. 27, 1941, 42.

16. Hopper interview, July 28, 1981; Dows interview, Oct. 31, 1963.

17. Hopper interview, July 28, 1981; Maria Ealand to author, Apr. 18, 1994; Ealand interview, Mar. 31, 1994.

18. Henry Varnum Poor, interview with Harlan B. Phillips, tape recording, 1964, AAA; Alice Graeme Korff, interview with Harlan B. Phillips, tape recording, Oct. 7, 1965, AAA.

19. Graeme Korff interview, Oct. 7, 1965; Jane Watson Crane, interview with author, telephone tape recording, Apr. 25, 1994; Dows interview, Oct. 31, 1963.

20. Bruce to FW, Aug. 21, 1940, 121/122 NA; Ealand interview, Mar. 31, 1994; Ealand to author, Apr. 18, 1994.

21. C. Adolph "Cook" Glassgold, interview with Harlan B. Phillips, tape recording, Dec. 9, 1964, AAA; Ealand to author, Apr. 18, 1994; Charlotte Partridge, interview with Harlan B. Phillips, tape recording, June 12, 1965, AAA.

22. "Roving eye" was a term Jane Watson Crane used to describe FW's womanizing. Crane interview, Apr. 25, 1994.

23. FW to Mrs. Edward Rowan, Feb. 2, 1934, ERP AAA; Leata Rowan to FW, Feb. 16, 1934, ERP AAA. FW's letter was written less than two months after Ed Rowan came to Washington. FW could not have met Mrs. Rowan on more than two occasions, those being when he lectured in Cedar Rapids, Iowa, in Nov. 1929. FW was a fast worker where the women were concerned.

24. Memorandum, FW to Director of Procurement, Feb. 20, 1935, 121/122 NA.

25. Memorandum, FW to Bruce, Dec. 14, 1934, 121/122 NA. By the seventh issue, Bruce looked to Dows for help in lowering the common denominator, writing him confidentially at his home to avoid offending Watson. "The *Bulletin* is not, I think, as good as it should be," he declared, generalizing from there. "Forbes has never had a particular flair for publicity. Certainly all the money which was spent by the Whitneys should have made more of the success than it was, and I think the *Bulletin* can [be] substantially improved." Nonplused, Dows asked for clarification at the same time defending both *The Arts* and Forbes's editorial approach to the *Bulletin*. Bruce withdrew his criticism of Watson in a subsequent letter, explaining, "what we want to do is get the artists of the country enthusiastically behind the movement and get as many of them rooters for it as we can." FW and Dows incorporated Bruce's suggestions into the next issue, number eight, following which they observed a greater response among readers. Bruce to Dows, Jan. 10, 1936, DC 40, CORTRAPFAS; Dows to Bruce, Jan. 14, 1936, DC 40, CORTRAPFAS; Bruce to Dows, Jan. 18, 1936, DC 40, CORTRAPFAS.

26. Bruce to Dows, Mar. 10, 1936, DC 40, CORTRAPFAS; Bruce, "Introduction," *Section Bulletin* 22 (Sept. 1940): 1.

27. C. J. Peoples, "Foreword," *Section Bulletin* 1 (Mar. 1, 1935): 5–6; "A Letter to Edward Bruce from Henry Varnum Poor," *Section Bulletin* 21 (Mar. 1940): 4; L.A.S. to FW, Oct. 5, 1938, FWP AAA.

28. FW to Bruce, Mar. 14, 1939, 121/122 NA; "Report of New York Trip, Thursday, Mar. 2, Sunday, Mar. 5 Inclusive," Apr. 3, 1939, p. 1, 121/129 NA.

29. FW to John Sloan, Jan. 27, 1939, FWP AAA; Dows, "The New Deal's Treasury Art Programs," 71. The SPS's sometimes elaborate efforts to oversee the content as well as the bureaucracy of all the mural projects around the country and respond to local citizens' concerns are recounted in at least four specialized studies of mural art under the New Deal. Marling *(Wall-to-Wall America)* and Marlene Park and Gerald Markowitz *(Democratic Vistas: Post Offices and Public Art in the New Deal* [Philadelphia: Temple Univ. Press, 1984]) detail the complications that often resulted from the section's efforts to get things right. Sue Bridwell Beckwith *(Depression Post Office Murals and Southern Culture* [Baton Rouge: Louisiana State Univ. Press, 1988]) examines the cultural implications of SPS murals on Southern society. Barbara Melosh *(Engendering Culture: Manhood and Womanhood in New Deal Public Art and Theater* [Washington D.C.: Smithsonian Institution Press, 1990]) focuses on the representation of gender in the images in New Deal murals, sculpture, and theater. Robert Carl Vitz ("Painters, Pickets, and Politics: The Artist Moves Left, 1925–1940" [Ph.D. diss., Univ. of North Carolina, 1971]) and McKinzie *(The New Deal for Artists)* describe some of the more farcical aspects of public and government interaction.

30. Press Release, June 21, 1939, FWP AAA; "Memorandum of the Jury in the 48-State Competition Held by the Section of Fine Arts, Oct. 10–14, 1939," DC 40, CORTRAPFAS;

"Special 48 State Mural Competition," *Section Bulletin* 19 (June 1939): 4. For a lively account of the "48-State Competition," see Marling, *Wall-to-Wall America.*

31. Payment to artists was usually made in three installments: the first upon acceptance of a design, a second upon half-completion, and the third at completion and final approval.

32. Cecil Jones to Robert Harshe, Apr. 5, 1937, FWP AAA; Ealand to Bernard Roufberg, Apr. 10, 1937, FWP AAA; Ealand to FW, Apr. 12, 1937, FWP AAA; FW, "Inspection Tour Made by Forbes Watson, Apr. 3 to May 24, 1937," undated typescript, p. 1, 121/128 NA. Nan's journal, which was almost as lengthy as FW's, offered interesting insights not only into the mechanics of the long cross-country trip but also into her own world and the kind of support she brought to their relationship. A curious medley of discerning professional observations about art and art conditions and chatty notes about shopping for shoes, people's manners, mending clothes, beauty-parlor appointments, and the cost of restaurants and hotels, the document reveals Nan's keen eye for detail and her own quiet streak of sardonic wit. That a number of phrases in Nan's journal and FW's final report are identical, including some of the most pungent, suggests that FW and Nan shared many observations and stories at the end of the day and on their long rides between towns. Clearly, Nan's record, with its volume of detail, including even arrival and departure times, hotel names, addresses of some of the people and places they visited, size and receptiveness of lecture audiences, and several statements of FW's in quotation marks, was meant to serve and refresh FW's recollections for his final report. What emerged most distinctly from her journal was a sense of her unwavering respect for her husband's expertise and talent. [Nan Watson], journal, Apr. 5–May 23, 1937, 121/122 NA.

33. Following FW's tour of California, Bernard Roufberg, California supervisor of TRAP, wrote Watson: "I have not heard any flashes by air, wire, or other means of communication concerning the success of your trip after we left the war-torn battle field at the Sir Francis Drake. We are very anxious to hear how things went along with you and whether there was any other state to rival California in its hospitality to a bacchanalian and epicurean cognoscente such as you." Bernard Roufberg to FW, May 24, 1937, FWP AAA; FW to Roufberg, May 29, 1937, FWP AAA. Even in 1939, when money had tightened considerably, Watson talked of personally financing another trip to the West Coast. Bruce would not subject him to the very heavy expense, however, and the second tour never materialized. Bruce to FW, Mar. 19 1939, 121/122 NA; FW to Bruce, Mar. 25 1939, 121/122 NA.

34. FW, "Inspection Tour Made by Forbes Watson," 10, 14, 35.

35. FW, "Inspection Tour Made by Forbes Watson," 2.

36. FW to Mrs. Stephen H. Beach, Oct. 28, 1937, FWP AAA; Ealand to Bruce, Sept. 19, 1935, DC 40, CORTRAPFAS. The restrictions on payment even applied to articles. When Simon ruled that FW's trip to New York to persuade the *New York Times* and the *Tribune* to publish articles about the government art programs could not be classified as official, Watson sold the articles to the newspapers. FW to Bruce, July 23, 1935, 121/125 NA.

37. FW, "Art Notes," *NYEP*, Nov. 7, 1914; FW, "The People and Their Art," undated typescript of lecture given at Howard University, p. 3, FWP AAA; FW "Art Notes," *NYEP*, Jan. 16, 1915; FW, "Americanism Unalloyed—A Defense of Alloys," *Brooklyn Daily Eagle*

Sunday Review, Dec. 17, 1933; FW to Dows, Sept. 7, 1938, ODL AAA; FW and Bruce, *Mural Designs,* 9.

38. FW, "Americanism Unalloyed"; FW to Theodore Sizer, May 21, 1934, 121/105 NA.

39. FW and Bruce, *Mural Designs,* 3–5.

40. Dows to Bruce, Mar. 5, 1936, DC 40, CORTRAPFAS; Hopper, [Report of trip to Cleveland, Ohio], Feb. 18 [1936], typescript, p. 5, DC 40, CORTRAPFAS.

41. FW to Bruce, Mar. 16, 1936, 121/122 NA. Richard McKinzie suggests that the motivation behind the publication of *Art in Federal Buildings* was self-serving and bordering on deception. "Edward Bruce and Forbes Watson in 1937 determined to write their own book, *Art in Federal Buildings.* The title page inscribed 'Volume I' and the introductory promise 'to publish further volumes which shall fully illustrate sculpture models, . . . and all other work in the fine arts created for the decoration of Federal buildings,' betrayed the expectations of the authors when they began. . . . Watson's articles about the Section and Section artists in the *Magazine of Art* had an easily recognizable tone—uncritical, tenderly egotistical, and suspicion inspiring for readers whose support the project needed most. Bruce fed selected anecdotes, photographs, and statistics to other writers, but never invited scholars or popular writers to move freely in the offices and files for an objective—and more believable—study." McKinzie, *The New Deal for Artists,* 182. Jane Watson Crane remembered it differently: "The initiative [for *Art in Federal Buildings*] came from Forbes, who dreamed of an ongoing project to acquaint the American public of this venture in which he, Bruce, and Olin Dows believed so fervently. The project was perhaps impractical and ill-advised, but I do not agree with Richard McKinzie that it was 'self-serving.'" Crane to author, Oct. 23, 1994. Erica Rubenstein, whose Harvard University dissertation, "Tax Payers' Murals," was completed in 1944, recalled "that both Watson and Ed Rowan [in the SPS office] were friendly and helpful and gave me the run of files and photographs." Erica Beckh Rubenstein to author, Mar. 24, 1994.

42. Five additional SPS members were shareholders: Bruce, Henry LaFarge, Ed Rowan, Inslee Hopper, and Maria Ealand.

43. Jane Watson Crane to author, Oct. 7, 1994.

44. Crane's memory is probably faulty with respect to the $5.00 figure. All official records specify an original price of $4.50 for the artists' edition.

45. At today's dollar value, the capitalization of volume 1 of *Art in Federal Buildings* would probably amount to $65,000. The price of each edition of the book would be at least $50 and $100, respectively. Crane to author, Oct. 23, 1994.

46. FW and Bruce, *Mural Designs,* 11, 23.

47. Crane interview, Apr. 25, 1994; [FW], *A Guide to the Painting and Sculpture in the Justice Department Building, Washington, District of Columbia,* Art Guides no. 1 (Washington, D.C.: Art in Federal Buildings Corporation, 1938), 3.

48. FW's request in 1938 for an increase in the stipend to fifty dollars per lecture was declined. FW to W. B. Dinsmoor, Nov. 10, 1938, FWP AAA; Dinsmoor to FW, Nov. 16, 1938, FWP AAA.

49. Tucker to FW, June 30, 1936, FWP AAA.

50. Korff interview, Oct. 7, 1965; Biddle interview, Dec. 9, 1964, AAA; Crane interview,

Apr. 25, 1994; Olin Dows, "The New Deal's Treasury Art Programs," *Arts in Society* 2 [1963]: 56; Glassgold interview, Dec. 9, 1964, AAA.

8. CONFIRMED NEW DEALER

1. FW to Bruce, Mar. 27, 1936, 121/122 NA.

2. Maria Ealand, interview with author, telephone tape recording, Mar. 31, 1994; Lloyd Goodrich, interview with author, tape recording, Mar. 16, 1985. See also FW to Scaravaglione, Oct. 4, 1948, CSP AAA.

3. FW to Bruce, July 29, 1936, 121/122 NA.

4. FW to Bruce, Dec. 19, 1935, 121/125 NA.

5. FW, "New Forces in American Art," *Kenyon Review* 1 (spring 1939): 122–24.

6. *American Painting Today,* with an essay by FW (Washington, D.C.: American Federation of Arts, 1939), 22. Jane Watson recalled that Allen Whiting felt that the staff of the *Magazine of Art* "could have done a better job in organizing the abundant material and in illustrating Forbes's very thoughtful summary" for *American Painting Today,* but "we were very busy at the time of its publication." Jane Watson Crane to author, Oct. 7, 1994.

7. FW, "The Unique Mr. Pascin—A Sketch," undated typescript, pp. 5, 6, FWP AAA.

8. FW, "The Return to the Facts," *AMA* 29 (Mar. 1936): 151; FW, "Woodstock Talk," undated typescript, pp. 5, 8, FWP AAA; FW, "This about America," undated typescript, pp. 7, 8, 13, 23, FWP AAA.

9. FW, "The Return to the Facts," *AMA* 29 (Mar. 1936): 152–53; FW, "The Gentle Removal of Charity," *MA* 34 (Feb. 1941): 61.

10. FW, "The Innocent Bystander," *AMA* 28 (Jan. 1935): 112; FW, "Max Weber—1941," *MA* 34 (Feb. 1941): 82.

11. FW, "A World without Elegance," *Parnassus* 7 (May 1935): 3, 4, 7, 8.

12. Ibid., 5–6.

13. FW, "The Arts Club of Chicago," *The Arts* 6 (Dec. 1924): 346, 342.

14. FW, "The Purpose of the Pittsburgh International," *AMA* 28 (Nov. 1935): 645–46.

15. FW, "Woodstock Talk," 9; FW to Esther Williams, May 4, 1947, EWP AAA. FW made the "brown shirts" remark concerning an Equity meeting in 1947.

16. FW, "The Innocent Bystander," *AMA* 28 (Mar. 1935): 173–74. The Artists Union was the recently reorganized version of the Unemployed Artists Group, which had attacked Juliana Force's administration of the New York regional committee of PWAP a year earlier.

17. FW, "The Chance in a Thousand," *AMA* 28 (Aug. 1935): 470–75; Davis, "Some Chance," 4, 7. See Ealand's statement quoted earlier (chap. 6, n. 35).

18. Biddle, *An American Artist's Story,* 287–88; FW to Dows, Sept. 7, 1938, ODL AAA; Bruce to FW, Feb. 16, 1940, 121/122 NA. Well into his retirement, Watson would gleefully share a rural neighbor's slighting description of architects: "'Hell, an architect is only a carpenter with his brains battered out.'" FW to Ealand, June 17, 1949, gift to author from Maria Ealand.

19. FW, "The Innocent Bystander," *AMA* 28 (June 1935): 373.

20. FW quoted the following statements from the committee's resolution: "Whereas the limitations of the olden state have been removed by the motion pictures, accompanied by sonancy, and the genius of dramatic authors and writers is no longer pent up in

the Utica of confination to small stages and auditoriums but ranges the United States so that the lesser villages may now receive the same presentations as the major cities, and instead of fustian and buckram the backgrounds of film dramas [always remembering 'sonancy'] are as realistic as if, as in many cases they are, they were the actual scenes of the words and actions of the plays shown on the film." Ibid. (brackets in original).

21. The artists' unions were overwhelmingly in favor of a federal art department to ensure jobs and security and had considerable input into the proposed bills. Carl Sandburg, Leopold Stokowski, and John Sloan were among those who supported the measure. Others, equally famous, opposed it. Fears of mediocrity in art and union control were major arguments raised against the bill.

As late as 1954, when asked by New Jersey representative Charles Howell for comments on his bill to create a nine-division federal fine arts commission, FW admonished: "Art is not a Sunday school teacher. . . . It is not a welfare department. It is a creative force by which our lives are enriched. . . . It's not a veteran's bureau nor a recreation center." FW did not send the letter containing these statements, but Congressman Howell's proposal never made it out of committee. FW to Congressman Howell, undated, FWP AAA.

22. Inslee Hopper, interview with Robert Brown, tape recording, July 28, 1981, AAA; Henry Morgenthau interview summary by Erica Rubenstein and Lewis Rubenstein, Nov. 9, 1964, AAA; Dows, "The New Deal's Treasury Art Programs," 72.

23. Morgenthau "said that he was very close to Roosevelt, perhaps closest of anyone in the cabinet in Washington. And that when Roosevelt had a job which no other cabinet member could or would do, it usually was given to Mr. Morgenthau. . . . Roosevelt relegated the art program to Morgenthau as one of these many jobs." Morgenthau interview summary, Nov. 9, 1964.

24. John M. Carmody to the President, Dec. 26, 1939, FWP AAA.

25. FW to Bruce, June 27, 1940, 121/122 NA.

26. FW to Bruce, Aug. 20, 1940, 121/122 NA; FW to Bruce, July 9, 1940, 121/122 NA.

27. FW to Bruce, Aug. 20, 1940.

28. Rubenstein, "Tax Payers' Murals," 74. Encouraged by Carmody's readiness to set aside fifty thousand dollars from the annual appropriation for the decoration of forty-two older federal buildings outside Washington, Bruce, FW, Rowan, and Hopper quietly appointed a jury of five recognized painters and sculptors to recommend artists for the commissions. There was no time for competitions. Unfortunately, the Bureau of the Budget ruled that to make the scheme legal, the word "decoration" must be inserted in the appropriation bill, to read: "alterations, improvement, 'decoration,' and preservation." This gave Congress the authority, for the first time, to pass on SFA activities, and it denied the request. Memorandum, Bruce to Commissioner of Public Buildings, June 20, 1941, DC 40, CORTRAPFAS; Bruce to W. E. Reynolds, Aug. 5, 1941, DC 40, CORTRAPFAS; "Memorandum Gotten from Mr. Melick's Office," undated, DC 40, CORTRAPFAS.

29. FW, "Slackers under the Skin," MA 32 (Oct. 1939): 557; FW, "Artists and Soldiers," MA 33 (June 1940): 333.

30. FW, "The Enemy Sees You," MA 33 (July 1940): 397; FW, "Unlimited Emergency," MA 34 (June–July 1941): 289; FW, "The Artist's Priorities," MA 34 (Dec. 1941): 503; FW, "What Can I Do?" MA 35 (Jan. 1942): 340.

31. Hopper to Lilian S. Saarinen, Jan. 30, 1942, DC 40, CORTRAPFAS; Resolutions Committee of Broadway Grange No. 647, "Resolution," [Jan. 1942], DC 40, CORTRAPFAS; Hopper to George C. Baer, Jan. 19, 1942, DC 40, CORTRAPFAS.

32. In addition to his two books on Treasury Department art, FW wrote two monographs during those years, one on the drawings of the gifted satirist Aaron Sopher and the other on Winslow Homer, part of Crown's American Artists Series. Both typically emphasized visual material over text. See FW, *Aaron Sopher* (Baltimore: Theodore Ember, 1940); and FW, *Winslow Homer* (New York: Crown, [1942]).

33. Ann Craton to FW, Sept. 24, 1934, FWP AAA.

34. FW to Edward Warder Rannells, Mar. 14, 1934, 121/105 NA. Everyone referred to Frederick Allen Whiting Jr., as "Allen," to distinguish him from his father, Frederick Allen Whiting, an executive in the American Federation of Arts.

35. Jane Watson Crane, interview with author, telephone tape recording, Apr. 25, 1994; Goodrich interview, Mar. 16, 1985; Harry Roberts Jr., "New Magazine—New Format," *MA* 30 (Jan. 1937): 4.

36. FW to Dows, Aug. 20, 1938, ODL AAA; FW to Louis Slobodkin, Sept. 8, 1938, FWP AAA; FW to Thomas La Farge, Sept. 7, 1938, FWP AAA; FW to Dows, Sept. 7, 1938, ODL AAA.

37. Dows to Robert Woods Bliss, Feb. 18, 1941, ODL AAA; Goodrich interview, Mar. 16, 1985.

38. FW, "The Benefit of Great Art," *MA* 34 (Mar. 1941): 113–14.

39. Thomas C. Parker to Dows, Apr. 23, 1941, ODL AAA; Parker to Dows, May 6, 1941, ODL AAA; George Hewitt Myers, "Mr. Watson's Day," *MA* 34 (May 1941): 230. The title of Myers's letter was an obvious reference to Eleanor Roosevelt's syndicated daily newspaper column, "My Day."

40. Robert W. Bliss to Dows, May 20, 1941, ODL AAA; Dows to "Dear Sir," [June 1941], FWP AAA. FW's was not the only salvo aimed at the Mellon bequest. Jane Watson's essay in the same issue traced the history of the national museum movement in Washington and found the Mellon gallery lacking both in the spirit and intention of the plan. Jane Watson, "A Nation in Search of a National Gallery," *MA* 34 (Mar. 1941): 144–47. The following month, Joseph Hudnut, dean of the Graduate School of Design at Harvard, published a scathing critique of the architectural layout of the National Gallery, in which he observed that museums of fine arts offered the "most favorable field for this pious collaboration of wealth and power with the priesthood of the Roman tradition." With its columns and dome, "forms emptied of purpose"; its "forty granite steps of majestic width . . . placed there, not to be used, but to be admired"; and other features of "professional hocus-pocus," it belonged to the "private Heaven of architects." Hudnut, "The Last of the Romans: Comment on the Building of the National Gallery of Art," *MA* 34 (Apr. 1941): 169–73.

41. FW to Dows, June 13, 1941, ODL AAA.

42. Dows to "Dear Sir," [June 1941] FWP AAA.

43. Jane Watson, "Nation in Search," 144–47; Crane interview, Apr. 25, 1994.

44. FW to Max Weber, Mar. 7, 1942, MWP AAA. The trustees of the American Federation of Art met in New York City that spring to consider "the whole situation of publication of the *Magazine of Art.*" By the end of the meeting, which included museum people, scholars, teachers, and other eminent persons in the art field, they agreed upon

an editorial board to oversee the magazine with Lloyd Goodrich as chairman. "Watson had lost control of the magazine at this point," Goodrich observed. "He was very much *in* control before." Goodrich interview, Mar. 16, 1985.

45. Goodrich interview, Mar. 16, 1985.

46. Flint, "Quick, Watson," 13, 39.

9. MAKING ART RELEVANT DURING WAR

1. Heinz Warneke to FW, Sept. 1942, FWP AAA. For a detailed account of the American Artists' Congress from its origins to decline, see *Artists against War and Fascism: Papers of the First American Artists' Congress,* with an introduction by Matthew Baigell and Julia Williams (New Brunswick, N.J.: Rutgers Univ. Press, 1986).

2. Rowan to Mina Ellis, Sept. 24, 1943, ERP AAA; Maurice Sterne to FW, Aug. 14, 1942, FWP AAA; Yasuo Kuniyoshi to FW, June 4, 1941, FWP AAA; Kuniyoshi to Bruce, Jan. 30, 1942, FWP AAA.

3. "Artists' Council for Victory," *Art News* 16 (Feb. 1, 1942): 32; *New York Times* article quoted in "Ten Thousand Artists Unite for Victory," *Art Digest* 16 (Feb. 1, 1942): 17. For a detailed account of the history of Artists for Victory, see Ellen G. Landau, *Artists for Victory: An Exhibition Catalog* (Washington, D.C.: Library of Congress, 1983).

4. *Advancing American Art: Politics and Aesthetics in the State Department Exhibition, 1946–48* (Montgomery, Ala.: Montgomery Museum of Fine Arts, 1984), 60–61; Rubenstein, "Tax Payers' Murals," 78. Typical of the early uses of art in the war effort was that of the National Woman's Division of the William Allen White Committee to Defend America by Aiding the Allies, which ran a nationwide contest in the fall of 1940 for posters "calculated to awaken public opinion to the need for all possible material aid to Great Britain and her Allies as America's first line of defense." FW, Peggy Bacon, and Henry Varnum Poor were members of the national jury that selected the winners during National Art Week. "Nation-wide Poster Contest," [Sept. 1940], DC 39, CORTRAPFAS.

5. Florence S. Berryman, "Guns and Brushes," MA 35 (Oct. 1942): 214–17.

6. Rowan to Harold Hartogensis, July 27, 1942, DC 38, CORTRAPFAS.

7. "A Call to Artists," *O.E.M. Art Bulletin* no. 1, undated, FWP AAA; FW, "Soldiers of Production: Exhibition of Paintings and Drawings by Eight American Artists Appointed by the Office for Emergency Management to Record Activities in Specific Defense Areas," undated, DC 40, CORTRAPFAS; F. Allen Whiting Jr., "A Call to Action," MA 35 (Mar. 1942): 96–101; Office for Emergency Management, "For Immediate Release," Feb. 3, 1942, FWP AAA; FW, *American Artists' Record of War and Defense, National Gallery of Art, Smithsonian Institution,* 1942, unpaged, 121/105 NA; *Red Cross Bulletin,* no. 1, Jan. 15, 1942, PHP AAA; Pauline Ehrlich to Donald B. Goodall, Apr. 30, 1942, DC 38, CORTRAPFAS.

8. "Pictorial War Correspondents," [June 1942], typescript, pp. [1], 6, FWP AAA. The plan was based on the successful British model of World War I.

9. Dows to Burt [W. E. Reynolds], July 27, 1942, ODL AAA; Dows to Mrs. Franklin D. Roosevelt, July 27, 1942, ODL AAA; Franklin D. Roosevelt to Gilmore D. Clarke, July 21, 1942, ODL AAA.

10. FW to Dows, July 18, 1942, ODL AAA; Dows to Burt [W. E. Reynolds], July 27, 1942.

11. FW, *The Edward Bruce Memorial Collection, Sept. 12 to 28, 1943* (Washington, D.C.: Corcoran Gallery of Art, [1943]), 3.

12. Olin Dows, interview with Harlan B. Phillips, tape recording, Oct. 31, 1963, AAA. "The Section of Fine Arts has continued nominally on the payroll of Public Buildings, reduced to a staff of one in the person of Edward Rowan," Rubenstein wrote, presumably some time between Bruce's death in Jan. 1943 and the SFA's termination in Aug. 1943, approximately twelve to seventeen months before her dissertation was submitted in 1943. "Tax Payers' Murals," 74.

13. The final mural, Anton Refregier's series of twenty-nine panels for the Rincon Annex Post Office, San Francisco, was completed in 1952. By then the supervising architect of the Procurement Division in the Treasury Department was in charge of the paintings. Beckh, "Government Art in the Roosevelt Era," 4.

14. Reeves Lewenthal to George Biddle, July 1943, in George Biddle, *Artist at War* (New York: Viking, 1944), 57–58.

15. Robert Cronbach, "Speech Delivered at a Session of the American Artists' Congress," June 8, 1941, typescript, [p. 1], DC 40, CORTRAPFAS; Peter Hurd, interview with Sylvia Loomis, tape recording, Mar. 28, 1964, AAA; Henry Morgenthau interview summary by Erica Rubenstein and Lewis Rubenstein, Nov. 9, 1964, AAA.

16. Dows interview, Oct. 31, 1963; Rubenstein, "Tax Payers' Murals," 179–80. Even Dows speculated as to whether Willem de Kooning, who became one of America's most prominent abstract-expressionist painters during the 1950s, had "painted down for the jury" when he won a SFA design competition for the maritime ship *SS President Jackson*. "It's handsome, utterly unlike anything he's done since," Dows noted. Dows interview, Oct. 31, 1963.

17. Goodrich interview, Mar. 16, 1985; Olin Dows, interview with Emily Williams, July 7, 1978, typescript, Franklin D. Roosevelt Library.

18. Henry Varnum Poor, interview with Harlan B. Phillips, tape recording, 1964, AAA; Dows interview, Oct. 31, 1963. Ashton noted a connection between government art programs and the genesis of abstract expressionism in the United States: "Throughout the nineteen-thirties the WPA was a central fact in the lives of nearly all the abstract expressionist painters. To them, the decade of the thirties represented the Project, and the Project meant the establishment of a milieu for the first time in the United States. If one conscientiously examines all the statements made subsequently by major artists of the forties and fifties, the obvious value the WPA had for them was that of artistic community." Ashton, *New York School*, 44. Although the majority of future abstract expressionists got their start in the WPA programs, several received opportunities in the SFA, namely, Adolph Gottlieb, Bradley Walker Tomlin (easel works), Philip Guston, and Willem de Kooning.

19. William Zorach to FW, May 24, 1938, FWP AAA; George Biddle, "Big Business Discovers Art," *48: The Magazine of the Year* 2 (Feb. 1948): 77.

20. Erica Beckh Rubenstein to author, Mar. 24, 1994.

21. World War II bonds were originally called Defense Savings Bonds; they changed to War Savings Bonds after Pearl Harbor.

22. "Buy Bonds! U.S. Spurs Drive to Draw in a Billion a Month," *Newsweek*, July 6, 1942, 46; John Morton Blum, *From the Morgenthau Diaries: Years of Urgency, 1938–1941* (Boston: Houghton Mifflin, 1965), 302.

23. Lawrence R. Samuel, *Pledging Allegiance: American Identity and the Bond Drive of World War II* (Washington, D.C.: Smithsonian Institution Press, 1997), 50; FW to Maurice

Sterne, July 29, 1942, FWP AAA; FW to Mr. and Mrs. Symeon Shimin, July 29, 1942, FWP AAA; *Art for Bonds: A National Exhibition of Original Paintings by American Artists Designed for Poster Use, Sponsored by the Treasury Department's National Committee of Honorary Patrons,* [1943], unpaginated catalog reproduced in Rubenstein, "Tax Payers' Murals," app. 25.

24. "Art for Bonds," *Art Digest* 17 (Apr. 15, 1943): 19; "Art for Bonds," *Art News* 42 (Apr. 15, 1943): 6; "Art for Bonds," *Brooklyn Museum Bulletin* 4 (Apr. 1, 1943). Elinor Morgenthau was chair for this drive, and Eleanor Roosevelt was honorary chair. The prominence of the seventy-eight honorary patrons alone would have assured wide notice. Some of the names on the list were: Marion Anderson, Dr. and Mrs. Nicholas Murray Butler, Mr. and Mrs. Walt Disney, Mr. and Mrs. Marshall Field, President and Mrs. Manuel Quezon, Secretary of War and Mrs. Stinson, Chief Justice and Mrs. Stone, Mr. and Mrs. Sumner Welles, and Mr. and Mrs. Wendell Willkie. *Art for Bonds,* n.p., reproduced in Rubenstein, "Tax Payers' Murals," app. 25.

25. "65,000 View U.S. Might as Big Army Show Opens," *Washington Post,* Sept. 10, 1943; "Mrs. R. to Talk at Museum," *The Sun, Baltimore,* Oct. 24, 1943; Mrs. R. at Museum," *The Sun, Baltimore,* Oct. 24, 1943; "Mrs. R. Speaks Here Tonight," *The Sun, Baltimore,* Oct. 26, 1943; "Mrs. Roosevelt Tells about Trip," *The Sun, Baltimore,* Oct. 27, 1943.

26. FW, Ed Rowan, and even Dows, in the capacity of soldier-artist, were involved in several of the Art Advisory Committee's activities, but the SFA, moribund by then, did not participate as a unit.

27. War Department Art Advisory Committee to David Fredenthal, Feb. 16, 1943, DFP AAA. In addition to Biddle, committee members included Edward Rowan, David Finley, Henry Varnum Poor, Reeves Lewenthal, and John Steinbeck.

28. Congressman Joe Starnes, a conservative representative from Alabama and member of the House Appropriations subcommittee that reviewed the War Department's budget, learned of "an American artist who had his 'easel set up' . . . facing a poppy-sprinkled wheat field strewn with wrecked cars and dead horses . . . calmly sketching the scene of death and destruction." The artist in question was George Biddle, a New Dealer and brother of Attorney General Francis Biddle. That Biddle had praised the army project as one of the most liberal ever devised could only have made matters worse. It did not take long for Starnes "to figure out that 'this piece of foolishness' was another government boondoggle, and he prevailed upon the House to slash the $125,000 item from the War Department budget." Gary O. Larson, *The Reluctant Patron: The United States Government and the Arts, 1943–1965* (Philadelphia: Univ. of Pennsylvania Press, 1983), 18–19.

29. FW, "The War and Art," Art Students League Lecture No. 7, Nov. 26, 1949, typescript, pp. 2, 4–5, FWP AAA. Originally, forty-two artists (twenty-three soldiers and nineteen civilians) were selected by the Art Advisory Committee. When Congress eliminated the funding from the War Department budget, the Corps of Engineers absorbed several of the civilian painters into a "Combat Arts Section"; numerous military artists worked with the Special Services and historical divisions of various theaters of operation; some of the civilian artists returned to the States. Of the civilians who remained, *Life* commissioned most to continue the project for publication in that magazine. One civilian artist, Howard Cook, joined the staff of *Collier's.* Larson, *Reluctant Patron,* 18–19; Peppino Mangravite, "Congress Vetoes Culture," MA 36 (Nov. 1943): 264.

30. FW to Dows, Nov. 18, 1943, ODL AAA; FW to Dows, Dec. 17, 1943, ODL AAA.

31. FW, "The War and Art," 5–6; Elinor F. Morgenthau, foreword to *The Army at War by American Artists: Paintings and Drawings Lent by the War Department and the Treasury Department* (Washington, D.C.: GPO, 1944); FW to Dows, Mar. 31, 1944, FWP AAA.

32. FW, "The War and Art," 5, 4, 6–8; FW to Dows, 18 May 1944, FWP AAA. Created early in the conflict as the War Savings Staff of the Treasury Department, "the name of the War Savings Staff was changed to War Finance Division by authority of Treasury Department order #50 dated June 25, 1943." *United States Government Printing Office Monthly Catalog* (Washington, D.C., Oct. 1943), 1243.

33. *The Army at War: A Graphic Record by American Artists* (Washington, D.C.: GPO, 1944), 44.

34. FW to Dows, Sept. 5, 1944, FWP AAA; FW to Concetta Scaravaglione, Nov. 25, 1944, CSP AAA; FW, "The War and Art," 6–8; FW to T/Sgt. Albert Gold, Aug. 16, 1944, FWP AAA.

35. FW, "The War and Art", 6–7.

36. Ibid., 6–8; FW to Dows, Jan. 12, 1945, FWP AAA. In a Nov. 1944 letter to Dows, FW indicated that Marshall Field's department store was the venue for the Chicago exhibition of the "Army at War" show. Evidently, the site was changed some time in late Nov. to the Chicago Art Institute, as FW indicated both in a letter written in Dec. and again in his Art Students League talk in 1949 that the exhibit took place at the Chicago Art Institute. FW to Dows, Nov. 16, 1944, ODL AAA; FW to T/Sgt. Savo Radulovich, Dec. 27, 1944, FWP AAA.

37. FW to Radulovich, Dec. 27, 1944; Leila Mechlin, "The Art World," *Sunday Star,* Feb. 27, 1944; Edward Alden Jewell, "'Army at War' Art in Roxy Theatre," *New York Times,* Oct. 11, 1944; Edward Alden Jewell, "'The Army' and Marsh," *New York Times,* Oct. 15, 1944; "Cinema War Art," *Art Digest* 19 (Jan. 1, 1945): 15; Robert M. Coates, "The Art Galleries," *New Yorker* 19 (Aug. 28, 1943): 57; Jerome Mellquist, "Feeble War Art," *Nation* 157 (Oct. 2, 1943): 388–89. Both Coates and Mellquist were writing on the occasion of a recent exhibition of art commissioned by *Life* magazine held at the Metropolitan Museum of Art. Many of the artists were those featured in FW's shows also, and he borrowed a substantial number of pictures from *Life.*

38. FW to Max Kuehne, July 7, 1944, FWP AAA; FW to Max Kuehne, July 24, 1944, FWP AAA.

39. FW to Dows, Sept. 5, 1944, FWP AAA; FW to Dows, Nov. 16, 1944.

40. [Helen Appleton Read], "In the Galleries—News & Comments," *Brooklyn Daily Eagle,* May 1, 1932; Alice Graeme, "Nan Watson Applauded for Artistic Frankness," *Washington Post,* Dec. 1, 1935; Graeme, "Works of Nan Watson, Washington Painter, on View at Arts Club," *Washington Post,* Mar. 30, 1941; "Frances Greenman Says," *Minneapolis Tribune,* Apr. 6, 1941.

41. FW to Dows, May 18, 1944, ODL AAA; FW to Dows, Mar. 31, 1944, FWP AAA; FW to Dows, Apr. 26, 1944, FWP AAA; "War Pictures by Americans: First Exhibition in London," *London Times,* Sept. 30, 1944; "American War Pictures," *London Times,* Sept. 30, 1944.

42. FW to Beatrice Winser, Apr. 19, 1945, FWP AAA; "Forbes Watson's Report on 'Fighting the Japs,' New York, Thursday Apr. 12 to Tuesday Apr. 17," Apr. 17 1945, typescript, FWP AAA.

43. [FW], "The War against Japan: Paintings by American Artists," undated typescript, FWP AAA; Ted R. Gamble, "The War against Japan: Paintings and Drawings by

American Artists," undated, FWP AAA. The sentences quoted were omitted from the final version of the introduction.

44. Clippings from Australian newspapers, Aug. 4, 1944–Jan. 10, 1945; "Realism in War Art," *Brisbane Courier Mail,* Sept. 16, 1944, clipping, FWP AAA.

45. FW, *Soldiers of Production: Exhibition of Paintings and Drawings by Eight American Artists Appointed by the Office for Emergency Management to Record Activities in Specific Defense Areas,* undated, DC 40, CORTRAPFAS; FW to Alfred H. Barr Jr. (draft of letter), July 3, 1944, FWP AAA; [FW], "News Release, National Gallery of Art, Washington, D.C.," May 26, 1945, p. 2, FWP AAA; FW, "The War and Art," 2.

46. Elinor F. Morgenthau, "Foreword," *Art for Bonds* (n.p., n.d.), reproduced in Rubenstein "Tax Payers' Murals," app. 25. FW was unquestionably the ghostwriter of this essay.

47. Samuel, *Pledging Allegiance,* 45. The Interallied Exhibition of Savings in Paris was also known as the Exposition for the French War and Reconstruction Bond Drive.

48. FW to Elinor Morgenthau, Sept. 17, 1945, FWP AAA.

49. FW mentioned figures of 11,000 and 13,000 in two separate letters to Nan. On July 19, he wrote, "Meanwhile my exhibition is going wonderfully, averaging an attendance of more than eleven thousand a day." A week later, he wrote, "In the afternoon . . . after I had been to my exhibition which is drawing about 13,000 people a day and is here considered a great success, . . ." [FW to Nan Watson], July 19, 1945, FWP AAA; [FW to Nan Watson], July 26, 1945, FWP AAA.

50. Memorandum, FW to Ted R. Gamble, Sept. 11, 1945, p. 2, FWP AAA; FW to M. Montfageon, July 20, 1945, FWP AAA; [FW to Nan Watson], July 29, 1945, FWP AAA. FW was very appreciative of the treatment accorded him by the army in Paris. He wrote Nan: "I am going to write to Dorothea and Eddie [Greenbaum] not only for friendship's sake, but also because the Army has been simply wonderful to us. Aside from the fact that they give me a car whenever I need it and that they lent us three huge searchlights for the exhibition and a specialist to run our little movie, the Commanding General invited me to a wonderful party and his aides from Colonels to lieutenants have done all sorts of favors from finding me a French teacher to letting me buy a pair of officer's combat boots. And these boots are the delight of my life." [FW to Nan Watson], July 26, 1945.

51. Memorandum, FW to Gamble, Sept. 11, 1945, 4; George Wolfenson to FW, Sept. 29, 1945, FWP AAA; Charles Adams to FW, July 31, 1945, FWP AAA.

52. [FW to Nan Watson], July 26, 1945; [FW to Nan Watson], July 25, 1945, FWP AAA.

53. [FW to Nan Watson], July 26, 1945; [FW to Nan Watson], July 31, 1945, FWP AAA; [FW to Nan Watson], July 25, 1945.

54. [FW to Nan Watson], Aug. 1, 1945, FWP AAA; [FW to Nan Watson], Aug. 4, 1945, FWP AAA; [FW to Nan Watson], Aug. 5, 1945, FWP AAA; [FW to Nan Watson], Aug. 8, 1945, FWP AAA.

55. [FW to Nan Watson], July 29, 1945.

56. [FW to Nan Watson], July 14, 1945, FWP AAA; [FW to Nan Watson], July 15, 1945, FWP AAA; FW to Elinor Morgenthau, Sept. 17, 1945, FWP AAA.

57. [FW to Nan Watson], July 26, 1945.

58. [FW to Nan Watson], Aug. 10, 1945, FWP AAA.

59. [FW to Nan Watson], Aug. 10, 1945.

60. [FW to Nan Watson], Aug. 10, 1945; FW to Mr. and Mrs. Wolfenson, Oct. 31, 1945; Elinor Morgenthau to FW, July 23, 1946, FWP AAA.

61. FW to Edytha Hart, Sept. 24, 1945, FWP AAA.

62. FW to M. Montfageon, Sept. 14, 1945, FWP AAA; FW to Mr. and Mrs. Wolfenson, Oct. 31, 1945.

63. FW wrote Olin Dows: "He [George Howe] says that Hannigan [sic] simply hates the whole idea of P.O. murals and that the plans which he, George, has drawn up allowing for splendid mural spaces infuriated the post office department. He said that the Post Office liaison officer between Public Buildings and the P.O. Department said that whether the murals were good or bad made no difference. If they were bad they interfered with business because people took up the postmaster's time complaining about them. If they were good they wanted to know about the artist or to get photographs and so took up the postmaster's time. The post office our cultivated liaison officer finally declared is no place to discuss art. It's a place to buy stamps." FW to Dows, Oct. 17, 1945, ODL AAA.

64. FW to Dows, Oct. 17, 1945; FW to Dows, Nov. 19, 1945, ODL AAA.

65. FW to Dows, Dec. 27, 1944, FWP AAA; FW to Dows, Jan. 12, 1945, FWP AAA.

66. FW to Elinor Morgenthau, Sept. 17, 1945, FWP AAA; "Memorandum of Meeting Relating to Proposed War Museum," Oct. 11, 1945, FWP AAA.

67. "The Function of a War Museum," [1945], typescript, pp. 3–5, FWP AAA.

68. FW to Dows, Nov. 19, 1945; FW to Marsden Hartley, Apr. 14, 1942, FWP AAA; Ward Lockwood to FW, July 21, 1942, FWP AAA; FW to Lockwood, July 29, 1942, FWP AAA; FW to Juliana Force, Jan. 12, 1943, WMAAA, Histories f.10.

69. Pène du Bois to FW, Dec. 12, 1944, FWP AAA; FW to Pène du Bois, Dec. 9, 1944, FWP AAA; Frank Jewett Mather Jr. to Pène du Bois, Jan. 13, 1945, quoted in Fahlman, "Guy Pène du Bois," 169. In an article published in 1977, John Baker describes a book Guy Pène du Bois worked on during the years 1941–45, *Apes and Angels in Art*, which consisted of four chapters: "Classicism," "Romanticism," "Realism," and "Modern Eclecticism." He never completed the book, however. John Baker, "Guy Pène du Bois on Realism," *Archives of American Art Journal* 17 (1977): 2–3.

70. FW to Dows, Jan. 11, 1946, ODL AAA. Samuel Golden was head of the American Artists Group Company, which published, among other books, *Gist of Art* by John Sloan, *Artist in Manhattan* by Jerome Myers, and *Artists Say the Silliest Things* by Guy Pène du Bois.

71. Ibid.; FW to Samuel Golden, Jan. 14, 1946, ODL AAA; FW to Norman Blaustein, Mar. 15, 1946, ODL AAA; FW to Dows, Apr. 15, 1946, ODL AAA. There were also 221 bundles of folded sheets, which were sufficient to bind into 2,300 volumes.

72. FW to Dows, Feb. 28, 1946, ODL AAA.

73. FW to Dows, June 17, 1946, ODL AAA.

74. Ibid.; Elinor Morgenthau to FW, July 23, 1946, FWP AAA.

75. FW to Dows, Aug. 21, 1946, ODL AAA; Elinor Morgenthau to FW, Sept. 17, 1946, FWP AAA; FW to Dows, Aug. 21, 1946, ODL AAA.

10. GAYLORDSVILLE

1. FW to Mr. and Mrs. George Wolfenson, Oct. 31, 1945, FWP AAA.

2. FW to Paul Laboulay, Sept. 24, 1945, FWP AAA.

3. Fred [Oliver] to Concetta Scaravaglione, Dec. 7, 1947, CSP AAA; Alexander, *Here the Country Lies,* 242; FW, "Have You a 20th Century Mind?" *Pic* 14 (Dec. 7, 1943): 39.

4. Lloyd Goodrich reminiscences, as recorded in talks with Harlan B. Phillips, 1963, AAA; David McCullough, *Truman* (New York: Simon and Schuster, 1992), 142; "Art," *Time* magazine, June 16, 1947, 51. For interesting accounts of the campaign to cancel the exhibition, see *Advancing American Art: Politics and Aesthetics in the State Department Exhibition, 1946–1948, Advancing American Art: Painting, Politics, and Cultural Confrontation at Mid-Century,* and Larson, *Reluctant Patron,* 23–31. The State Department, capitulating without a struggle, turned over the seventy-nine paintings, originally purchased for $49,000, to the War Assets Administration, which sold them on June 24, 1948, according to war-surplus guidelines, for $5,526.65. Lacking legal authority to sell the paintings, the State Department turned them over to a reluctant War Assets Administration, which sold the paintings according to an elaborate set of procedures and priorities. Under the war-surplus rules, certain tax-supported institutions were entitled to discounts as high as 95 percent. The biggest gainers under those guidelines were the Univ. of Oklahoma and Auburn Univ., each of which purchased thirty-six paintings. Jo Gibbs, "State Department Art Classed as War Surplus," *Art Digest* 22 (June 1, 1948): 9, 37; Alonzo Lansford, "Sic Transit," *Art Digest* 22 (July 1, 1948): 13; *Advancing American Art,* 24–26.

5. Olin Dows, interview with Harlan B. Phillips, tape recording, Oct. 31, 1963, AAA; FW to Jane Jones, Mar. 12, 1957, WJP AAA. Harlan Phillips commented that FW had the feelings of a "firebrand; he glowed. . . . It was compulsive with him."

6. An editorial note to a 1947 article by Watson stated: "He is now at work on a book on changing tastes in contemporary art." *47: The Magazine of the Year,* 16. FW's papers do not contain drafts of a monograph on this subject. However, FW prepared two lectures on taste for the Art Students League in 1949: FW, "Lecture V [untitled]," undated, but between Oct. 14 and Nov. 11, 1949, typescript, FWP AAA; FW, "What the Public Buys," Art Students League Talk No. 8, Dec. 2, 1949, typescript, FWP AAA.

7. FW to Concetta Scaravaglione, Mar. 27, 1948, CSP AAA; FW to Peggy Bruce, Nov. 11, 1952, FWP AAA; FW to Pène du Bois, Dec. 8, 1953, GPBP AAA; FW to Ernest Fiene, Mar. 17, 1955, EFP AAA; Ira Glackens to FW, Dec. 8, 1955, FWP AAA.

8. FW to Esther Williams, Apr. 20, 1947, EWP AAA; FW to Dows, May 19, 1947, ODL AAA; FW to Howland, Dec. 7, 1948, IHP AAA; FW to Howland, June 28, 1948, IHP AAA; FW to Howland, Jan. 3, 1949, IHP AAA.

9. FW to Edward Millman, Jan. 22, 1948, FWP AAA; FW to Dows, Feb. 27, 1947, FWP AAA.

10. FW to Howland, Aug. 21, 1948, IHP AAA; FW to Howland, Mar. 30, 1948, IHP AAA.

11. FW to Jane Jones, Mar. 19, 1957, WJP AAA; FW to Leon Kroll, Feb. 3, 1947, LKP AAA; FW to Millman, Jan. 22, 1948, FWP AAA.

12. *Harvard Fiftieth Anniversary Report,* 654; FW to Ealand, June 1949.

13. FW to Dows, Feb. 7, 1954, FWP AAA; FW to Jane Jones, Mar. 19, 1957; FW to Ealand, June 1949.

14. FW to Millman, Jan. 22, 1948; FW to Jones, June 25, 1957, WJP AAA; FW to Scaravaglione, Apr. 15, 1955, CSP AAA; FW to Howland, Dec. 7, 1948; FW to Howland, Jan. 3, 1949, IHP AAA; FW to Howland, [1949], IHP AAA.

15. FW to Howland, June 6, 1948, IHP AAA; Alice Paterson to Scaravaglione, Oct. 27, 1949, CSP AAA.

16. FW to Symeon Shimin, Jan. 25, 1943, FWP AAA; FW to Juliana Force, Jan. 12, 1943, WMAAA, Histories f.10. In 1948, upon learning that the merger was off because the Metropolitan and the Whitney could not agree on the status of modern art, Watson was delighted but speculated that the real reason was Juliana Force's death. He was mistaken; the issue had been, as given out, the status of modern art. FW to Scaravaglione, Oct. 4, 1948, CSP AAA. For a detailed account of the proposed merger of the Whitney and the Metropolitan, see Berman, *Rebels on Eighth Street,* 431, 437–38, 451–53, 458–60, 464–65, 475, 485–86, 489, 495–96, 498, 499, 501, 505.

17. FW to Pène du Bois, Dec. 8, 1953. Born in Germany in 1893, George Grosz moved to the United States, settling in New York in 1933. FW continued to consider him German in orientation, however.

18. Annie [Mrs. Henry Varnum] Poor to Nan and FW, Sept. 27, (n.d.o.), FWP AAA.

19. FW, "Belief and Painting," *47: The Magazine of the Year* 1 (Dec. 1947): 20. The magazine editors described the new publication as "the only national magazine owned and controlled by people who write, paint, and photograph professionally." "A Statement of Intention," *47: The Magazine of the Year* 1 (Mar. 1947): 1. A number of the stockholders were friends of FW's, including Olin Dows and Henry Varnum Poor.

20. FW to Howland, Sept. 30, 1947, IHP AAA.

21. FW to Ernest Fiene, Nov. 11, 1948, EFP AAA; FW to Scaravaglione, Mar. 27, 1948, CSP AAA.

22. FW to Howland, May 27, 1949, IHP AAA. Typical of the verses FW composed for Howland was "Wild Beasts in Sportive Outbursts" (undated, IHP AAA):

In Van Dyck's oven lair they prowled
They bit, they cuffed, they leaped, they growled
Wild beasts in sportive outbursts they
And when they love-patted in play
They struck with such a mighty force
It would have killed the strongest horse
The listening frightened neighbors say
That with love's winning of the day
The wild beasts' roaring howls of joy
Were clearly heard in Perth Amboy.

23. FW to Howland, Dec. 20, 1947, IHP AAA; FW to Howland, "The First Day after the Third Sacred Tuesday, 1949," IHP AAA.

24. FW to Ealand, June 1949; *The Metropolitan Museum of Art Presents the 75th Anniversary Exhibition of Painting & Sculpture by 75 Artists Associated with the Art Students League of New York* (New York: Art Students League of New York, 1951). Watson wrote introductory essays on Louis Bouché, Alexander Brook, Kenyon Cox, Andrew Dasburg, Jo Davidson, Thomas W. Dewing, Preston Dickinson, Guy Pène du Bois, Jerome Myers, and Maurice Sterne.

25. FW to Scaravaglione, Mar. 27, 1948.

26. FW to Scaravaglione, Oct. 4, 1948; *Juliana Force and American Art: A Memorial Exhibition, Sept. 24–Oct. 30, 1949* (New York: Whitney Museum of American Art, 1949), 54–63; FW, "The Achievement of Two Ladies," Art Students League Talk No. 6, Nov. 18, 1949, typescript, FWP AAA.

27. FW, "Sargent—Boston—And Art," *Arts & Decoration* 7 (Feb. 1917): 197; FW, "Twentieth Century American Painting—The Calm before the Storm," Apr. 2, 1950, typescript of lecture, p. 12, FWP AAA.

28. FW, "Metropolitan Museum Talk No. 3—Twentieth Century American Painting—Assertions and Experiments," Apr. 30 1950, typescript, pp. 1, 5, FWP AAA; FW, "A Note on Henry Lee McFee," MA 30 (Mar. 1937): 142.

29. Bruce Bliven, ed., *Twentieth Century Unlimited: From the Vantage Point of the First Fifty Years* (Philadelphia: J. B. Lippincott, 1950). The book was comprised largely of essays originally published in *New Republic* magazine.

30. FW, "American Art," in *Twentieth Century Unlimited,* 217, 216, 228, 226.

31. Ibid., 224, 218, 219.

32. Ibid., 226–29.

33. Ibid., 232.

34. Ibid., 232–33.

35. Dows interview, Oct. 31, 1963; FW to Howland, July 26, 1948, IHP AAA; FW to Pène du Bois, Dec. 8, 1953.

36. FW to Peggy Bruce, Nov. 11, 1952.

37. C. Adolph "Cook" Glassgold, interview with Harlan B. Phillips, tape recording, Dec. 9, 1964, AAA; George Biddle, interview with Harlan B. Phillips, tape recording, 1963, AAA; Ealand interview, Mar. 31, 1994. Biddle recalled a letter from FW around 1950 in response to Biddle's inquiry concerning ways the Fine Arts Commission, of which he was a member, could be improved. "I remember very well his anger with me that I could simply take part in any discussion of a government program after having known what was done under Roosevelt and Bruce," Biddle recalled.

Biddle remembered correctly that FW's hostility toward the Fine Arts Commission had not abated since the early years of the SPS, and FW's letter to Biddle reflected that. However FW's letter did not express anger at Biddle. The facts were that FW, when told by a friend in Washington that Biddle had resigned his position on the Fine Arts Commission, had misunderstood the reason. FW wrote Biddle to "congratulate" him, then launched into a two-page attack on the Fine Arts Commission for its past abuses of Biddle; for "being stupidly reactionary" in its "underhandedly unfair treatment" of Biddle's Justice Department murals in 1934; and for rejecting Biddle's original suggestions to Roosevelt concerning government-sponsored art. FW also expressed skepticism that any recommendations from the commission would receive serious consideration from the Democrats or the Republicans in an election year. In response to FW's letter, Biddle explained that the only reason he was resigning from the commission was to go to Rome as an artist in residence at the American Academy. Biddle interview, 1963; FW to Biddle, Sept. 1951, FWP AAA; Biddle to FW, Sept. 15, 1951, FWP AAA.

38. Biddle interview, 1963. Biddle commented that with Bruce's stroke, "that must have been mud in his mouth, must have left him, and did leave him, a bitter, angry man. . . . He at times felt that I was doing things that were interfering with his program and he would get furious with me and not speak to me for months. But I think that was largely due to the fact that he was sitting in a wheel chair and he must have been filled with bitter rage at the time because he wasn't able to do what he had done all his life and that was to sit up till three o'clock and drink and then be up at seven o'clock and

put in a twelve-hour day's work and then go bowling afterward, which was really the cause of his tragic stroke."

39. FW to Fiene, Nov. 13, 1957, EFP AAA; FW to Fiene, Nov. 11, 1948.

40. FW interview summary by Rosalind Irvine, Feb. 18, 1949, WMAAA H.1/f38.

41. FW to Scaravaglione, Nov. 28, 1950, CSP AAA.

42. FW to Leon Hartl, Mar. 8, 1938, LHP AAA.

43. FW to Pène du Bois, Dec. 8, 1953; FW to Dows, Feb. 7, 1954.

44. FW, "Arthur Bowen Davies," MA 45 (Dec. 1952): 365, 368.

45. FW, "John Sloan," MA 45 (Feb. 1952): 69, 70, 68.

46. FW, "Maurice Prendergast," [1955], manuscript, FWP AAA.

47. In a letter to Ira Glackens, FW referred to the Prendergast essay as an article; in a letter to Concetta Scaravaglione, he referred to it as a chapter, probably in his projected book. FW to Glackens, Mar. 19, 1955, FWP AAA; FW to Scaravaglione, Apr. 14, 1955, CSP AAA; FW, "Maurice Prendergast," [1955], typescript, FWP AAA.

48. Joseph T. Fraser Jr. to FW, Apr. 29, 1954, FWP AAA; FW, "William James Glackens," in *The Pennsylvania Academy of Fine Arts One Hundred and Fiftieth Anniversary Exhibition, Jan. 15, through Mar. 13, 1955* (Philadelphia: Pennsylvania Academy of the Fine Arts, 1955), 124–29; FW, "William Glackens: An Artist Who Seizes the Colorful and Interesting Aspects of Life," *Arts & Decoration* 45 (Dec. 1920): 103, 152.

49. Ira Glackens to FW, Nov. 20, 1954, FWP AAA. FW never lost his craving for cigarettes. Beginning in 1954, letter after letter to friends tabulated the days since he had smoked. As late as Mar. 1957, he still began a letter to Jane Jones, "It's 2073 days since I have smoked." FW to Jones, Mar. 19, 1957. He recorded the "impressive figure" of 2,363 on the dateline of a letter to Guy Pène du Bois's daughter, Yvonne. FW to Mrs. James Harvey McKenney, Jan. 5, 1958, GPBP AAA.

50. See Glackens, *William Glackens and The Eight*. Describing a rare outburst by Sloan over a damaged picture, Brooks inserted a footnote: "Unlike Glackens, who sometimes threw his palette and brushes across the room, Sloan rarely indulged in tantrums while at his work." Van Wyck Brooks, *John Sloan: A Painter's Life* (New York: E. P. Dutton, 1955), 69; Glackens to FW, Mar. 9, 1955, FWP AAA.

51. When Tucker's widow, Euphrasia, founded the Allen Tucker Memorial in Apr. 1944, FW was appointed to the board of trustees and named chair. Other trustees were Philippa Gerry Offner, Charles Downing Lay, and Frederick S. Hoppin. In 1956 the trustees were FW, Robert C. McIntyre, Philippa Gerry Offner, and Henry Allen Moe. In 1980 the Allen Tucker Memorial was transferred to the Art Students League.

52. FW to Jones, Mar. 24, 1957; FW to Jones, Apr. 21, 1957, WJP AAA; Maria Ealand, "Recollections of Nan and Forbes Watson," Jan. 17, 1988, typescript, p. 2, gift to author from Maria Ealand.

53. FW to Jones, May 3, 1957, WJP AAA.

54. FW to Jones, Sept. 19, 1957, WJP AAA; FW to Mrs. James Harvey McKenney, July 22, 1958, GPBP AAA; FW to Jones, Sept. 1, 1958, WJP AAA; FW to Jones, Feb. 9, 1959, WJP AAA; FW to Jones, Feb. 28, 1959, WJP AAA.

55. Nan Watson to Jones, May 27, 1960, WJP AAA.

56. Biddle interview, 1963, AAA.

57. Dows, "Nan and Forbes Watson," in *Still-Lifes by Nan Watson: Loan Exhibition,*

Nov. 10–Dec. 4, 1960, Wadsworth Atheneum, Hartford ([Hartford, Conn.: Wadsworth Atheneum, 1960]).

58. Nan Watson to Hartl, Jan. 1, 1963, LHP AAA; Alice Graeme Korff, interview with Harlan B. Phillips, tape recording, Oct. 7, 1965, AAA; Ealand, "Recollections of Nan and Forbes Watson," 2.

59. *Homage to Forbes Watson and The Arts: Spring Exhibition, Apr. 18–May 30, 1967* (Washington, D.C.: Adams, Davidson, [1967]).

60. Lloyd Goodrich reminiscences, as recorded in talks with Harlan B. Phillips, 1963, AAA; Dows interview, Oct. 31, 1963.

61. Max Weber to FW, Jan. 13, 1940, FWP AAA.

ANNOTATED BIBLIOGRAPHY

ARCHIVE AND MANUSCRIPT SOURCES

The resources of the Archives of American Art of the Smithsonian Institution, particularly the papers of Forbes Watson, have been invaluable to this study. Donated to the archives by Watson's widow, artist Nan Watson, and microfilmed in eleven reels, D47 to D57, the Forbes Watson Papers contain correspondence, drafts of articles and lectures, newspaper and magazine clippings, photographs, and exhibition catalogs. The largest group of papers pertains to the 1930s and 1940s, with relatively little from Watson's early years. The papers also include several drafts of reminiscences for a book Watson worked on but did not complete; unfortunately, these are extremely fragmentary. The Forbes Watson Papers are grouped together roughly by period but are not arranged chronologically. Many of the documents are undated, and pages of individual documents are not necessarily sequential, which sometimes creates difficulties in developing a coherent biographical line. Used in conjunction with other papers of artists, dealers, and art commentators in the archives, a chronological framework can be constructed, and a social and artistic milieu emerges with some clarity. The papers of Olin Dows, Edward B. Rowan, George Biddle, Isabella Howland, Concetta Scaravaglione, Guy Pène du Bois, Leon Kroll, Henry Schnakenberg, and Wendell Jones are particularly valuable for this purpose. For specific topics and issues, the papers of Ernest Fiene, David Fredenthal, Max Weber, Henry McBride, Julian E. Levi, Leon Hartl, Esther Williams, Gertrude Vanderbilt Whitney, Lucile Blanch, Edward Bruce, Helen Appleton Read, and Peter Hurd are useful.

The Archives of American Art Oral History Program, begun in 1959 to document the history of the visual arts in the United States primarily through taped interviews with figures in art, provide varied insights about Forbes Watson and his times. Harlan B. Phillips and others' interviews with Lloyd Goodrich, Olin Dows, Alice Graeme Korff, Inslee Hopper, C. Adolph "Cook" Glassgold, Henry Varnum Poor, George Biddle, Alexander Brook, Raphael Soyer, Isabel Bishop, Dorothy Varian, and Peter Hurd are particularly enlightening. (The interview with Lloyd Goodrich, entitled "Reminiscences," was also edited into a two-part article in *The Archives of American Art Journal*.) Interviews with John Clancy, Charles Sheeler, Mildred Baker, Charlotte Partridge, Dewey Albinson, John Davis Hatch, and Stuart Klonis, while not central to the development of Watson's thought and career, nonetheless provide perspectives on the art scene.

Watson's years as critic and editor of *The Arts* are documented further in the Archives of the Whitney Museum of American Art. The papers of Lloyd Goodrich, specifically two years of correspondence during the time he was European editor of *The*

Arts, offer a view from the operational side. The Whitney Museum archive is rich in material on Juliana Force, Gertrude Vanderbilt Whitney, and the early Whitney galleries with which Watson was closely associated during the 1920s.

For information about Watson's New Deal years, the National Archives is the major repository, principally Record Group 121, Inventory Entries 105, 106, 108, 109, 114, 115, 116, 122, 124, 125, 126, and 133. The *Preliminary Inventory of the Records of the Public Buildings Service (Record Group 121),* compiled by W. Lane Van Neste and Virgil E. Baugh (Washington, D.C.: The National Archives and Records Service, 1958), is a useful finding aid and reduces some of the difficulty in accessing the National Archives vast holdings. In addition, the Archives of American Art's "New Deal and the Arts" collection, a project underwritten by the Ford Foundation in 1964, contains selected microfilmed documents from the National Archives' Record Group 121. Arranged under Public Works of Art Project, Section of Fine Arts, Works Progress Administration, and Treasury Relief Art Project, the microfilm collections facilitate topical access to pertinent materials in the National Archives. For this study, I used the following groups from the "New Deal and the Arts" series: Selected Records of the Public Works of Art Project, 1933–35 (DC 1–DC 4, DC 8); Public Works of Art Project Final Reports, Report Materials, and Project Issuances, 1933–36 (DC 12); Selected Records of the Treasury Relief Art Project, 1935–38, (DC 14); and Selected Records of the Central Office Records of the Treasury Relief Art Project and the Section of Fine Arts of the Public Buildings Administration 1934–43 (DC 38–DC 42). The Archives of American Art also tape recorded interviews with New Deal arts figures as part of the "New Deal and the Arts" project. Many of the interviews described in the previous section were acquired as part of the project.

The Waldo Pierce Papers in the Manuscript Division, Library of Congress offers interesting sidelights on artists and the art scene during Watson's time. From the Eleanor Roosevelt Oral History Collection of the Franklin D. Roosevelt Library in Hyde Park, New York, an interview with Olin Dows offers background both on Dows and the Roosevelt family. Conducted fifteen years after Harlan B. Phillips's interview for the Archives of American Art Oral History Program, it supplements Dows's earlier comments on the New Deal art projects. The New Haven Colony Historical Society contains correspondence between officials of the Public Works of Art Project and the United States Naval Academy in Annapolis, Maryland, concerning a mural for the school.

Of the innumerable official documents issued by the various Treasury art projects, three provide comprehensive overviews. The Public Works of Art Project's *Report of the Assistant Secretary of the Treasury to Federal Emergency Relief Administrator, December 8, 1933–June 30, 1934* (Washington, D.C.: Government Printing Office, 1934) contains statistical data along with a concise, if somewhat biased, summary of the Public Works of Art Project. The exhibition catalog of the Public Works of Art Project national exhibition, *National Exhibition of Art by the Public Works of Art Project, April 24, 1934 to May 20, 1934* (Washington, D.C.: Government Printing Office, 1934), details the range and scope of art and artists who participated in the project. The twenty-four issues of the *Bulletin of the Section of Fine Arts* (Mar. 1935–May 1941) that Watson edited offer a more or less sequential account from the administrators' standpoint of competitions and other projects the Section of Fine Arts and the Treasury Relief Art Project.

Information relating to the New Deal arts programs is updated in the *Federal Art*

Patronage Notes, a newsletter edited by Francis V. O'Connor. O'Connor's bibliography in the summer 1979 issue (College Park, Md., vol. 3, no. 3) is especially useful.

INTERVIEWS AND WRITTEN COMMUNICATIONS

Unfortunately, I found no close relatives of Forbes or Nan Watson to supplement the somewhat sparse biographical data. To clarify and augment Watson's fragmentary, sometimes contradictory reminiscences of his childhood and youth, I relied on census reports, records of vital statistics, and documents from Browne and Nichols Preparatory School, Andover Academy, Harvard University, New York Law School, and Columbia Law School. For perspectives and details of his adult life and career, I was able to interview either in person or in taped telephone conversations several persons who knew Forbes and Nan Watson personally during the twenties, thirties, and forties: Lloyd Goodrich, a close associate and friend during *The Arts* years; Antoinette Kraushaar, daughter of the art dealer John Kraushaar, who remembered Watson from the twenties; and Maria K. Ealand and Jane Watson Crane, his friends and colleagues of the New Deal years. Their recollections provided informal glimpses into Watson's personality and relationships and a vivid sense of the times. In addition, letters from Ira Glackens, Erica Beckh Rubenstein (who interviewed Forbes Watson for her dissertation), Jane Watson Crane, and Maria Ealand helped fill gaps and answer specific questions.

FORBES WATSON'S WRITINGS

No truer source of Watson's thought exists than *The Arts* magazine and its successor, *Arts Weekly*, to which he contributed beginning in 1921 and edited from 1923 until 1932. In addition, his monthly and weekly articles and editorials in the *American Magazine of Art, Magazine of Art*, the *New York Evening Post*, and *New York World* and his books, monographs, articles, and essays in other magazines and exhibition catalogs compose a more or less continuous record of Watson's ideas. The following is a selected chronological list of Forbes Watson's writings other than regular columns in the *New York Evening Post, The Arts, Arts Weekly, New York World, American Magazine of Art*, and *Magazine of Art*. Besides documenting Watson's point of view, many such as *Art in Federal Buildings, American Painting Today*, and monographs on individual artists serve also as general sources on the history of American art during the years between the Armory Show and World War II.

"Eugene Speicher—A New Arrival." *International Studio Supplement* 46 (Mar. 1912): 19–22.

Yearbook of American Etching; With an Introduction by Forbes Watson. New York: John Lane, 1914.

"Allen Tucker: A Painter with a Fresh Vision." *International Studio Supplement* 52 (Mar. 1914): 19–21.

"The Association of American Etchers." *International Studio Supplement* 52 (May 1914): 79–86.

"American Etchers of the Present Day." *Arts & Decoration* 4 (Aug. 1914): 381–84.

"Four Great Paintings." *Ladies Home Journal* 33 (July 1916): 16–20.

"Four Great Paintings." *Ladies Home Journal* 33 (Oct. 1916): 16–20.

"Sargent—Boston—and Art." *Arts & Decoration* 7 (Feb. 1917): 194–97.

"Serving 10,000 Meals a Day." *Red Cross Magazine* (Mar. 18, 1918): 29–34.

"Playing the Game." *Arts & Decoration* 12 (Feb. 1920): 239, 299.

"The Swan-Song of Impressionism." *Arts & Decoration* 12 (Feb. 1920): 254, 288.

"Rockwell Kent, Incorporated." *Arts & Decoration* 12 (Mar. 1920): 324–25.

"John H. Twachtman: A Painter Pure and Simple." *Arts & Decoration* 12 (Apr. 1920): 395, 434.

"The American Art Exhibition in Venice." *Arts & Decoration* 13 (Aug. 1920): 152–53, 213–14.

"Prince, Bourgeois and Bolshevist: The Coming of the New Rule in Art." *Arts & Decoration* 13 (Sept. 1920): 228–29.

"At the Galleries." *Arts & Decoration* 14 (Dec. 1920): 98–99, 144.

"William Glackens." *Arts & Decoration* 14 (Dec. 1920): 103, 152.

"Art in Every Home." *Arts & Decoration* 14 (Jan. 1921): 195–97.

"At the Galleries." *Arts & Decoration* 14 (Jan. 1921): 214–15, 230.

"At the Galleries." *Arts & Decoration* 14 (Feb. 1921): 304–5.

"Institutional versus Individual Collectors." *Arts & Decoration* 14 (Feb. 1921): 274–75, 340.

Introduction to *Second Annual Exhibition American and European Art*. Dallas, Tex.: Dallas Art Association, 1921.

Preface to *French Institute in the United States Museum of French Art Loan Exhibition of Works, March 16 to April 3, 1921*. New York: Gallery of the Museum, 1921.

Preface to *Exhibition of Contemporary Art: Catalogue, March–April 1921*. London: Grafton Galleries, 1921.

William Glackens. Arts Monographs. New York: Duffield and *The Arts*, 1923.

Foreword to *John Quinn 1870–1925* [sic]: *Collection of Paintings, Water Colors, Drawings, and Sculpture*. Huntington, N.Y.: Pidgeon Hill Press, [1926].

"Stepfathers of Art." *New Yorker* 1 (May 14, 1927): 32–34.

"The Sculpture of Charles Despiau." *Vanity Fair* 29 (Jan. 1928): 64.

"Our Land Grows Keenly Aware of Art." *New York Times Magazine*, Mar. 4, 1928.

"A Note on Edward Hopper." *Vanity Fair* 32 (Feb. 1929): 64, 98, 107.

"All the World's a Critic." *Space* 1 (Jan. 1930): 6–7.

"Robert Henri: Introduction." *The Art Spirit* by Robert Henri, 5–10. Philadelphia: J. B. Lippincott, 1930.

Allen Tucker. American Artists Series. New York: Whitney Museum of American Art, 1932.

Mary Cassatt. American Artists Series. New York: Whitney Museum of American Art, 1932.

"Gallery Explorations." *Parnassus* 4 (Dec. 1932): 1–5, 32.

"The Universal Diplomat." *Parnassus* 5 (Jan. 1933): 1–4.

"Gallery Explorations." *Parnassus* 5 (Feb. 1933): 1–5, 30.

"Gallery Explorations." *Parnassus* 5 (Apr. 1933): 1–5.

"Rockwell Kent, Idol of Laymen." *Brooklyn Daily Eagle Sunday Review*, Oct. 29, 1933.

"The Rise of Edward Hopper." *Brooklyn Daily Eagle Sunday Review*, Nov. 5, 1933.

"George Luks: Last of the Romantics." *Brooklyn Daily Eagle Sunday Review*, Nov. 19, 1933.

"The Important Decade." *Brooklyn Daily Eagle Sunday Review*, Dec. 3, 1933.

"Two Biennials that Beat as One." *Parnassus* 5 (Dec. 1933): 4–8.

"Americanism Unalloyed—A Defense of Alloys." *Brooklyn Daily Eagle Sunday Review,* Dec. 17, 1933.

"The Public Works of Art Project: Federal, Republican, or Democratic?" *American Magazine of Art* 27 (Jan. 1934): 6–9.

"The U.S.A. Challenges the Artists." *Parnassus* 6 (Jan. 1934): 1–2.

"The Vicissitudes of Women in Art." *Brooklyn Daily Eagle Sunday Review,* Feb. 25, 1934.

"A Steady Job." *American Magazine of Art* 27 (Apr. 1934): 168–82.

"The Artist Becomes a Citizen." *Forum* 91 (May 1934): 277–79.

"Pittsburgh Postpones its Awakening." *Parnassus* 6 (Nov. 1934): 12–14.

"An Afternoon with George Picken." *Parnassus* 6 (Dec. 1934): 7–9.

"Art and the Government in 1934." *Parnassus* 7 (Jan. 1935): 12–16.

"Bryson Burroughs." *Parnassus* 7 (Jan. 1935): 3.

"A World without Elegance." *Parnassus* 7 (May 1935): 3–8, 48.

"The Chance in a Thousand." *American Magazine of Art* 28 (Aug. 1935): 470–75, 506–8.

"The Return to the Facts." *American Magazine of Art* 29 (Mar. 1936): 146–53.

"Is There—Will There Be—An American Art?" *New York Times Magazine,* May 24, 1936.

Mural Designs, 1934–1936 (coauthored with Edward Bruce). Vol. 1 of *Art in Federal Buildings: An Illustrated Record of the Treasury Department's New Program in Painting and Sculpture.* Washington, D.C.: Art in Federal Buildings Corporation, 1936.

"Realism Undefeated." *Parnassus* 9 (Mar. 1937): 11–14, 37–38.

"The Matter of Subject." *Parnassus* 9 (Oct. 1937): 13–18.

A Guide to the Painting and Sculpture in the Justice Department Building, Washington, District of Columbia. Art Guides no. 1. Washington, D.C.: Art in Federal Buildings Corporation, 1938.

A Guide to the Painting and Sculpture in the Post Office Department Building, Washington, District of Columbia. Art Guides no. 2. Washington, D.C.: Art in Federal Buildings Corporation, 1938.

"New Forces in American Art." *Kenyon Review* 1 (spring 1939): 119–34.

Essay for *American Painting Today.* Washington, D.C.: American Federation of Arts, 1939.

Essay for *William Glackens Memorial Exhibition, May 19th to June 10th, 1939.* Arts Club of Chicago illustrated catalog. Chicago: American Federation of Arts, 1939.

Essay for *Allen Tucker: Memorial Exhibition, December 6, 1939 to January 3, 1940.* New York: Whitney Museum of American Art, 1939.

Aaron Sopher. Baltimore: Theodore Ember, 1940.

Winslow Homer. New York: Crown, [1942].

Introduction to *The Edward Bruce Memorial Collection, September 12 to 28, 1943.* Washington, D.C.: Corcoran Gallery of Art, [1943].

"Have You a 20th Century Mind?" *Pic,* Dec. 7, 1943, 39.

"Belief and Painting." *47: The Magazine of the Year* 1 (Dec. 1947): 16–20.

Foreword to *Paintings by Allen Tucker, October 13–November 1, 1947.* New York: Macbeth Gallery, 1947.

Essay for *Juliana Force and American Art: A Memorial Exhibition September 24–October 30, 1949.* New York: Whitney Museum of American Art, 1949.

"American Art." In *Twentieth Century Unlimited: From the Vantage Point of the First Fifty Years,* 213–33. Philadelphia: J. B. Lippincott, 1950.

"Thomas W. Dewing," "Kenyon Cox," "Jerome Myers," "Maurice Sterne," "Jo Davidson," "Guy Pène du Bois," "Andrew Dasburg," "Preston Dickinson," "Louis Bouché," "Alexander Brook." In *The Metropolitan Museum of Art Presents the 75th Anniversary Exhibition of Painting and Sculpture by 75 Artists Associated with the Art Students League of New York.* New York: Art Students League of New York, 1951.

"Arthur Bowen Davies." *Magazine of Art* 45 (Dec. 1952): 362–69.

"John Sloan." *Magazine of Art* 45 (Feb. 1952): 62–70.

"William James Glackens." In *The Pennsylvania Academy of Fine Arts One Hundred and Fiftieth Anniversary Exhibition, January 15 through March 13, 1955,* 124–29. Philadelphia: Pennsylvania Academy of the Fine Arts, 1955.

MEMOIRS AND CONTEMPORARY ACCOUNTS

Art criticism, which appeared regularly in major American newspapers and general periodicals by the time of the Armory Show in 1913, reflected the public's interests. Among these magazines, *Dial, Arts & Decoration,* and *International Studio Supplement* provided specialized coverage of art currents during the years 1910–19. Alfred Stieglitz's *Camera Work* was the definitive periodical in the United States for avant-garde art. Other than *The Arts* and *Arts Weekly,* the most useful magazines for information about contemporary American art during the 1920s were *Arts & Decoration* and *Creative Art.* The *American Magazine of Art* represented the conservative point of view. In addition, a number of general-interest magazines such as *Scribner's* and *Vanity Fair* routinely carried articles on art. During the 1930s, the *American Magazine of Art, Magazine of Art,* and *Parnassus* were dependable sources for regular coverage of New Deal art. *Art Digest* and *Art Front* were also attentive to New Deal projects. For general art news during the 1930s and 1940s, *Art Digest* and *Art News* kept readers informed.

In addition to interviews, the written memoirs of contemporaries offer authentic and distinctive perspectives on personalities and issues of the day. The following is a selected list of memoirs and contemporary books and articles published during Watson's career.

BOOKS

Army at War: A Graphic Record by American Artists. Washington, D.C.: GPO, 1944.

Army at War by American Artists: Paintings and Drawings Lent by the War Department and the Treasury Department. Washington, D.C.: GPO, 1944.

Barker, Virgil. *A Critical Introduction to American Painting.* New York: William Edwin Rudge for the Whitney Museum of American Art, 1931.

Barr, Alfred H., Jr. *Defining Modern Art: Selected Writings of Alfred H. Barr, Jr.* Edited by Irving Sandler and Amy Newman. New York: Harry N. Abrams, 1986.

Barrett, James Wyman. *The World, the Flesh, and Messrs. Pulitzer.* New York: Vanguard Press, 1931.

———. *The End of the World: A Post-Mortem, by Its Intangible Assets.* New York: Harper and Brothers, 1931.

Benton, Thomas Hart. *An Artist in America.* 4th ed. Columbia: Univ. of Missouri Press, 1983.

———. *An American in Art: A Professional and Technical Autobiography.* Lawrence: Univ. Press of Kansas, 1969.

Biddle, George. *An American Artist's Story.* Boston: Little, Brown, 1939.

———. *Artist at War.* New York: Viking Press, 1944.

Blanch, Arnold. *Arnold Blanch.* New York: American Artists Group, 1946.

Boswell, Peyton, Jr. *Modern American Painting.* New York: Dodd, Mead, 1948.

Brancusi vs. United States: The Historic Trial, 1928. English ed. Paris: Societé nouvelle Adam Biro, 1999.

Brook, Alexander. *Alexander Brook.* New York: American Artists Group, 1945.

Civilization in the United States: An Inquiry by Thirty Americans. Edited by Harold E. Stearns. New York: Harcourt, Brace, 1922.

Cowley, Malcolm. *Exile's Return: A Literary Odyssey of the 1920's.* New York: Viking Press, 1934.

Coyle, Edward Royal. *Ambulancing on the French Front.* New York: Britton, 1918.

Craven, Thomas. *Modern Art: The Men, the Movements, the Meaning.* Rev. ed. Garden City, N.J.: Halcyon House, 1940.

Davis, Stuart. *Stuart Davis.* New York: American Artists Group, 1945.

Dewey, John. *Art as Experience.* New York: Minton, Balch, 1934.

Dows, Olin. *Franklin Roosevelt at Hyde Park.* New York: American Artists Group, 1949.

Flannagan, John B. *Letters of John B. Flannagan.* New York: Curt Valentin, 1942.

The Forum Exhibition of Modern American Painters, March 13 to March 25, 1916, on View at the Anderson Galleries, New York. New York: Mitchell Kennerley, 1916.

Henri, Robert. *The Art Spirit.* Philadelphia: J. B. Lippincott, 1960.

Hoffman, Malvina. *Yesterday Is Tomorrow: A Personal History.* New York: Crown, 1965.

Josephson, Matthew. *Infidel in the Temple.* New York: Alfred A. Knopf, 1967.

Karfiol, Bernard. *Bernard Karfiol.* New York: American Artists Group, 1945.

Kent, Rockwell. *It's Me, O Lord: The Autobiography of Rockwell Kent.* New York: Dodd, Mead, 1955.

Keppel, Frederick Paul, and R. L. Duffus. *The Arts in American Life.* New York: McGraw-Hill, 1933.

Kroll, Leon. *A Spoken Memoir.* Edited by Nancy Hale and Fredson Bowers. Charlottesville: Univ. Press of Virginia, 1983.

Kuhn, Walt. *The Story of the Armory Show.* New York: Walt Kuhn, 1938.

Kuniyoshi, Yasuo. *Yasuo Kuniyoshi.* New York: American Artists Group, 1945.

Luhan, Mabel Dodge. *Movers and Shakers.* Albuquerque: Univ. of New Mexico Press, 1936.

McBride, Henry. *The Flow of Art: Essays and Criticisms of Henry McBride.* Edited by Daniel Catton Rich. New York: Atheneum, 1975.

Myers, Jerome. *Artist in Manhattan.* New York: American Artists Group, 1940.

Nevins, Allan. *The Evening Post: A Century of Journalism.* New York: Boni and Liveright, 1922.

The New Deal Art Projects: An Anthology of Memoirs. Edited by Francis V. O'Connor. Washington, D.C.: Smithsonian Institution Press, 1972.

One Third of a Nation: Lorena Hickok Reports on The Great Depression. Edited by Richard Lowitt and Maurine Beasley. Urbana: Univ. of Illinois Press, 1981.

Overmyer, Grace. *Government and the Arts.* New York: W. W. Norton, 1939.

Pach, Walter. *Modern Art in America.* New York: C. W. Kraushaar Art Galleries, 1928.

———. *Queer Thing, Painting: Forty Years in the World of Art.* New York: Harper and Brothers, 1938.

Paintings and Sculpture by Living Americans, Ninth Loan Exhibition, December 2, 1930 to January 20, 1931. New York: Museum of Modern Art, 1930.

Paintings by Nineteen Americans, December 13, 1929 to January 12, 1930. New York: Museum of Modern Art, 1930.

Pemberton, Murdock. *Picture Book.* New York: Alfred A. Knopf, 1930.

Pène du Bois, Guy. *Artists Say the Silliest Things.* New York: American Artists Group, 1940.

Pierce, Waldo. *Waldo Pierce.* New York: American Artists Group, 1945.

Rosenfeld, Paul. *Port of New York: Essays on Fourteen American Moderns.* New York: Harcourt, Brace, 1924.

Saint-Gaudens, Homer. *The American Artist and His Times.* New York: Dodd, Mead, 1941.

Scudder, Janet. *Modeling My Life.* New York: Harcourt, Brace, 1925.

Sloan, John. *Gist of Art.* New York: American Artists Group, 1939.

———. *John Sloan's New York Scene: From the Diaries, Notes and Correspondence 1906–1913.* Edited by Bruce St. John. New York: Harper and Row, 1965.

Soyer, Raphael. *Raphael Soyer.* New York: American Artists Group, 1946.

Stearns, Harold E. *Rediscovering America.* New York: Liveright, 1934.

Sterne, Maurice. *Shadow and Light: The Life, Friends, and Opinions of Maurice Sterne.* Edited by Charlotte Leon Mayerson. New York: Harcourt, Brace, and World, 1952.

Still-Lifes by Nan Watson: Loan Exhibition, November 10–December 4, 1960, Wadsworth Atheneum, Hartford. Foreword by Olin Dows. [Hartford, Conn.: Wadsworth Atheneum, 1960.]

Terkel, Studs. *Hard Times: An Oral History of the Great Depression.* New York: Avon, 1970.

Villard, Oswald Garrison. *Fighting Years: Memoirs of a Liberal Editor.* New York: Harcourt, Brace, 1939.

Walkowitz, Abraham. *A Demonstration of Objective, Abstract, and Non-Objective Art.* Girard, Kans.: Haldeman-Julius, 1945.

Warshawsky, Abel L. *The Memories of an American Impressionist.* Kent, Ohio: Kent State Univ. Press, 1980.

Zigrosser, Carl. *My Own Shall Come to Me: A Personal Memoir and Picture Chronicle.* Philadelphia: Casa Laura, 1971.

Zorach, William. *Art Is My Life: The Autobiography of William Zorach.* New York: World, 1967.

ARTICLES

(Contemporary newspaper and magazine reviews of the government art shows cited in the text are not included in the bibliography except where more general issues were also discussed.)

Barker, Virgil. "The Search for Americanism." *American Magazine of Art* 27 (Feb. 1934): 51–52.

———. "Americanism in Painting." *Yale Review* 25 (June 1936): 778–93.

Benson, E. M. "Art on Parole." *American Magazine of Art* 29 (Nov. 1936): 694–709, 770.

Berryman, Florence S. "Guns and Brushes." *Magazine of Art* 35 (Oct. 1942): 214–17.

Biddle, George. "An Art Renascence under Federal Patronage." *Scribner's Magazine* 95 (June 1934): 428–31.

———. "Art under Five Years of Federal Patronage." *American Scholar* 9 (Summer 1940): 327–38.

———. "The Government and the Arts: A Proposal by George Biddle, with Comment and Criticisms by Others." *Harper's Magazine* 187 (Oct. 1943): 427–34.

———. "Big Business Discovers Art." *48: The Magazine of the Year* 2 (Feb. 1948): 71–78.

Bruce, Edward. "Implications of the Public Works of Art Project." *American Magazine of Art* 27 (Mar. 1934): 113–15.

———. "Public Works of Art Project—Address by Edward Bruce." *Congressional Record*, 73d Cong., 2d sess., 1934, vol. 78, pt. 1:765–67.

Burchfield, Charles. "On the Middle Border." *Creative Art* 3 (Sept. 1928): 25–32.

Cortissoz, Royal. "The Field of Art." *Scribner's Magazine* 78 (Oct. 1925): 440–50.

Craven, Thomas. "Men of Art: American Style." *American Mercury* 6 (Dec. 1925): 425–32.

———. "Have Painters Minds?" *American Mercury* 10 (Mar. 1927): 257–62.

———. "Our Art Becomes American." *Harper's Monthly* 171 (Sept. 1935): 430–41.

Davis, Stuart. "The Artist Today: The Standpoint of the Artists' Union." *American Magazine of Art* 28 (Aug. 1935): 476–78, 506.

———. "Some Chance." *Art Front* 1 (Nov. 1935): 4, 7.

———. "What About Modern Art and Democracy?" *Harper's* 188 (Dec. 1943): 16–23.

Demuth, Charles. "Across a Greco Is Written." *Creative Art* 5 (Sept. 1929): 629–34.

Dow, Arthur Wesley. "Modernism in Art." *American Magazine of Art* 8 (Jan. 1917): 113–16.

Dows, Olin. "The New Deal's Treasury Art Programs." *Arts in Society* 2 [1963]: 51–88.

"Eight Critics of Art; without Whom no Artistic 'Movement' Can Be Launched in New York." *Vanity Fair* 4 (June 1915): 34.

"Emergency Relief for the Artist." *Art Forum* 1 (Jan. 1934): 2–7.

"The Evening Post Introduces Mr. Forbes Watson." *New York Evening Post Saturday Magazine*, Mar. 31, 1917.

Flint, Ralph. "Quick, Watson—The American Way." *Art News* 40 (Apr. 15, 1941): 13, 36, 39.

Goodrich, Lloyd. "Lloyd Goodrich Reminisces: Part I." *Archives of American Art Journal* 20 (1980): 2–18.

———. "'The Arts' Magazine: 1920–1931." *American Art Journal* 5 (May 1973): 79–85.

———. "Lloyd Goodrich Reminisces: Part II." *Archives of American Art Journal* 23 (1983): 8–21.

McFee, Henry Lee. "My Painting and Its Development." *Creative Art* 4 (Mar. 1929): 29–31.

McMahon, Audrey. "May the Artist Live?" *Parnassus* 5 (Oct. 1933): [1]–4.

———. "The Trend of the Government in Art." *Parnassus* 8 (Jan. 1936): 3–6.

Mangravite, Peppino. "Congress Vetoes Culture." *Magazine of Art* 36 (Nov. 1943): 264–65.

Odegard, Peter H., and Alan Barth. "Millions for Defense." *Public Opinion Quarterly* 5 (fall 1941): 399–411.

Parrish, Wayne W. "American Art Scrapes Off French Veneer." *Literary Digest* 117 (June 30, 1934): 22, 35.

Pearl, Philip. "The World Passes." *Saturday Review of Literature* 7 (Mar. 14, 1931): 663.

Pemberton, Murdock. "Painting America's Portrait." *Travel* 72 (Feb. 1939): 6–13, 44–45.

Pickering, Ruth. "American Art Comes Home." *Forum* 94 (Sept. 1935): 182–86.

Rowan, Edward B. "Will Plumber's Wages Turn the Trick?" *American Magazine of Art* 27 (Feb. 1934): 80–83.

Taylor, Francis Henry. "Pork Barrel Renaissance." *Magazine of Art* 31 (Mar. 1938): 157, 186–87.

"Tragedy." *Art Digest* 8 (Apr. 1934): 3, 4, 11.

Whiting, Frederick A., Jr. "Five Important Years." *Magazine of Art* 32 (Dec. 1939): 676–82, 729.

Wright, Willard Huntington. "The New Painting and American Snobbery." *Arts & Decoration* 7 (Jan. 1917): 129–30, [152], 154.

SELECTED EXHIBITION CATALOGS OF THE SECTION OF FINE ARTS

Painters and Sculptors Represented in the First Annual Exhibition of Mural Designs and Sculpture Models by Appointed and Competing Artists Submitted for Federal Building Projects, The Corcoran Gallery of Art, October 27th to November 21st, 1935. Washington, D.C.: Section of Painting and Sculpture Public Works Branch, Procurement Division, Treasury Department, [1935].

Painting and Sculpture for Federal Buildings, Treasury Department Art Projects, November Seventeenth to December Thirteenth Nineteen Hundred and Thirty-Six. Washington, D.C.: Corcoran Gallery of Art, [1936].

Loan Exhibition of Mural Designs for Federal Buildings from the Section of Fine Arts, Washington, D.C., Feb. 27 to March 17, 1940. New York: Whitney Museum of American Art, [1940].

Exhibition Painting and Sculpture Designed for Federal Buildings, The Corcoran Gallery of Art, Washington, D.C., November 2 through November 21, 1939. (Forty-eight State Competition Winners.) [Washington, D.C.]: Section of Fine Arts, Public Buildings Administration, Federal Works Agency, [1939].

Mural Designs for Federal Buildings from the Section of Fine Arts, Washington, D.C. Ottawa: National Gallery of Canada, 1940.

An Exhibition of Two Hundred American Water Colors, Selected by John Marin, Charles Burchfield, Buk Ulreich, and Eliot O'Hara for the Carville, Louisiana, Marine Hospital from a National Competition Held by the Section of Fine Arts, Federal Works Agency, Public Buildings Administration from May 15 through June 4, 1941, National Gallery of Art, Smithsonian Institution. Washington, D.C.: [National Gallery of Art, 1941].

SECONDARY SOURCES

BOOKS

Adams, Henry. *Thomas Hart Benton: An American Original.* New York: Alfred A. Knopf, 1989.

Alexander, Charles C. *Here the Country Lies: Nationalism and the Arts in Twentieth-Century America.* Bloomington: Indiana Univ. Press, 1980.

Allen, Frederick Lewis. *Only Yesterday: An Informal History of the Nineteen-Twenties.* New York: Bantam, 1946.

The American Field Service Archives of World War I, 1914–1917. Compiled by L. D. Geller. New York: Greenwood Press, 1989.

American Paintings in the Ferdinand Howald Collection. Catalogue by Marcia Tucker. Columbus, Ohio: Columbus Gallery of Fine Arts, 1969.

Artists against War and Fascism: Papers of the First American Artists' Congress. Introduction by Matthew Baigell and Julia Williams. New Brunswick, N.J.: Rutgers Univ. Press, 1986.

Ashton, Dore. *The New York School: A Cultural Reckoning.* New York: Viking Press, 1973.

Avant-Garde Painting and Sculpture in America 1910–1925: Delaware Art Museum, April 4–May 18, 1975. Wilmington, Del.: Delaware Art Museum, 1975.

Baigell, Matthew. *The American Scene: American Painting of the 1930s.* New York: Praeger, 1974.

Baker, John. *Henry Lee McFee and Formalist Realism in American Still Life, 1923–1936.* Lewisburg. Penn.: Bucknell Univ. Press, 1987.

Baur, John Ireland Howe. *Revolution and Tradition in Modern American Art.* Cambridge, Mass.: Harvard Univ. Press, 1951.

Beckham, Sue Bridwell. *Depression Post Office Murals and Southern Culture: A Gentle Reconstruction.* Baton Rouge: Louisiana State Univ. Press, 1988.

Beer, Thomas. *The Mauve Decade: American Life at the End of the Nineteenth Century.* New York: Vintage, 1926.

Berman, Avis. *Rebels on Eighth Street: Juliana Force and the Whitney Museum of American Art.* New York: Atheneum, 1990.

Bohan, Ruth L. *The Société Anonyme's Brooklyn Exhibition: Katherine Dreier and Modernism in America.* Ann Arbor, Mich.: UMI Research Press, 1982.

Brooks, Van Wyck. *The Writer in America.* New York: E. P. Dutton, 1953.

Brown, Milton W. *American Painting from the Armory Show to the Depression.* Princeton, N.J.: Princeton Univ. Press, 1955.

———. *The Story of the Armory Show.* 2d ed. New York: Abbeville Press, 1988.

Burns, James McGregor. *Roosevelt: The Lion and the Fox.* New York: Harcourt, Brace, and World, 1956.

———. *Roosevelt: The Soldier of Freedom.* New York: Harcourt, Brace, Jovanovich, 1970.

Burns, Sarah. *Inventing the Modern Artist: Art and Culture in Gilded Age America.* New Haven, Conn.: Yale Univ. Press, 1996.

Bustard, Bruce I. *A New Deal for the Arts.* Washington, D.C.: National Archives and Records Administration, 1997.

Contreras, Belisario Ramon. *Tradition and Innovation in New Deal Art.* Lewisburg, Penn.: Bucknell Univ. Press, 1983.

Davidson, Abraham A. *Early American Modernist Painting, 1910–1935.* New York: Harper and Row, 1981.

Davis, Ronald L., ed. *The Social and Cultural Life of the 1920s.* New York: Holt, Rinehart, and Winston, 1972.

Davis, Stuart. *Stuart Davis.* Edited by Diane Kelder. New York: Praeger, 1971.

The Decade of the Armory Show: New Directions in American Art 1910–1920. New York: Whitney Museum of American Art, 1963.

Doezema, Marianne. *George Bellows and Urban America.* New Haven, Conn.: Yale Univ. Press, 1992.

Doss, Erika. *Benton, Pollock, and the Politics of Modernism: From Regionalism to Abstract Expressionism.* Chicago: Univ. of Chicago Press, 1991.

Ekirch, Arthur A., Jr. *Ideologies and Utopias: The Impact of the New Deal on American Thought*. Chicago: Quadrangle, 1969.

Eliot, Thomas H. *Two Schools in Cambridge: The Story of Browne & Nichols and Buckingham*. Cambridge, Mass.: Windflower Press, 1982.

Fink, Lois Marie, and Joshua C. Taylor. *Academy: The Academic Tradition in American Art: An Exhibition Organized on the Occasion of the One Hundred and Fiftieth Anniversary of the National Academy of Design: 1825–1975*. Washington, D.C.: Smithsonian Institution Press, 1975.

Fort, Ilene Susan. *The Figure in American Sculpture: A Question of Modernity*. Los Angeles County Museum of Art, 1995.

Friedman, Bernard Harper. *Gertrude Vanderbilt Whitney*. Garden City, N.J.: Doubleday, 1978.

Gerdts, William H. *William Glackens*. New York: Abbeville Press, 1996.

The Gilded Age. Edited by H. Wayne Morgan. Rev. and enlarged ed. Syracuse: Syracuse Univ. Press, 1970.

Glackens, Ira. *William Glackens and The Eight*. New York: Horizon Press, 1983.

Goldman, Eric Frederick. *Rendezvous with Destiny*. New York: Alfred A. Knopf, 1966.

Goldsmith, Barbara. *Little Gloria . . . Happy at Last*. New York: Alfred A. Knopf, 1980.

Greenfeld, Howard. *The Devil and Dr. Barnes*. New York: Viking, 1987.

Greenwich Village: Culture and Counterculture. Edited by Rick Beard and Leslie Cohen Berlowitz. Brunswick, N.J.: Rutgers Univ. Press, 1993.

Gurney, George. *Sculpture and the Federal Triangle*. Washington, D.C.: Smithsonian Institution Press, 1985.

Hale, Nancy. *Mary Cassatt*. Reading, Mass.: Addison-Wesley, 1987.

Haskell, Barbara. *Charles Demuth*. New York: Whitney Museum of American Art, 1987.

Heller, Nancy, and Julia Williams. *The Regionalists*. New York: Watson-Guptil Publications, 1976.

Hoffman, Frederick J. *The Twenties: American Writing in the Postwar Decade*. Rev. ed. New York: Free Press, 1962.

Hofstadter, Richard. *The Age of Reform*. New York: Vintage, 1955.

Homage to Forbes Watson and The Arts, Spring Exhibition, April 18–May 30, 1967. Washington, D.C.: Adams, Davidson, [1967].

Homer, William Innes. *Alfred Stieglitz and the American Avant-Garde*. Boston: New York Graphic Society, 1976.

———. *Robert Henri and His Circle*. New York: Hacker Art, 1988.

Hughes, Robert. *American Visions: The Epic History of Art in America*. New York: Alfred A. Knopf, 1997.

Kahn, E. J., Jr. *The World of Swope*. New York: Simon and Schuster, 1965.

Kouwenhoven, John A. *Made in America: The Arts in Modern Civilization*. Garden City, N.J.: Doubleday, 1948.

Landau, Ellen G. *Artists for Victory: An Exhibition Catalog*. Washington, D.C.: Library of Congress, 1983.

Landgren, Marchal E. *Years of Art: The Story of the Art Students League of New York*. New York: McBride, 1940.

Larkin, Oliver W. *Art and Life in America*. Rev. ed. New York: Holt, Rinehart, and Winston, 1960.

Larson, Gary O. *The Reluctant Patron: The United States Government and the Arts, 1943–1965.* Philadelphia: Univ. of Pennsylvania Press, 1983.

Levin, Gail. *Edward Hopper: An Intimate Biography.* New York: Alfred A. Knopf, 1995.

Lindemann, Edna M. *The Art Triangle: Artist, Dealer, Collector.* Buffalo, N.Y.: Burchfield Art Center, 1989.

Littleton, Taylor D., and Maltby Sykes. *Advancing American Art: Painting, Politics, and Cultural Confrontation at Mid-Century.* Tuscaloosa: Univ. of Alabama Press, 1989.

Loughery, John. *John Sloan: Painter and Rebel.* New York: Henry Holt, 1995.

Lynes, Barbara Buhler. *O'Keeffe, Stieglitz, and the Critics, 1916–1929.* Ann Arbor, Mich.: UMI Research Press, 1989.

McCullough, David. *Truman.* New York: Simon and Schuster, 1992.

McDonald, William F. *Federal Relief Administration and the Arts.* Columbus: Ohio State Univ. Press, 1969.

McKinzie, Richard D. *The New Deal for Artists.* Princeton, N.J.: Princeton Univ. Press, 1973.

Marling, Karal Ann. *Wall-to-Wall America: A Cultural History of Post-Office Murals in the Great Depression.* Minneapolis: Univ. of Minnesota Press, 1982.

Marx, Leo. *The Machine in the Garden.* New York: Oxford Univ. Press, 1977.

May, Henry F. *The End of American Innocence: A Study of the First Years of Our Own Time, 1912–1917.* New York: Alfred A. Knopf, 1969.

Mecklenburg, Virginia. *Advancing American Art: Politics and Aesthetics in the State Department Exhibition, 1946–1948.* Montgomery, Ala.: Montgomery Museum of Fine Arts, 1984.

———. *The Public as Patron: A History of the Treasury Department Mural Program Illustrated with Paintings from the Collection of the University of Maryland Art Gallery.* College Park: University of Maryland Department of Art, 1979.

Melosh, Barbara. *Engendering Culture: Manhood and Womanhood in New Deal Public Art and Theater.* Washington, D.C.: Smithsonian Institution Press, 1990.

Morgan, Charles H. *George Bellows: Painter of America.* New York: Reynal, 1965.

Morgan, H. Wayne. *Keepers of Culture: The Art-Thought of Kenyon Cox, Royal Cortissoz, and Frank Jewett Mather Jr.* Kent, Ohio: Kent State Univ. Press, 1989.

———. *Kenyon Cox, 1856–1919: A Life in American Art.* Kent, Ohio: Kent State Univ. Press, 1994.

———. *New Muses: Art in American Culture, 1865–1920.* Norman: Univ. of Oklahoma Press, 1978.

Mowry, George E. *The Era of Theodore Roosevelt and the Birth of Modern America, 1900–1912.* New York: Harper and Row, 1958.

Nash, Roderick. *The Nervous Generation: American Thought, 1917–1930.* Chicago: Rand, McNally, 1970.

O'Connor, Francis V. *Federal Art Patronage 1933–1943: An Exhibition, April 6 to May 13, 1966.* College Park: University of Maryland Art Gallery, 1966.

———. *Federal Support for the Visual Arts: The New Deal and Now.* Greenwich, Conn.: New York Graphic Society, 1969.

Olson, Arlene Rita. *Art Critics and the Avant-Garde: New York, 1900–1913.* Ann Arbor, Mich.: UMI Research Press, 1980.

Park, Marlene, and Gerald E. Markowitz. *Democratic Vistas: Post Offices and Public Art in the New Deal.* Philadelphia: Temple Univ. Press, 1984.

Perlman, Bennard B. *The Immortal Eight: American Painting from Eakins to the Armory Show, 1870–1913.* Westport, Conn.: North Light, 1979.

Perrett, Geoffrey. *Days of Sadness, Years of Triumph: The American People 1939–1945.* Baltimore: Penguin, 1973.

Platt, Susan Noyes. *Modernism in the 1920s: Interpretations of Modern Art in New York from Expressionism to Constructivism.* Ann Arbor, Mich.: UMI Research Press, 1985.

Reid, B. L. *The Man from New York: John Quinn and His Friends.* New York: Oxford Univ. Press, 1968.

Roeder, George H., Jr. *The Censored War: American Visual Experience during World War Two.* New Haven, Conn.: Yale Univ. Press, 1993.

———. *Forum of Uncertainty: Confrontations with Modern Painting in Twentieth-Century American Thought.* Ann Arbor, Mich.: UMI Research Press, 1980.

Rose, Barbara. *American Art since 1900.* Rev. ed. New York: Praeger, 1972.

———. *Readings in American Art, 1900–1975.* New York: Praeger, 1975.

Samuel, Lawrence R. *Pledging Allegiance: American Identity and the Bond Drive of World War II.* Washington, D.C.: Smithsonian Institution Press, 1997.

Schapiro, Meyer. *Modern Art: 19th & 20th Centuries.* New York: George Braziller, 1978.

Schwab, Arnold T. *James Gibbons Huneker: Critic of the Seven Arts.* Stanford, Calif.: Stanford Univ. Press, 1963.

Sherwood, Robert E. *Roosevelt and Hopkins: An Intimate History.* New York: Harper and Brothers, 1948.

Steiner, Raymond J. *The Art Students League of New York: A History.* Saugerties, N.Y.: CSS, 1999.

Turner, Elizabeth Hutton. *American Artists in Paris, 1919–1929.* Ann Arbor, Mich.: UMI Research Press, 1988.

Underwood, Sandra Lee. *Charles H. Caffin: A Voice for Modernism, 1897–1918.* Ann Arbor, Mich.: UMI Research Press, 1983.

U.S. Treasury. *A History of the United States Savings Bond Program.* Washington, D.C.: U.S. Treasury, 1984.

Weber, Nicholas Fox. *Patron Saints: Five Rebels Who Opened America to a New Art, 1928–1943.* New York: Alfred A. Knopf, 1992.

The Whitney Studio Club and American Art, 1900–1932. New York: Whitney Museum of American Art, 1975.

Wiebe, Robert H. *The Search for Order, 1877–1920.* New York: Hill and Wang, 1967.

Wilson, Edmund. *The American Earthquake: A Documentary of the Twenties and Thirties.* Garden City, N.J.: Doubleday, 1958.

Woodstock: An American Art Colony, 1902–1977; Vassar College Art Gallery, January 23–March 4, 1977. Poughkeepsie, N.Y.: Hamilton Reproductions, 1977.

Woodstock Artists Association. *Woodstock's Art Heritage.* Woodstock, N.Y.: Overlook Press, 1987.

Zilczer, Judith. *"The Noble Buyer": John Quinn: Patron of the Avant-Garde.* Washington, D.C.: Smithsonian Institution Press, 1978.

ARTICLES

Beckh, Erica. "Government Art in the Roosevelt Era: An Appraisal of Federal Art Patronage in the Light of Present Needs." *Art Journal* 20 (fall 1960): 2–8.

Fenton, Charles A. "Ambulance Drivers in France and Italy, 1914–1918." *American Quarterly* 3 (winter 1951): 326–43.

Knight, Christopher. "On Native Ground: U.S. Modern." *Art in America* 71 (Oct. 1983): 166–74.

Mathews, Jane De Hart. "Arts and the People: The New Deal Quest for a Cultural Democracy." *Journal of American History* 62 (Sept. 1975): 316–39.

Vitz, Robert Carl. "Struggle and Response: American Artists and the Great Depression." *New York History* (Jan. 1976): 81–98.

Weinberg, Jonathan. "Cruising with Paul Cadmus." *Art in America* 80 (Nov. 1992): 102–9.

THESES AND DISSERTATIONS

Contreras, Belisario R. "The New Deal Treasury Department Art Programs and the American Artist: 1933 to 1943." Ph.D. diss., American University, 1967.

Davidson, Abraham Aba. "Some Early American Cubists, Futurists and Surrealists: Their Paintings, Their Writings, and Their Critics." Ph.D. diss., Columbia University, 1965.

Fahlman, Betsy Lee. "Guy Pène du Bois: Painter, Critic, Teacher." Ph.D. diss., University of Delaware, 1981.

Levy, Robert Jonathan. "Art for the Public's Sake, 1920–1943." Ph.D. diss., University of Wisconsin, 1978.

Lucchesi, Joseph Edward. "*American Painting Today:* Forbes Watson, the Section of Fine Arts, the 1930s, and the American Search for a Cultural Identity." Master's thesis, University of North Carolina, 1990.

McRoberts, Jerry William. "The Conservative Realists' Image of America in the 1920s: Modernism, Traditionalism and Nationalism." Ph.D. diss., University of Illinois, 1979.

Marling, Karal Ann Rose. "Federal Patronage and the Woodstock Colony." Ph.D. diss., Bryn Mawr College, 1971.

Mecklenburg, Virginia McCord. "American Aesthetic Theory, 1908–1917: Issues in Conservative and Avant-Garde Thought." Ph.D. diss., University of Maryland, 1983.

Petruck, Peninah R. Y. "American Art Criticism: 1910–1939." Ph.D. diss., New York University, 1979.

Pietan, Norman. "Federal Government and the Arts." Ph.D. diss., Columbia University, 1950.

Platt, Susan Noyes. "Responses to Modern Art in New York in the 1920s." Ph.D. diss., University of Texas, 1981.

Risatti, Howard Anthony. "American Critical Reaction to European Modernism, 1908 to 1917." Ph.D. diss., University of Illinois, 1977.

Rubenstein, Erica Beckh. "Tax Payers' Murals." Ph.D. diss., Harvard University, 1944.

Vitz, Robert Carl. "Painters, Pickets, and Politics: The Artist Moves Left, 1925–1940." Ph.D. diss., University of North Carolina, 1971.

Werthman, Joan B. "The New Deal Federal Art Programs, 1935–1939." Ph.D. diss., St. John's University, 1971.

Zilczer, Judith Katy. "The Aesthetic Struggle in America, 1913–1918: Abstract Art and Theory in the Stieglitz Circle." Ph.D. diss., University of Delaware, 1975.

INDEX

Abbott, Jere, 86
Abbott Laboratories of Chicago, 158, 160, 163
Abstract art, 147, 178, 189
Abstract expressionism, 161, 178, 188, 189, 196
Abstractionism, 47, 112, 178, 190
Adams, Charles W., 170, 172
Administrative Reorganization Act, 148–49
American Academy of Fine Arts, 25
American Art Dealers Association, 87
American Art Research Council, 189
American Art Student, 53
American Federation of Arts, 66, 78, 100, 120, 137, 138, 144, 152–54
American Indian art, 112
American Magazine of Art, 115, 137–38, 144, 152–53, 155, 184, 190
American Painting Today, 144
American Red Cross, 42, 159
American Scene movement, 97, 101, 121, 178
American scene subject matter, 111–12, 118, 121, 123
Ankeney, John S., 112
Ardsley Studios, 52
Arensberg, Walter, 23, 26–27
Armory Show, 23, 36, 46–47, 74, 79, 187, 190, 196
"Army at War" show. *See* War art
Art Digest, 114
Art for Bonds. See War art
Art Front, 146
Art galleries: Adams, Davidson Gallery, 195; Arden Gallery, 43; Bourgeois Gallery, 23; Brummer Galleries, 74; Carroll Gallery, 23; Corcoran Gallery, 117, 141, 167; Daniel Gallery, 23; de Zayas Gallery, 47; Downtown Galleries, 71; Dudensing Gallery, 74; Durand-Ruel Galleries, 74, 83; Feragil Galleries, 74; Fine Arts Galleries, 185;

Folsom Gallery, 12; Keppel Galleries, 74; Knoedler Galleries, 28, 43, 48, 74; Kraushaar Galleries, 84, 92, 100; Layton Art Gallery, Milwaukee, 166; Little Gallery, Cedar Rapids, 65, 110; Macbeth Galleries, 8, 11–12, 74, 97, 184; MacDowell Club Gallery, 28; Madison Gallery, 12; Modern Gallery, 23, 47; Montross Gallery, 12; National Gallery, London, 168; National Gallery of Art, Washington, 153–54, 158, 164, 169; Phillips Gallery, 167; Rehn Gallery, 73; Smithsonian Gallery of Art, 149; Marie Sterner Gallery, 168, 184; Washington Square Gallery, 23; Weyhe Gallery, 47; Whitney Gallery, 168
Art in Federal Buildings, 137–39
Art Institute of Chicago, 80, 166
Art News, 49, 156
Art Students League, 12–13, 15, 52, 93, 184–86, 192, 194
Artists organizations: Allied Artists of America, 113; American Artists' Congress, 157; American Artists Professional League, 78, 100, 113; Artists Council for Victory, 158; Artists Equity, 179, 185; Artists Union, 161; Artists War Corps, 164; Associated American Artists, 168; Association of American Painters and Sculptors, 21, 25; Beaux Arts Architects Society, 113; College Art Association, 95, 102, 120; Friends of the Young Artists, 39, 121; Municipal Art League of Chicago, 115; Municipal Art Society of New York, 113; National Sculpture Society, 70; People's Art Guild, 29; Society of American Artists, 25; United Scenic Artists of the American Federation of Labor, 114; Washington Artists' Guild, 141. *See also* Art Students League; Society of Independent Artists

Forbes Watson: Independent Revolutionary
was designed and composed by Christine Brooks
in 10/13.5 Minion with display type
in 16/27 Futura Condensed Bold;
printed on 60# Supple Opaque stock
and notch bound in signatures
by Thomson-Shore, Inc. of Dexter, Michigan;
and published by The Kent State University Press
Kent, Ohio 44242